WEBSTER'S CONCISE SPANISH-ENGLISH ENGLISH-SPANISH DICTIONARY

WEBSTER'S
CONCISE
SPANISH–ENGLISH
ENGLISH–SPANISH
DICTIONARY

Books
Are Fun® Ltd
Reader's Digest. Company

This edition published 2004 for Books Are Fun by Geddes & Grosset,
David Dale House, New Lanark ML11 9DJ, Scotland

This book is not published by the original publishers of
Webster's Dictionary or by their successors

ISBN 1 84205 418 X

Printed and bound in Poland, OZGraf S.A.

Spanish–English Dictionary

A

a *prep* to; in; at; according to; on; by; for; of.
abadía *f* abbey.
abajo *adv* under, underneath; below.
abalanzarse *vr* to rush forward.
abandonado/da *adj* derelict; abandoned; neglected.
abandonar *vt* to abandon; to leave: —**~se** *vr* **~ a** to give oneself up to.
abarcar *vt* to include; to monopolize.
abarrotado/da *adj* packed.
abarrotar *vt* to tie down; (*mar*) to stow.
abastecer *vt* to purvey.
abatido/da *adj* dejected, low-spirited; abject.
abatimiento *m* low spirits *pl*, depression.
abatir *vt* to knock down; to humble.
abdicar *vt* to abdicate.
abdomen *m* abdomen.
abdominal *adj* abdominal.
abecedario *m* alphabet; spelling book, primer.
abeja *f* bee.
aberración *f* aberration.
abertura *f* aperture, chink, opening.
abeto *m* fir tree.
abierto/ta *adj* open; sincere; frank.
abismal *adj* abysmal.
abismo *m* abyss; gulf; hell.
ablandar *vt*, *vi* to soften.
abnegado/da *adj* selfless.
abogacía *f* legal profession.
abogado/a *m/f* lawyer; barrister.
abogar *vi* to intercede:—**~ por** to advocate.
abolir *vt* to abolish.
abollar *vt* to dent.
abonado/da *adj* paid-up:—*m/f* subscriber.
abonar *vt* to settle; to fertilize.
abono *m* payment; subscription; dung, manure.
aborrecer *vt* to hate, abhor.
abortar *vi* to miscarry; to have an abortion.
aborto *m* abortion; monster.
abotonar *vt* to button.
abovedado/da *adj* vaulted.
abrasar *vt* to burn; to parch:—**~se** *vr* to burn oneself.
abrazar *vt* to embrace; to surround; to contain.
abrazo *m* embrace.
abrebotellas *m invar* bottle opener.
abrelatas *m invar* can opener.
abreviar *vt* to abridge, cut short.
abridor *m* opener.
abrigar *vt* to shelter; to protect.
abrigo *m* shelter; protection; aid.
abril *m* April.
abrillantar *vt* to polish.
abrir *vt* to open; to unlock.
abrochar *vt* to button; to do up.
abrumar *vt* to overwhelm.
absolución *f* forgiveness, absolution.
absoluto/ta *adj* absolute.
absorber *vt* to absorb.
absorción *f* absorption; takeover.
absorto *adj* engrossed.
abstemio *adj* teetotal.
abstracción *f* abstraction.
abstracto/ta *adj* abstract.
abstraer *vt* to abstract:—**~se** *vr* to be absorbed.
absuelto/ta *adj* absolved.
absurdo *adj* absurd.
abuela *f* grandmother.
abuelo *m* grandfather.
abulia *f* lethargy.
abultado/da *adj* bulky, large, massive.
abultar *vt* to increase, enlarge:—*vi* to be bulky.
abundante *adj* abundant, copious.
aburrido/da *adj* boring, bored.
aburrir *vt* to bore, weary.
abusar *vt* to abuse.
acá *adv* here.
acabado/da *adj* perfect, accomplished; old.
acabar *vt* to finish, complete; to achieve: —**~se** *vr* to finish, expire.
academia *f* academy; literary society.
acaecer *vi* to happen.
acallar *vt* to quiet, hush; to soften, appease.
acalorado/da *adj* heated.
acampar *vt* (*mil*) to encamp.
acanalado/da *adj* grooved; fluted.
acaparar *vt* to monopolize; to hoard.
acariciar *vt* to fondle, caress.
acarrear *vt* to transport; to occasion.
acaso *m* chance:—*adv* perhaps.
acatarrarse *vr* to catch cold.
acceder *vi* to agree:—**~ a** to have access to.
accesible *adj* attainable; accessible.
acceso *m* access; fit.
accidentado/da *adj* uneven; hilly; eventful.
accidental *adj* accidental; casual.
accidente *m* accident.
acción *f* action, operation; share.
accionar *vt* to work.
accionista *m* shareholder.
acebo *m* holly tree.
acechar *vt* to lie in ambush for; to spy on.
aceite *m* oil.

aceituna *f* olive.
aceitunado/da *adj* olive-green.
aceleración *f* acceleration.
aceleradamente *adv* swiftly, hastily.
acelerar *vt* to accelerate; to hurry.
acento *m* accent.
aceptar *vt* to accept, admit.
acera *f* sidewalk.
acerca *prep* about, relating to.
acercar *vt* to move nearer:—**~se** *vr* **~ a** to approach.
acero *m* steel.
acertar *vt* to hit; to guess right.
acertijo *m* riddle.
achacar *vt* to impute.
achaque *m* ailment; excuse; subject, matter.
achicar *vt* to diminish; to humiliate; to bale (out).
achicharrar *vt* to scorch; to overheat.
aciago/ga *adj* unlucky; ominous.
ácido *m* acid:—**~/da** *adj* acid, sour.
acierto *m* success; solution; dexterity.
aclamar *vt* to applaud, acclaim.
aclaración *f* clarification.
aclarar *vt* to clear; to brighten; to explain; to clarify.
acobardar *vt* to intimidate.
acodarse *vr* to lean.
acoger *vt* to receive; to welcome; to harbor:—**~se** *vr* to take refuge.
acogida *f* reception; asylum.
acometida *f* attack, assault.
acomodar *vt* to accommodate, arrange:—**~se** *vr* to comply.
acompañar *vt* to accompany; to join; (*mus*) to accompany.
acompasado/da *adj* measured; well-proportioned.
acondicionar *vt* to arrange; to condition.
acongojar *vt* to distress.
aconsejar *vt* to advise:—**~se** *vr* to take advice.
acontecer *vi* to happen.
acontecimiento *m* event, incident.
acoplar *vt* to couple; to fit; to connect.
acordar *vt* to agree; to remind:—**~se** *vr* to agree; to remember.
acorde *adj* harmonious:—*m* chord.
acordeón *m* accordion.
acorralar *vt* to round up; to intimidate.
acortar *vt* to abridge, shorten:—**~se** *vr* to become shorter.
acostar *vt* to put to bed; to lay down: —**~se** *vr* to go to bed; to lie down.
acostumbrar *vi* to be used to:—*vt* to accustom:—**~se** *vr* **~ a** to become used to.
acotar *vt* to set bounds to; to annotate.
ácrata *m/f* anarchist.
acreditar *vt* to guarantee; to assure; to authorize.
acreedor *m* creditor.
acribillar *vt* to riddle with bullets; to molest, torment.
acta *f* act:—**~s** *fpl* records *pl*.
actitud *f* attitude; posture.
actividad *f* activity; liveliness.
activo/va *adj* active; diligent.
acto *m* act, action; act of a play; ceremony.
actor *m* actor; plaintiff.
actriz *f* actress.
actuación *f* action; behavior; proceedings *pl*.
actual *adj* actual, present.
actualizar *vt* to update.
actuar *vt* to work; to operate:—*vi* to work; to act.
acuarela *f* watercolor.
acudir *vi* to go to; to attend; to assist.
acuerdo *m* agreement:—**de ~** OK.
acumular *vt* to accumulate, collect.
acurrucarse *vr* to squat; to huddle up.
adelantado/da *adj* advanced; fast.
adelantar *vt, vi* to advance, accelerate; to pass.
adelante *adv* forward(s):—*excl* come in!
adelanto *m* advance; progress; improvement.
adelgazar *vt* to make thin or slender; to discuss with subtlety.
además *adv* moreover, besides:—**~ de** besides.
adentro *adv* in; inside.
aderezar *vt* to dress, adorn; to prepare; to season.
adeudar *vt* to owe:—**~se** *vr* to run into debt.
adherir *vi*:—**~ a** to adhere to; to espouse.
adiestrar *vt* to guide; to teach, to instruct.
adiós *excl* goodbye; hello.
adivinar *vt* to foretell; to guess.
admirar *vt* to admire; to surprise:—**~se** *vr* to be surprised.
admitir *vt* to admit; to let in; to concede; to permit.
admonición *f* warning.
adobar *vt* to dress; to season.
adobe *m* adobe, sun-dried brick.
adobo *m* dressing; pickle sauce.
adolecer *vi* to suffer from.
adolescencia *f* adolescence.
adónde *adv* where.
adoptar *vt* to adopt.
adoquín *m* paving stone.
adorar *vt* to adore; to love.
adormecer *vt* to put to sleep:—**~se** *vr* to fall asleep.

adornar *vt* to embellish, adorn.
adosado/da *adj* semi-detached.
adquirir *vt* to acquire.
adrede *adv* on purpose.
aduana *f* customs *pl.*
adueñarse *vr*:—~ **de** to take possession of.
adular *vt* to flatter.
adulterio *m* adultery.
adulto/ta *adj*, *m/f* adult, grown-up.
advenedizo *m* upstart.
advenimiento *m* arrival; accession.
adversidad *f* adversity; setback.
advertencia *f* warning, foreword.
advertir *vt* to notice; to warn.
aerodeslizador *m* hovercraft.
aeronave *f* spaceship.
aeropuerto *m* airport.
afán *m* hard work; desire.
afanar *vt* to harass; (*col*) to pinch:—~**se** *vr* to strive.
afear *vt* to deform, misshape.
afección *f* affection; fondness, attachment; disease.
afectar *vt* to affect, feign.
afectuoso/sa *adj* affectionate; moving; tender.
afeitar *vt*:—~**se** *vr* to shave.
aferrar *vt* to grapple, grasp, seize.
afianzar *vt* to strengthen; to prop up.
aficionado/da *adj* keen:—*m/f* lover, devotee; amateur.
afilado *adj* sharp.
afilar *vt* to sharpen, grind.
afín *m* related; similar.
afinar *vt* to tune; to refine.
afincarse *vr* to settle.
afirmar *vt* to secure, fasten; to affirm, assure.
aflicción *f* affliction, grief.
aflictivo/va *adj* distressing.
aflojar *vt* to loosen, slacken, relax.
aflorar *vi* to emerge.
afluente *adj* flowing:—*m* tributary.
afónico/ca *adj* hoarse; voiceless.
afortunado/da *adj* fortunate, lucky.
afrenta *f* outrage; insult.
afrontar *vt* to confront; to bring face to face.
afuera *adv* out, outside.
agacharse *vr* to stoop, squat.
agarradero *m* handle.
agarrar *vt* to grasp, seize:—~**se** *vr* to hold on tightly.
agasajar *vt* to receive and treat kindly; to regale.
agenciarse *vr* to obtain.
agenda *f* diary.
agente *m* agent; policeman.
ágil *adj* agile.
agilidad *f* agility, nimbleness.
agitar *vt* to wave; to move:—~**se** *vr* to become excited; to become worried.
aglomeración *f* crowd; jam.
agobiar *vt* to weigh down; to oppress; to burden.
agolparse *vr* to assemble in crowds.
agonía *f* agony.
agorar *vt* to predict.
agostar *vt* to parch.
agosto *m* August.
agotado/da *adj* exhausted; finished; sold out.
agotar *vt* to exhaust; to drain; to misspend.
agradable *adj* pleasant; lovely.
agradar *vt* to please, gratify.
agradecer *vt* to be grateful for; to thank.
agradecido/da *adj* thankful.
agrandar *vt* to enlarge; to exaggerate.
agrario/ria *adj* agrarian; agricultural.
agravante *f* further difficulty.
agraviar *vt* to wrong; to offend:—~**se** *vr* to be aggrieved; to be piqued.
agredir *vt* to attack.
agregar *vt* to aggregate, heap together; to collate; to appoint.
agreste *adj* rustic, rural.
agrícola *adj* farming *compd.*
agricultor/ra *m/f* farmer.
agrietarse *vr* to crack.
agrimensor *m* surveyor.
agrio *adj* sour, acrid; rough, craggy; sharp, rude, unpleasant.
agrupar *vt* to group, cluster; to crowd.
agua *f* water.
aguacate *m* avocado pear.
aguacero *m* cloudburst, downpour.
aguado/da *adj* watery.
aguafuerte *m* etching.
aguamarina *f* aquamarine (gem stone).
aguanieve *f* sleet.
aguantar *vt* to bear, suffer; to hold up.
aguardar *vt* to wait for.
aguarrás *f* turpentine.
agudo/da *adj* sharp; keen-edged; smart; fine; acute; witty; brisk.
aguijón *m* sting of a bee, wasp, etc; stimulation.
águila *f* eagle; genius.
aguileño/ña *adj* aquiline; sharp-featured.
aguja *f* needle; spire; hand; magnetic needle; (*ferro*) points *pl.*
agujerear *vt* to pierce, bore.
agujero *m* hole.
ahí *adv* there.
ahijada *f* goddaughter.
ahijado *m* godson.
ahínco *m* earnestness; eagerness.

ahogar *vt* to smother; to drown; to suffocate; to oppress; to quench.
ahora *adv* now, at present; just now.
ahorrar *vt* to save; to avoid.
ahumar *vt* to smoke, cure (in smoke): —**~se** *vr* to fill with smoke.
ahuyentar *vt* to drive off; to dispel.
aire *m* air; wind; aspect; musical composition.
aislar *vt* to insulate; to isolate.
ajardinado/da *adj* landscaped.
ajedrez *m* chess.
ajedrezado/da *adj* chequered.
ajeno/na *adj* someone else's; foreign; ignorant; improper.
ajetreo *m* activity; bustling.
ajo *m* garlic.
ajorca *f* bracelet.
ajustar *vt* to regulate, adjust; to settle (a balance); to fit.
al = **a el.**
ala *f* wing; aisle; row, file; brim:—*m/f* winger.
alabar *vt* to praise; to applaud.
alacena *f* cupboard, closet.
alacrán *m* scorpion.
alambre *m* wire.
alameda *f* avenue; poplar grove.
álamo *m* poplar.
alargar *vt* to lengthen; to extend.
alarido *m* outcry, shout:—**dar ~s** to howl.
alarma *f* alarm.
alba *f* dawn.
albañil *m* mason, bricklayer.
albarán *m* invoice.
albaricoque *m* apricot.
albedrío *m* free will.
albergue *m* shelter:—**~ de juventud** youth hostel.
albóndiga *f* meatball.
albornoz *m* burnous:—**~ de baño** bath robe.
alboroto *m* noise; disturbance, riot.
alborozo *m* joy.
albricias *fpl* good news *pl*.
albufera *f* lagoon.
álbum *m* album.
alcachofa *f* artichoke.
alcalde *m* mayor.
alcaldesa *f* mayoress.
alcantarilla *m* sewer; gutter.
alcanzar *vt* to reach; to get, obtain; to hit.
alcaparra *f* caper.
alcayata *f* hook.
alcázar *m* castle, fortress.
alcornoque *m* cork tree.
aldea *f* village.
aleatorio/ria *adj* random.
aleccionar *vt* to instruct; to train.
alegar *vt* to allege; to quote.
alegrar *vt* to cheer; to poke; to liven up:—**~se** *vr* to get merry.
alegre *adj* happy; merry, joyful; content.
alegría *f* happiness; merriment.
alejar *vt* to remove; to estrange:—**~se** *vr* to go away.
alemán/ana *adj, m/f* German:—*m* German language.
alentar *vt* to encourage.
alergia *f* allergy.
alero *m* gable-end; eaves *pl*.
alertar *vt* to alert.
aleta *f* fin; wing; flipper; fender.
alfabeto *m* alphabet.
alfarería *f* pottery.
alféizar *m* window sill.
alfiler *m* pin; clip; clothes pin.
alfombra *f* carpet; rug.
alga *f* (*bot*) seaweed.
algo *pn* something; anything:—*adv* somewhat.
algodón *m* cotton; cotton plant; cotton wool.
alguien *pn* someone, somebody; anyone, anybody.
alguno/na *adj* some; any; no:—*pn* someone, somebody.
alhaja *f* jewel.
aliado/da *adj* allied.
alianza *f* alliance, league; wedding ring.
alicates *mpl* pincers *pl*, nippers *pl*.
aliciente *m* attraction; incitement.
aliento *m* breath; respiration.
aligerar *vt* to lighten; to alleviate; to hasten; to ease.
alijo *m* lightening of a ship; alleviation; cache.
alimentar *vt* to feed, nourish:—**~se** *vr* to feed.
aliñar *vt* to adorn; to season.
alinear *vt* to arrange in line:—**~se** *vr* to line up.
alisar *vt* to plane; to polish; to smooth.
aliviar *vt* to lighten; to ease; to relieve, mollify.
allá *adv* there; over there; then.
allanar *vt* to level, flatten; to subdue; to burgle.
allí *adv* there, in that place.
alma *f* soul; human being.
almacén *m* warehouse, store; magazine.
almacenar *vt* to store (up).
almeja *f* clam.
almena *f* battlement.
almendra *f* almond.

almíbar *m* syrup.
almirez *m* mortar.
almizcle *m* musk.
almohada *f* pillow; cushion.
almorranas *fpl* hemorrhoids *pl*.
almuerzo *m* lunch.
alocado/da *adj* crazy; foolish; inconsiderate.
alojamiento *m* lodgings, rooming house; housing.
alpargata *f* rope-soled shoe.
alpinismo *m* mountaineering.
alquilar *vt* to let, rent; to hire.
alquitrán *m* tar, liquid pitch.
alrededor *adv* around.
alta *f* (*mil*) discharge from hospital.
altanero/ra *adj* haughty, arrogant, vain, proud.
altavoz *m* loudspeaker, amplifier.
alterar *vt* to alter, change; to disturb.
altercado *m* altercation, controversy; quarrel.
alterno/na *adj* alternate; alternating.
Alteza *f* Highness (title).
altibajos *mpl* ups and downs *pl*.
altitud *f* height; altitude.
altivo/va *adj* haughty, proud, high-flown.
alto/ta *adj* high; tall:—*m* height; story; highland; (*mil*) halt; (*mus*) alto: —**¡~!/¡~ ahí!** *interj* stop!
altura *f* height; depth; mountain summit; altitude.
alubia *f* kidney bean.
alucinar *vt* to blind, deceive:—*vi* to hallucinate.
alumbrado *m* lighting; illumination.
alumbrar *vt* to light:—*vi* to give birth.
alumno/na *m/f* student, pupil.
alza *f* rise; sight.
alzar *vt* to raise, lift up:—**~se** *vr* to get up; to rise in rebellion.
ama *f* mistress, owner; housewife; foster mother.
amable *adj* kind, nice.
amagar *vt* to threaten; to shake one's fist at:—*vi* to feint.
amamantar *vt* to suckle.
amanecer *vi* to dawn:—**al ~** at daybreak.
amanerado/da *adj* affected.
amansar *vt* to tame; to soften; to subdue:—**~se** *vr* to calm down.
amante *m/f* lover.
amapola *f* (*bot*) poppy.
amar *vt* to love.
amargo/ga *adj* bitter, acrid; painful: —*m* bitterness.
amarillo/lla *adj* yellow:—*m* yellow.
amarrar *vt* to moor; to tie, fasten.
amasar *vt* to knead; (*fig*) to arrange, settle; to prepare.
ámbar *m* amber.
ambiente *m* atmosphere; environment.
ambiguo/gua *adj* ambiguous; doubtful, equivocal.
ámbito *m* circuit, circumference; field; scope.
ambos/bas *adj, pn* both.
ambulante *adj* traveling.
ambulatorio *m* state-run clinic.
amenazar *vt* to threaten.
ameno/na *adj* pleasant; delicious; flowery (of language).
América *f* America:—**~ del Norte/del Sur** North/South America.
amianto *m* asbestos.
amiga *f* (female) friend.
amigo *m* friend; comrade; lover:—**~/ga** *adj* friendly.
aminorar *vt* to diminish; to reduce.
amistad *f* friendship.
amistoso/sa *adj* friendly, cordial.
amo *m* owner; boss.
amoldar *vt* to mold; to adapt:—**~se** *vr* to adapt oneself.
amor *m* love; fancy; lover:—**~ mio** my love:—**por ~ de Dios** for God's sake: —**~ propio** self-love.
amortiguador *m* shock absorber.
amortizar *vt* to redeem, pay, liquidate, discharge (a debt).
amperio *m* amp.
ampliar *vt* to amplify, enlarge; to extend; to expand.
amplificador *m* amplifier.
amplio/lia *adj* ample, extensive.
ampolla *f* blister; ampoule.
amueblar *vt* to furnish.
anacoreta *m* anchorite, hermit.
anacronismo *m* anachronism.
añadir *vt* to add.
analfabeto/ta *adj* illiterate.
analgésico *m* painkiller.
análisis *m* analysis.
anaranjado/da *adj* orange-colored.
anarquía *f* anarchy.
ancho/cha *adj* broad, wide, large:—*m* breadth, width.
anchoa *f* anchovy.
anchura *f* width, breadth.
anciano/na *adj* old:—*m/f* old man/woman.
ancla *f* anchor.
anclaje *m* anchorage.
andamiaje *m* scaffolding.
andar *vi* to go, walk; to fare; to act, proceed.
andén *m* sidewalk; (*ferro*) platform; quayside.

andrajo *m* rag.
anegar *vt* to inundate, submerge;.
añejo/ja *adj* old; stale, musty.
anexión *f* annexation.
anfibio/bia *adj* amphibious.
anfitrión/ona *m/f* host(ess).
ángel *m* angel.
angosto/ta *adj* narrow, close.
anguila *f* eel.
angula *f* elver.
angular *adj* angular:—**piedra ~** *f* cornerstone.
ángulo *m* angle, corner.
angustia *f* anguish; heartache.
anhelar *vi* to gasp:—*vt* to long for.
anidar *vi* to nestle, make a nest; to dwell, inhabit.
añil *m* indigo plant; indigo.
anillo *m* ring.
ánima *f* soul.
animación *f* liveliness; activity.
animado/da *adj* lively.
animal *adj*, *m* animal.
animar *vt* to animate, liven up; to comfort; to revive:—**~se** *vr* to cheer up.
ánimo *m* soul; courage; mind; intention:—*excl* come on!
anís *m* aniseed; anisette.
aniversario/ria *adj* annual:—*m* anniversary.
ano *m* anus.
año *m* year.
anoche *adv* last night.
anochecer *vi* to grow dark:—*m* nightfall.
anónimo/ma *adj* anonymous.
añoranza *f* longing.
anormal *adj* abnormal.
anotar *vt* to comment, note.
anquilosamiento *m* paralysis.
ánsar *m* goose.
ansiar *vt* to desire.
ansiedad *f* anxiety.
antagónico/ca *adj* antagonistic; opposed.
antaño *adv* formerly.
ante *m* suede:—*prep* before; in the presence of; faced with.
anteanoche *adv* the night before last.
anteayer *adv* the day before yesterday.
antebrazo *m* forearm.
antelación *f*:—**con ~** in advance.
antemano *adv*:—**de ~** beforehand.
antena *f* feeler, antenna; aerial.
antepasado/da *adj* passed, elapsed: —**~s** *mpl* ancestors *pl*.
anterior *adj* preceding; former.
antes *prep*, *adv* before:—*conj* before.
antibiótico *m* antibiotic.
anticiclón *m* anticyclone.
anticipar *vt* to anticipate; to forestall; to advance.
anticonceptivo *m* contraceptive.
anticongelante *m* antifreeze.
anticuado/da *adj* antiquated.
anticuerpo *m* antibody.
antiestético/ca *adj* unsightly.
antifaz *m* mask.
antiguamente *adv* in ancient times, of old.
antiguo/gua *adj* antique, old, ancient.
antipático/ca *adj* unpleasant.
antojo *m* whim, fancy; longing.
antorcha *f* torch; taper.
antro *m* (*poet*) cavern, den, grotto.
antropófago *m* cannibal.
antropología *f* anthropology.
anual *adj* annual.
anudar *vt* to knot; to join:—**~se** *vr* to get into knots.
anular *vt* to annul; to revoke; to cancel:—*adj* annular.
anunciar *vt* to announce; to advertise.
anuncio *m* advertisement.
anzuelo *m* hook; allurement.
apacible *adj* affable; gentle; placid, quiet.
apaciguar *vt* to appease; to pacify, calm.
apagar *vt* to put out; to turn off; to quench, extinguish.
apañar *vt* to grasp; to pick up; to patch: —**~se** *vr* to manage.
aparador *m* sideboard; store window.
aparato *m* apparatus; machine; radio or television set; ostentation, show; (*med*) bandage, dressing.
aparcamiento *m* parking lot.
aparcar *vt*, *vi* to park.
aparecer *vi* to appear:—**~se** *vr* to appear.
aparentar *vt* to look; to pretend; to deceive.
apariencia *f* outward appearance.
apartamento *m* flat, apartment.
apartar *vt* to separate, divide; to remove; to sort;.
aparte *m* aside; new paragraph:—*adv* apart, separately; besides; aside.
apasionado/da *adj* passionate; devoted; fond; biased.
apeadero *m* halt, stopping place; station.
apearse *vr* to dismount; to get down/out/off.
apechugar *vt* to face up to.
apego *m* attachment, fondness.
apelar *vi* (*jur*) to appeal:—**~ a** to have recourse to.
apellido *m* surname; family name; epithet.
apenar *vt* to grieve; to embarrass:—**~se** *vr* to grieve; to be embarrassed.
apenas *adv* scarcely, hardly:—*conj* as soon as.
apéndice *m* appendix, supplement.

apercibirse *vr* to notice.
aperitivo *m* aperitif; appetizer.
apero *m* agricultural implement.
apesadumbrar *vt* to sadden.
apestar *vt* to infect:—*vi* ~ **a** to stink of.
apetito *m* appetite.
apiadarse *vr* to take pity.
apilar *vt* to pile up:—~**se** *vr* to pile up.
apiñado/da *adj* crowded; pyramidal; pine-shaped.
apio *m* (*bot*) celery.
apisonadora *f* steamroller.
aplacar *vt* to appease, pacify:—~**se** *vr* to calm down.
aplastar *vt* to flatten, crush.
aplatanarse *vr* to get weary.
aplaudir *vt* to applaud; to extol.
aplauso *m* applause; approbation, praise.
aplazar *vt* to postpone.
aplicado/da *adj* studious; industrious.
aplicar *vt* to apply; to clasp; to attribute:—~**se** *vr* ~ **a** to devote oneself to.
aplique *m* wall light.
aplomo *m* self-assurance.
apocado/da *adj* timid.
apoderado/da *adj* powerful:—*m* proxy, attorney; agent.
apodo *m* nickname, sobriquet.
apogeo *m* peak.
apósito *m* (*med*) external dressing.
aposta *adv* on purpose.
apostar *vt* to bet, wager; to post soldiers:—*vi* to bet.
apóstol *m* apostle.
apoteosis *f* apotheosis.
apoyar *vt* to rest; to favor, patronize, support:—~**se** *vr* to lean.
apreciar *vt* to appreciate; to estimate, value.
aprecio *m* appreciation; esteem.
apremiante *adj* urgent.
aprender *vt* to learn:—~ **de memoria** to learn by heart.
aprensión *f* apprehension.
apresar *vt* to seize, grasp.
apresurar *vt* to accelerate, hasten, expedite:—~**se** *vr* to hurry.
apretar *vt* to compress, tighten; to constrain:—*vi* to be too tight.
aprisa *adv* quickly, swiftly; promptly.
aprobar *vt* to approve; to pass:—*vi* to pass.
apropiado/da *adj* appropriate.
aprovechar *vt* to use; to exploit; to profit from; to take advantage of:—*vi* to be useful; to progress:—~**se** *vr* ~ **de** to use; to take advantage of.
aproximar *vt* to approach:—~**se** *vr* to approach.
aptitud *f* aptitude, fitness, ability.
apto/ta *adj* apt; fit, able; clever.
apuesta *f* bet, wager.
apuñalar *vt* to stab.
apuntar *vt* to aim; to level, point at; to mark:—*vi* to begin to appear or show itself; to prompt (theater):—~**se** *vr* to score; to enrol.
apurado/da *adj* poor, destitute of means; exhausted; hurried.
aquél/~ la *pn* that (one):—~ **los/~ las** *pl* those (ones).
aquel/~la *adj* that:—~**los/~las** *pl* those.
aquello *pn* that.
aquí *adv* here; now.
árabe *adj*, *m/f*, *m* (*ling*) Arab, Arabic.
arado *m* plough.
araña *f* spider; chandelier.
arañar *vt* to scratch; to scrape; to corrode.
arancel *m* tariff.
arandela *f* washer.
arar *vt* to plough.
árbitro *m* arbitrator; referee; umpire.
árbol *m* tree; (*mar*) mast; shaft.
arbolado/da *adj* forested; wooded: —*m* woodland.
arbusto *m* shrub.
arca *f* chest, wooden box.
arcada *f* arch; arcade:—~**s** *fpl* retching.
arce *m* maple tree.
archivar *vt* to file.
arcilla *f* clay.
arco *m* arc; arch; fiddle bow; hoop: —~**iris** rainbow.
arder *vi* to burn, blaze.
ardilla *f* squirrel.
área *f* area.
arena *f* sand; grit; arena.
arenque *m* herring:—~ **ahumado** red herring.
argolla *f* large ring.
argucia *f* subtlety.
argumentar *vt*, *vi* to argue, dispute; to conclude.
árido/da *adj* dry; barren.
arisco/ca *adj* fierce; rude; intractable.
arlequín *m* harlequin, buffoon.
arma *f* weapon, arms.
armado/da *adj* armed; reinforced.
armador *m* shipowner; privateer; jacket, jerkin.
armar *vt* to man; to arm; to fit:—~**la** to kick up a fuss.
armario *m* wardrobe; cupboard.
armazón *f* chassis; skeleton; frame.
armonía *f* harmony.
armonizar *vt* to harmonize; to reconcile.

arnés *m* harness:—**~eses** *mpl* gear, trappings *pl.*
aro *m* ring; earring.
aroma *m* aroma, fragrance.
arpa *f* harp.
arpía *f* (*poet*) harpy, shrew.
arpillera *f* sackcloth.
arpón *m* harpoon.
arqueado/da *adj* arched, vaulted.
arquero *m* archer.
arquitectónico/ca *adj* architectural.
arrabal *m* suburb; slum.
arraigado *adj* deep-rooted; established.
arraigar *vi* to root; to establish:—*vt* to establish;.
arrancar *vt* to pull up by the roots; to pull out:—*vi* to start; to move.
arrasar *vt* to demolish, destroy.
arrastrar *vt* to drag:—*vi* to creep, crawl; to lead a trump at cards:—**~se** *vr* to crawl; to grovel.
arrebatar *vt* to carry off, snatch; to enrapture.
arrebato *m* fury; rapture.
arrecife *m* reef.
arreglar *vt* to regulate; to tidy; to adjust:—**~se** *vr* to come to an understanding.
arrellanarse *vr* to sit at ease; to make oneself comfortable.
arrendar *vt* to rent, let out, lease.
arrendatario/ria *m/f* tenant.
arrepentirse *vr* to repent.
arrestar *vt* to arrest; to imprison.
arriate *m* flowerbed; causeway.
arriba *adv* above, over, up; high, on high, overhead; aloft.
arribista *m/f* upstart.
arriendo *m* lease; farm rent.
arriesgado *adj* risky, dangerous; daring.
arriesgar *vt* to risk, hazard; to expose to danger:—**~se** *vr* to take a chance.
arrimar *vt* to approach, draw near; (*mar*) to stow (cargo):—**~se** *vr* to sidle up; to lean.
arrinconar *vt* to put in a corner; to lay aside.
arrodillarse *vr* to kneel down.
arrogante *adj* arrogant; haughty, proud; stout.
arrojar *vt* to throw, fling; to dash; to emit; to shoot, sprout:—**~se** *vr* to hurl oneself.
arrollar *vt* to run over; to defeat heavily.
arropar *vt* to clothe, dress:—**~se** *vr* to wrap up.
arroyo *m* stream; gutter.
arroz *m* rice.
arrozal *m* ricefield.
arrugar *vt* to wrinkle; to rumple; to fold:—**~ la frente** to frown:—**~se** *vr* to shrivel.
arruinar *vt* to demolish; to ruin:—**~se** *vr* to go bankrupt.
arrullar *vt* to lull:—*vi* to coo.
artesanía *f* craftsmanship.
ártico/ca *adj* arctic, northern:—*m* **el A~** the Arctic.
articular *vt* to articulate; to joint.
artículo *m* article; clause; point; (*gr*) article; condition.
artífice *m* artisan; artist.
artificio *m* workmanship, craft; artifice, cunning trick.
artimaña *f* trap; cunning.
artista *m* artist; craftsman.
arzobispo *m* archbishop.
as *m* ace.
asa *f* handle; lever.
asado *m* roast meat; barbecue.
asaltar *vt* to assault; to storm (a position); to assail.
asamblea *f* assembly, meeting.
asar *vt* to roast.
ascender *vi* to be promoted; to rise:—*vt* to promote.
ascenso *m* promotion; ascent.
ascensor *m* elevator.
asco *m* nausea; loathing.
ascua *f* red-hot coal.
asear *vt* to clean; to tidy.
asedio *m* siege.
asegurar *vt* to secure; to insure; to affirm; to bail:—**~se** *vr* to make sure.
asentar *vt* to sit down; to affirm, assure; to note:—*vi* to suit.
asentir *vi* to acquiesce, concede.
aseo *m* cleanliness; neatness:—**~s** *mpl* rest room.
aséptico/ca *adj* germ-free.
asequible *adj* attainable; obtainable.
aserrar *vt* to saw.
aserrín *m* sawdust.
asesinar *vt* to assassinate; to murder.
asesorar *vt* to advise; to act as consultant:—**~se** *vr* to consult.
asfalto *m* asphalt.
asfixiar *vt* to suffocate:—**~se** *vr* to suffocate.
así *adv* so, thus, in this manner; like this; therefore; so that; also:—**~ que** so that; therefore:—**así/así** so-so; middling.
asiento *m* chair; bench, stool; seat; contract; entry; residence.
asignar *vt* to assign, attribute.
asignatura *f* subject; course.
asilo *m* asylum, refuge.
asimismo *adv* similarly, in the same manner.
asir *vt* to grasp, seize; to hold, grip:—*vi* to take root.

asistencia *f* audience; presence; assistance, help.
asistir *vi* to be present; to assist:—*vt* to help.
asma *f* asthma.
asno *m* ass.
asociación *f* association; partnership.
asolear *vt* to expose to the sun:—**~se** *vr* to sunbathe.
asomar *vi* to appear:—**~se** *vr* to appear, show up.
asombrar *vt* to amaze; to astonish:—**~se** *vr* to be amazed; to get a fright.
aspa *f* cross; sail.
aspecto *m* appearance; aspect.
áspero/ra *adj* rough, rugged; craggy, knotty; horrid; harsh, hard; severe, austere; gruff.
aspiración *f* breath; pause.
asqueroso/sa *adj* disgusting.
asta *f* lance; horn; handle.
astilla *f* chip (of wood), splinter.
astillero *m* dockyard.
astral *adj* astral.
astro *m* star.
astrología *m* astrology.
astronomía *f* astronomy.
astucia *f* cunning, slyness.
astuto/ta *adj* cunning, sly; astute.
asumir *vt* to assume.
asunto *m* subject, matter; affair, business.
asustar *vt* to frighten:—**~se** *vr* to be frightened.
atacar *vt* to attack.
atajo *m* short cut.
atañer *vi*:—**~ a** to concern.
atar *vt* to tie; to fasten.
atardecer *vi* to get dark:—*m* dusk; evening.
atascar *vt* to jam; to hinder:—**~se** *vr* to become bogged down.
ataúd *m* coffin.
atemorizar *vt* to frighten:—**~se** *vr* to get scared.
atención *f* attention, heedfulness; civility; observance, consideration.
atender *vi* to be attentive:—*vt* to attend to; to heed, expect, wait for; to look at.
atenerse *vr*:—**~ a** to adhere to.
atentamente *adv*:—**le saluda ~** yours faithfully.
atento/ta *adj* attentive; heedful; observing; mindful; polite, courteous, mannerly.
atenuar *vt* to diminish; to lessen.
ateo/a *adj*, *m/f* atheist.
aterciopelado/da *adj* velvety.
aterrar *vt* to terrify:—**~se** *vr* to be terrified.
aterrizar *vi* to land.
aterrorizar *vt* to frighten, terrify.
atesorar *vt* to treasure *or* hoard up (riches).
atestado/da *adj* packed:—*m* affidavit.
atestiguar *vt* to witness, attest.
atiborrar *vt* to stuff:—**~se** *vr* to stuff oneself.
ático *m* attic.
atinado/da *adj* wise; correct.
atizar *vt* to stir (the fire) with a poker; to stir up.
atlántico/ca *adj* atlantic.
atleta *m* athlete.
atletismo *m* athletics.
atomizador *m* spray.
átomo *m* atom.
atónito/ta *adj* astonished, amazed.
atontado/da *adj* stunned; silly.
atornillar *vt* to screw on; to screw down.
atosigar *vt* to poison; to harass; to oppress.
atracar *vt* to moor; to rob:—**~se** *vr* **~ (de)** to stuff oneself (with).
atractivo/va *adj* attractive; magnetic:—*m* charm.
atraer *vt* to attract, allure.
atragantarse *vr* to stick in the throat, choke.
atrapar *vt* to trap; to nab; to deceive.
atrás *adv* backward(s); behind; previously: —**hacia ~** backward(s).
atrasar *vi* to be slow:—*vt* to postpone: —**~ el reloj** to put back a watch:—**~se** *vr* to stay behind; to be late.
atravesado/da *adj* oblique; cross; perverse; mongrel; degenerate.
atravesar *vt* to cross; to pass over; to pierce; to go through:—**~se** *vr* to get in the way; to meddle.
atreverse *vr* to dare, venture.
atribuir *vt* to attribute, ascribe; to impute.
atril *m* lectern; bookrest.
atrio *m* porch; portico.
atrocidad *f* atrocity.
atropellar *vt* to trample; to run down; to hurry; to insult:—**~se** *vr* to hurry.
atroz *adj* atrocious, heinous; cruel.
atuendo *m* attire.
atún *m* tuna (fish).
aturdir *vt* to stun, confuse; to stupefy.
audaz *adj* audacious, bold.
audiencia *f* audience.
auge *m* boom; climax.
augurio *m* omen.
aula *f* lecture room.
aullar *vi* to howl.
aumentar *vt* to augment, increase; to magnify; to put up:—*vi* to increase; to grow larger.
aún *adv* even:—**~ asi** even so.
aunque *adv* though, although.
auricular *m* receiver:—**~es** *mpl* headphones *pl*.

aurora *f* dawn.
ausencia *f* absence.
ausente *adj* absent.
auspicio *m* auspice; prediction; protection.
austero/ra *adj* austere, severe.
auténtico/ca *adj* authentic.
autoadhesivo/va *adj* self-adhesive.
autobús *m* bus.
autocar *m* bus, coach.
autóctono/na *adj* native.
autodefensa *f* self-defense.
autodeterminación *f* self-determination.
autoescuela *f* driving school.
automovilismo *m* motoring; motor racing.
autónomo/ma *adj* autonomous.
autopista *f* motorway.
autopsia *f* post mortem, autopsy.
autor/ra *m/f* author; maker; writer.
autoridad *f* authority.
autorizar *vt* to authorize.
autorretrato *m* self-portrait.
autoservicio *m* self-service store; restaurant.
autostop *m* hitch-hiking.
autosuficiencia *f* self-sufficiency.
autovía *f* state highway.
auxiliar *vt* to aid, help, assist; to attend:—*adj* auxiliary.
aval *m* guarantee; guarantor.
avanzar *vt*, *vi* to advance.
avaricia *f* avarice.
avaro/ra *adj* miserly:—*m/f* miser.
ave *f* bird; fowl.
avecinarse *vr* to approach.
avellana *f* hazelnut.
avena *f* oats *pl*.
avenida *f* avenue.
aventajar *vt* to surpass, excel.
aventura *f* adventure; event, incident.
avergonzar *vt* to shame, abash:—**~se** *vr* to be ashamed.
avería *f* breakdown.
averiado/da *adj* broken down; out of order.
averiguar *vt* to find out; to inquire into; to investigate.
avestruz *m* ostrich.
aviación *f* aviation; air force.
avicultura *f* poultry farming.
avidez *f* covetousness.
avinagrado/da *adj* sour.
avión *m* airplane.
avioneta *f* light aircraft.
avisar *vt* to inform; to warn; to advise.
aviso *m* notice; warning; hint.
avispa *f* wasp.
avispado/da *adj* lively, brisk; vivacious.
¡ay! *excl* alas!; ow!:—**¡~ de mi!** alas! poor me!
ayer *adv* yesterday.
ayuda *f* help, aid; support:—*m* deputy, assistant.
ayudar *vt* to help, assist; to further.
ayunar *vi* to fast, abstain from food.
ayuntamiento *m* town/city hall.
azabache *m* jet.
azafata *f* air hostess.
azafrán *m* saffron.
azahar *m* orange or lemon blossom.
azar *m* fate:—**por ~** by chance:—**al ~** at random.
azotar *vt* to whip, lash.
azotea *f* flat roof of a house.
azúcar *m* sugar.
azufre *m* sulfur, brimstone.
azul *adj* blue:—**~ celeste** sky blue.
azulejo *m* tile.

B

baba *f* dribble, spittle.
babero *m* bib.
babia *f*:—**estar en ~** to be absent-minded *or* dreaming.
baca *f* (*auto*) luggage rack.
bacalao *m* cod.
bache *m* pothole.
bachillerato *m* baccalaureate.
bahía *f* bay.
bailar *vi* to dance.
bailarín/ina *m/f* dancer.
baja *f* fall; casualty.
bajada *f* descent; inclination; slope; ebb.
bajamar *f* low tide.
bajar *vt* to lower, let down; to lessen; to humble; to go/come down.
bajo/ja *adj* low; abject, despicable; common; humble:—*prep* under, underneath, below:—*adv* softly; quietly:—*m* (*mus*) bass; low place.
bala *f* bullet.
balance *m* hesitation; balance sheet; balance; rolling (of a ship).
balanza *f* scale; balance; judgement.
balar *vi* to bleat.
balcón *m* balcony.
balde *m* bucket:—**de ~** *adv* gratis, for nothing:—**en ~** in vain.

baldío/dia *adj* waste; uncultivated.
baldosa *f* floor; tile; flagstone.
ballena *f* whale; whalebone.
balneario *m* spa.
baloncesto *m* basketball.
balonmano *m* handball.
balonvolea *m* volleyball.
balsa *f* balsa wood; pool; raft, float; ferry.
bañador *m* swimsuit.
bañar *vt* to bathe; to dip; to coat (with varnish):—**~se** *vr* to bathe; to swim.
bancarrota *f* bankruptcy.
banco *m* bench; work bench; bank.
banda *f* band; sash; ribbon; troop; party; gang; touchline.
bandada *f* flock; shoal.
bandeja *f* tray, salver.
bandera *f* banner, standard; flag.
bando *m* faction, party; edict.
bandolero *m* bandit.
bañera *f* bath (tub).
baño *m* bath; dip; bathtub; varnish; crust of sugar; coating.
banqueta *f* three-legged stool; sidewalk.
banquete *m* banquet; formal dinner.
banquillo *m* dock.
bar *m* bar.
baraja *f* deck of cards.
barandilla *f* small balustrade, small railing.
barato/ta *adj* cheap:—**de ~** gratis:—*m* cheapness; bargain sale.
barba *f* chin; beard:—**~ a ~** face to face.
barbaridad *f* barbarity, barbarism; outrage.
bárbaro/ra *adj* barbarous; cruel; rude; rough.
barbecho *m* first ploughing, fallow land.
barbero *m* barber.
barbilampiño/ña *adj* clean-shaven; (*fig*) inexperienced.
barbilla *f* chin.
barca *f* boat.
barco *m* boat; ship.
barnis *m* varnish; glaze.
barómetro *m* barometer.
barquillo *m* wafer; cornet, cone.
barra *m* bar; rod; lever; French loaf; sandbank.
barraca *f* hut.
barranco *m* gully, ravine; (*fig*) great difficulty.
barrenar *vt* to drill, bore; (*fig*) to frustrate.
barrendero *m* sweeper, garbage man.
barrer *vt* to sweep.
barrera *f* barrier; turnpike, claypit.
barriga *f* abdomen; belly.
barril *m* barrel; cask.
barrio *m* area, district.
barro *m* clay, mud.
barrote *m* ironwork of doors, windows, tables; crosspiece.
barruntar *vt* to guess; to foresee; to conjecture.
bártulos *mpl* gear, belongings *pl*.
barullo *m* uproar.
basar *vt* to base:—**~se** *vr* **~ en** to be based on.
báscula *f* scales *pl*.
base *f* base, basis.
básico/ca *adj* basic.
bastante *adj* sufficient, enough:—*adv* quite.
bastar *vi* to be sufficient, be enough.
bastidor *m* embroidery frame:—**~es** *mpl* scenery (on stage).
basto/ta *adj* coarse, rude, unpolished.
bastón *m* cane, stick; nightstick; (*fig*) command.
bastos *mpl* clubs *pl* (one of the four suits at cards).
basura *f* trash, garbage.
bata *f* bathrobe; overall; laboratory coat.
batalla *f* battle, combat; fight.
batata *f* sweet potato.
batería *m* battery; percussion.
batir *vt* to beat; to whisk; to dash; to demolish; to defeat.
baúl *m* trunk.
bautisar *vt* to baptize, christen.
baza *f* card-trick.
bazo *m* spleen.
beato/ta *adj* happy; blessed; devout: —*m* lay brother:—*m/f* pious person.
bebé *m/f* baby.
beber *vt* to drink.
bebida *f* drink, beverage.
beca *f* fellowship; grant, bursary, scholarship; sash; hood.
bedel *m* head porter; uniformed employee.
belén *m* nativity scene.
bélico/ca *adj* warlike, martial.
belladona *f* (*bot*) deadly nightshade.
belleza *f* beauty.
bello/lla *adj* beautiful; handsome; lovely; fine.
bellota *f* acorn.
bemol *m* (*mus*) flat.
bendecir *vt* to bless; to consecrate; to praise.
bendito/ta *adj* saintly; blessed; simple; happy.
beneficiar *vt* to benefit; to be of benefit to.
beneficio *m* benefit, advantage; profit; benefit night.
beneficioso/sa *adj* beneficial.
beneplácito *m* consent, approbation.
benévolo/la *adj* benevolent, kind-hearted.
benigno/na *adj* benign; kind; mild.

berberecho *m* cockle.
berenjena *f* eggplant.
bergantín *m* (*mar*) brig.
berrear *vi* to low, bellow.
berrinche *m* anger, rage, tantrum (applied to children).
berrinchudo/da *adj* bad-tempered.
berro *m* watercress.
berza *f* cabbage.
besar *vt* to kiss:—**~se** *vr* to kiss.
bestia *f* beast, animal; idiot.
besugo *m* sea bream.
betún *m* shoe polish.
biberón *m* feeding bottle.
bibliófilo/la *m/f* book-lover, bookworm.
bibliografía *f* bibliography.
biblioteca *f* library.
bicarbonato *m* bicarbonate.
bicho *m* small animal; bug:—**mal ~** villain.
bici *f* (*fam*) bike.
bicicleta *f* bicycle.
bidé *m* bidet.
bien *m* good, benefit; profit:—**~es** *mpl* goods *pl*, property; wealth:—*adv* well, right; very; willingly; easily:—**~ que** *conj* although:—**está ~** very well.
bienestar *m* well-being.
bienhechor/ra *m/f* benefactor.
bienvenida *f* welcome.
bifurcación *f* fork.
bigote *m* mustache; whiskers *pl*.
bilingüe *adj* bilingual.
bilis *f* bile.
billar *m* billiards *pl*.
billete *m* note, bill; ticket; (*ferro*) ticket:—**~ sencillo** single ticket:—**~ de ida y vuelta** return ticket.
biografía *f* biography.
biología *f* biology.
biombo *m* screen.
birlar *vt* to knock down at one blow; to pinch (*fam*).
bis *excl* encore.
bisabuela *f* great-grandmother.
bisabuelo *m* great-grandfather.
bisagra *f* hinge.
bisiesto *adj*:—**año ~** leap year.
bisnieto/ta *m/f* great-grandson/daughter.
bistec *m* steak.
bisturí *m* scalpel.
bisutería *f* costume jewelry.
bisco/ca *adj* cross-eyed.
biscocho *m* sponge cake; biscuit; ship's biscuit.
blanco/ca *adj* white; blank:—*m* whiteness; white person; blank, blank space; target (to shoot at).
blando/da *adj* soft, smooth; mild, gentle; (*fam*) cowardly.
blanquear *vt* to bleach; to whitewash; to launder (money).
blasfemar *vi* to blaspheme.
bledo *m*:—**no me importa un ~** I don't give a damn (*sl*).
blindado/da *adj* armor-plated; bullet-proof.
bloc *m* writing pad.
bloque *m* block.
bloquear *vt* to block; to blockade.
blusa *f* blouse.
bobada *f* folly, foolishness.
bobina *f* bobbin.
bobo/ba *m/f* idiot, fool; clown, funny man:—*adj* stupid, silly.
boca *f* mouth; entrance, opening; mouth of a river:—**~ en ~** *adv* by word of mouth:—**a pedir de ~** to one's heart's content.
bocacalle *f* entrance to a street.
bocadillo *m* sandwich, roll.
bocado *m* mouthful.
bocazas *m invar* big-mouth.
boceto *m* sketch; design; mock-up.
bochorno *m* sultry weather, scorching heat; blush.
bocina *f* (*mus*) trumpet; (*auto*) horn.
bocinar *vi* to sound a horn, hoot.
boda *f* wedding.
bodega *f* wine cellar; warehouse; bar.
bofetada *f* slap (in the face).
boina *f* beret.
boj *m* box, box tree.
bola *f* ball; marble; globe; (*fam*) lie, fib.
bolera *f* bowling alley.
bolero *m* bolero jacket; bolero dance.
boletín *m* bulletin; journal, review.
boleto *m* ticket.
boliche *m* jack at bowls; bowls, bowling alley; dragnet.
bolígrafo *m* (ballpoint) pen.
bollo *m* bread roll; lump.
bolo *m* ninepin; (large) pill.
bolsa *f* purse; bag; pocket; sac; stock exchange.
bolsillo *m* pocket; purse.
bomba *f* pump; bomb; surprise:—**dar a la ~** to pump:—**~ de gaso- lina** gas pump.
bombero *m* fireman.
bombilla *f* light bulb.
bombo *m* large drum.
bombón *m* chocolate.
bondad *f* goodness, kindness; courtesy.
bondadoso/sa *adj* good, kind.
boñiga *f* cow pat.
bonito *adj* pretty, nice-looking; pretty good, passable:—*m* tuna (fish).

boquerón *m* anchovy; large hole.
boquilla *f* mouthpiece of a musical instrument; nozzle.
borde *m* border; margin; (*mar*) board.
bordear *vi* (*mar*) to tack:—*vt* to go along the edge of; to flank.
bordillo *m* curb.
bordo *m* (*mar*) board of a ship.
boreal *adj* boreal, northern.
borracho/cha *adj* drunk, intoxicated; blind with passion:—*m/f* drunk, drunkard.
borrador *m* first draft; scribbling pad; eraser.
borrar *vt* to erase, rub out; to blur; to obscure.
borrasca *f* storm; violent squall of wind; hazard; danger.
borrico/ca *m/f* donkey, ass; blockhead.
borrón *m* blot, blur.
bosque *m* forest; wood.
bosquejo *m* sketch (of a painting); unfinished work.
bostezar *vi* to yawn; to gape.
bota *f* leather wine-bag; boot.
botánica *f* botany.
bote *m* bounce; thrust; tin, can; boat.
botella *f* bottle.
botijo *m* earthenware pitcher.
botín *m* high boot, half-boot; gaiter; booty.
botiquín *m* medicine chest.
botón *m* button; knob (of a radio etc); (*bot*) bud.
bóveda *f* arch; vault, crypt.
boxeo *m* boxing.
boya *f* (*mar*) buoy.
boyante *adj* buoyant, floating; (*fig*) fortunate, successful.
bozo *m* down (on the upper lip or chin); headstall (of a horse).
braga *f* sling, rope; nappy, diaper:—**~s** *fpl* breeches *pl*; panties *pl*.
bragueta *f* fly, flies *pl* (of pants/trousers).
brasa *f* live coal:—**estar hecho una ~** to be very flushed.
bravío/vía *adj* ferocious, savage, wild; coarse.
bravo/va *adj* brave, valiant; bullying; savage, fierce; rough; sumptuous; excellent, fine: —*excl* well done!
braza *f* fathom.
brazo *m* arm; branch (of a tree); enterprise; courage:—**luchar a ~ par-tido** to fight hand-to-hand.
brea *f* pitch; tar.
brebaje *m* potion.
brecha *f* (*mil*) breach; gap, opening.
breva *f* early fig; early large acorn.
breve *m* papal brief:—*f* (*mus*) breve: —*adj* brief, short:—**en ~** shortly.
brezo *m* (*bot*) heather.
bribón/ona *adj* dishonest, rascally.
bricolaje *m* do-it-yourself.
brida *f* bridle; clamp, flange.
brigada *f* brigade; squad, gang.
brillante *adj* brilliant; bright, shining:—*m* diamond.
brillar *vi* to shine; to sparkle, glisten; to shine, be outstanding.
brincar *vi* to skip; to leap, jump; to gambol; to fly into a passion.
brindis *m invar* toast.
brío *m* spirit, dash.
brisca *f* card game.
broca *f* reel; drill; shoemaker's tack.
brocado *m* gold or silver brocade:—**~/ da** *adj* embroidered, like brocade.
brocha *f* large brush:—**~ de afeitar** shaving brush.
broche *m* clasp; brooch; cufflink.
broma *f* joke.
bromear *vi* to joke.
bronca *f* row.
bronceado/da *adj* tanned:—*m* bronzing, suntan.
brotar *vi* (*bot*) to bud, germinate; to gush, rush out; (*med*) to break out.
bruces *adv*:—**a ~/de ~** face down-ward(s).
bruja *f* witch.
brújula *f* compass.
bruma *f* mist; (*mar*) sea mist.
bruñir *vt* to polish; to put rouge on.
brusco/ca *adj* rude; sudden; brusque.
brutal *adj* brutal, brutish:—*m* brute.
bruto *m* brute, beast:—**~/ ta** *adj* stupid; gross; brutish.
bucal *adj* oral.
bucear *vi* to dive.
bucle *m* curl.
buen *adj* (*before m nouns*) good.
bueno/na *adj* good, perfect; fair; fit, proper; good-looking:—**¡buenos días!** good morning!:—**¡buenas tardes!** good afternoon:—**¡buenas noches!** good night!:—**¡~!** right!
buey *m* ox, bullock.
bufanda *f* scarf.
bufete *m* desk, writing-table; lawyer's office.
bufo/fa *adj* comic:—**opera ~a** *f* comic opera.
buhardilla *f* attic.
búho *m* owl; unsocial person.
buitre *m* vulture.
bujía *f* candle; spark plug.
bullicio *m* bustle; uproar.
bulto *m* bulk; tumor, swelling; bust; baggage.

buñuelo *m* doughnut; fritter.
buque *m* vessel, ship, tonnage, capacity (of a ship); hull (of a ship).
burbuja *f* bubble.
burdel *m* brothel.
burguesía *f* bourgeoisie.
burlar *vt* to hoax; to defeat; to play tricks on, deceive; to frustrate:—**~se** *vr* to joke, laugh at.
burro *m* ass, donkey; idiot; saw-horse.
bursátil *adj* stock exchange *compd*.
buscar *vt* to seek, search for; to look for; to hunt after:—*vi* to look, search, seek.
busilis *m* difficulty, snag.
busto *m* bust.
butaca *f* armchair; seat.
butano *m* butane.
butifarra *f* Catalan sausage.
butrón *m* burglary.
buzo *m* diver.
buzón *m* mailbox; conduit, canal; cover of a jar.

C

cabalgar *vi* to ride, go riding.
cabalgata *f* procession.
caballa *f* mackerel.
caballería *f* mount, steed; cavalry; cavalry horse; chivalry; knighthood.
caballero *m* knight; gentleman; rider, horseman.
caballete *m* ridge of a roof; painter's easel; trestle; bridge (of the nose).
caballo *m* horse; (at chess) knight; queen (in cards):—**a ~** on horseback.
cabecera *f* headboard; head; far end; pillow; headline; vignette.
cabecilla *m* ringleader.
cabello *m* hair.
caber *vi* to fit.
cabeza *f* head; chief, leader; main town, chief center.
cabida *f* room, capacity.
cabildo *m* chapter (of church); meeting of a chapter; corporation of a town.
cabina *f* cabin; telephone booth.
cabizbajo/ja, cabizcaido/da *adj* crestfallen; pensive, thoughtful.
cable *m* cable, lead, wire.
cabo *m* end, extremity; cape, headland; (*mar*) cable, rope.
cabra *f* goat.
cabrón *m* cuckold:—**¡~!** (*fam*) bastard! (*sl*).
cacahuete *m* peanut.
cacao *m* (*bot*) cacao tree; cocoa.
cacarear *vi* to crow; to brag, boast.
cacerola *f* pan, saucepan; casserole.
cachalote *m* sperm whale.
cacharro *m* pot.
cachivache *m* pot; piece of junk.
cachondo/da *adj* randy; funny.
cachorro/ra *m/f* puppy; cub.
caco *m* pickpocket; coward.
cada *adj invar* each; every.
cadáver *m* corpse, cadaver.
cadena *f* chain; series, link; radio or TV network.
cadera *f* hip.
caducar *vi* to become senile; to expire, lapse; to deteriorate.
caer *vi* to fall; to tumble down; to lapse; to happen; to die:—**~se** *vr* to fall down.
café *m* coffee; cafe, coffee house.
cafetera *f* coffee pot.
cagar *vi* (*fam*) to have a shit (*sl*).
caimán *m* caiman, alligator.
caja *f* box, case; casket; cashbox; cash desk; supermarket check-out: —**~ de ahorros** savings bank:—**~ de cambios** gearbox.
cajón *m* bureau; locker.
cal *f* lime:—**~ viva** quick lime.
calabacín *m* small marrow, zucchini.
calabaza *f* pumpkin, squash.
calamar *m* squid.
calar *vt* to soak, drench; to penetrate, pierce; to see through; to lower:—**~se** *vr* to stall (of a car).
calavera *f* skull; madcap.
calcar *vt* to trace, copy.
calcetín *m* sock.
calcio *m* calcium.
calcomanía *f* transfer.
calculadora *f* calculator.
calcular *vt* to calculate, reckon; to compute.
caldear *vt* to weld; to warm, heat up.
calderada *f* stew.
calderilla *f* small change.
caldo *m* stock; broth.
calefacción *f* heating.
calendario *m* calendar.
calentar *vt* to warm up, heat up:—**~se** *vr* to grow hot; to dispute.
calidad *f* grade, quality, condition; kind.
cálido/da *adj* hot; (*fig*) warm.
caliente *adj* hot; fiery:—**en ~** in the heat of the moment.

callado/da *adj* silent, quiet.
callar *vi*, **~se** *vr* to be silent, keep quiet.
calle *f* street; road.
callejear *vi* to loiter about the streets.
callejón *m* alley.
callo *m* corn; callus:—**~s** *mpl* tripe.
calmante *m* (*med*) sedative.
calmar *vt* to calm, quiet, pacify:—*vi* to become calm.
calor *m* heat, warmth; ardor, passion.
calumnia *f* calumny, slander.
calvo/va *adj* bald; bare, barren.
calzado *m* footwear.
calzoncillos *mpl* underpants, shorts *pl*.
cama *f* bed:—**hacer la ~** to make the bed.
cámara *f* hall; chamber; room; camera; cine camera.
camarada *m/f* comrade, companion.
camarera *f* waitress.
camarero *m* waiter.
camarón *m* shrimp, prawn.
camarote *m* berth, cabin.
cambalache *m* exchange, swap.
cambiar *vt* to exchange; to change:—*vi* to change, alter:—**~se** *vr* to move house.
cambio *m* change, exchange; rate of exchange; bureau de change.
camelar *vt* to flirt with.
camello *m* camel; drug dealer.
camilla *f* couch; cot; stretcher.
caminar *vi* to travel; to walk, go.
camino *m* road; way.
camión *m* truck.
camisa *f* shirt; chemise.
camiseria *f* dry goods store.
camiseta *f* T-shirt; undershirt.
camisón *m* nightgown.
campamento *m* (*mil*) encampment.
campana *f* bell.
campanario *m* belfry.
campeón/ona *m/f* champion.
campesino/na, campestre *adj* rural.
campo *m* country; field; camp; ground; pitch.
caña *f* cane, reed; stalk; shinbone; glass of beer:—**~ dulce** sugar cane.
cañada *f* gully; glen; sheep-walk.
canal *m* channel, canal.
canalla *f* mob, rabble.
cáñamo *m* hemp.
canas *fpl* gray hair:—**peinar ~** to grow old.
cañaveral *m* reedbed.
cancelar *vt* to cancel; to write off.
cancha *f* (tennis) court.
canción *f* song.
candado *m* padlock.
candilejas *fpl* footlights *pl*.
canela *f* cinnamon.
cangrejo *m* crab; crayfish.
canica *f* marble.
canilla *f* shinbone; arm-bone; tap of a cask; spool.
canjear *vt* to exchange.
cano/na *adj* gray-haired; white-haired.
canoso/sa *adj* gray-haired; white-haired.
cansancio *m* tiredness, fatigue.
cansar *vt* to tire, tire out; to bore:—**~se** *vr* to get tired, grow weary.
cantante *m/f* singer.
cantar *m* song:—*vt* to sing; to chant: —*vi* to sing; to chirp.
cántaro *m* pitcher; jug:—**llover a ~s** to rain heavily, pour.
cantera *f* quarry.
cantidad *f* quantity, amount; number.
cantina *f* buffet, refreshment room; canteen; cellar; snack bar; bar.
canto *m* stone; singing; song; edge.
canuto *m* (*fam*) joint (*sl*), marijuana cigarette.
caño *m* tube, pipe; sewer.
cañón *m* tube, pipe; barrel; gun; canyon.
caoba *f* mahogany.
caos *m* chaos; confusion.
capa *f* cloak; cape; layer, stratum; cover; pretext.
capacidad *f* capacity; extent; talent.
capataz *m* foreman, overseer.
capaz *adj* capable; capacious, spacious, roomy.
capeo *m* challenging of a bull with a cloak.
caperuza *f* hood.
capirote *m* hood.
capital *m* capital; capital sum:—*f* capital, capital city:—*adj* capital; principal.
capítulo *m* chapter of a cathedral; chapter (of a book).
capó *m* (*auto*) hood.
capote *m* greatcoat; bullfighter's cloak.
capricho *m* caprice, whim, fancy.
captar *vt* to captivate; to understand; (*rad*) to tune in to, receive.
capturar *vt* to capture.
capucha *f* cap, cowl, hood of a cloak.
capullo *m* cocoon of a silkworm; rosebud.
cara *f* face; appearance:—**~ a ~** face to face.
cárabe *m* amber.
caracol *m* snail; seashell; spiral.
carácter *m* character; quality; condition; hand-writing.
característico/ca *adj* characteristic.
caradura *m/f*:—**es un ~** he's got a nerve.
caramba *excl* well!

carámbano *m* icicle.
carambola *f* cannon (at billiards); trick.
caravana *f* trailer; queue; tailback (traffic).
carbón *m* coal; charcoal; carbon; carbon paper.
carboncillo *m* charcoal.
carbono *m* (*quim*) carbon.
carburador *m* carburettor.
carcajada *f* (loud) laugh.
cárcel *f* prison, penitentiary; jail.
carcoma *f* deathwatch beetle; woodworm; anxious concern.
cardenal *m* cardinal; cardinal bird; (*med*) bruise, weal.
cardo *m* thistle.
carecer *vi*:—~ **de** to want, lack.
cargar *vt* to load, burden; to charge: —*vi* to charge; to load (up); to lean.
cargo *m* burden, loading; employment, post; office; charge, care; obligation; accusation.
carguero *m* freighter.
caricia *f* caress.
caridad *f* charity.
caries *f* (*med*) tooth decay, caries.
cariño *m* fondness, tenderness; love.
carmesí *adj*, *m* crimson.
carmín *m* carmine; rouge; lipstick.
carne *f* flesh; meat; pulp (of fruit).
carné, carnet *m* driver's license:—~ **de identidad** identity card.
carnicería *f* butcher's (store); carnage, slaughter.
caro/ra *adj* dear; affectionate; dear, expensive:—*adv* dearly.
carpa *f* carp (fish); tent.
carpeta *f* table cover; folder, file, portfolio.
carpintero *m* carpenter.
carraca *f* carrack (ship); rattle.
carrera *f* career; course; race; run, running; route; journey:—**a ~ abierta**, at full speed.
carrete *m* reel, spool, bobbin.
carretera *f* highway.
carril *m* lane (of highway); furrow.
carrillo *m* cheek; pulley.
carro *m* cart; car.
carrocería *f* bodywork, coachwork.
carta *f* letter; map; document; playing card; menu:—~ **blanca** carte blanche:—~ **credencial** *o* **de creencia** credentials *pl*:—~ **certificada** registered letter:—~ **de crédito** credit card:—~ **verde** green card.
cartabón *m* square (tool).
cartel *m* placard; poster; wall chart; cartel.
cartera *f* satchel; purse, handbag; briefcase.
carterista *m/f* pickpocket.
cartero *m* mailman.
cartón *m* cardboard, pasteboard; cartoon.
casa *f* house; home; firm, company: —~ **de campo** country house:—~ **de moneda** mint:—~ **de huéspedes** boarding house, rooming house.
casar *vt* to marry; to couple; to abrogate; to annul:—~**se** *vr* to marry, get married.
cascabel *m* small bell; rattlesnake.
cascada *f* cascade, waterfall.
cascanueces *m invar* nutcracker.
cascar *vt* to crack, break into pieces; (*fam*) to beat:—~**se** *vr* to be broken open.
cáscara *f* rind, peel; husk, shell; bark.
casco *m* skull; helmet; fragment; shard; hulk (of a ship); crown (of a hat); hoof; empty bottle, returnable bottle.
cascote *m* rubble, fragment of material used in building.
caserío *m* country house; hamlet.
casero *m* landlord; janitor:—~/**ra**, *adj* domestic; household *compd*; home-made.
caset(t)e *m* cassette:—*f* cassette-player.
casi *adv* almost, nearly:—~ **nada** next to nothing:—~ **nunca** hardly ever, almost never.
caso *m* case; occurrence, event; hap, casuality; occasion; (*gr*) case:—**en ese ~** in that case:—**en todo ~** in any case:—~ **que** in case.
caspa *f* dandruff; scurf.
castaño *m* chestnut tree:—~/ **na** *adj* chestnut(-colored), brown.
castañuela *f* castanet.
castellano *m* Castilian, Spanish.
castigar *vt* to castigate, punish; to afflict.
castillo *m* castle.
castizo/za *adj* pure, thoroughbred.
casto/ta *adj* pure, chaste.
castor *m* beaver.
castrar *vt* to geld, castrate; to prune; to cut the honeycombs out of (beehives).
casualidad *f* chance, accident.
cataplasma *f* poultice.
catar *vt* to taste; to inspect, examine; to look at; to esteem.
catarata *f* (*med*) cataract; waterfall.
catarro *m* catarrh; cold.
cátedra *f* professor's chair.
categoría *f* category; rank.
católico/ca *adj*, *m/f* catholic.
catorce *adj*, *m* fourteen.
catre *m* cot.
cauce *m* riverbed; (*fig*) channel.
caucho *m* rubber; tire.
caudal *m* volume, flow; property, wealth; plenty.

causa *f* cause; motive, reason; lawsuit:—**a ~ de** considering, because of.
causar *vt* to cause; to produce; to occasion.
cautela *f* caution, cautiousness.
cautivar *vt* to take prisoner in war; to captivate, charm.
cauto/ta *adj* cautious, wary.
cavar *vt* to dig up, excavate:—*vi* to dig, delve; to think profoundly.
caverna *f* cavern, cave.
cavidad *f* cavity, hollow.
cavilar *vt* to ponder, consider carefully.
cazador/ra *m/f* hunter; *m* huntsman: —**~ furtivo** poacher.
cazar *vt* to chase, hunt; to catch.
cazo *m* saucepan; ladle.
cazuela *f* casserole; pan.
cebada *f* barley.
cebar *vt* to feed (animals), fatten.
cebo *m* feed, food; bait, lure; priming.
cebolla *f* onion; bulb.
cebra *f* zebra.
cedazo *m* sieve, strainer.
ceder *vt* to hand over; to transfer, make over; to yield, give up:—*vi* to submit, comply, give in; to diminish, grow less.
cedro *m* cedar.
cédula *f* certificate; document; slip of paper; bill:—**~ de cambio** bill of exchange.
cegar *vi* to grow blind:—*vt* to blind; to block up.
ceja *f* eyebrow.
cejar *vi* to go backward(s); to slacken, give in.
celebrar *vt* to celebrate; to praise:—**~ misa** to say mass.
célebre *adj* famous, renowned; witty, funny.
celeste *adj* heavenly; sky-blue.
celestial *adj* heavenly; delightful.
celo *m* zeal; rut (in animals):—**~s** *mpl* jealousy.
celoso/sa *adj* zealous; jealous.
célula *f* cell.
cementerio *m* graveyard.
cena *f* supper.
cenar *vt* to have for dinner:—*vi* to have supper, have dinner.
cenegal *m* quagmire.
cenicero *m* ashtray.
ceniza *f* ashes *pl*:—**miércoles de ~** Ash Wednesday.
censo *m* census; tax; ground rent:—**~ electoral** electoral roll.
censurar *vt* to review, criticize; to censure, blame.
centella *f* lightning; spark.
centenar *m* hundred.
centeno *m* rye.
centésimo/ma *adj* hundredth:—*m* hundredth.
centígrado *m* centigrade.
centímetro *m* centimeter.
céntimo *m* cent.
centinela *f* sentry, guard.
central *adj* central:—*f* head office, headquarters; (telephone) exchange.
centro *m* center:—**~ comercial** shopping center.
centuplicar *vt* to increase a hundredfold.
ceñido/da *adj* tight-fitting; sparing, frugal.
ceñudo/da *adj* frowning, grim.
cepa *f* stock (of a vine); origin (of a family).
cepillo *m* brush; plane (tool).
cepo *m* branch, bough; trap; snare; poorbox.
cera *f* wax:—**~s** *fpl* honeycomb.
cerámica *f* pottery.
cerca *f* enclosure; fence:—**~s** *mpl* objects *pl* in the foreground of a painting:—*adv* near, at hand, close by:—**~ de** close, near.
cercano/na *adj* near, close by; neighboring, adjoining.
cerciorar *vt* to assure, ascertain, affirm:—**~se** *vr* to find out.
cerdo *m* pig, hog.
cerebro *m* brain.
cereza *f* cherry.
cerilla *f* wax taper; ear wax:—**~s** *fpl* matches, safety matches *pl*.
cero *m* nothing, zero.
cerrado/da *adj* closed, shut; locked; overcast, cloudy; broad (of accent).
cerrajero *m* locksmith.
cerrar *vt* to close, shut; to block up; to lock:—**~ la cuenta** to close an account:—**~se** *vr* to close; to heal; to cloud over:—*vi* to close, shut; to lock.
cerro *m* hill; neck (of an animal); backbone; combed flax or hemp:—**en ~** bareback.
cerrojo *m* bolt (of a door).
certamen *m* competition, contest.
certero *adj* accurate; well-aimed.
certeza, certidumbre *f* certainty.
certificado *m* certificate:—**~/ da** *adj* registered (of a letter).
cerveza *m* beer.
cesar *vt* to cease, stop; to fire (*sl*); to remove from office:—*vi* to cease, stop; to retire.
cese *m* suspension; dismissal.
cesión *f* cession; transfer.
césped *m* grass; lawn.
cesta *f* basket, pannier.

chabola *f* shack.
chal *m* shawl.
chalado/da *adj* crazy.
chale(t) *m* detached house.
chaleco *m* vest.
champán *m* champagne.
champiñón *m* mushroom.
champú *m* shampoo.
chamuscar *vt* to singe, scorch.
chantaje *m* blackmail.
chapa *f* metal plate; panel; (*auto*) license plate.
chaparrón *m* heavy shower (of rain).
chapuza *f* badly done job.
chaqueta *f* jacket.
charco *m* pool, puddle.
charcutería *f* store selling pork meat products.
charlar *vi* to chat.
charlatán/ana *m/f* chatterbox.
charol *m* varnish; patent leather.
chasco *m* disappointment; joke, jest.
chasis *m invar* (*auto*) chassis.
chasquido *m* crack; click.
chatarra *f* scrap.
chato/ta *adj* flat, flattish; snub-nosed.
chaval/la *m/f* lad/lass.
chicle *m* chewing gum.
chico/ca *adj* little, small:—*m/f* boy/girl.
chiflado/da *adj* crazy.
chile *m* chilli pepper.
chillar *vi* to scream, shriek; to howl; to creak.
chimenea *f* chimney; fireplace.
china *f* pebble; porcelain, chinaware; China silk.
chincheta *f* thumbtack.
chino/na *adj*, *m/f* Chinese:—*m* Chinese language.
chirriar *vi* to hiss; to creak; to chirp.
chisme *m* tale; thingummyjig.
chispa *f* spark; sparkle; wit; drop (of rain); drunkenness.
chiste *m* funny story, joke.
chivo/va *m/f* billy/nanny goat.
chocar *vi* to strike, knock; to crash:—*vt* to shock.
chochear *vi* to dodder, be senile; to dote.
chocolate *m* chocolate.
chófer *m* driver.
chopo *m* (*bot*) black poplar.
chorizo *m* pork sausage.
chorro *m* gush; jet; stream:—**a ~s** abundantly.
chuchería *f* trinket.
chulear *vi* to brag.
chuleta *f* chop.
chulo *m* rascal; pimp.
chupar *vt* to suck; to absorb.
churro *m* fritter.
ciática *f* sciatica.
cicatriz *f* scar.
cicatrizar *vt* to heal.
ciclista *m/f* cyclist.
ciclo *m* cycle.
cicuta *f* (*bot*) hemlock.
ciego/ga *adj* blind.
cielo *m* sky; heaven; atmosphere; climate.
ciempiés *m invar* centipede.
cien *adj*, *m* a hundred.
ciénaga *f* swamp.
ciencia *f* science.
cieno *m* mud; mire.
cierto/ta *adj* certain, sure; right, correct:—**por ~** certainly.
ciervo *m* deer, hart, stag:—**~ volante** stag beetle.
cierzo *m* cold northerly wind.
cifra *f* number, numeral; quantity; cipher; abbreviation.
cigarra *f* cicada.
cigarro *m* cigar; cigarette.
cigüeña *f* stork; crank (of a bell).
cilindro *m* cylinder.
cima *f* summit; peak; top.
cimiento *m* foundation, groundwork; basis, origin.
cinc *m* zinc.
cincelar *vt* to chisel, engrave.
cinco *adj*, *m* five.
cincuenta *adj*, *m* fifty.
cine *m* cinema.
cínico/ca *adj* cynical.
cinta *f* band, ribbon; reel.
cintura *f* waist.
cinturón *m* belt, girdle; (*fig*) zone:—**~ de seguridad** seatbelt.
ciprés *m* cypress tree.
circo *m* circus.
circuito *m* circuit; circumference.
circular *adj* circular; circulatory:—*vt* to circulate:—*vi* (*auto*) to drive.
círculo *m* circle; (*fig*) scope, compass.
circunspecto/ta *adj* circumspect, cautious.
circunstancia *f* circumstance.
circunvalacion *f*:—**carretera de ~** bypass.
cirio *m* wax candle.
ciruela *f* plum:—**~ pasa** prune.
cirugía *f* surgery.
cisne *m* swan.
citar *vt* to make an appointment with; to quote; (*jur*) to summon.
ciudad *f* city; town.
ciudadano/na *m/f* citizen:—*adj* civic.

clamor *m* clamor, outcry; peal of bells.
clandestino/na *adj* clandestine, secret, concealed.
clara *f* egg-white.
claraboya *f* skylight.
clarear *vi* to dawn:—**~se** *vr* to be transparent.
clarín *m* bugle; bugler.
clarinete *m* clarinet:—*m/f* clarinetist.
claro/ra *adj* clear, bright; evident, manifest:—*m* opening; clearing (in a wood).
clase *f* class; rank; order.
clasificar *vt* to classify.
claudicar *vi* to limp; to act deceitfully; to back down.
claustro *m* cloister; faculty (of a university).
cláusula *f* clause.
clavar *vt* to nail.
clave *f* key; (*mus*) clef:—*m* harpsichord.
clavel *m* (*bot*) carnation.
clavicordio *m* clavichord.
clavícula *f* clavicle, collar bone.
clavija *f* pin, peg.
clavo *m* nail; corn (on the feet); clove.
clemente *adj* clement, merciful.
clérigo *m* priest; clergyman.
cliente *m/f* client.
clima *m* climate.
climatizado/da *adj* air-conditioned.
clínica *f* clinic; private hospital.
clip *m* paper clip.
cloaca *f* sewer.
coacción *f* coercion, compulsion.
coagular *vt*, **~se** *vr* to coagulate; to curdle.
coartada *f* (*jur*) alibi.
coartar *vt* to limit, restrict, restrain.
cobalto *m* cobalt.
cobarde *adj* cowardly, timid.
cobaya *f* guinea pig.
cobertizo *m* small shed; shelter.
cobijar *vt* to cover; to shelter.
cobrar *vt* to recover:—**~se** *vr* (*med*) to come to.
cobre *m* copper; kitchen utensils *pl*; (*mus*) brass.
cocear *vt* to kick; (*fig*) to resist.
cocer *vt* to boil; to bake (bricks):—*vi* to boil; to ferment:—**~se** *vr* to suffer intense pain.
cochambroso/sa *adj* nasty; filthy, stinking.
coche *m* car; coach, carriage; pram, baby carriage:—(*ferro*) **~ cama** sleeping car:—**~ restaurante** restaurant car.
cochino/na *adj* dirty, filthy; nasty:—*m* pig, hog.
cocina *f* kitchen; stove; cookery.
cocinero/ra *m/f* cook.
coco *m* coconut; bogeyman.
cocodrilo *m* crocodile.
codazo *m* blow given with the elbow.
codear *vt*, *vi* to elbow:—**~se** *vr* **~se con** to rub shoulders with.
codiciar *vt* to covet, desire.
código *m* code; law; set of rules.
codillo *m* knee of a four-legged animal; angle; (*tec*) elbow (joint).
codo *m* elbow.
codorniz *f* quail.
coetáneo/nea *adj* contemporary.
coexistir *vi* to coexist.
cofia *f* (nurse's) cap.
cofradía *f* brotherhood, fraternity.
cofre *m* trunk.
coger *vt* to catch, take hold of; to occupy, take up:—**~se** *vr* to catch.
cogollo *m* heart of a lettuce or cabbage; shoot of a plant.
cogote *m* back of the neck.
cohecho *m* bribery.
coherencia *f* coherence.
cohete *m* rocket.
cohibido/da *adj* shy.
coincidir *vi* to coincide.
coito *m* intercourse, coitus.
cojear *vi* to limp, hobble; (*fig*) to go astray.
cojín *m* cushion.
cojo/ja *adj* lame, crippled.
col *f* cabbage.
cola *f* tail; queue; last place; glue.
colaborar *vi* to collaborate.
colada *f* wash, washing; (*quím*) bleach; sheep run.
colador *m* sieve.
colar *vt* to strain, filter:—*vi* to ooze: —**~se en** to get into without paying.
colcha *f* bedspread, counterpane.
colchón *m* mattress.
coleccionar *vt* to collect.
colecta *f* collection (for charity).
colectivo/va *adj* collective.
colega *m/f* colleague.
colegial *m* schoolboy.
colegiala *f* schoolgirl.
colegio *m* college; school.
colegir *vt* to collect; to deduce, infer.
cólera *f* bile; anger; fury, rage; cholera.
coleta *f* pigtail.
colgar *vt* to hang; to suspend; to decorate with tapestry:—*vi* to be suspended.
colibrí *m* hummingbird.
coliflor *m* cauliflower.
colina *f* hill.
colisión *f* collision; friction.
colmar *vt* to heap up:—*vi* to fulfill, realize.

colmena *f* hive, beehive.
colmillo *m* eyetooth; tusk.
colmo *m* height, summit; extreme:—**a ~** plentifully.
colocar *vt* to arrange; to place; to provide with a job:—**~se** *vr* to get a job.
collar *m* necklace; (dog) collar.
colono *m* colonist; farmer.
coloquio *m* conversation; conference.
color *m* color, hue; dye; rouge; suit (of cards).
colorado/da *adj* ruddy; red.
colorete *m* rouge.
columna *f* column.
columpio *m* swing, seesaw.
colza *f* (*bot*) rape; rape seed.
coma *f* (*gr*) comma:—*m* (*med*) coma.
comadreja *f* weasel.
comandante *m* commander.
comarca *f* territory, district.
combatir *vt* to combat, fight; to attack:—*vi* to fight.
combinar *vi* to combine.
combustible *adj* combustible:—*m* fuel.
comedia *f* comedy; play, drama.
comedido/da *adj* moderate, restrained.
comedor/ra *m/f* glutton:—*m* dining room.
comentar *vt* to comment on, expound.
comentario *m* comment, remark; commentary.
comenzar *vi* to commence, begin.
comer *vt* to eat; to take (a piece at chess):—*vi* to have lunch.
comercial *adj* commercial.
comercio *m* trade, commerce; business.
comestible *adj* eatable:—*mpl* **~s** food, foodstuffs *pl.*
cometa *m* comet:—*f* kite.
cometer *vt* to commit, charge; to entrust.
cómico/ca *adj* comic, comical.
comida *f* food; eating; meal; lunch.
comillas *fpl* quotation marks *pl.*
comino *m* cumin (plant or seed).
comisaría *f* police station; commissariat.
como *adv* as; like; such as.
cómo *adv* how?; why?:—*excl* what?
cómoda *f* bureau.
cómodo/da *adj* convenient; comfortable.
compacto/ta *adj* compact; close, dense.
compadecer *vt* to pity:—**~se** *vr* to agree with each other.
compaginar *vt* to arrange, put in order:—**~se** *vr* to tally.
compañero/ra *m/f* companion, friend; comrade; partner.
compañía *f* company.
comparar *vt* to compare.
compartimento *m* compartment.
compartir *vt* to share.
compás *m* compass; pair of compasses; (*mus*) measure, beat.
compatible *adj*:—**~ con** compatible with, consistent with.
compensar *vt* to compensate; to recompense.
competencia *f* competition, rivalry; competence.
competente *adj* competent; adequate.
compilar *vt* to compile.
compinche *m* pal, mate (*sl*).
complacencia *f* pleasure; indulgence.
complacer *vt* to please:—**~se** *vr* to be pleased with.
complejo *m* complex:—**~/ja** *adj* complex.
complementario/ria *adj* complementary.
complemento *m* complement.
completar *vt* to complete.
completo/ta *adj* complete; perfect.
complicar *vt* to complicate.
cómplice *m/f* accomplice.
complot *m* plot.
componer *vt* to compose; to constitute; to mend, repair; to strengthen, restore; to compose, calm:—**~se** *vr* **~se de** to consist of.
comportamiento *m* behavior.
compostura *f* composition, composure; mending, repairing; discretion; modesty, demureness.
compota *f* stewed fruit.
comprar *vt* to buy, purchase.
comprender *vt* to include, contain; to comprehend, understand.
compresa *f* sanitary napkin.
comprimido *m* pill.
comprimir *vt* to compress; to repress, restrain.
comprobar *vt* to verify, confirm; to prove.
comprometer *vt* to compromise; to embarrass; to implicate; to put in danger:—**~se** *vr* to compromise oneself.
compuerta *f* hatch; sluice.
compuesto *m* compound:—**~/ta** *adj* composed; made up of.
compulsar *vt* to collate, compare; to make an authentic copy.
compungirse *vr* to feel remorseful.
comulgar *vt* to administer communion to:—*vi* to receive communion.
común *adj* common, usual, general: —*m* community; public:—**en ~** in common.
comunicar *vt* to communicate:—**~se** *vr* to communicate (with each other).
comunidad *f* community.

con prep with; by:—~ **que** so then, providing that.
coñac *m* brandy, cognac.
cóncavo/va *adj* concave.
concebir *vt* to conceive:—*vi* to become pregnant.
conceder *vt* to give; to grant; to concede, allow.
concejal/la *m/f* member of a council.
concentrar *vt*:—~**se** *vr* to concentrate.
concepto *m* conceit, thought; judgement, opinion.
concernir *v imp* to regard, concern.
concertar *vt* to coordinate; to settle; to adjust; to agree; to arrange, fix up:—*vi* (*mus*) to harmonize, be in tune.
concesión *f* concession.
concha *f* shell; tortoise-shell.
conciencia *f* conscience.
concienciar *vt* to make aware:—~**se** *vr* to become aware.
concierto *m* concert; agreement; concerto: —**de** ~ in agreement, in concert.
conciliar *vt* to reconcile:—*adj* conciliar, council.
conciso/sa *adj* concise, brief.
concluir *vt* to conclude, end, complete; to infer, deduce:—~**se** *vr* to conclude.
concordar *vt* to reconcile, make agree:—*vi* to agree, correspond.
concordia *f* conformity, agreement.
concretar *vt* to make concrete; to specify.
concubina *f* concubine.
concurrido/da *adj* busy.
concursante *m/f* competitor.
concurso *m* crowd; competition; help, cooperation.
conde *m* earl, count.
condenable *adj* culpable.
condenar *vt* to condemn; to find guilty:—~**se** *vr* to blame oneself; to confess (one's guilt).
condensar *vt* to condense.
condescender *vi* to acquiesce, comply.
condición *f* condition, state; quality; status; rank; stipulation.
condimentar *vt* to flavor, season.
condolerse *vr* to sympathize.
condón *m* condom.
conducir *vt* to convey, conduct; to drive; to manage:—*vi* to drive:—~ **(a)** to lead (to):—~**se** *vr* to conduct oneself.
conducta *f* conduct, behavior; management.
conducto *m* conduit, pipe; drain; (*fig*) channel.
conductor/ra *m/f* conductor, guide; (*ferro*) guard; driver.
conectar *vt* to connect.
conejo *m* rabbit.
conexión *f* connection; plug; relationship.
confección *f* preparation; clothing industry.
conferencia *f* conference; telephone call.
confesar *vt* to confess; to admit.
confianza *f* trust; confidence; conceit; familiarity:—**en** ~ confidential.
confiar *vt* to confide, entrust:—*vi* to trust.
configurar *vt* to shape, form.
confinar *vt* to confine:—*vi* ~ **con** to border upon.
confirmar *vt* to confirm; to corroborate.
confiscar *vt* to confiscate.
confitería *f* sweet store.
confitura *f* preserve; jam.
conflicto *m* conflict.
conformar *vt* to shape; to adjust, adapt:—*vi* to agree:—~**se** *vr* to conform; to resign oneself.
conforme *adj* alike, similar; agreed: —*prep* according to.
confortar *vt* to comfort; to strengthen; to console.
confundir *vt* to confound, jumble; to confuse:—~**se** *vr* to make a mistake.
confusión *f* confusion.
congelado/da *adj* frozen:—*mpl* ~**s** frozen food.
congelar *vt* to freeze:—~**se** *vr* to congeal.
congeniar *vi* to get on well.
congoja *f* anguish, distress, grief.
congraciarse *vr* to ingratiate oneself.
congregar(se) *vt* (*vr*) to assemble, meet, collect.
conjetura *f* conjecture, guess.
conjugar *vt* (*gr*) to conjugate; to combine.
conjunto/ta *adj* united, joint:—*m* whole; (*mus*) ensemble, band; team.
conjurar *vt* to exorcize:—*vi* to conspire, plot.
conmemorar *vt* to commemorate.
conmigo *pn* with me.
conmover *vt* to move; to disturb.
conmutador *m* switch.
conmutar *vt* (*jur*) to commute; to exchange.
connotar *vt* to imply.
cono *m* cone.
conocer *vt* to know, understand:—~**se** *vr* to know one another.
conocimiento *m* knowledge, understanding; (*med*) consciousness; acquaintance; (*mar*) bill of lading.
conquistar *vt* to conquer.
consabido/da *adj* well-known; above-mentioned.
consagrar *vt* to consecrate.

consanguíneo/nea *adj* related by blood.
consecuencia *f* consequence; conclusion; consistency:—por ~ therefore.
consecuente *adj* consistent.
conseguir *vt* to attain; to get, obtain.
consejo *m* advice; council.
consentir *vt* to consent to; to allow; to admit; to spoil (a child).
conserje *m* doorman; janitor.
conservar *vt* to conserve; to keep; to preserve (fruit).
conservas *fpl* canned food.
conservatorio *m* (*mus*) conservatoire.
consideración *f* consideration; respect.
considerar *vt* to consider.
consigna *f* (*mil*) watchword; order, instruction; (*ferro*) left-luggage office.
consignar *vt* to consign, dispatch; to assign; to record, register.
consigo *pn* (*m*) with him; (*f*) with her; (*vd*) with you; (*refl*) with oneself.
consiguiente *adj* consequent.
consistente *adj* consistent; firm, solid.
consistir *vi*:—~ **en** to consist of; to be due to.
consola *f* control panel.
consolar *vt* to console, comfort, cheer.
consolidar *vt* to consolidate.
consonante *m* rhyme:—*f* (*gr*) consonant:—*adj* consonant, harmonious.
consorcio *m* partnership.
consorte *m/f* consort, companion, partner; accomplice.
conspirar *vi* to conspire, plot.
constante *adj* constant; firm.
constar *vi* to be evident, be certain; to be composed of, consist of.
constatar *vt* to note; to check.
consternar *vt* to dismay; to shock.
constipado/da *adj*:—**estar** ~ to have a cold.
constituir *vt* to constitute; to establish; to appoint.
construir *vt* to form; to build, construct; to construe.
consuegro/gra *m/f* father-in-law/mother-in-law of one's son or daughter.
consuelo *m* consolation, comfort.
cónsul *m* consul.
consultar *vt* to consult, ask for advice.
consultor/ra *m/f* adviser, consultant.
consultorio *m* (*med*) consulting room, doctor's rooms.
consumar *vt* to consummate, finish; to carry out.
consumir *vt* to consume; to burn, use; to waste, exhaust:—~**se** *vr* to waste away, be consumed.
contabilidad *f* accounting; bookkeeping.
contacto *m* contact; (*auto*) ignition.
contado/da *adj*:—~**s** scarce, few:—*m* **pagar al** ~ to pay (in) cash.
contador *m* meter; counter in a cafe: — ~/~**a** *m/f* accountant.
contagiar *vt* to infect:—~**se** *vr* to get infected.
contaminar *vt* to contaminate; to pollute; to corrupt.
contar *vt* to count, reckon; to tell:—*vi* to count:—~ **con** to rely upon.
contemplar *vt* to look at; to contemplate, consider; to meditate.
contemporáneo/nea *adj* contemporary.
contenedor *m* container.
contener *vt* to contain, hold; to hold back; to repress:—~**se** *vr* to control oneself.
contentar *vt* to content, satisfy; to please:—~**se** *vr* to be pleased or satisfied.
contento/ta *adj* glad; pleased; content:—*m* contentment; (*jur*) release.
contestador *m*:—~ **automatico** answering machine.
contestar *vt* to answer, reply; to prove, corroborate.
contienda *f* contest, dispute.
contigo *pn* with you.
contiguo/gua *adj* contiguous, close.
continente *m* continent, mainland:—*adj* continent.
contingencia *f* risk; contingency.
continuar *vt*, *vi* to continue.
continuo/nua *adj* continuous.
contorno *m* environs *pl*; contour, outline:—**en** ~ round about.
contra *prep* against; contrary to; opposite.
contrabajo *m* (*mus*) double bass; bass guitar; low bass.
contrabando *m* contraband; smuggling.
contrachapado *m* plywood.
contradecir *vt* to contradict.
contraer *vt* to contract, shrink; to make (a bargain):—~**se** *vr* to shrink, contract.
contrahecho/cha *adj* deformed; hunchbacked; counterfeit, fake, false.
contralto *m* (*mus*) contralto.
contrapartida *f* (*com*) balancing entry.
contrapelo *adv*:—**a** ~ against the grain.
contrapeso *m* counterpoise; counterweight.
contraproducente *adj* counterproductive.
contrariar *vt* to contradict, oppose; to vex.
contrariedad *f* opposition; setback; annoyance.
contrario/ria *m/f* opponent:—*adj* contrary, opposite:—**por el** ~ on the contrary.
contrarrestar *vt* to return a ball; (*fig*) to counteract.

contraseña *f* countersign; (*mil*) watch word.
contrasentido *m* contradiction.
contrastar *vt* to resist; to contradict; to assay (metals); to verify (measures and weights):—*vi* to contrast.
contratar *vt* to contract; to hire, engage.
contratiempo *m* setback; accident.
contrato *m* contract, agreement.
contravenir *vi* to contravene, transgress; to violate.
contraventana *f* shutter.
contribución *f* contribution; tax.
contribuir *vt*, *vi* to contribute.
contrincante *m* competitor.
controlar *vt* to control; to check.
contumaz *adj* obstinate, stubborn; (*jur*) guilty of contempt of court.
contundente *adj* overwhelming; blunt.
contusión *f* bruise.
convalecer *vi* to recover from sickness, convalesce.
convencer *vt* to convince.
conveniencia *f* suitability; usefulness; agreement:—**~s** *fpl* property.
convenir *vi* to agree, suit.
convento *m* convent, nunnery; monastery.
conversar *vi* to talk, converse.
convicto/ta *adj* convicted (found guilty).
convidar *vt* to invite.
convocar *vt* to convoke, assemble.
convocatoria *f* summons; notice of a meeting.
conyugal *adj* conjugal, married.
cónyuge *m/f* spouse.
cooperar *vi* to cooperate.
coordinar *vt* to arrange, coordinate.
copa *f* cup; glass; top of a tree; crown of a hat:—**~s** *fpl* hearts *pl* (at cards).
copiar *vt* to copy; to imitate.
copla *f* verse; (*mus*) popular song, folk song.
copo *m* small bundle; flake of snow.
coquetear *vi* to flirt.
coraje *m* courage; anger, passion.
coral *m* coral; choir:—*adj* choral.
corazón *m* heart; core:—**de ~** willingly.
corazonada *f* inspiration; quick decision; presentiment.
corbata *f* tie.
corchete *m* clasp; hook and eye.
corcho *m* cork; float (for fishing); cork bark.
cordel *m* cord, rope; (*mar*) line.
cordero *m* lamb; lambskin; meek, gentle person.
cordial *adj* cordial, affectionate:—*m* cordial.
cordillera *f* range of mountains.
cordón *m* cord, string; lace; cordon.
cornada *f* thrust with a bull's horn.
coro *m* choir; chorus.
corona *f* crown; coronet; top of the head; crown (of a tooth); tonsure; halo.
coronilla *f* crown of the head.
corpiño *m* bodice.
corporal *adj* corporal.
corpulento/ta *adj* corpulent, bulky.
corral *m* yard; farmyard; corral; playpen.
correa *f* leather strap, thong; flexibility.
correcto/ta *adj* exact, correct.
corregir *vt* to correct, amend; to reprehend:—**~se** *vr* to reform.
correo *m* post, mail; courier; mailman:—**a vuelta de ~** by return of post:—**~s** *mpl* post office.
correr *vt* to run; to flow; to travel over; to pull (a drape):—*vi* to run, rush; to flow; to blow (applied to the wind):—**~se** *vr* to be ashamed; to slide, move; to run (of colors).
correspondencia *f* correspondence; communication; agreement.
corresponder *vi* to correspond; to answer; to be suitable; to belong; to concern:—**~se** *vr* to love one another.
corresponsal *m/f* correspondent.
corriente *f* current; course, progression; (electric) current:—*adj* current; common, ordinary, general; fluent; flowing, running.
corro *m* circle of people.
corroer *vt* to corrode, erode.
corromper *vt* to corrupt; to rot; to turn bad; to seduce; to bribe:—**~se** *vr* to rot; to become corrupted:—*vi* to stink.
cortacesped *m* lawn mower.
cortado *m* coffee with a little milk:—**~/ da** *adj* cut; sour; embarrassed.
cortar *vt* to cut; to cut off, curtail; to intersect; to carve; to chop; to cut (at cards); to interrupt:—**~se** *vr* to be ashamed or embarrassed; to curdle.
corte *m* cutting; cut; section; length (of cloth); style:—*f* (royal) court; capital (city):—**C~s** *fpl* Spanish Parliament.
cortejo *m* entourage; courtship; procession; lover.
cortés/esa *adj* courteous, polite.
cortesía *f* courtesy, good manners *pl*.
corteza *f* bark; peel; crust; (*fig*) outward appearance.
cortina *f* curtain.
corto/ta *adj* short; scanty, small; stupid; bashful:—**a la ~a** *o* **a la larga** sooner or later.
corzo/za *m/f* roe deer, fallow deer.
cosa *f* thing; matter, affair:—**no hay tal ~** nothing of the sort!

cosecha *f* harvest; harvest time:—**de su ~** of one's own invention.
coser *vt* to sew; to join.
cosquillas *fpl* tickling; (*fig*) agitation.
costa *f* cost, price; charge, expense; coast, shore:—**a toda ~** at all events.
costado *m* side; (*mil*) flank; side of a ship.
costal *m* sack, large bag.
costar *vt* to cost; to need.
coste *m* cost, expense.
costero/ra *adj* coastal; (*mar*) coasting.
costilla *f* rib; cutlet:—**~s** *fpl* back, shoulders *pl.*
costra *f* crust; (*med*) scab.
costumbre *f* custom, habit.
cotejar *vt* to compare.
cotidiano/na *adj* daily.
cotilla *m/f* gossip.
cotizar *vt* to quote:—**~se** *vr* **~ a** to sell at; to be quoted at.
coto *m* enclosure; reserve; boundary stone.
cotorra *f* small parrot; (*col*) chatterbox.
covacha *f* small cave, grotto.
coyuntura *f* joint, articulation; juncture.
coz *f* kick; recoil (of a gun); ebbing (of a flood); (*fig*) insult.
cráneo *m* skull.
crear *vt* to create, make; to establish.
crecer *vi* to grow, increase; to rise.
crecida *f* swell (of rivers).
creciente *f* crescent (moon); (*mar*) flood tide:—*adj* growing; crescent.
crecimiento *m* increase; growth.
crédito *m* credit; belief, faith; reputation.
creer *vt*, *vi* to believe; to think; to consider.
crema *f* cream; custard.
cremallera *f* zipper.
crepúsculo *m* twilight.
cresta *f* crest (of birds).
creyente *m/f* believer.
cría *f* breeding; young.
criadero *m* (*bot*) nursery; breeding place.
criadilla *f* testicle; small loaf; truffle.
crianza *f* breeding, rearing.
criar *vt* to create, produce; to breed; to breast-feed; to bring up.
criatura *f* creature; child.
crimen *m* crime.
criminal *adj*, *m/f* criminal.
crin *f* mane; horsehair.
crío/a *m/f* (*fam*) kid.
cripta *f* crypt.
crisis *f invar* crisis.
crisol *m* crucible; melting pot.
crispar *vt* to set on edge; to tense up.
cristal *m* crystal; glass; pane; lens.
cristalino/na *adj* crystalline.
cristalizar *vt* to crystallize.
cristiano/na *adj*, *m/f* Christian.
criterio *m* criterion.
crítica *m/f* criticism.
criticar *vt* to criticize.
croar *vi* to croak.
cromo *m* chrome.
crónica *f* chronicle; news report; feature.
crónico/ca *adj* chronic.
cronista *m/f* chronicler; reporter, columnist.
cronómetro *m* stopwatch.
cruce *m* crossing; crossroads.
crucero *m* cruiser; cruise; transept; crossing.
crucifijo *m* crucifix.
crucigrama *m* crossword.
crudo/da *adj* raw; green, unripe; crude; cruel; hard to digest.
cruel *adj* cruel.
crueldad *f* cruelty.
crujiente *adj* crunchy.
crujir *vi* to crackle; to rustle.
crustáceo *m* crustacean.
cruz *f* cross; tails (of a coin).
cruzar *vt* to cross; (*mar*) to cruise:—**~se** *vr* to cross; to pass each other.
cuaderno *m* notebook; exercise book; logbook.
cuadra *f* block; stable.
cuadrado/da *adj*, *m* square.
cuadrante *m* quadrant; dial.
cuadrar *vt*, *vi* to square; to fit, suit, correspond.
cuadrilátero/ra *adj*, *m* quadrilateral.
cuadrilla *f* party, group; gang, crew.
cuadro *m* square; picture, painting; window frame; scene; chart.
cuadrúpedo/da *adj* quadruped.
cuajar *vt* to coagulate; to thicken; to adorn; to set:—**~se** *vr* to coagulate, curdle; to set; to fill up.
cual *pn* which; who; whom:—*adv* as; like: —*adj* such as.
cuál *pn* which (one).
cualidad *f* quality.
cualquier *adj* any.
cualquiera *adj* anyone, anybody; someone, somebody; whoever; whichever.
cuando *adv* when; if; even:—*conj* since:—**de ~ en ~** from time to time: —**~ más/~ mucho** at most, at best: —**~ menos** at least.
cuándo *adv* when:—**¿de cuándo acá?** since when?
cuánto *adj* what a lot of; how much?: —**¿~s?** how many?:—*pn*, *adv* how; how much; how many.

cuanto/ta *adj* as many as; as much as; all; whatever:—*adv* **en ~** as soon as:—**en ~ a** as regards:—**~ más** moreover, the more as.
cuarenta *adj*, *m* forty.
cuaresma *f* Lent.
cuarto *m* fourth part; quarter; room, apartment; span:—**~s** *mpl* cash, money: —**~/ta** *adj* fourth.
cuarzo *m* quartz.
cuatro *adj*, *m* four.
cuatrocientos/tas *adj* four hundred.
cuba *f* cask; tub; (*fig*) drunkard.
cubierta *f* cover; deck of a ship; (*auto*) hood; tire; pretext.
cubierto *m* cover; shelter; place at table; meal at a fixed charge:—**~s** *mpl* cutlery, silverware.
cubo *m* cube; bucket; can:—**~de la basura** garbage can.
cubrir *vt* to cover; to disguise; to protect; to roof a building:—**~se** *vr* to become overcast.
cucaracha *f* cockroach.
cuchara *f* spoon.
cucharada *f* spoonful; ladleful.
cucharadita *f* teaspoonful.
cuchichear *vi* to whisper.
cuchillo *m* knife.
cuclillas *adv*:—**en ~** squatting.
cuclillo *m* cuckoo; (*fig*) cuckold.
cuello *m* neck; collar.
cuenca *m* bowl, deep valley; hollow; socket of the eye.
cuenta *f* calculation; account; check, bill (in a restaurant); count, counting; bead; importance.
cuento *m* tale, story, narrative.
cuerda *f* rope; string; spring.
cuerdo/da *adj* sane; prudent, judicious.
cuerno *m* horn.
cuero *m* hide, skin, leather.
cuerpo *m* body; cadaver, corpse.
cuesta *f* slope, hill; incline:—**ir ~ abajo** to go downhill:—**~ arriba** uphill.
cuestión *f* question, matter; dispute; quarrel; problem.
cueva *f* cave; cellar.
cuidado *m* care, worry, concern; charge.
cuidar *vt* to care for; to mind, look after.
culebra *f* snake.
culo *m* backside; bum (*sl*); bottom.
culpa *f* fault, blame; guilt.
culpable *adj* culpable; guilty:—*m/f* culprit.
cultivar *vt* to cultivate.
culto/ta *adj* cultivated, cultured; refined, civilized:—*m* culture; worship.
cumbre *f* top, summit.
cumplir *vt* to carry out, fulfil; to serve (a prison sentence); to carry out (death penalty); to attain, reach (a certain age):—**~se** *vr* to be fulfilled; to expire, be up.
cuna *f* cradle.
cuña *f* wedge.
cuñado/da *m/f* brother/sister-in-law.
cura *m* priest:—*f* cure; treatment.
curar *vt* to cure; to treat, dress (a wound); to salt; to dress; to tan.
curioso/sa *adj* curious:—*m/f* bystander.
currar *vi* (*fam*)to work.
curso *m* course, direction; year (at university); subject.
curtir *vt* to tan leather:—**~se** *vr* to become sunburned; to become inured.
curva *f* curve, bend.
custodia *f* custody, safekeeping, care; monstrance.
cutis *m* skin.
cutre *adj* (*fam*) mean, grotty.
cuyo/ya *pn* whose, of which, of whom.

D

dado *m* die (*pl* dice).
daga *f* dagger.
dama *f* lady, gentlewoman; mistress; queen; actress of principal parts.
damnificar *vt* to hurt, injure, damage.
dañar *vt* to hurt, injure; to damage.
dañino/na *adj* harmful; noxious; mischievous.
danza *f* dance.
dar *vt* to give; to supply, administer, afford; to deliver.
dátil *m* (*bot*) date.
dato *m* fact.
de *prep* of; from; for; by; on; to; with.
debajo *adv* under, underneath, below.
debatir *vt* to debate, argue, discuss.
debe *m* (*com*) debit:—**~ y haber** debit and credit.
deber *m* obligation, duty; debt:—*vt* to owe; to be obliged to:—*vi* **debe (de)** it must, it should.
debidamente *adv* justly, duly; exactly, perfectly.
débil *adj* feeble, weak; sickly; frail.

debilitar *vt* to debilitate, weaken.
decadencia *f* decay, decline.
decena *f* ten.
decencia *f* decency.
decepción *f* disappointment.
decidir *vt* to decide, determine.
décimo/ma *adj*, *m* tenth.
decir *vt* to say; to tell; to speak; to name.
decisión *f* decision; determination, resolution; sentence.
declamar *vi* to declaim; to harangue.
declarar *vt* to declare; to manifest; to expound; to explain; (*jur*) to decide:—**~se** *vr* to declare one's opinion:—*vi* to testify.
declinar *vi* to decline; to decay, degenerate:—*vt* (*gr*) to decline.
declive *m* slope; decline.
decorar *vt* to decorate, adorn; to illustrate.
decrecer *vi* to decrease.
decrépito/ta *adj* decrepit, worn out with age.
decretar *vt* to decree, determine.
dedal *m* thimble; very small drinking glass.
dedicar *vt* to dedicate, devote; to consecrate:—**~se** *vr* to apply oneself to.
dedo *m* finger; toe; small bit:—**~ meñique** little finger:—**~ pulgar** thumb:—**~ del corazón** middle finger:—**~ anular** ring finger.
deducir *vt* to deduce, infer; to allege in pleading; to subtract.
defecto *m* defect; defectiveness.
defectuoso/sa *adj* defective, imperfect, faulty.
defender *vt* to defend, protect; to justify, assert;to resist, oppose.
defensor/ra *m/f* defender, protector; lawyer, defense counsel.
deferir *vi* to defer; to yield (to another's opinion):—*vt* to communicate.
deficiente *adj* defective.
definir *vt* to define, describe, explain; to decide.
definitivo/va *adj* definitive; positive.
deformar *vt* to deform:—**~se** *vr* to become deformed.
deforme *adj* deformed; ugly.
defraudar *vt* to defraud, cheat; to usurp; to disturb.
defunción *f* death; funeral.
degenerar *vi* to degenerate.
degollar *vt* to behead; to destroy, ruin.
degradar *vt* to degrade:—**~se** *vr* to degrade or demean oneself.
degustar *vt* to taste.
dehesa *f* pasture.
dejadez *f* slovenliness, neglect.
dejar *vt* to leave, quit; to omit; to let; to permit, allow; to forsake; to bequeath; to pardon:—**~ de** to stop; to fail to:—**~se** *vr* to abandon oneself.
del *adj* of the (contraction of *de* and *el*).
delantal *m* apron.
delante *adv* in front; opposite; ahead: —**~ de** in front of; before.
delantero/ra *adj* front:—*m* forward.
delegar *vt* to delegate; to substitute.
deleitar *vt* to delight.
deletrear *vt* to spell; to examine; to conjecture.
delfín *m* dolphin; dauphin.
delgado/da *adj* thin; delicate, fine; light; slender, lean.
deliberadamente *adv* deliberately.
deliberar *vi* to consider, deliberate: —*vt* to debate; to consult.
delicado/da *adj* delicate, tender; faint; exquisite; delicious, dainty; slender, subtle.
delicioso/sa *adj* delicious; delightful.
delincuencia *f* delinquency.
delineante *m/f* draftsman/woman.
delirar *vi* to rave; to talk nonsense.
delito *m* offence; crime.
demacrado/da *adj* pale and drawn.
demandar *vt* to demand; to ask; to claim; to sue.
demarcar *vt* to mark out (limits).
demás *adj* other; remaining:—*pn* **los/las ~** the others, the rest:—**estar ~** to be over and above; to be useless or superfluous:—**por ~** in vain.
demasiado/da *adj* too; excessive:—*adv* too, too much.
demencia *f* madness.
demoler *vt* to demolish; to destroy.
demonio *m* demon.
demorar *vt* to delay:—**~se** *vr* to be delayed:—*vi* to linger.
demostrar *vt* to prove, demonstrate; to manifest.
denegar *vt* to deny; to refuse.
denigrar *vt* to blacken; to insult.
denominar *vt* to name; to designate.
denotar *vt* to denote; to express.
denso/sa *adj* dense, thick; compact.
dentado/da *adj* toothed; indented.
dentadura *f* set of teeth.
dentífrico *m* toothpaste.
dentista *m/f* dentist.
dentro *adv* within:—*pn* **~ de** in, inside.
denunciar *vt* to advise; to denounce; to report.
depender *vi*:—**~ de** to depend on, be dependent on.

dependiente *m* sales clerk:—*adj* dependent.
depilatorio *m* hair remover.
deponer *vt* to depose; to declare; to displace; to deposit.
deportar *vt* to deport.
deporte *m* sport.
deportista *m/f* sportsman/woman.
depositar *vt* to deposit; to confide; to put away for safekeeping.
depravación *f* depravity.
deprimir *vt* to depress:—**~se** *vr* to become depressed.
deprisa *adv* quickly.
depurar *vt* to cleanse, purify; to filter.
derecho/cha *adj* right; straight; just; perfect; certain:—*m* right, justice; law; just claim; tax, duty; fee:—*adv* straight.
derivar *vt, vi* to derive; (*mar*) to drift.
derogar *vt* to derogate, abolish; to reform.
derramar *vt* to drain off (water); to spread; to spill, scatter; to waste, shed: —**~se** *vr* to pour out.
derretir *vt* to melt; to consume; to thaw:—**~se** *vr* to melt.
derribar *vt* to demolish; to flatten.
derrochar *vt* to dissipate; to squander.
derrotar *vt* to destroy; to defeat.
derruir *vt* to demolish.
derrumbar *vt* to throw down:—**~se** *vr* to collapse.
desabrido/da *adj* tasteless, insipid; rude; unpleasant.
desacato *m* disrespect, incivility.
desacertado/da *adj* mistaken; unwise; inconsiderate.
desaconsejar *vt* to advise against.
desacostumbrado/da *adj* unusual.
desacuerdo *m* blunder; disagreement; forgetfulness.
desafiar *vt* to challenge; to defy.
desafinar *vi* to be out of tune.
desafuero *m* outrage; excess.
desagradable *adj* disagreeable, unpleasant.
desagradecido/da *adj* ungrateful.
desagüe *m* channel, drain; drainpipe; drainage.
desahogar *vt* to ease; to vent:—**~se** *vr* to recover; to relax.
desahuciar *vt* to cause to despair; to give up; to evict.
desajustar *vt* to make uneven; to unbalance:—**~se** *vr* to get out of order.
desalentar *vt* to put out of breath; to discourage.
desaliño *m* slovenliness; carelessness.
desalmado/da *adj* cruel, inhuman.
desalojar *vt* to eject; to move out:—*vi* to move out.
desamparar *vt* to forsake, abandon; to relinquish.
desangrar *vt* to bleed; to drain (a pond); (*fig*) to exhaust (one's means):—**~se** *vr* to lose a lot of blood.
desanimar *vt* to discourage:—**~se** *vr* to lose heart.
desaparecer *vi* to disappear.
desapercibido/da *adj* unnoticed.
desaprobar *vt* to disapprove; to condemn; to reject.
desaprovechado/da *adj* useless; unprofitable; backward; slack.
desaprovechar *vt* to waste, turn to a bad use.
desarmar *vt* to disarm; to disband (troops); to dismantle; (*fig*) to pacify.
desarraigar *vt* to uproot; to root out; to extirpate.
desarrollar *vt* to develop; to unroll; to unfold:—**~se** *vr* to develop; to be unfolded; to open.
desasosiego *m* restlessness; anxiety.
desastre *m* disaster; misfortune.
desatar *vt* to untie, loose; to separate; to solve:—**~se** *vr* to come undone; to break.
desatascar *vt* to unblock; to clear.
desatender *vt* to pay no attention to; to disregard.
desatinar *vi* to talk nonsense; to reel, stagger.
desatornillar *vt* to unscrew.
desayunar *vt* to have for breakfast:—**~se** *vr* to breakfast:—*vi* to have breakfast.
desazón *f* disgust; uneasiness; annoyance.
desbarrar *vi* to talk nonsense.
desbordar *vt* to exceed:—**~se** *vr* to overflow.
descalabrado/da *adj* wounded on the head; imprudent.
descalificar *vt* to disqualify; to discredit.
descalzo/za *adj* barefooted; (*fig*) destitute.
descaminado/da *adj* (*fig*) misguided.
descansar *vt* to rest:—*vi* to rest; to lie down.
descansillo *m* landing.
descapotable *m* convertible.
descarado/da *adj* cheeky, barefaced.
descargar *vt* to unload, discharge:—**~se** *vr* to unburden oneself.
descarriar *vt* to lead astray; to misdirect:—**~se** *vr* to lose one's way; to stray; to err.
descarrilar *vi* (*ferro*) to leave or run off the rails.

descartar *vt* to discard; to dismiss; to rule out.
descendencia *f* descent, offspring.
descender *vt* to take down:—*vi* to descend, walk down; to flow; to fall:—~ **de** to be derived from.
descenso *m* descent; drop.
descifrar *vt* to decipher; to unravel.
descollar *vi* to excel.
descolorido/da *adj* pale, colorless.
descomunal *adj* uncommon; huge.
desconcertar *vt* to disturb; to confound; to disconcert:—**~se** *vr* to be bewildered; to be upset.
desconectar *vt* to disconnect.
desconfiar *vi*:—~ **de** to mistrust, suspect.
descongelar *vt* to defrost.
desconocer *vt* to disown, disavow; to be totally ignorant of (a thing); not to know (a person); not to acknowledge (a favor received).
desconsuelo *m* distress; trouble; despair.
descontar *vt* to discount; to deduct.
descontento *m* dissatisfaction; disgust.
descortés/esa *adj* impolite, rude.
descoser *vt* to unseam; to separate:—**~se** *vr* to come apart at the seams.
descreído/da *adj* incredulous.
descremado/da *adj* skimmed.
describir *vt* to describe; to draw, delineate.
descuartizar *vt* to quarter; to carve.
descubrir *vt* to discover, disclose; to uncover; to reveal; to show:—**~se** *vr* to reveal oneself; to take off one's hat; to confess.
descuento *m* discount; decrease.
descuidado/da *adj* careless, negligent.
descuidar *vt* to neglect:—*vi* **~se** *vr* to be careless.
desde *prep* since; after; from:—~ **lue-go** of course:—~ **entonces** since then.
desdén *m* disdain, scorn.
desdeñar *vt* to disdain, scorn:—**~se** *vr* to be disdainful.
desdentado/da *adj* toothless.
desdicha *f* misfortune, calamity; great poverty.
desdoblar *vt* to unfold, spread open.
desear *vt* to desire, wish; to require, demand.
desecar *vt* to dry up.
desechar *vt* to depreciate; to reject; to refuse; to throw away.
desecho *m* residue:—**~s** *mpl* trash.
desembarcar *vt* to unload, disembark:—*vi* to disembark, land.
desembolsar *vt* to pay out.
desempatar *vi* to hold a play-off.
desempeñar *vt* to redeem; to extricate from debt; to fulfil (any duty or promise); to acquit:—**~se** *vr* to get out of debt.
desempleo *m* unemployment.
desencadenar *vt* to unchain:—**~se** *vr* to break loose; to burst.
desencajar *vt* to disjoint; to dislocate; to disconnect.
desencanto *m* disenchantment.
desenchufar *vt* to unplug.
desenfado *m* ease; facility; calmness, relaxation.
desenfocado/da *adj* out of focus.
desenfreno *m* wildness; lack of self-control.
desengañar *vt* to disillusion:—**~se** *vr* to become disillusioned.
desenganchar *vt* to unhook; to uncouple.
desengrasar *vt* to take the grease off.
desenlace *m* climax; outcome.
desenredar *vt* to disentangle.
desenroscar *vt* to untwist; to unroll.
desentenderse *vr* to feign not to understand; to pass by without noticing.
desenterrar *vt* to exhume; to dig up.
desentonar *vi* to be out of tune; to clash.
desenvolver *vt* to unfold; to unroll; to decipher, unravel; to develop:—**~se** *vr* to develop; to cope.
deseo *m* desire, wish.
desequilibrado/da *adj* unbalanced.
desertar *vt* to desert; (*jur*) to abandon (a cause).
desesperar *vi*, **~se** *vr* to despair:—*vt* to make desperate.
desestabilizar *vt* to destabilize.
desfachatez *f* impudence.
desfalco *m* embezzlement.
desfallecer *vi* to get weak; to faint.
desfasado/da *adj* old-fashioned.
desfavorable *adj* unfavorable.
desfiladero *m* gorge.
desfilar *vi* (*mil*) to parade.
desfogarse *vr* to give vent to one's passion or anger.
desgana *f* disgust; loss of appetite; aversion, reluctance.
desgañitarse *vr* to scream, bawl.
desgarrar *vt* to tear; to shatter.
desgaste *m* wear (and tear).
desgracia *f* misfortune; disgrace; accident; setback.
desgreñado/da *adj* disheveled.
deshabitado/da *adj* deserted, uninhabited; desolate.
deshacer *vt* to undo, destroy; to cancel, efface; to rout (an army); to solve; to melt; to break up, divide; to dissolve in a liquid;

to violate (a treaty); to diminish; to disband (troops):—**~se** *vr* to melt; to come apart.
deshelar *vt* to thaw:—**~se** *vr* to thaw, melt.
desheredar *vt* to disinherit.
deshidratar *vt* to dehydrate.
deshinchar *vt* to deflate:—**~se** *vr* to go flat, go down.
deshonesto/ta *adj* indecent.
deshonrar *vt* to affront, insult, defame; to dishonor.
deshuesar *vt* to rid of bones; to stone.
desidia *f* idleness, indolence.
desierto/ta *adj* deserted; solitary:—*m* desert; wilderness.
designar *vt* to design; to intend; to appoint; to express, name.
desigual *adj* unequal, unlike; uneven, craggy, cliffy.
desilusionar *vt* to disappoint:—**~se** *vr* to become disillusioned.
desinfectar *vt* to disinfect.
desinflar *vt* to deflate.
desinteresado/da *adj* disinterested; unselfish.
desistir *vi* to desist, cease.
desleal *adj* disloyal; unfair.
desleír *vt* to dilute; to dissolve.
deslenguado/da *adj* foul-mouthed.
desligar *vt* to untie; to separate.
deslizar *vt* to slip, slide; to let slip (a comment):—**~se** *vr* to slip; to skid; to flow softly; to creep in.
deslumbrar *vt* to dazzle; to puzzle.
desmayar *vi* to be dispirited or faint-hearted:—**~se** *vr* to faint.
desmedido/da *adj* disproportionate.
desmemoriado/da *adj* forgetful.
desmentir *vt* to give the lie to:—**~se** *vr* to contradict oneself.
desmenuzar *vt* to crumble; to chip at; to fritter away; to examine minutely.
desmesurado/da *adj* excessive; huge; immeasurable.
desmoralizar *vt* to demoralize.
desnatado/da *adj* skimmed.
desnivel *m* unevenness of the ground.
desnudar *vt* to undress; to strip; to discover, reveal:—**~se** *vr* to undress.
desnutrido/da *adj* undernourished.
desobedecer *vt*, *vi* to disobey.
desocupar *vt* to vacate; to empty:—**~se** *vr* to retire from a business; to withdraw from an arrangement.
desodorante *m* deodorant.
desolado/da *adj* desolate, disconsolate.
desordenar *vt* to disorder; to untidy: —**~se** *vr* to get out of order.
desorganizar *vt* to disorganize.
desorientar *vt* to mislead; to confuse: —**~se** *vr* to lose one's way.
desovar *vi* to spawn.
despabilado/da *adj* watchful, vigilant; wide-awake.
despacho *m* dispatch, expedition; cabinet; office; commission; warrant, patent; expedient; smart answer.
despachurrar *vt* to squash, crush; to mangle.
despacio *adv* slowly, leisurely; little by little:—**¡~!** softly!, gently!
desparramar *vt* to disseminate, spread; to spill; to squander, lavish: —**~se** *vr* to be dissipated.
despavorido *adj* frightened.
despecho *m* indignation; displeasure; spite; dismay, despair; deceit; derision, scorn: —**a ~ de** in spite of.
despectivo/va *adj* pejorative, derogatory.
despedir *vt* to discharge; to dismiss (from office); to see off:—**~se** *vr* **~ de** to say goodbye to.
despegar *vt* to unglue; to take off:—**~se** *vr* to come loose.
despegue *m* take-off.
despeinar *vt* to ruffle.
despejado/da *adj* sprightly, quick; clear.
despellejar *vt* to skin.
despensa *f* pantry, larder; provisions *pl*.
desperdiciar *vt* to squander.
desperdigar *vt* to separate; to scatter.
desperfecto *m* slight damage; flaw.
despertador *m* alarm clock.
despertar *vt* to wake up, rouse from sleep; to excite:—*vi* to wake up; to grow lively or sprightly:—**~se** *vr* to wake up.
despiadado/da *adj* heartless; merciless.
despido *m* dismissal.
despierto/ta *adj* awake; vigilant; fierce; brisk, sprightly.
despistar *vt* to mislead; to throw off the track:—**~se** *vr* to take the wrong way; to become confused.
desplazar *vt* to move; to scroll:—**~se** *vr* to travel.
desplegar *vt* to unfold, display; to explain, elucidate; (*mar*) to unfurl:—**~se** *vr* to open out; to travel.
desplomarse *vr* to fall to the ground; to collapse.
despoblar *vt* to depopulate; to desolate: —**~se** *vr* to become depopulated.
despojar *vt*:—**~ (de)** to strip (of); to deprive (of):—**~se** *vr* to undress.
desposar *vt* to marry, betroth:—**~se** *vr* to be betrothed or married.
desposeer *vt* to dispossess.

déspota *m* despot.
despreciar *vt* to offend; to despise.
desprender *vt* to unfasten, loosen; to separate:—**~se** *vr* to give way; to fall down; to extricate oneself.
despreocupado/da *adj* careless; unworried.
desprevenido/da *adj* unawares, unprepared.
desproporcionado/da *adj* disproportionate.
desprovisto/ta *adj* unprovided.
después *adv* after, afterwards; next.
despuntar *vt* to blunt:—*vi* to sprout; to dawn:—**al ~ del dia** at break of day.
desquiciar *vt* to upset; to discompose; to disorder.
desquite *m* recovery of a loss; revenge, retaliation.
destacamento *m* (*mil*) detachment.
destacar *vt* to emphasize; (*mil*) to detach (a body of troops):—**~se** *vr* to stand out.
destajo *m* piecework.
destapar *vt* to uncover; to open:—**~se** *vr* to be uncovered.
destartalado/da *adj* untidy.
destello *m* signal light; sparkle.
desteñir *vt* to discolor:—**~se** *vr* to fade.
desternillarse *vr*:—**~ de risa** to roar with laughter.
desterrar *vt* to banish; to expel, drive away.
destetar *vt* to wean.
destilar *vt*, *vi* to distil.
destinar *vt* to destine for, intend for.
destinatario/a *m/f* addressee.
destino *m* destiny; fate, doom; destination; office.
destornillador *m* screwdriver.
destreza *f* dexterity, cleverness, cunning, expertness, skill.
destrozar *vt* to destroy, break into pieces; (*mil*) to defeat.
destruir *vt* to destroy.
desvalido/da *adj* helpless; destitute.
desvalijar *vt* to rob; to burgle.
desván *m* garret.
desvanecer *vt* to dispel:—**~se** *vr* to grow vapid, become insipid; to vanish; to be affected with giddiness.
desvarío *m* delirium; giddiness; inconstancy, caprice; extravagance.
desvelar *vt* to keep awake:—**~se** *vr* to stay awake.
desventaja *f* disadvantage; damage.
desventura *f* misfortune; calamity.
desvergüenza *f* impudence; shamelessness.
desvestir *vt*:—**~se** *vr* to undress.
desviar *vt* to divert; to dissuade; to parry (at fencing):—**~se** *vr* to go off course.
detallar *vt* to detail, relate minutely.
detener *vt* to stop, detain; to arrest; to keep back; to reserve; to withhold: —**~se** *vr* to stop; to stay.
detenidamente *adv* carefully.
detergente *m* detergent.
deteriorar *vt* to damage.
determinar *vt* to determine:—**~se** *vr* to decide.
detestar *vt* to detest, abhor.
detonar *vi* to detonate.
detrás *adv* behind; at the back, in the back.
deuda *f* debt; fault; offence.
devanar *vt* to reel; to wrap up.
devastar *vt* to devastate.
devengar *vt* to accrue.
devoción *f* devotion, piety; strong affection; ardent love.
devolver *vt* to return; to send back; to refund:—*vi* to be sick.
devorar *vt* to devour, swallow up.
día *m* day.
diablo *m* devil.
diablura *f* prank.
diana *f* (*mil*) reveille; bull's-eye.
diapositiva *f* transparency, slide.
diario *m* journal, diary; daily newspaper; daily expenses *pl*:—**~/ ria** *adj* daily.
diarrea *f* diarrhea.
dibujar *vt* to draw, design.
diccionario *m* dictionary.
dicha *f* happiness, good fortune:—**por ~** by chance.
diciembre *m* December.
dictamen *m* opinion, notion; suggestion; judgement.
dictar *vt* to dictate.
diecinueve *adj*, *m* nineteen.
dieciocho *adj*, *m* eighteen.
dieciséis *adj*, *m* sixteen.
diecisiete *adj*, *m* seventeen.
diente *m* tooth; fang; tusk.
diestro/tra *adj* right; dexterous, skillful, clever; sagacious, prudent; sly, cunning: —*m* skillful fencer; halter; bridle.
dieta *f* diet, regimen; diet, assembly; daily salary of judges.
diez *adj*, *m* ten.
diezmar *vt* to decimate.
difamar *vt* to defame, libel.
diferencia *f* difference.
diferenciar *vt* to differentiate, distinguish: —**~se** *vr* to differ, distinguish oneself.
diferente *adj* different, unlike.
diferido/da *adj* recorded.
difícil *adj* difficult.
dificultad *f* difficulty.
difundir *vt* to diffuse, spread; to divulge:—**~se** *vr* to spread (out).

difunto/ta *adj* dead, deceased; late.
digerir *vt* to digest; to bear with patience; to adjust, arrange.
dignarse *vr* to condescend, deign.
digno/na *adj* worthy; suitable.
dilatado/da *adj* large; numerous; prolix; spacious, extensive.
dilatar *vt* to dilate, expand; to spread out; to defer, protract.
dilema *m* dilemma.
diligencia *f* diligence; affair, business; call of nature; stage coach.
dilucidar *vt* to elucidate, explain.
diluir *vt* to dilute.
diluviar *vi* to rain in torrents.
diminuto/ta *adj* minute, small.
dimitir *vt* to give up:—*vi* to resign.
dinamita *f* dynamite.
dinamo *f* dynamo.
dineral *m* large sum of money.
dinero *m* money.
dios *m* god.
diosa *f* goddess.
diplomado/da *adj* qualified.
dique *m* dam.
dirección *f* direction, guidance; administration; steering.
directo/ta *adj* direct, straight; apparent, evident; live.
director/ra *m/f* director; conductor; president; manager.
dirigir *vt* to direct; to conduct; to regulate, govern:—**~se** *vr* to go towards; to address oneself to.
discernir *vt* to discern, distinguish.
discípulo *m* disciple; scholar.
disco *m* disc; record; discus; light; face (of the sun or moon); lens (of a telescope).
díscolo/la *adj* ungovernable; peevish.
discordante *adj* dissonant, discordant.
discreción *f* discretion; acuteness of mind.
discrepar *vi* to differ.
discreto/ta *adj* discreet; ingenious; witty, eloquent.
disculpar *vt* to exculpate, excuse; to acquit, absolve:—**~se** *vr* to apologize; to excuse oneself.
discurrir *vi* to ramble about; to run to and fro; to discourse (on a subject): —*vt* to invent, contrive; to meditate.
discurso *m* speech; conversation; dissertation; space of time.
discutir *vt*, *vi* to discuss.
disecar *vt* to dissect; to stuff.
diseminar *vt* to scatter; to disseminate, propagate.
diseñar *vt* to draw; to design.
disentir *vi* to dissent, disagree.
disfrazar *vt* to disguise, conceal; to cloak, dissemble:—**~se** *vr* to disguise oneself as.
disfrutar *vt* to enjoy:—**~se** *vr* to enjoy oneself.
disgustar *vt* to disgust; to offend:—**~se** *vr* to be displeased; to fall out.
disidente *adj* dissident:—*m/f* dissident, dissenter.
disimular *vt* to hide; to tolerate.
disipar *vt* to dissipate, disperse, scatter; to lavish.
dislocarse *vr* to be dislocated or out of joint.
disminuir *vt* to diminish; to decrease.
disolver *vt* to loosen, untie; to dissolve; to disunite; to melt, liquefy; to interrupt.
disparar *vt* to shoot, discharge, fire; to let off; to throw with violence:—*vi* to shoot, fire.
disparate *m* nonsense, absurdity, extravagance.
displicencia *f* displeasure; dislike.
disponer *vt* to arrange, prepare; to dispose.
disponible *adj* available; disposable.
dispositivo *m* device.
disputar *vt* to dispute, controvert, question:—*vi* to debate, argue.
disquete *m* floppy disk.
distancia *f* distance; interval; difference.
distante *adj* distant, far off.
distinguido/da *adj* distinguished, conspicuous.
distinguir *vt* to distinguish; to discern:—**~se** *vr* to distinguish oneself.
distinto/ta *adj* distinct, different; clear.
distraer *vt* to distract:—**~se** *vr* to be absent-minded, be inattentive.
distraído/da *adj* absent-minded, inattentive.
distribuir *vt* to distribute.
distrito *m* district; territory.
disturbio *m* riot; disturbance, interruption.
disuadir *vt* to dissuade.
diurno/na *adj* daily.
diva *f* prima donna.
divagar *vt* to digress.
divergencia *f* divergence.
diversidad *f* diversity; variety of things.
diversificar *vt* to diversify; to vary.
diversión *f* diversion; sport; amusement; (*mil*) diversion.
divertir *vt* to divert (the attention); to amuse, entertain; (*mil*) to draw off: —**~se** *vr* to amuse oneself.
dividir *vt* to divide; to disunite; to separate; to share out.

divieso *m* (*med*) boil.
divino/na *adj* divine, heavenly; excellent.
divorcio *m* divorce; separation, disunion.
divulgar *vt* to publish, divulge.
dobladillo *m* hem; turn-up.
doblar *vt* to double; to fold; to bend: —*vi* to turn; to toll:—**~se** *vr* to bend, bow, submit.
doble *adj* double; dual; deceitful:—**al ~** doubly:—*m* double.
doblegar *vt* to bend:—**~se** *vr* to yield.
doblez *m* crease; fold; turn-up:—*f* duplicity.
doce *adj*, *m* twelve.
docena *f* dozen.
dócil *adj* docile, tractable.
doctor/ra *m/f* doctor.
documento *m* document; record.
dogma *m* dogma.
dólar *m* dollar.
doler *vt*, *vi* to feel pain; to ache:—**~se** *vr* to feel for the sufferings of others; to complain.
dolor *m* pain; aching, ache; affliction.
domar *vt* to tame; to subdue, master.
domesticar *vt* to domesticate.
domicilio *m* domicile; home, abode.
dominar *vt* to dominate; to be fluent in:—**~se** *vr* to moderate one's passions.
domingo *m* Sunday; (Christian) Sabbath.
donar *vt* to donate; to bestow.
donativo *m* contribution.
doncella *f* virgin, maiden; lady's maid.
donde *relative adv* where
¿dónde? *interrogative adv* where?:—**¿de dónde?** from where?
dondequiera *adv* wherever.
dorado/da *adj* gilt *compd*; golden:—*m* gilding.
dormir *vi* to sleep:—**~se** *vr* to fall asleep.
dos *adj*, *m* two.
doscientos/tas *adj pl* two hundred.
dosis *f invar* dose.
dotado/da *adj* gifted.
drama *m* drama.
dramatizar *vt* to dramatize.
droga *f* drug; stratagem; artifice, deceit.
droguería *f* hardware store.
ducha *f* shower; (*med*) douche.
ducho/cha *adj* skilled, experienced.
dudar *vt* to doubt.
duelo *m* grief, affliction; mourning.
duende *m* elf, hobgoblin.
dueño/ña *m/f* owner; landlord/lady; employer.
dulce *adj* sweet; mild, gentle, meek; soft:—*m* sweet, candy.
dúo *m* (*mus*) duo, duet.
duodécimo/ma *adj* twelfth.
duplicar *vt* to duplicate; to repeat.
duradero/ra *adj* lasting, durable.
durante *adv* during.
durar *vi* to last, continue.
durazno *m* peach; peach tree.
dureza *f* hardness; harshness:—**~ de oido** hardness of hearing.
duro/ra *adj* hard; cruel; harsh, rough: —*m* five peseta coin:—*adv* hard.

E

e *conj* and (before words starting with *i* and *hi*).
ébano *m* ebony.
ebrio/ia *adj* drunk.
ebullición *f* boiling.
echar *vt* to throw; to add; to pour out; to mail:—**~se** *vr* to lie down.
eco *m* echo.
económico/ca *adj* economic; cheap; thrifty; financial; avaricious.
ecuánime *adj* level-headed.
ecuménico/ca *adj* ecumenical; universal.
edad *f* age.
edición *f* edition; publication.
edificar *vt* to build, construct; to edify.
edificio *m* building; structure.
editar *vt* to edit; to publish.
educación *f* education; upbringing; (good) manners *pl*.
educar *vt* to educate, instruct; to bring up.
efectivamente *adv* exactly; really; in fact.
efecto *m* effect; consequence; purpose: —**~s** *mpl* effects *pl*, goods *pl*:—**en ~** in fact, really.
efectuar *vt* to effect, carry out.
eficaz *adj* efficient; effective.
eficiente *adj* efficient.
egoísta *m/f* self-seeker:—*adj* selfish.
eje *m* axle; axis.
ejecutar *vt* to execute, perform; to put to death; (*jur*) to distrain, seize.
ejecutivo/va *adj* executive:—*m/f* executive.
ejemplar *m* specimen; copy; example:—*adj* exemplary.
ejemplo *m* example:—**por ~** for example, for instance.
ejercer *vt* to exercise; *vi* to apply oneself to the functions of an office.

ejercicio *m* exercise.
ejercitar *vt* to exercise.
ejército *m* army.
el *art, m* the.
él *pn* he, it.
elaborar *vt* to elaborate.
elástico/ca *adj* elastic.
elección *f* election; choice.
eléctrico/ca *adj* electric, electrical.
electrocutar *vt* to electrocute.
electrodomesticos *mpl* (electrical) household appliances *pl*.
electrotecnia *f* electrical engineering.
elefante *m* elephant.
elegante *adj* elegant, fine.
elegir *vt* to choose, elect.
elemento *m* element:—**~s** *mpl* elements, rudiments, first principles *pl*.
elevar *vt* to raise; to elevate:—**~se** *vr* to rise; to be enraptured; to be conceited.
eliminar *vt* to eliminate, remove.
eliminatoria *f* preliminary (round).
ella *pn* she; it.
ello *pn* it.
elogiar *vt* to praise, eulogize.
eludir *vt* to elude, escape.
emanar *vi* to emanate.
embadurnar *vt* to smear, bedaub.
embalaje *m* packing, package.
embaldosar *vt* to pave with tiles.
embalse *m* reservoir.
embarazada *f* pregnant woman:—*adj* pregnant.
embarazoso/sa *adj* difficult; intricate, entangled.
embarcación *f* embarkation; any vessel or ship.
embarcar *vt* to embark:—**~se** *vr* to go on board; (*fig*) to get involved (in a matter).
embargo *m* embargo:—**sin ~** still, however.
embarque *m* embarkation.
embaucar *vt* to deceive; to trick.
embeber *vt* to soak; to saturate:—*vi* to shrink:—**~se** *vr* to be enraptured; to be absorbed.
embeleso *m* amazement, enchantment.
embellecer *vt* to embellish, beautify.
embestir *vt* to assault, attack.
emblanquecer *vt* to whiten:—**~se** *vr* to grow white; to bleach.
embobado/da *adj* amazed; fascinated.
émbolo *m* plunger; piston.
embolsar *vt* to put money into (a purse); to pocket.
emborrachar *vt* to intoxicate, inebriate:—**~se** *vr* to get drunk.
emboscada *f* (*mil*) ambush.
embotar *vt* to blunt:—**~se** *vr* to go numb.
embotellamiento *m* traffic jam.
embotellar *vt* to bottle (wine).
embozar *vt* to muffle (the face); (*fig*) to cloak, conceal.
embrague *m* clutch.
embriagar *vt* to intoxicate, inebriate; to transport, enrapture.
embrión *m* embryo.
embrollo *m* muddle.
embromar *vt* to tease; to cajole, wheedle.
embrujar *vt* to bewitch.
embrutecer *vt* to brutalize:—**~se** *vr* to become depraved.
embudo *m* funnel.
embustero/ra *m/f* impostor, cheat; liar:—*adj* deceitful.
embutido *m* sausage; inlay.
emerger *vi* to emerge, appear.
emigrar *vi* to emigrate.
eminente *adj* eminent, high; excellent, conspicuous.
emisora *f* broadcasting station.
emitir *vt* to emit; to issue; to broadcast.
emoción *f* emotion; feeling; excitement.
emocionar *vt* to excite; to move, touch.
emotivo/va *adj* emotional.
empacho *m* (*med*) indigestion.
empalagoso/sa *adj* cloying; tiresome.
empalmar *vt* to join.
empanada *f* (meat) pie.
empanar *vt* to cover with bread-crumbs.
empantanarse *vr* to get swamped; to get bogged down.
empapar *vt* to soak; to soak up:—**~se** *vr* to soak.
empapelar *vt* to paper.
empaquetar *vt* to pack, parcel up.
emparedado *m* sandwich.
emparrado *m* vine arbor.
empastar *vt* to paste; to fill (a tooth).
empatar *vi* to draw.
empedernido/da *adj* inveterate; heartless.
empedrado *m* paving.
empeine *m* instep.
empellón *m* push; heavy blow.
empeñar *vt* to pawn, pledge:—**~se** *vr* to pledge oneself to pay debts; to get into debt:—**~se en algo** to insist on something.
empeorar *vt* to make worse:—*vi* **~se** *vr* to grow worse.
empequeñecer *vt* to dwarf; (*fig*) to belittle.
empezar *vt* to begin, start.
emplazamiento *m* summons; location.
empleado/da *m/f* official; employee.
emplear *vt* to employ; to occupy; to commission.

empobrecer *vt* to reduce to poverty: *—vi* to become poor.
empollar *vt* to incubate; to hatch; (*fam*) to swot (up).
empolvar *vt* to powder; to sprinkle powder upon.
empotrado/da *adj* built-in.
emprender *vt* to embark on; to tackle; to undertake.
empresa *f* (*com*) company; enterprise, undertaking.
empujar *vt* to push; to press forward.
empujón *m* push; impulse:—**a ~ones** in fits and starts.
emular *vt* to emulate, rival.
en *prep* in; for; on, upon.
enaguas *fpl* petticoat.
enamorado/da *adj* in love, lovesick.
enamorar *vt* to inspire love in:—**~se** *vr* to fall in love.
enano/na *adj* dwarfish:—*m* dwarf.
enardecer *vt* to fire with passion, inflame.
enarenar *vt* to fill with sand.
encabezar *vt* to head; to put a heading to; to lead.
encadenar *vt* to chain, link together; to connect, unite.
encajar *vt* to insert; to drive in; to encase; to intrude:—*vi* to fit (well).
encaje *m* lace.
encalar *vt* to whitewash.
encallar *vi* (*mar*) to run aground.
encaminar *vt* to guide, show the way: —**~se** *vr* **~ a** to take the road to.
encandilar *vt* to dazzle.
encanecer *vi* to grow gray; to grow old.
encantado/da *adj* bewitched; delighted; pleased.
encantador/ra *adj* charming:—*m/f* magician.
encantar *vt* to enchant, charm; (*fig*) to delight.
encarcelar *vt* to imprison.
encarecimiento *m* price increase:—**con ~** insistently.
encargado/da *adj* in charge:—*m/f* representative; person in charge.
encargar *vt* to charge; to commission.
encariñarse *vr*:—**~ con** to grow fond of.
encarnar *vt* to embody, personify.
encasillar *vt* to pigeonhole; to typecast.
encastillarse *vr* to refuse to yield.
encausar *vt* to prosecute.
encauzar *vt* to channel.
encebollado *m* casseroled beef or lamb and onions, seasoned with spice.
encenagado/da *adj* muddy, mud-stained.
encendedor *m* lighter.
encender *vt* to kindle, light, set on fire; to inflame, incite; to switch on, to turn on:—**~se** *vr* to catch fire; to flare up.
encerado *m* blackboard.
encerar *vt* to wax; to polish.
encerrar *vt* to shut up, confine; to contain: —**~se** *vr* to withdraw from the world.
enchufar *vt* to plug in; to connect.
enchufe *m* plug; outlet, socket; connection; (*fam*) contact, connection.
encía *f* gum (of the teeth).
encierro *m* confinement; enclosure; prison, penitentiary; bull-pen; penning (of bulls).
encima *adv* above; over; at the top; besides:—**~ de** *prep* above; over; at the top of; besides.
encina *f* evergreen oak.
encinta *adj* pregnant.
enclenque *adj* weak, sickly:—*m* weakling.
encoger *vt* to contract, shorten; to shrink; to discourage:—**~se** *vr* to shrink; (*fig*) to cringe.
encolar *vt* to glue.
encolerizar *vt* to provoke, irritate:—**~se** *vr* to get angry.
encomendar *vt* to recommend; to entrust: —**~se** *vr* **~ a** to entrust oneself to; to put one's trust in.
encontrar *vt* to meet, encounter:—*vr* **~se con** to run into:—*vi* to assemble, come together.
encrucijada *f* four way stop, intersection; junction.
encuadernar *vt* to bind (books).
encubierto/ta *adj* hidden, concealed.
encubrir *vt* to hide, conceal.
encuesta *f* inquiry; opinion poll.
encurtir *vt* to pickle.
endeble *adj* feeble, weak.
endemoniado/da *adj* possessed with the devil; devilish.
enderezar *vt* to straighten out; to set right: —**~se** *vr* to stand upright.
endeudarse *vr* to get into debt.
endosar *vt* to endorse.
endrino *m* blackthorn, sloe.
endulzar *vt* to sweeten; to soften.
endurecer *vt* to harden, toughen:—**~se** *vr* to become cruel; to grow hard.
enebro *m* (*bot*) juniper.
enemistar *vt* to make an enemy:—**~se** *vr* to become enemies; to fall out.
energía *f* energy, power, drive; strength of will.
energúmeno/na *m/f* (*fam*) madman/woman.
enero *m* January.
enfadar *vt* to anger, irritate; to trouble:—**~se** *vr* to become angry.

énfasis *m* emphasis.
enfermar *vi* to fall ill:—*vt* to make sick; to weaken.
enfermedad *f* illness.
enfermero/ra *m/f* nurse.
enfermo/ma *adj* sick, ill:—*m/f* invalid, sick person; patient.
enfocar *vt* to focus; to consider (a problem).
enfoque *m* focus.
enfrentar *vt* to confront; to put face to face:—**~se** *vr* to face each other; to meet (two teams).
enfrente *adv* over against, opposite; in front.
enfriar *vt* to cool; to refrigerate:—**~se** *vr* to cool down; (*med*) to catch a cold.
enfurecer *vt* to madden, enrage:—**~se** *vr* to get rough (of the wind and sea); to become furious or enraged.
enfurruñarse *vr* to get sulky; to frown.
engañar *vt* to deceive, cheat:—**~se** *vr* to be deceived; to make a mistake.
enganchar *vt* to hook, hang up; to hitch up; to couple, connect; to recruit into military service:—**~se** *vr* (*mil*) to enlist.
engañoso/sa *adj* deceitful, artful, false.
engastar *vt* to set, mount.
engatusar *vt* to coax.
engendrar *vt* to beget, engender; to produce.
englobar *vt* to include.
engordar *vt* to fatten:—*vi* to grow fat; to put on weight.
engorroso/sa *adj* troublesome, cumbersome.
engranaje *m* gear; gearing.
engrasar *vt* to grease, lubricate.
engreído/da *adj* conceited, vain.
engullir *vt* to swallow; to gobble, devour.
enharinar *vt* to cover or sprinkle with flour.
enhebrar *vt* to thread.
enhorabuena *f* congratulations *pl*:—*adv* all right; well and good.
enhoramala *interj* good riddance!
enjalbegar *vt* to whitewash.
enjambre *m* swarm of bees; crowd, multitude.
enjuagar *vt* to rinse out; to wash out.
enjuiciar *vt* to prosecute, try; to pass judgement on, judge.
enlace *m* connection, link; relationship.
enladrillar *vt* to pave with bricks.
enlazar *vt* to join, unite; to tie.
enlodar *vt* to cover in mud; (*fig*) to stain.
enloquecer *vt* to madden, drive crazy:—*vi* to go mad.
enmarañar *vt* to entangle; to complicate; to confuse:—**~se** *vr* to become entangled; to get confused.
enmendar *vt* to correct; to reform; to repair, compensate for; to amend:—**~se** *vr* to mend one's ways.
enmohecer *vt* to make moldy; to rust:—**~se** *vr* to grow moldy or musty; to rust.
enmudecer(se) *vt* to silence:—**~se** *vr* to grow dumb; to be silent.
ennegrecer *vt* to blacken; to darken; to obscure.
enojar *vt* to irritate, make angry; to annoy; to upset; to offend:—**~se** *vr* to get angry.
enorgullecerse *vr*:—**~ (de)** to be proud (of).
enorme *adj* enormous, vast, huge; horrible.
enredadera *f* climbing plant; bindweed.
enredar *vt* to entangle, ensnare, confound, perplex; to puzzle; to sow discord among:—**~se** *vr* to get entangled; to get complicated; to get embroiled.
enrejado *m* trelliswork.
enrevesado/da *adj* complicated.
enriquecer *vt* to enrich; to adorn:—**~se** *vr* to grow rich.
enrojecer *vt* to redden:—*vi* to blush.
enrolar *vt* to recruit:—**~se** *vr* (*mil*) to join up.
enrollar *vt* to roll (up).
enroscar *vt* to twist:—**~se** *vr* to curl or roll up.
ensalada *f* salad.
ensalmo *m* enchantment, spell.
ensalzar *vt* to exalt, aggrandize; to exaggerate.
ensamblar *vt* to assemble.
ensañar *vt* to irritate, enrage:—**~se con** *vr* to treat brutally.
ensanchar *vt* to widen; to extend; to enlarge:—**~se** *vr* to expand; to assume an air of importance.
ensangrentar *vt* to stain with blood.
ensartar *vt* to string (beads, etc).
ensayar *vt* to test; to rehearse.
ensayo *m* test, trial; rehearsal of a play; essay.
enseñar *vt* to teach, instruct; to show.
ensimismarse *vr* to be or become lost in thought.
ensordecer *vt* to deafen:—*vi* to grow deaf.
ensuciar *vt* to stain, soil; to defile:—**~se** *vr* to wet oneself; to dirty oneself.
ensueño *m* fantasy; daydream; illusion.
entablar *vt* to board (up); to strike up (conversation).
entablillar *vt* (*med*) to put in a splint.
entallar *vt* to tailor (a suit):—*vi* to fit.
ente *m* organization; entity, being; (*fam*) odd character.
entender *vt*, *vi* to understand, comprehend; to remark, take notice (of); to reason, think:—**a mi ~** in my opinion: —**~se** *vr* to understand each other.

enterar *vt* to inform; to instruct:—**~se** *vr* to find out.
enternecer *vt* to soften; to move (to pity):—**~se** *vr* to be moved.
entero/ra *adj* entire, complete; perfect; honest; resolute:—**por ~** entirely, completely.
enterrar *vt* to inter, bury.
entidad *f* entity; company; body; society.
entierro *m* burial; funeral.
entonar *vt* to tune, intonate; to intone; to tone:—*vi* to be in tune:—**~se** *vr* to give oneself airs.
entonces *adv* then, at that time.
entornar *vt* to half close.
entorpecer *vt* to dull; to make lethargic; to hinder; to delay.
entrada *f* entrance, entry; (*com*) receipts *pl*; entree; ticket (for cinema, theater, etc).
entrampar *vt* to trap, snare; to mess up; to burden with debts:—**~se** *vr* get into debt.
entrañable *adj* intimate; affectionate.
entrañas *fpl* entrails *pl*, intestines *pl*.
entrar *vi* to enter, go in; to commence.
entre *prep* between; among(st); in:—**~ manos** in hand.
entrecejo *m* space between the eyebrows; frown.
entredicho *m* (*jur*) injunction:—**estar en ~** to be banned:—**poner en ~** to cast doubt on.
entregar *vt* to deliver; to hand over: —**~se** *vr* to surrender; to devote oneself.
entremeses *mpl* hors d'oeuvres.
entrenarse *vr* to train.
entrepierna *f* crotch.
entresuelo *m* entresol; mezzanine.
entretanto *adv* meanwhile.
entretejer *vt* to interweave.
entretela *f* interfacing, stiffening, interlining.
entretener *vt* to amuse; to entertain, divert; to hold up; to maintain:—**~se** *vr* to amuse oneself; to linger.
entrever *vt* to have a glimpse of.
entrevistar *vt* to interview:—**~se** *vr* to have an interview.
entristecer *vt* to sadden.
entrometer *vt* to put (one thing) between (others):—**~se** *vr* to interfere.
entumecido/da *adj* numb, stiff.
enturbiar *vt* to make cloudy; to obscure, confound:—**~se** *vr* to become cloudy; (*fig*) to get confused.
entusiasmar *vt* to excite, fill with enthusiasm; to delight.
enumerar *vt* to enumerate.
envalentonar *vt* to give courage to:—**~se** *vr* to boast.
envanecer *vt* to make vain; to swell with pride:—**~se** *vr* to become proud.
envaramiento *m* stiffness; numbness.
envasar *vt* to pack; to bottle; to can.
envase *m* packing; bottling; canning; container; package; bottle; can.
envejecer *vt* to make old:—*vi* **~se** *vr* to grow old.
envenenar *vt* to poison; to embitter.
envés *m* wrong side (of material).
enviar *vt* to send, transmit, convey, dispatch.
enviciar *vt* to vitiate, corrupt:—**~se** *vr* to get corrupted.
envidia *f* envy; jealousy.
envidiar *vt* to envy; to grudge; to be jealous of.
envilecer *vt* to vilify, debase:—**~se** *vr* to degrade oneself.
envío *m* (*com*) dispatch, remittance of goods; consignment.
enviudar *vi* to become a widower or widow.
envolver *vt* to involve; to wrap up.
enyesar *vt* to plaster; (*med*) to put in a plaster cast.
enzarzarse *vr* to get involved in a dispute; to get oneself into trouble.
épico/ca *adj* epic.
epígrafe *f* epigraph, inscription; motto; headline.
episodio *m* episode, installment.
época *f* epoch; period, time.
epopeya *f* epic.
equidad *f* equity, honesty; impartiality, justice.
equilibrar *vt* to balance; to poise.
equilibrio *m* balance, equilibrium.
equipaje *m* luggage; equipment.
equipar *vt* to fit out, equip, furnish.
equipararse *vr*:—**~ con** to be on a level with.
equipo *m* equipment; team; shift.
equitación *f* horsemanship; riding.
equitativo/va *adj* equitable; just.
equivaler *vi* to be of equal value.
equivocación *f* mistake, error; misunderstanding.
equivocar *vt* to mistake:—**~se** *vr* to make a mistake, be wrong.
equívoco/ca *adj* equivocal, ambiguous:—*m* equivocation; quibble.
era *f* era, age; threshing floor.
erario *m* treasury, public funds *pl*.
erguir *vt* to erect, raise up straight:—**~se** *vr* to straighten up.
erial *m* fallow land.

erigir *vt* to erect, raise, build; to establish.
erizarse *vr* to bristle; to stand on end.
erizo *m* hedgehog:—~ **de mar** sea urchin.
ermita *f* hermitage.
erotismo *m* eroticism.
errar *vi* to be mistaken; to wander.
errata *f* misprint.
erre: —~ **que** ~ *adv* obstinately.
error *m* error, mistake, fault.
eructar *vi* to belch, burp.
esbelto/ta *adj* slim, slender.
esbirro *m* bailiff; henchman; killer.
esbozo *m* outline.
escabeche *m* pickle; pickled fish.
escabroso/sa *adj* rough, uneven; craggy; rude, risqué, blue.
escabullirse *vr* to escape, evade; to slip through one's fingers.
escafandra *f* diving suit; space suit.
escala *f* ladder; (*mus*) scale; stopover.
escalar *vt* to climb.
escalera *f* staircase; ladder.
escalfar *vt* to poach (eggs).
escalofriante *adj* chilling.
escalón *m* step of a stair; rung.
escama *f* (fish) scale.
escamar *vt* to scale, take off scales:—~**se** *vr* to flake off; to become suspicious.
escamotear *vt* to swipe; to make disappear.
escampar *vi* to stop raining.
escándalo *m* scandal; uproar.
escaño *m* bench with a back; seat (parliament).
escapar *vi* to escape:—~**se** *vr* to get away; to leak (water, etc).
escaparate *m* store window; wardrobe.
escape *m* escape, flight; leak; exhaust (of motor).
escarabajo *m* beetle.
escaramuza *f* skirmish; dispute, quarrel.
escarbar *vt* to scratch (the earth as hens do); to inquire into.
escarcha *f* white frost.
escarlata *adj* scarlet.
escarlatina *f* scarlet fever.
escarmentar *vi* to learn one's lesson: —*vt* to punish severely.
escarola *f* (*bot*) endive.
escarpado/da *adj* sloped; craggy.
escaso/sa *adj* small, short, little; sparing; scarce; scanty.
escenario *m* stage; set.
escéptico/ca *adj* sceptic, sceptical.
esclarecer *vt* to lighten; to illuminate; to illustrate; to shed light on (problem, etc).
esclavo/va *m/f* slave; captive.
esclusa *f* sluice, floodgate.
escoba *f* broom, brush.
escocer *vt* to sting; to burn:—~**se** *vr* to chafe.
escoger *vt* to choose, select.
escolar *m/f* schoolboy/girl:—*adj* scholastic.
escollo *m* reef, rock.
escoltar *vt* to escort.
escombros *mpl* trash; debris.
esconder *vt* to hide, conceal:—~**se** *vr* to be hidden.
escondite *m* hiding place:—**juego de** ~ hide-and-seek.
escoplo *m* chisel.
escorbuto *m* scurvy.
escote *m* low neck (of a dress).
escribir *vt* to write; to spell.
escrito *m* document; manuscript, text.
escritor/ra *m/f* writer, author.
escritorio *m* writing desk; office, study.
escrúpulo *m* doubt, scruple, scrupulousness.
escuchar *vt* to listen to, heed.
escudilla *f* bowl.
escudo *m* shield.
escudriñar *vt* to search, examine; to pry into.
escuela *f* school.
esculpir *vt* to sculpt.
escupir *vt* to spit.
escurreplatos *m invar* plate rack.
escurrir *vt* to drain; to drip:—~**se** *vr* to slip away; to slip, slide:—*vi* to wring out.
ese/esa *adj* that:—**esos/as** *pl* those.
ése/ésa *pn* that (one):—**ésos/as** *pl* those (ones).
esencial *adj* essential; principal.
esfera *f* sphere; globe.
esforzarse *vr* to exert oneself, make an effort.
esfuerzo *m* effort.
esfumarse *vr* to fade away.
esgrima *f* fencing.
esguince *m* (*med*) sprain.
eslabón *m* link of a chain; steel; shackle.
esmalte *m* enamel.
esmerado/da *adj* careful, neat.
esmeralda *m* emerald.
esmero *m* careful attention, great care.
eso *pn* that.
esos/as; ésos/as *pl* of **ese/a; ése/a**.
espabilar *vt* to wake up:—~**se** *vr* to wake up; (*fig*) to get a move on.
espaciar *vt* to spread out; to space (out).
espacio *m* space; (radio or TV) program.
espada *f* sword; ace of spades.
espalda *f* back, back-part:—~**s** *fpl* shoulders *pl*.
español/la *adj* Spanish:—*m/f* Spaniard:—*m* Spanish language.

espantajo *m* scarecrow; bogeyman.
espantar *vt* to frighten; to chase or drive away.
esparadrapo *m* adhesive tape.
esparcir *vt* to scatter; to divulge:—**~se** *vr* to amuse oneself.
espárrago *m* asparagus.
espátula *f* spatula.
especia *f* spice.
especial *adj* special; particular:—**en ~** especially.
especie *f* species; kind, sort; matter.
especificar *vt* to specify.
espectáculo *m* spectacle; show.
espectador/ra *m/f* spectator.
especular *vt* to speculate.
espejismo *m* mirage.
espejo *m* mirror.
espeluznante *adj* horrifying.
esperanza *f* hope.
esperar *vt* to hope; to expect, wait for.
esperma *f* sperm.
espeso/sa *adj* thick, dense.
espesor *m* thickness.
espía *m/f* spy.
espiga *f* ear (of corn).
espigón *m* ear of corn; sting; (*mar*) breakwater.
espina *f* thorn; fishbone.
espinaca *f* (*bot*) spinach.
espinilla *f* shinbone.
espino *m* hawthorn.
espiral *adj*, *f* spiral.
espirar *vt* to exhale.
espíritu *m* spirit, soul; mind; intelligence: —**el E~ Santo** the Holy Ghost:—**~s** *pl* demons, hobgoblins *pl*.
espléndido/da *adj* splendid.
espliego *m* (*bot*) lavender.
espolón *m* spur (of a cock); spur (of a mountain range); sea wall; jetty; (*mar*) buttress.
espolvorear *vt* to sprinkle.
esponja *f* sponge.
espontáneo/nea *adj* spontaneous.
esposa *f* wife.
esposas *fpl* handcuffs *pl*.
esposo *m* husband.
espuma *f* froth, foam.
espumar *vt* to skim, take the scum off.
espumoso/sa *adj* frothy, foamy; sparkling (wine).
esputo *m* spit, saliva.
esqueje *m* cutting (of plant).
esquela *f* note, slip of paper.
esqueleto *m* skeleton.
esquema *m* scheme; diagram; plan.
esquí *m* ski; skiing.
esquina *f* corner, angle.
esquirol *m* blackleg.
esquivar *vt* to shun, avoid, evade.
esta *adj f* this:—**~s** *pl* these.
ésta *pn f* this:—**~s** *pl* these.
estable *adj* stable.
establecer *vt* to establish.
establo *m* stable.
estaca *f* stake; stick; post.
estación *f* season (of the year); station; railroad station, terminus:—**~ de autobuses** bus station:—**~ de servicio** service station.
estacionar *vt* to park; (*mil*) to station.
estadio *m* phase; stadium.
estado *m* state, condition.
Estados Unidos *mpl* United States (of America).
estafar *vt* to deceive, defraud.
estallar *vi* to crack; to burst; to break out.
estambre *m* stamen.
estamento *m* estate; body; layer; class.
estampa *f* print; engraving; appearance.
estampar *vt* to print.
estancar *vt* to check (a current); to monopolize; to prohibit, suspend:—**~se** *vr* to stagnate.
estancia *f* stay; bedroom; ranch; (*poet*) stanza.
estanco *m* tobacconist's (store):—**~/ca** *adj* watertight.
estándar *adj*, *m* standard.
estaño *m* tin.
estanque *m* pond, pool; reservoir.
estantería *f* shelves *pl*, shelving.
estar *vi* to be; to be (in a place).
estatua *f* statue.
este[1] *m* east;
este[2]**/ta** *adj* this:—**estos/tas** *pl* these.
estera *f* mat.
estéreo *adj invar*, *m* stereo.
estereotipo *m* stereotype.
estéril *adj* sterile, infertile.
esterlina *adj*:—**libra ~** pound sterling.
estético/ca *adj* esthetic:—*f* esthetics.
estiércol *m* dung; manure.
estilo *m* style; fashion; stroke (swimming).
estima *f* esteem.
estimar *vt* to estimate, value; to esteem; to judge; to think.
estimular *vt* to stimulate, excite; to goad.
estío *m* summer.
estipular *vt* to stipulate.
estirar *vt* to stretch out.
esto *pn* this.
estofado *m* stew.
estómago *m* stomach.

estopa *f* tow.
estorbar *vt* to hinder; (*fig*) to bother: *—vi* to be in the way.
estornudar *vi* to sneeze.
estos/as, éstos/tas *pl* of **este/ta, éste/ta.**
estrado *m* drawing room; stage, platform.
estrafalario/ria *adj* slovenly; eccentric.
estrago *m* ruin, destruction; havoc.
estrangular *vt* to strangle; (*med*) to strangulate.
estraperlo *m* black market.
estratagema *f* stratagem, trick.
estrato *m* stratum, layer.
estraza *f* rag:—**papel de ~** brown paper.
estrechar *vt* to tighten; to contract, constrain; to compress:—**~se** *vr* to grow narrow; to embrace:—**~ la mano** to shake hands.
estrecho *m* straits *pl*:—**~/ cha** *adj* narrow, close; tight; intimate; rigid, austere; short (of money).
estrella *f* star.
estrellar *vt* to dash to pieces:—**~se** *vr* to smash; to crash; to fail.
estremecer *vt* to shake, make tremble:—**~se** *vr* to shake, tremble.
estrenar *vt* to wear for the first time; to move into (a house); to show (a movie) for the first time:—**~se** *vr* to make one's debut.
estreñido/da *adj* constipated.
estrépito *m* noise, racket; fuss.
estribillo *m* chorus.
estribo *m* buttress; stirrup; running board: —**perder los ~s** to fly off the handle (*fam*).
estribor *m* (*mar*) starboard.
estricto/ta *adj* strict; severe.
estrofa *f* (*poet*) verse, strophe.
estropajo *m* scourer.
estropear *vt* to spoil; to damage:—**~se** *vr* to get damaged.
estructura *f* structure.
estruendo *m* clamor, noise; confusion, uproar; pomp, ostentation.
estuche *m* case (for scissors, etc); sheath.
estudiar *vt* to study.
estufa *f* heater, fire.
estupefaciente *m* narcotic.
estupefacto *adj* speechless; thunderstruck.
estupendo/da *adj* terrific, marvelous.
estúpido *adj* stupid.
etapa *f* stage; stopping place; (*fig*) phase.
etcétera *adv* etcetera, and so on.
eterno/na *adj* eternal.
ético/ca *adj* ethical, moral.
etiqueta *f* etiquette; label.
evacuar *vt* to evacuate, empty.
evadir *vt* to evade, escape.
evaluar *vt* to evaluate.
evaporar *vt* to evaporate:—**~se** *vr* to vanish.
eventual *adj* possible; temporary, casual (worker).
evidente *adj* evident, clear.
evitar *vt* to avoid.
evolucionar *vi* to evolve.
ex *adj* ex.
ex profeso *adv* on purpose.
exacerbar *vt* to exacerbate; to irritate.
exacto/ta *adj* exact; punctual; accurate.
exagerar *vt* to exaggerate.
exaltar *vt* to exalt, elevate; to praise, extol: —**~se** *vr* to get excited.
examen *m* exam, examination, test, inquiry.
examinar *vt* to examine.
exasperar *vt* to exasperate, irritate.
excavar *vt* to excavate, dig out.
exceder *vt* to exceed, surpass, excel, outdo.
excelente *adj* excellent.
excéntrico/ca *adj* eccentric.
excepto *adv* excepting, except (for).
exceso *m* excess.
excitar *vt* to excite:—**~se** *vr* to get excited.
exclamar *vt* to exclaim, cry out.
excluir *vt* to exclude.
excremento *m* excrement.
excursión *f* excursion, trip.
excusa *f* excuse, apology.
excusado *m* bathroom.
excusar *vt* to excuse; to avoid:—**~ de** to exempt from:—**~se** *vr* to apologize.
exento/ta *adj* exempt, free.
exhalar *vt* to exhale; to give off; to heave (a sigh).
exhausto/ta *adj* exhausted.
exhibir *vt* to exhibit.
exhortar *vt* to exhort.
exhumar *vt* to disinter, exhume.
exigir *vt* to demand, require.
exiliado/da *adj* exiled:—*m/f* exile.
existir *vi* to exist, be.
éxito *m* outcome; success; (*mus,etc*) hit:—**tener ~** to be successful.
exorbitante *adj* exhorbitant, excessive.
exótico/ca *adj* exotic.
expandir *vt* to expand.
expatriarse *vr* to emigrate; to go into exile.
expectativa *f* expectation; prospect.
expedición *f* expedition.
expediente *m* expedient; means; (*jur*) proceedings *pl*; dossier, file.
expedir *vt* to send, forward, dispatch.
expensas *fpl*:—**a ~ de** at the expense of.
experimentar *vt* to experience:—*vi* **~ con** to experiment with.

experto/ta *adj* expert; experienced.
expiar *vt* to atone for; to purify.
expirar *vi* to expire.
explayarse *vr* to speak at length.
explicar *vt* to explain, expound:—**~se** *vr* to explain oneself.
explorar *vt* to explore.
explotar *vt* to exploit; to run:—*vi* to explode.
exponer *vt* to expose; to explain.
exportar *vt* to export.
exposición *f* exposure; exhibition; explanation; account.
expresar *vt* to express.
expreso/sa *adj* express, clear, specific; fast (train).
exprimir *vt* to squeeze out.
expropriar *vt* to expropriate.
expulsar *vt* to expel, drive out.
éxtasis *m* ecstasy, enthusiasm.
extender *vt* to extend, stretch out:—**~se** *vr* to extend; to spread.
extenso/sa *adj* extensive.
extenuar *vt* to exhaust, debilitate.
exterior *adj* exterior, external:—*m* exterior, outward appearance.
exterminar *vt* to exterminate.
externo/na *adj* external, outer:—*m/f* day pupil.
extinguir *vt* to wipe out; to extinguish.
extintor *m* (fire) extinguisher.
extra *adj invar* extra; good quality:—*m/f* extra:—*m* bonus.
extraer *vt* to extract.
extrañar *vt* to find strange; to miss: —**~se** *vr* to be surprised; to grow apart.
extranjero/ra *m/f* stranger; foreigner:—*adj* foreign, alien.
extraño/ña *adj* foreign; rare; singular, strange, odd.
extraviar *vt* to mislead:—**~se** *vr* to lose one's way.
extremidad *f* extremity; brim; tip:—**~es** *fpl* extremities *pl*.
extremo/ma *adj* extreme, last:—*m* extreme, highest degree:—**en ~/por ~** extremely.
extrovertido/da *adj*, *m/f* extrovert.
exuberancia *f* exuberance; luxuriance.

F

fábrica *f* factory.
fabricar *vt* to build, construct; to manufacture; (*fig*) to fabricate.
fábula *f* fable; fiction; rumor, common talk.
fabuloso/sa *adj* fabulous, fictitious.
facción *f* (political) faction; feature.
fachada *f* facade, face, front.
fácil *adj* facile, easy.
facilitar *vt* to facilitate.
fácilmente *adv* easily.
factor *m* (*mat*) factor; (*com*) factor, agent.
factura *f* invoice.
facultativo/va *adj* optional:—*m/f* doctor, practitioner.
faena *f* task, job; hard work.
faisán *m* pheasant.
fajo *m* bundle; wad.
falaz *adj* deceitful, fraudulent; fallacious.
falda *f* skirt; lap; flap; train; slope, hillside.
fallar *vt* (*jur*) to pronounce sentence on, judge:—*vi* to fail.
fallecer *vi* to die.
falso/sa *adj* false, untrue; deceitful; fake.
falta *f* fault, defect; want; flaw, mistake; (*dep*) foul.
faltar *vi* to be wanting; to fail; not to fulfil one's promise; to need; to be missing.
fama *f* fame; reputation, name.
familia *f* family.
familiar *adj* familiar; homely, domestic:—*m/f* relative, relation.
famoso/sa *adj* famous.
fanfarrón *m* bully, braggart.
fango *m* mire, mud.
fantasía *f* fancy; fantasy; caprice; presumption.
fantasma *f* phantom, ghost.
fardo *m* bale, parcel.
farmacia *f* drugstore.
faro *m* (*mar*) lighthouse; (*auto*) headlamp; floodlight.
farola *f* street light.
fascículo *m* part, installment.
fascinar *vt* to fascinate; to enchant.
fase *f* phase.
fastidiar *vt* to annoy; to offend; to spoil.
fatal *adj* fatal; mortal; awful.
fatiga *f* weariness, fatigue.
fatuo/tua *adj* fatuous, stupid, foolish; conceited.
fauces *fpl* jaws *pl*, gullet.
favor *m* favor; protection; good turn.
favorecer *vt* to favor, protect.
fe *f* faith, belief.
febrero *m* February.
fecha *f* date (of a letter etc).

fecundar *vt* to fertilize.
felicitar *vt* to congratulate.
feliz *adj* happy, fortunate.
felpa *f* plush; toweling.
felpudo *m* doormat.
femenino/na *adj* feminine; female.
feo/ea *adj* ugly; bad, nasty.
feria *f* fair, rest day; village market.
fermentar *vi* to ferment.
feroz *adj* ferocious, savage; cruel.
ferretería *f* hardware store.
ferrocarril *m* railway.
fértil *adj* fertile, fruitful.
festejo *m* courtship; feast.
festivo/va *adj* festive, merry; witty: —**dia ~** holiday.
feto *m* fetus.
fiable *adj* trustworthy; reliable.
fiambre *m* cold meat.
fianza *f* (*jur*) surety.
fiar *vt* to entrust, confide; to bail; to sell on credit:—**~se** *vr* to trust.
fibra *f* fibre.
ficha *f* token, counter (at games); (index) card.
fidelidad *f* fidelity; loyalty.
fideos *mpl* noodles *pl*.
fiebre *f* fever.
fiel *adj* faithful, loyal:—*mpl* **los ~es** the faithful *pl*.
fieltro *m* felt.
fiera *f* wild beast.
fiesta *f* party; festivity:—**~s** *fpl* vacations *pl*.
figura *f* figure, shape.
figurar *vt* to figure:—**~se** *vr* to fancy, imagine.
fijar *vt* to fix, fasten:—**~se** *vr* to become fixed:—**~se en** to notice.
fijo/ja *adj* fixed, firm; settled, permanent.
fila *f* row, line; (*mil*) rank:—**en ~** in a line, in a row.
filete *m* fillet; fillet steak.
filmar *vt* to film.
filo *m* edge, blade.
filosofía *f* philosophy.
filtro *m* filter.
fin *m* end; termination, conclusion; aim, purpose:—**al ~** at last:—**en ~** (*fig*) well then:—**por ~** finally, lastly.
finalmente *adv* finally, at last.
financiar *vt* to finance.
finca *f* land, property, real estate; country house; farm.
fingir *vt* to feign, fake:—**~se** *vr* to pretend to be:—*vi* to pretend.
fino/na *adj* fine, pure; slender; polite; acute; dry (of sherry).
firma *f* signature; (*com*) company.
firmamento *m* firmament, sky, heaven.
firme *adj* firm, stable, strong, secure; constant; resolute:—*m* road surface.
fiscal *adj* fiscal:—*m/f* district attorney.
fisco *m* treasury, exchequer.
fisgar *vt* to pry into.
física *f* physics.
flaco/ca *adj* lean, skinny; feeble.
flan *m* crème caramel.
flauta *f* (*mus*) flute.
flecha *f* arrow.
flequillo *m* fringe (of hair).
flete *m* (*mar*) freight; charter.
flexible *adj* flexible; compliant; docile.
flojo/ja *adj* loose; flexible; slack; lazy.
flor *f* flower.
florecer *vi* to blossom.
florero *m* vase.
flotador *m* float; rubber ring.
flotar *vi* to float.
fluctuar *vi* to fluctuate; to waver.
fluir *vi* to flow.
foco *m* focus; center; source; floodlight; (light)bulb.
fogón *m* stove; hearth.
fogoso/sa *adj* fiery; ardent, fervent; impetuous, boisterous.
folleto *m* pamphlet; folder, brochure.
follón *m* (*fam*) mess; fuss.
fomentar *vt* to encourage; to promote.
fondo *m* bottom; back; background; space: —**~s** *mpl* stock, funds *pl*, capital:—**a ~** perfectly, completely.
fontanero/ra *m/f* plumber.
forjar *vt* to forge; to frame; to invent.
forma *f* form, shape; pattern; (*med*) fitness; (*dep*) form; means, method: —**de ~ que** in such a manner that.
formación *f* formation; form, figure; education; training.
formar *vt* to form, shape.
fornido/da *adj* well-built.
forro *m* lining; book jacket.
fortuna *f* fortune; wealth.
forzar *vt* to force.
forzoso/sa *adj* indispensable, necessary.
fosa *f* grave; pit.
fósforo *m* phosphorus:—**~s** *mpl* matches *pl*.
fotocopia *f* photocopy.
fotografía *f* photography; photograph.
fracasar *vi* to fail.
frágil *adj* fragile, frail.
fraguar *vt* to forge; to contrive:—*vi* to solidify, harden.
fraile *m* friar, monk.

frambuesa *f* raspberry.
francés/sa *adj* French:—*m* French language:—*m/f* Frenchman/woman.
frasco *m* flask.
frase *f* phrase.
fraternal *adj* fraternal, brotherly.
fraude *m* fraud, deceit; cheat.
frazada *f* blanket.
frecuencia *f* frequency.
fregar *vt* to scrub; to wash up.
freír *vt* to fry.
frenar *vt* to brake; (*fig*) to check.
frenesí *m* frenzy.
freno *m* bit; brake; (*fig*) check.
frente *f* front; face:—**~ a ~** face to face:—**en ~** opposite; (*mil*) front:—*m* forehead.
fresa *f* strawberry.
fresco/ca *adj* fresh; cool; new; ruddy: —*m* fresh air:—*m/f* (*fam*) shameless or impudent person.
fresno *m* ash tree.
frigorífico *m* fridge.
frijol *m* kidney bean.
frío/fría *adj* cold; indifferent:—*m* cold; indifference.
friso *m* frieze; wainscot.
frito/ta *adj* fried.
frívolo/la *adj* frivolous.
frondoso/sa *adj* leafy.
frontera *f* frontier.
frontón *m* (*dep*) pelota court; pelota.
frotar *vt* to rub.
fructificar *vi* to bear fruit; to come to fruition.
frugal *adj* frugal, sparing.
fruncir *vt* to pleat; to knit; to contract:—**~ las cejas** to knit the eyebrows.
frustrar *vt* to frustrate.
fruta *f* fruit:—**~ del tiempo** seasonal fruit.
frutal *m* fruit tree.
frutilla *f* strawberry.
fuego *m* fire.
fuente *f* fountain; spring; source; large dish.
fuera *adv* out(side); away:—**~ de** *prep* outside:—**¡~!** out of the way!
fuerte *m* (*mil*) fortification, fort; forte: —*adj* vigorous, tough; strong; loud; heavy: —*adv* strongly; hard.
fuerza *f* force, strength; (*elec*) power; violence:—**a ~ de** by dint of:—**~s** *mpl* troops *pl*.
fugarse *vr* to escape, flee.
fugaz *adj* fleeting.
fullero *m* cardsharper, cheat.
fumar *vt*, *vi* to smoke.
función *f* function; duties *pl*; show, performance.
funcionar *vi* to function; to work (of a machine).
funcionario/ria *m/f* official; civil servant.
funda *f* case, sheath:—**~ de almohada** pillowcase.
fundar *vt* to found; to establish; to ground.
fundir *vt* to fuse; to melt; to smelt; (*com*) to merge; to bankrupt; (*elec*) to fuse, blow.
fúnebre *adj* mournful, sad; funereal.
furgoneta *f* pick-up (truck).
furioso/sa *adj* furious.
furtivo/va *adj* furtive.
fusible *m* fuse.
fusión *f* fusion; (*com*) merger.
fútbol *m* soccer.
futuro/ra *adj*, *m* future.

G

gabardina *f* gabardine; raincoat.
gabinete *m* (*pol*) cabinet, study; office (of solicitors, etc).
gafas *fpl* glasses *pl*, spectacles *pl*.
gafe *m* jinx.
gai (*fam*) *adj invar*, *m* gay (*sl*), homosexual.
gajo *m* segment (of orange).
galápago *m* tortoise.
galardón *m* reward, prize.
galbana *f* laziness, idleness.
galera *f* (*mar*) galley; wagon; galley (of type).
galería *f* gallery.
galgo *m* grayhound.
gallardo/da *adj* graceful, elegant; brave, daring.
galleta *f* biscuit.
gallina *f* hen:—*m/f* (*fig*) coward:—**~ ciega** blindman's buff.
gallo *m* cock.
gama *f* (*mus*) scale; (*fig*) range, gamut; doe.
gamba *f* shrimp.
gamberro/rra *m/f* hooligan.
gamuza *f* chamois.
gana *f* desire, wish; appetite; will, longing:—**de buena ~** with pleasure, voluntarily:—**de mala ~** unwillingly, with reluctance.
ganado *m* livestock, cattle *pl*:—**~ mayor** horses and mules *pl*:—**~ menor** sheep, goats and hogs *pl*.
ganar *vt* to gain; to win; to earn:—*vi* to win.

gancho *m* hook; crook.
gandul *adj*, *m/f* layabout.
ganga *f* bargain.
ganso/sa *m/f* gander; goose; (*fam*) idiot.
garabatear *vi*, *vt* to scrawl, scribble.
garaje *m* garage.
garantía *f* warranty, guarantee.
garbanzo *m* chickpea, garbanzo.
garbo *m* gracefulness, elegance; stylishness; generosity.
garganta *f* throat, gullet; instep; neck (of a bottle); narrow pass between mountains or rivers.
gárgara *f* gargling, gargle.
garra *f* claw; talon; paw.
garrafa *f* carafe; (gas) cylinder.
garrafal *adj* great, vast, huge.
garrotillo *m* (*med*) croup.
garrucha *f* pulley.
garza *f* heron.
gasa *f* gauze.
gaseoso/sa *adj* fizzy:—*f* lemonade.
gasoil *m* diesel (oil).
gasolina *f* gas.
gasolinera *f* gas station.
gastar *vt* to spend; to expend; to waste; to wear away; to use up:—**~se** *vr* to wear out; to waste.
gata *f* she-cat:—**a ~s** on all fours.
gato *m* cat; jack.
gavilán *m* sparrow hawk.
gavilla *f* sheaf of corn.
gaviota *f* seagull.
gazpacho *m* Spanish cold tomato soup.
gelatina *f* jelly; gelatine.
gemelo/la *m/f* twin.
gemir *vi* to groan, moan.
generación *f* generation; progeny, race.
general *m* general:—*adj* general:—**en ~** generally, in general.
género *m* genus; kind, type; gender; cloth, material:—**~s** *mpl* goods, commodities *pl*.
generoso/sa *adj* noble, generous.
genio *m* nature, character; genius.
genital *adj* genital:—*mpl* **~es** genitals *pl*.
gente *f* people; nation; family.
gentileza *f* grace; charm; politeness.
genuino/na *adj* genuine; pure.
geografía *f* geography.
geología *f* geology.
geometría *f* geometry.
geranio *m* (*bot*) geranium.
gerente *m/f* manager; director.
germinar *vi* to germinate, bud.
gestión *f* management; negotiation.
gesto *m* face; grimace; gesture.
gigante *m* giant:—*adj* gigantic.
gilipollas *adj invar* (*fam*) stupid:—*m/f invar* wimp (*sl*).
gimnasia *f* gymnastics.
ginebra *f* gin.
ginecólogo/ga *m/f* gynecologist.
gira *f* trip, tour.
girar *vt* to turn around; to swivel:—*vi* to go round, revolve.
girasol *m* sunflower.
gitano/na *m/f* Gipsy.
glacial *adj* icy.
glándula *f* gland.
globo *m* globe; sphere; orb; balloon: —**~ aerostatico** air balloon.
glorieta *f* bower, arbor; traffic circle.
glosar *vt* to gloss; to comment on.
glotón/ona *m/f* glutton.
gobierno *m* government.
goce *m* enjoyment.
gol *m* goal.
golondrina *f* swallow.
golosina *f* dainty, titbit; sweet.
golpe *m* blow, stroke, hit; knock; clash; coup:—**de ~** suddenly.
goma *f* gum; rubber; elastic.
gordo/da *adj* fat, plump, big-bellied; first, main; (*fam*) enormous.
gorjear *vi* to twitter, chirp.
gorrión *m* sparrow.
gorro *m* cap; bonnet.
gorrón/ona *m/f* scrounger.
gota *f* drop; (*med*) gout.
gotera *f* leak.
gozar *vt* to enjoy, have, possess:—**~se** *vr* to enjoy oneself, rejoice.
gozne *m* hinge.
gozo *m* joy, pleasure.
grabado *m* engraving.
grabar *vt* to engrave; to record.
gracia *f* grace, gracefulness; wit:—**¡(muchas) ~s!** thanks (very much): —**tener ~** to be funny.
gracioso/sa *adj* graceful; beautiful; funny; pleasing:—*m* comic character.
grada *f* step of a staircase; tier, row:—**~s** *fpl* seats *pl* of stadium or theater.
grado *m* step; degree:—**de buen ~** willingly.
gráfico/ca *adj* graphic:—*m* diagram: —*f* graph.
grajo *m* rook.
gramo *m* gram(me).
gran *adj* = **grande**.
granada *f* pomegranate.
granate *m* garnet (precious stone).
grande *adj* great; big; tall; grand:—*m/f* adult.
grandioso/sa *adj* grand, magnificent.
granel *adv*:—**a ~** in bulk.

granizado *m* iced drink.
granizo *m* hail.
granja *f* farm.
grano *m* grain.
granuja *m/f* rogue; urchin.
grapa *f* staple; clamp.
grasa *f* suet, fat; grease.
gratis *adj* free.
grato/ta *adj* pleasant, agreeable.
gravamen *m* charge, obligation; nuisance; tax.
grave *adj* weighty, heavy; grave, important; serious.
gravilla *f* gravel.
gravoso/sa *adj* onerous, burdensome; costly.
graznar *vi* to croak; to cackle; to quack.
gremio *m* union, guild; society; company, corporation.
greña *f* tangle; shock of hair.
gresca *f* clatter; outcry; confusion; wrangle, quarrel.
grieta *f* crevice, crack, chink.
grifo *m* faucet, tap; gas station.
grillo *m* cricket; bud, shoot.
gripe *f* flu, influenza.
gris *adj* gray.
gritar *vi* to cry out, shout, yell.
grosella *f* redcurrant:—~ **negra** blackcurrant.
grosero/ra *adj* coarse; rude, bad-mannered.
grúa *f* crane (machine); derrick.
grueso/sa *adj* thick; bulky; large; coarse:—*m* bulk.
grulla *f* crane (bird).
gruñir *vi* to grunt; to grumble; to creak (of hinges, etc).
grupo *m* group.
gruta *f* grotto.
guadaña *f* scythe.
guante *m* glove.
guapo/pa *adj* good-looking; handsome; smart.
guardabosque *m* gamekeeper; ranger.
guardacostas *m invar* coastguard vessel.
guardaespaldas *m/f invar* bodyguard.
guardar *vt* to keep, preserve; to save (money); to guard:—~**se** *vr* to be on one's guard:—~**se de** to avoid, abstain from.
guardarropa *f* wardrobe; cloakroom.
guardia *f* guard; (*mar*) watch; care, custody: —*m/f* guard; police officer: —*m* (*mil*) guardsman.
guarecer *vt* to protect; to shelter:—~**se** *vr* to take refuge.
guarnecer *vt* to provide, equip; to reinforce; to garnish, set (in gold, etc); to adorn.
guasa *f* joke.
gubernativo/va *adj* governmental.
guía *m/f* guide:—*f* guidebook.
guiar *vt* to guide; (*auto*) to steer.
guijarro *m* pebble.
guiñar *vt* to wink.
guinda *f* cherry.
guindilla *f* chilli pepper.
guión *m* hyphen; script (of movie).
guisante *m* (*bot*) pea.
guisar *vt* to cook.
guitarra *f* guitar.
gula *f* gluttony.
gusano *m* maggot, worm.
gustar *vt* to taste; to sample:—*vi* to please, be pleasing:—**me gusta. . .** I like. . .

H

haba *f* bean.
haber *vt* to get, lay hands on; to occur:—*v imp* **hay** there is, there are: —*v aux* to have:—~**se** *vr* **habérselas con uno** to have it out with somebody:—*m* income, salary; assets *pl*; (*com*) credit.
hábil *adj* able, clever, skillful, dexterous, apt.
habitación *f* habitation, abode, rooming house, dwelling, residence; room.
habitar *vt* to inhabit, live in.
hábito *m* dress; habit, custom.
habitual *adj* habitual, customary.
hablar *vt, vi* to speak; to talk.
hacendoso/sa *adj* industrious.
hacer *vt* to make; to do; to put into practice; to perform; to effect; to prepare; to imagine; to force; (*mat*) to amount to, make:—*vi* to act, behave:—~**se** *vr* to become.
hacha *f* torch; ax, hatchet.
hacia *adv* toward(s); about:—~ **arriba/abajo** up(wards)/ down(wards).
hada *f* fairy.
halagar *vt* to cajole, flatter.
halcón *m* falcon.
hallar *vt* to find; to meet with; to discover:—~**se** *vr* to find oneself; to be.
hambre *f* hunger; famine; longing.
harina *f* flour.
harto/ta *adj* full; fed up:—*adv* enough.
hasta *prep* up to; down to; until, as far as:—*adv* even.

haya *f* beech tree.
hazaña *f* exploit, achievement.
hebilla *f* buckle.
hebra *f* thread; vein of minerals or metals; grain of wood.
hebreo/ea *m/f, adj* Hebrew; Israeli:—*m* Hebrew language.
hechizar *vt* to bewitch, enchant; to charm.
hecho/cha *adj* made; done; mature; ready-to-wear; cooked:—*m* action; act; fact; matter; event.
hectárea *f* hectare.
helado/da *adj* frozen; glacial, icy; astonished; astounded:—*m* ice cream.
helar *vt* to freeze; to congeal; to astonish, amaze:—**~se** *vr* to be frozen; to turn into ice; to congeal:—*vi* to freeze; to congeal.
helecho *m* fern.
hélice *f* helix; propeller.
hembra *f* female.
heno *m* hay.
heredar *vt* to inherit.
hereje *m/f* heretic.
herir *vt* to wound, hurt; to beat, strike; to affect, touch, move; to offend.
hermana *f* sister.
hermano *m* brother:—**~/na** *adj* matched; resembling.
hermético/ca *adj* hermetic, airtight.
hermoso/sa *adj* beautiful, handsome, lovely; large, robust.
héroe *m* hero.
herradura *f* horseshoe.
herrero *m* smith.
hervir *vt* to boil; to cook:—*vi* to boil; to bubble; to seethe.
hiedra *f* ivy.
hiel *f* gall, bile.
hielo *m* frost; ice.
hierba *f* grass; herb.
hierro *m* iron.
hígado *m* liver; (*fig*) courage, pluck.
higiene *f* hygiene.
higo *m* fig.
hijo/ja *m/f* son/daughter; child; offspring.
hilera *f* row, line, file.
hilo *m* thread; wire.
hincar *vt* to thrust in, drive in.
hinchar *vt* to swell; to inflate; (*fig*) to exaggerate:—**~se** *vr* to swell; to become vain.
hinojo *m* (*bot*) fennel.
hipo *m* hiccups *pl*.
hipócrita *adj* hypocritical:—*m/f* hypocrite.
hipódromo *m* racetrack.
hipoteca *f* mortgage.
historia *f* history; tale, story.
historieta *f* short story; short novel; comic strip.
hocico *m* snout:—**meter el ~ en todo** to meddle in everything.
hogar *m* hearth, fireplace; (*fig*) house, home; family life.
hogaza *f* large loaf of bread.
hoguera *f* bonfire; blaze.
hoja *f* leaf; petal; sheet of paper; blade.
hojalata *f* tin (plate).
hojaldre *f* puff pastry.
hojear *vt* to turn the pages of.
hola *excl* hello!
holgado/da *adj* loose, wide, baggy; at leisure; idle, unoccupied; well-off.
hollín *m* soot.
hombre *m* man; human being.
hombro *m* shoulder.
homenaje *m* homage.
homicidio *m* murder.
hondo/da *adj* deep, profound.
honesto/ta *adj* honest; modest.
hongo *m* mushroom; fungus.
honor *m* honor.
honorario/ria *adj* honorary:—**~s** *mpl* fees *pl*.
honra *f* honor, reverence; self-esteem; reputation; integrity:—**~s funebres** *pl* funeral honors *pl*.
hora *f* hour; time.
horario/ria *adj* hourly, hour *compd*: —*m* schedule.
horchata *f* tiger-nut milk.
horma *f* mold, form.
hormiga *f* ant.
hormigón *m* concrete.
horno *m* oven; furnace.
horquilla *f* pitchfork; hairpin.
hórreo *m* granary.
horrible *adj* horrid, horrible.
horror *m* horror, fright; atrocity.
hortaliza *f* vegetable.
hospedar *vt* to put up, lodge; to entertain.
hospicio *m* orphanage; hospice.
hospital *m* hospital.
hostal *m* small hotel.
hostelería *f* hotel business or trade.
hostia *f* host; wafer; (*fam*) whack (*sl*), punch.
hostil *adj* hostile; adverse.
hotel *m* hotel.
hoy *adv* today; now, nowadays:—**de ~ en adelante** from now on, henceforward.
hoyo *m* hole, pit; excavation.
hoz *f* sickle; gorge.
hucha *f* money-box.

hueco/ca *adj* hollow, concave; empty; vain, ostentatious:—*m* interval; gap, hole; vacancy.
huelga *f* strike.
huella *f* track, footstep.
huérfano/na *adj, m/f* orphan.
huerta *f* market garden; irrigated region.
hueso *m* bone; stone, core.
huésped/da *m/f* guest, lodger, roomer; innkeeper.
huevo *m* egg.
huir *vi* to flee, escape.
humano/na *adj* human; humane, kind.
húmedo/da *adj* humid; wet; damp.
humilde *adj* humble.
humillar *vt* to humble; to subdue:—**~se** *vr* to humble oneself.
humo *m* smoke; fumes *pl*.
humor *m* mood, temper; humor.
hundir *vt* to submerge; to sink; to ruin:—**~se** *vr* to sink, go to the bottom; to collapse; to be ruined.
huraño/ña *adj* shy; unsociable.
hurtadillas *adv*:—**a ~** by stealth.
hurtar *vt* to steal, rob.
husmear *vt* to scent; to pry into.

I

ictericia *f* jaundice.
ida *f* departure, going:—**(viaje de) ~** outward journey:—**~ y vuelta** round trip:—**~s y venidas** comings and goings *pl*.
idea *f* idea; scheme.
ídem *pn* ditto.
idéntico/ca *adj* identical.
idioma *m* language.
idiota *m/f* idiot.
idóneo/nea *adj* suitable, fit.
iglesia *f* church.
ignorar *vt* to be ignorant of, not to know.
igual *adj* equal; similar; the same:—**al ~** equally.
ilegal *adj* illegal, unlawful.
ileso/sa *adj* unhurt.
ilimitado/da *adj* unlimited.
iluminar *vt* to illumine, illuminate, enlighten.
ilusión *f* illusion; hope:—**hacerse ~ones** to build up one's hopes.
ilustre *adj* illustrious, famous.
imagen *f* image.
imaginar *vt* to imagine; to think up:—*vi* **~se** *vr* to imagine.
imán *m* magnet.
imitar *vt* to imitate, copy; to counterfeit.
impaciente *adj* impatient.
impar *adj* odd.
imparcial *adj* impartial.
impedir *vt* to impede, hinder; to prevent.
impeler *vt* to drive, propel; to impel; to incite, stimulate.
impenetrable *adj* impenetrable, impervious; incomprehensible.
impenitente *adj* impenitent.
imperdible *m* safety pin.
imperdonable *adj* unforgivable.
imperfecto/ta *adj* imperfect.
impermeable *adj* waterproof:—*m* raincoat.
imperturbable *adj* imperturbable; unruffled.
implacable *adj* implacable, inexorable.
implicar *vt* to implicate, involve.
imponer *vt* to impose; to command: —**~se** *vr* to assert oneself; to prevail.
impopular *adj* unpopular.
importante *adj* important, considerable.
importar *vi* to be important, matter: —*vt* to import; to be worth.
importe *m* amount, cost.
importunar *vt* to bother, pester.
imposible *adj* impossible; extremely difficult; slovenly.
impostor/ra *m/f* impostor, fraud.
impotencia *f* impotence.
impracticable *adj* impracticable, unworkable.
impreciso/sa *adj* imprecise, vague.
imprenta *f* printing; press; printing office.
imprescindible *adj* essential.
impresión *f* impression; stamp; print; edition.
impresionar *vt* to move; to impress:—**~se** *vr* to be impressed; to be moved.
imprevisto/ta *adj* unforeseen, unexpected.
imprimir *vt* to print; to imprint; to stamp.
improbable *adj* improbable, unlikely.
improvisar *vt* to extemporize; to improvise.
improviso/sa *adj*:—**de ~** unexpectedly.
imprudente *adj* imprudent; indiscreet; unwise.
impúdico/ca *adj* shameless; lecherous.
impuesto/ta *adj* imposed:—*m* tax, duty.
impulso *m* impulse; thrust; (*fig*) impulse.
impune *adj* unpunished.
impuro/ra *adj* impure; foul.
inaccesible *adj* inaccessible.
inadvertido/da *adj* unnoticed.
inagotable *adj* inexhaustible.

inaguantable *adj* unbearable, intolerable.
inalterable *adj* unalterable.
inapreciable *adj* imperceptible; invaluable.
inaudito/ta *adj* unheard-of.
inaugurar *vt* to inaugurate.
incalculable *adj* incalculable.
incansable *adj* untiring, tireless.
incapaz *adj* incapable, unable.
incauto/ta *adj* incautious, unwary.
incendio *m* fire.
incentivo *m* incentive.
incertidumbre *f* doubt, uncertainty.
incierto/ta *adj* uncertain, doubtful.
incineración *f* incineration; cremation.
incitar *vt* to incite, excite.
inclemencia *f* inclemency, severity; inclemency (of the weather).
inclinar *vt* to incline; to nod, bow (the head):—**~se** *vr* to bow; to stoop.
incluir *vt* to include, comprise; to incorporate; to enclose.
incluso/sa *adj* included:—*adv* inclusively; even.
incógnito/ta *adj* unknown:—**de ~** incognito.
incombustible *adj* incombustible, fireproof.
incómodo/da *adj* uncomfortable; annoying; inconvenient.
incomparable *adj* incomparable, matchless.
incompasivo *adj* unsympathetic.
incompleto/ta *adj* incomplete.
incomunicado/da *adj* isolated, cut off; in solitary confinement.
inconcebible *adj* inconceivable.
incondicional *adj* unconditional; wholehearted; staunch.
inconfundible *adj* unmistakable.
inconsciente *adj* unconscious; thoughtless.
inconstante *adj* inconstant, variable, fickle.
incorporar *vt* to incorporate:—**~se** *vr* to sit up; to join (an organization), become incorporated.
incorrecto/ta *adj* incorrect.
incrédulo/la *adj* incredulous.
increíble *adj* incredible.
incremento *m* increment, increase; growth; rise.
inculcar *vt* to inculcate.
inculto/ta *adj* uncultivated; uneducated; uncouth.
incumbencia *f* obligation; duty.
incurable *adj* incurable; irremediable.
indagar *vt* to inquire into.
indebido/da *adj* undue; illegal, unlawful.
indeciso/sa *adj* hesitant; undecided.
indefenso/sa *adj* defenseless.
indemnizar *vt* to indemnify, compensate.
independiente *adj* independent.
indeterminado/da *adj* indeterminate; indefinite.
indicador *m* indicator; gage.
indicar *vt* to indicate.
índice *m* ratio, rate; hand (of a watch or clock); index, table of contents; catalog; forefinger, index finger.
indicio *m* indication, mark; sign, token; clue.
indiferencia *f* indifference, apathy.
indígena *adj* indigenous, native:—*m/f* native.
indignar *vt* to irritate; to provoke, tease:—**~se** *vr* **~ por** to get indignant about.
indigno/na *adj* unworthy, contemptible, low.
indirecta *f* innuendo, hint.
indiscreción *f* indiscretion, tactlessness; gaffe.
individual *adj* individual; single (of a room):—*m* (*dep*) singles.
individuo *m* individual.
índole *f* disposition, nature, character; soft, kind.
indolente *adj* indolent, lazy.
indómito/ta *adj* untamed, ungoverned.
inducir *vt* to induce, persuade.
indudable *adj* undoubted; unquestionable.
indultar *vt* to pardon; to exempt.
industria *f* industry; skill.
inédito/ta *adj* unpublished; (*fig*) new.
ineficaz *adj* ineffective; inefficient.
inepto/ta *adj* inept, unfit, useless.
inercia *f* inertia, inactivity.
inerte *adj* inert; dull; sluggish, motionless.
inesperado/da *adj* unexpected, unforeseen.
inevitable *adj* unavoidable.
inexacto/ta *adj* inaccurate, untrue.
inexperto/ta *adj* inexperienced.
infame *adj* infamous.
infancia *f* infancy, childhood.
infantil *adj* infantile; childlike; children's.
infarto *m* heart attack.
infatigable *adj* tireless, untiring.
infectar *vt* to infect.
infeliz *adj* unhappy, unfortunate.
inferior *adj* inferior.
infernal *adj* infernal, hellish.
infiel *adj* unfaithful; disloyal; inaccurate.
infierno *m* hell.
infiltrarse *vr* to infiltrate.
ínfimo/ma *adj* lowest; of very poor quality.
infinidad *f* infinity; immensity.
infinito/ta *adj* infinite; immense.
inflamable *adj* inflammable.
inflar *vt* to inflate, blow up; (*fig*) to exaggerate.
inflexible *adj* inflexible.
influir *vt* to influence.
información *f* information; news; (*mil*) intelligence; investigation, judicial inquiry.

informal *adj* irregular, incorrect; untrustworthy; informal.
informar *vt* to inform; to reveal, make known:—**~se** *vr* to find out: —*vi* to report; (*jur*) to plead; to inform.
informática *f* computer science, information technology.
informe *m* report, statement; piece of information, account:—*adj* shapeless, formless.
infortunio *m* misfortune, ill luck.
infracción *f* infraction; breach, infringement.
infructuoso/sa *adj* fruitless, unproductive, unprofitable.
infundado/da *adj* groundless.
ingeniero/ra *m/f* engineer.
ingenio *m* talent; wit; ingenuity; engine:—**~ de azúcar** sugar mill.
ingenuo/nua *adj* naive.
ingerir *vt* to ingest; to swallow; to consume.
ingle *f* groin.
inglés/esa *adj* English:—*m* English language: —*m/f* Englishman/woman.
ingrato/ta *adj* ungrateful, thankless; disagreeable.
ingresar *vt* to deposit:—*vi* to come in.
inhabilitar *vt* to disqualify, disable.
inhabitable *adj* uninhabitable.
inhibir *vt* to inhibit; to restrain.
iniciar *vt* to initiate; to begin.
ininteligible *adj* unintelligible.
injertar *vt* to graft.
injuriar *vt* to insult, wrong.
injusto/ta *adj* unjust.
inmediaciones *fpl* neighborhood.
inmediatamente *adv* immediately, at once.
inmobiliario/ria *adj* real-estate *compd*:—*f* estate agency.
inmortal *adj* immortal.
inmóvil *adj* immovable, still.
inmueble *m* property:—*adj* **bienes ~s** real estate.
inmundo/da *adj* filthy, dirty; nasty.
inmune *adj* (*med*) immune; free, exempt.
innato/ta *adj* inborn, innate.
innecesario/ria *adj* unnecessary.
innegable *adj* undeniable.
innumerable *adj* innumerable, countless.
inocente *adj* innocent.
inodoro *m* washroom:—**~/ra** *adj* odorless, without smell.
inofensivo/va *adj* harmless.
inolvidable *adj* unforgettable.
inoxidable *adj*:—**acero ~** stainless steel.
inquietar *vt* to worry, disturb:—**~se** *vr* to worry, get worried.
inquilino/na *m/f* tenant; roomer, lodger.
inquirir *vt* to inquire into, investigate.
inscribir *vt* to inscribe; to list, register.
insecto *m* insect.
insensato/ta *adj* senseless, stupid; mad.
insensible *adj* insensitive; imperceptible; numb.
inseparable *adj* inseparable.
insertar *vt* to insert.
inservible *adj* useless.
insignia *f* badge:—**~s** *fpl* insignia *pl*.
insinuar *vt* to insinuate:—**~se** *vr* **~ en** to worm one's way into.
insípido/da *adj* insipid.
insistir *vi* to insist.
insolación *f* (*med*) sunstroke.
insolencia *f* insolence, rudeness, effrontery.
insólito/ta *adj* unusual.
insolvente *adj* insolvent.
insomnio *m* insomnia.
insondable *adj* unfathomable; inscrutable.
insoportable *adj* unbearable.
inspeccionar *vt* to inspect; to supervize.
inspector/ra *m/f* inspector; superintendent.
inspirar *vt* to inspire; (*med*) to inhale.
instalar *vt* to install.
instantáneo/nea *adj* instantaneous: —*f* snap(shot):—**café ~** instant coffee.
instante *m* instant:—**al ~** immediately, instantly.
instigar *vt* to instigate.
instinto *m* instinct.
instructivo/va *adj* instructive; educational.
instrumento *m* instrument; tool, implement.
insuficiente *adj* insufficient, inadequate.
insulso/sa *adj* insipid; dull.
insultar *vt* to insult.
insuperable *adj* insuperable, insurmountable.
intacto/ta *adj* untouched; entire; intact.
integral *adj* integral, whole:—**pan ~** whole-wheat bread.
intemperie *f*:—**a la ~** out in the open.
intencionado/da *adj* meaningful; deliberate.
intenso/sa *adj* intense, strong; deep.
intentar *vt* to try, attempt.
intercalar *vt* to insert.
intercambio *m* exchange, swap.
interés *m* interest; share, part; concern, advantage; profit.
interesar *vt* to be of interest to, interest:—**~se** *vr* **~ en** *o* **por** to take an interest in:—*vi* to be of interest.
interferir *vt* to interfere with; to jam (a telephone):—*vi* to interfere.
interfono *m* intercom.

interino/na *adj* provisional, temporary:—*m/f* temporary holder of a post; stand-in.
interior *adj* interior, internal:—*m* interior, inside.
intermedio/dia *adj* intermediate:—*m* interval.
interminable *adj* interminable, endless.
intermitente *adj* intermittent; *m* (*auto*) indicator.
internado *m* boarding school.
interno/na *adj* interior, internal:—*m/f* boarder.
interpretar *vt* to interpret, explain; (*teat*) to perform; to translate.
interrogación *f* interrogation; question mark.
interrogatorio *m* questioning; (*jur*) examination; questionnaire.
interrumpir *vt* to interrupt.
interruptor *m* switch.
intervenir *vt* to control, supervise; (*com*) to audit; (*med*) to operate on: —*vi* to participate; to intervene.
intestino/na *adj* internal, interior:—*m* intestine.
íntimo/ma *adj* internal, innermost; intimate, private.
intranquilo/la *adj* worried.
intransitable *adj* impassable.
intrépido/da *adj* intrepid, daring.
intrigar *vt*, *vi* to intrigue.
introducir *vt* to introduce; to insert.
introvertido/da *adj*, *m/f* introvert.
intruso/sa *adj* intrusive:—*m/f* intruder.
inundar *vt* to inundate, overflow; to flood.
inusitado/da *adj* unusual.
inútil *adj* useless.
inválido/da *adj* invalid, null and void:—*m/f* invalid.
invencible *adj* invincible.
invernadero *m* greenhouse.
inverosímil *adj* unlikely, improbable.
inverso/sa *adj* inverse; inverted; contrary.
invertir *vt* (*com*) to invest; to invert.
investigar *vt* to investigate; to do research into.
invierno *m* winter.
invitar *vt* to invite; to entice; to pay for.
invocar *vt* to invoke.
ir *vi* to go; to walk; to travel:—**~se** *vr* to go away, depart.
ira *f* anger, wrath.
iris *m* iris (eye):—**arco ~** rainbow.
ironía *f* irony.
irracional *adj* irrational.
irreal *adj* unreal.
irreflexión *f* rashness, thoughtlessness.
irregular *adj* irregular; abnormal.
irremediable *adj* irremediable; incurable.
irresistible *adj* irresistible.
irreverente *adj* irreverent; disrespectful.
irrisorio/ria *adj* derisory, ridiculous.
irritar *vt* to irritate, exasperate; to stir up; to inflame.
isla *f* island, isle.
istmo *m* isthmus.
italiano/na *adj* Italian:—*m* Italian language: —*m/f* Italian.
itinerario *m* itinerary.
izquierdo/da *adj* left; left-handed:—*f* left; left(-wing).

J

jabalí *m* wild boar.
jabón *m* soap.
jaca *f* pony.
jacinto *m* hyacinth.
jadear *vi* to pant.
jaleo *m* racket, uproar.
jamás *adv* never:—**para siempre ~** for ever.
jamón *m* ham:—**~ de York** cooked ham:—**~ serrano** cured ham.
jaque *m* check (at game of chess):—**~ mate** checkmate.
jaqueca *f* migraine.
jarabe *m* syrup.
jardín *m* garden.
jarra *f* jug, jar, pitcher:—**en ~s, de ~s** with hands to the sides.
jaula *f* cage; cell for mad people.
jazmín *m* jasmin.
jefe *m* chief, head, leader:—(*ferro*) **~ de tren** guard, conductor.
jerarquía *f* hierarchy.
jerigonza *f* jargon, gibberish.
jeringa *f* syringe.
jeroglífico/ca *adj* hieroglyphic:—*m* hieroglyph, hieroglyphic.
jersey *m* sweater, pullover.
jilguero *m* goldfinch.
jinete/ta *m/f* horseman/woman, rider.
jipijapa *m* straw hat.
jirón *m* rag, shred.
jornada *f* journey; day's journey; working day.
jornal *m* day's wage.

jornalero *m* (day) laborer.
joroba *f* hump:—*m/f* hunchback.
jota *f* jot, iota; Spanish dance.
joven *adj* young:—*m/f* youth; young woman.
jovial *adj* jovial, cheerful.
joya *f* jewel:—**~s** *fpl* jewelry.
juanete *m* (*med*) bunion.
jubilar *vt* to pension off; to superannuate; to discard:—**~se** *vr* to retire.
júbilo *m* joy, rejoicing.
judía *f* bean:—**~ verde** French bean.
judicial *adj* judicial.
judío/día *adj* Jewish:—*m/f* Jewish man/woman.
juego *m* play; amusement; sport; game; gambling.
jueves *m invar* Thursday.
juez *m/f* judge.
jugar *vt*, *vi* to play, sport, gamble.
jugo *m* sap, juice.
juguete *m* toy, plaything.
juicio *m* judgement, reason; sanity; opinion.
julio *m* July.
junco *m* (*bot*) rush; junk (Chinese ship).
junio *m* June.
junta *f* meeting; assembly; congress; council.
juntar *vt* to join; to unite:—**~se** *vr* to meet, assemble; to draw closer.
junto/ta *adj* joined; united; near; adjacent:—**~s** together:—*adv* **todo ~** all at once.
jurar *vt*, *vi* to swear.
jurídico/ca *adj* lawful, legal; juridical.
justicia *f* justice; equity.
justificante *m* voucher; receipt.
justo/ta *adj* just; fair, right; exact, correct; tight:—*adv* exactly, precisely; just in time.
juventud *f* youthfulness, youth; young people *pl*.
juzgado *m* tribunal; court.

K

kilogramo *m* kilogram(me).
kilómetro *m* kilometer.
kiosco *m* kiosk.

L

la *art f* the:—*pn* her; you; it.
labio *m* lip; edge.
labor *f* labor, task; needlework; farmwork; ploughing.
laborioso/sa *adj* laborious; hard-working.
labrar *vt* to work; to carve; to farm; (*fig*) to bring about.
laca *f* lacquer; hairspray.
lacio/cia *adj* faded, withered; languid; lank (hair).
lacrar *vt* to seal (with sealing wax).
lactancia *f* lactation; breast-feeding.
lácteo/tea *adj*:—**productos ~s** dairy products.
ladera *f* slope.
ladino/na *adj* cunning, crafty.
lado *m* side; faction, party; favor, protection; (*mil*) flank:—**al ~ de** beside:—**poner a un ~** to put aside:—**por todos ~s** on all sides.
ladrar *vt* to bark.
ladrillo *m* brick.
ladrón/ona *m/f* thief, robber.
lagar *m* wine press.
lagartija *f* (small) lizard.
lagarto *m* lizard.
lago *m* lake.
lágrima *f* tear.
laguna *f* lake; lagoon; gap.
laico/ca *adj* lay.
lamentar *vt* to be sorry about; to lament, regret:—*vi* **~se** *vr* to lament, complain; to mourn.
lamer *vt* to lick, lap.
lámina *f* plate, sheet of metal; engraving.
lámpara *f* lamp.
lana *f* wool.
lancha *f* barge, lighter; launch.
langosta *f* locust; lobster.
lanzar *vt* to throw; (*dep*) to bowl, pitch; to launch, fling; (*jur*) to evict.
lápida *f* flat stone, tablet.
lápiz *m* pencil; mechanical pencil.
largamente *adv* for a long time.
largo/ga *adj* long; lengthy, generous; copious:—**a la ~a** in the end, eventually.

las *art fpl* the:—*pn* them; you.
lascivo/va *adj* lascivious; lewd.
láser *m* laser.
lástima *f* compassion, pity; shame.
lastimar *vt* to hurt; to wound; to feel pity for:—**~se** *vr* to hurt oneself.
lastre *m* ballast.
lata *f* tin; tin can; (*fam*) nuisance.
latido *m* (heart)beat.
latifundio *m* large estate.
latir *vi* to beat, palpitate.
latitud *f* latitude.
latón *m* brass.
latoso/sa *adj* annoying; boring.
laúd *f* lute (musical instrument).
laudable *adj* laudable, praise-worthy.
laurel *m* (*bot*) laurel; reward.
lavabo *m* washbasin; washroom.
lavadora *f* washing machine.
lavanda *f* lavender.
lavar *vt* to wash; to wipe away:—**~se** *vr* to wash oneself.
laxante *m* (*med*) laxative.
lazarillo *m*:—**perro ~** guide dog.
lazo *m* knot; bow; snare, trap; tie; bond.
le *pn* him; you; (*dativo*) to him; to her; to it; to you.
leal *adj* loyal; faithful.
lebrel *m* greyhound.
lección *f* reading; lesson; lecture; class.
leche *f* milk.
lecho *m* bed; layer.
lechón *m* sucking pig.
lechuga *f* lettuce.
lechuza *f* owl.
leer *vt, vi* to read.
legado *m* bequest, legacy; legate.
legal *adj* legal; trustworthy.
legaña *f* sleep (in eyes).
legislar *vt* to legislate.
legítimo/ma *adj* legitimate, lawful; authentic.
legumbres *fpl* pulses *pl*.
lejano/na *adj* distant, remote; far.
lejía *f* bleach.
lejos *adv* at a great distance, far off.
lelo/la *adj* stupid, ignorant:—*m/f* idiot.
lema *m* motto; slogan.
leña *f* firewood, kindling.
lencería *f* linen, drapery.
lengua *f* tongue; language.
lenguado *m* sole.
lenguaje *m* language.
lente *m/f* lens.
lenteja *f* lentil.
lentilla *f* contact lens.
lento/ta *adj* slow.
león *m* lion.
leopardo *m* leopard.
leotardos *mpl* tights, pantihose.
lesión *f* wound; injury; damage.
letal *adj* mortal, deadly.
letanía *f* litany.
letargo *m* lethargy.
letra *f* letter; handwriting; printing type; draft of a song; bill, draft:—**~s** *fpl* letters *pl*, learning.
letrero *m* sign; label.
leucemia *f* leukemia.
levadura *f* yeast; brewer's yeast.
levantar *vt* to raise, lift up; to build; to elevate; to hearten, cheer up:—**~se** *vr* to get up; to stand up.
levante *m* Levant; east; east wind.
levantisco *adj* turbulent, restless.
leve *adj* light; trivial.
léxico *m* vocabulary.
ley *f* law; standard (for metal).
leyenda *f* legend.
liar *vt* to tie, bind; to confuse.
libélula *f* dragonfly.
liberal *adj* liberal, generous:—*m/f* liberal.
libertad *f* liberty, freedom.
libra *f* pound:—**~ esterlina** pound sterling.
libre *adj* free; exempt; vacant.
librería *f* book store.
libreta *f* notebook:—**~ de ahorros** savings book.
libro *m* book.
licencia *f* license; licentiousness.
licenciado/da *adj* licensed:—*m/f* graduate.
lícito/ta *adj* lawful, fair; permissible.
líder *m/f* leader.
liebre *f* hare.
lienzo *f* linen; canvas; face or front of a building.
liga *f* suspender; birdlime; league; coalition; alloy.
ligar *vt* to tie, bind, fasten:—**~se** *vr* to commit oneself:—*vi* to mix, blend; (*fam*) to pick up.
ligero/ra *adj* light, swift; agile; superficial.
liguero *m* suspender belt.
lijar *vt* to smooth, sandpaper.
lima *f* file.
límite *m* limit, boundary.
limón *m* lemon.
limosna *f* alms *pl*, charity.
limpiar *vt* to clean; to cleanse; to purify; to polish; (*fig*) to clean up.
linaza *f* linseed.
lince *m* lynx.
lindar *vi* to be adjacent.
lindo/da *adj* pretty; lovely.
línea *f* line; cable; outline.

lino *m* flax.
linterna *f* lantern, lamp; torch.
lío *m* bundle, parcel; (*fam*) muddle, mess.
liquidar *vt* to liquidate; to settle (accounts).
líquido/da *adj* liquid.
lirio *m* (*bot*) iris.
lirón *m* dormouse; (*fig*) sleepy- head.
liso/sa *adj* plain, even, flat, smooth.
lisonja *f* adulation, flattery.
lista *f* list; register; catalog; menu.
listo/ta *adj* ready; smart, clever.
litera *f* berth; bunk, bunk bed.
litigio *m* lawsuit.
litoral *adj* coastal:—*m* coast.
litro *m* liter (measure).
liviano/na *adj* light; fickle; trivial.
llama *f* flame; llama (animal).
llamar *vt* to call; to name; to summon; to ring up, telephone:—*vi* to knock at the door; to ring up, telephone:—**~se** *vr* to be named.
llano/na *adj* plain; even, level, smooth; clear, evident:—*m* plain.
llanta *f* (wheel) rim; tire; inner (tube).
llanura *f* evenness, flatness; plain, prairie.
llave *f* key:—**~ maestra** master key.
llegar *vi* to arrive:—**~ a** to reach:—**~se** *vr* to come near, approach.
llenar *vt* to fill; to cover; to fill out (a form); to satisfy, fulfil:—**~se** *vr* to gorge oneself.
llevar *vt* to take; to wear; to carry; to convey, transport; to drive; to lead; to bear: —**~se** *vr* to carry off, take away.
llorar *vt*, *vi* to weep, cry.
llover *vi* to rain.
lluvia *f* rain.
lo *pn* it; him; you:—*art* the.
lobo *m* wolf.
lóbulo *m* lobe.
local *adj* local:—*m* place, site.
loco/ca *adj* mad:—*m/f* mad person.
locutor/ra *m/f* (*rad*) announcer; (*TV*) newsreader.
lodo *m* mud, mire.
lograr *vt* to achieve; to gain, obtain.
lombarda *f* red cabbage.
lombriz *f* worm.
lomo *m* loin; back (of an animal); spine (of a book):—**llevar** *o* **traer a ~** to carry on the back.
lona *f* canvas.
loncha *f* slice; rasher.
longaniza *f* pork sausage.
longitud *f* length; longitude.
loro *m* parrot.
los *art mpl* the:—*pn* them; you.
losa *f* flagstone.
lote *m* lot; portion.
loza *f* crockery.
lucero *m* morning star, bright star.
luchar *vi* to struggle; to wrestle.
luciérnaga *f* glowworm.
lucir *vt* to light (up); to show off:—*vi* to shine:—**~se** *vr* to make a fool of oneself.
luego *adv* next; afterward(s):—**desde ~** of course.
lugar *m* place, spot; village; reason: —**en ~ de** instead of, in lieu of.
lúgubre *adj* lugubrious; sad, gloomy.
lujo *m* luxury; abundance.
lujuria *f* lust.
lumbre *f* fire; light.
luna *f* moon; glass plate for mirrors; lens.
lunar *m* mole, spot:—*adj* lunar.
lunes *m invar* Monday.
lupa *f* magnifying glass.
lupanar *m* brothel.
luto *m* mourning (dress); grief.
luz *f* light.

M

maceta *f* flowerpot.
machacar *vt* to pound, crush:—*vi* to insist, go on.
macho *adj* male; (*fig*) virile:—*m* male; (*fig*) he-man.
macizo/za *adj* massive; solid:—*m* mass, chunk.
madera *f* wood; lumber.
madrastra *f* stepmother.
madre *f* mother; womb.
madreselva *f* honeysuckle.
madriguera *f* burrow; den.
madrugar *vi* to get up early; to get ahead.
maduro/ra *adj* ripe, mature.
maestro *m* master; teacher:—**~/tra** *adj* masterly, skilled; principal.
magia *f* magic.
magisterio *m* teaching; teaching profession; teachers *pl*.
magnetofón, magnetófono *m* tape recorder.
magnífico/ca *adj* magnificent, splendid.
mago/ga *m/f* magician.
magullar *vt* to bruise; to damage; to bash (*sl*).
mahometano/na *m/f*, *adj* Muslim.
maíz *m* maize, Indian corn.
majadero/ra *adj* dull; silly, stupid:—*m* idiot.

majo/ja *adj* nice; attractive; smart.
majuelo *m* vine newly planted; hawthorn.
mal *m* evil; hurt; harm, damage; misfortune; illness:—*adj* (before masculine nouns) bad.
malcriado/da *adj* rude, ill-behaved; naughty; spoiled.
maldad *f* wickedness.
maldecir *vt* to curse.
maldito/ta *adj* wicked; damned, cursed.
malecón *m* pier.
maleducado/da *adj* bad-mannered, rude.
malestar *m* discomfort; (*fig*) uneasiness; unrest.
maleta *f* suitcase; (*auto*) trunk.
maleza *f* weeds *pl*; thicket.
malgastar *vt* to waste, ruin.
malhablado/da *adj* foul-mouthed.
malhechor/ra *m/f* malefactor; criminal.
malhumorado/da *adj* cross, bad-tempered.
malla *f* mesh, network:—**~s** *fpl* leotard.
malo/la *adj* bad; ill; wicked:—*m/f* villain.
maltratar *vt* to ill-treat, abuse, mistreat.
malva *f* (*bot*) mallow.
malvado/da *adj* wicked, villainous.
mama *f* teat; breast.
mamá *f* (*fam*) mum, mummy.
mamar *vt*, *vi* to suck.
mamífero *m* mammal.
manada *f* flock, herd; pack; crowd.
manantial *m* source, spring; origin.
manchar *vt* to stain, soil.
manco/ca *adj* one-armed; one-handed; maimed; faulty.
mancomunidad *f* union, fellowship; community; (*jur*) joint responsibility.
mandar *vt* to command, order; to bequeath; to send.
mandarina *f* tangerine.
mandíbula *f* jaw.
mandil *m* apron.
manera *f* manner, way; fashion; kind.
manga *f* sleeve; hose.
mango *m* handle; mango.
manguera *f* hose; pipe.
maní *m* peanut.
manifestación *f* manifestation; show; demonstration; mass meeting.
manifestar *vt* to manifest, declare.
maniobrar *vt* to maneuvre; to handle.
manipular *vt* to manipulate.
maniquí *m* dummy:—*m/f* model.
manivela *f* crank.
mano *f* hand; hand (of clock, etc); foot, paw (of animal); coat (of paint); lot, series; hand (at game):—**a ~** by hand:—**a ~s llenas** liberally, generously.
manojo *m* handful, bunch.
manopla *f* wash cloth; mitten; gauntlet.
manosear *vt* to handle; to mess up.
manso/sa *adj* tame; gentle, soft.
manta *f* blanket.
manteca *f* fat:—**~ de cerdo** lard.
mantel *m* tablecloth.
mantener *vt* to maintain, support; to nourish; to keep:—**~se** *vr* to hold one's ground; to support oneself.
mantequilla *f* butter.
manzana *f* apple.
manzanilla *f* camomile; camomile tea; manzanilla sherry.
maña *f* handiness, dexterity, cleverness, cunning; habit, custom; trick.
mañana *f* morning:—*adv* tomorrow.
mapa *m* map.
maquillar *vt* to make up:—**~se** *vr* to put on make-up.
máquina *f* machine; (*ferro*) engine; camera; (*fig*) machinery; plan, project.
maquinilla *f*:—**~ de afeitar** razor.
maquinista *m* (*ferro*) train driver; operator; (*mar*) engineer.
mar *m/f* sea.
maravilla *f* wonder.
marca *f* mark; stamp; make, brand.
marcar *vt* to mark; to dial; to score; to record; to set (hair):—*vi* to score; to dial.
marchar *vi* to go; to work:—**~se** *vr* to go away.
marco *m* frame; framework; (*dep*) goalposts *pl*.
marea *f* tide.
marear *vt* (*mar*) to sail, navigate; to annoy, upset:—**~se** *vr* to feel sick; to feel faint; to feel dizzy.
marfil *m* ivory.
margarita *f* daisy.
margen *m* margin; border:—*f* bank (of river).
marido *m* husband.
marinero/ra *adj* sea *compd*; seaworthy:—*m* sailor.
marioneta *f* puppet.
mariposa *f* butterfly.
mariquita *f* ladybird.
marisco *m* shellfish *pl*.
mármol *m* marble.
marrano *m* hog, boar.
marrón *adj* brown.
martes *m invar* Tuesday.
martillo *m* hammer.
marzo *m* March.
mas *adv* but, yet.
más *adv* more; most; besides, moreover:—**a ~ tardar** at latest:—**sin ~ ni ~** without more ado.

masa *f* dough, paste; mortar; mass.
mascar *vt* to chew.
máscara *m/f* masked person:—*f* mask.
mascullar *vt* to mumble, mutter.
mástil *m* (*mar*) mast.
mastín *m* mastiff.
mata *f* shrub; sprig, blade; grove, group of trees; mop of hair.
matadero *m* slaughterhouse.
matar *vt* to kill; to execute; to murder:—**~se** *vr* to kill oneself, commit suicide.
matasellos *m invar* postmark.
mate *m* checkmate:—*adj* matt.
material *adj* material, physical:—*m* equipment, materials *pl*.
maternidad *f* motherhood.
matinal *adj* morning *compd*.
matiz *m* shade of color; shading.
matrícula *f* register, list; (*auto*) registration number; license plate.
matrimonio *m* marriage, matrimony.
matriz *f* matrix; womb; mold, form.
maullar *vi* to mew.
mayo *m* May.
mayor *adj* main, chief; (*mus*) major; biggest; eldest; greater, larger; elderly:—*m* chief, boss; adult:—**al por ~** wholesale:—**~es** *mpl* forefathers.
mayoría *f* majority, greater part:—**~ de edad** coming of age.
mayúsculo/la *adj* (*fig*) tremendous: —*f* capital letter.
mazo *m* bunch; club, mallet; bat.
mazorca *f* ear of corn.
me *pn* me; to me.
mear *vi* (*fam*) to pee, piss (*sl*).
mecanógrafo/fa *m/f* typist.
mecer *vt* to rock; to dandle (a child).
mechar *vt* to lard; to stuff.
mechón *m* lock of hair; large bundle of threads or fibres.
media *f* stocking; sock; average.
medianoche *f* midnight.
mediante *prep* by means of.
mediar *vi* to intervene; to mediate.
medicamento *m* medicine.
médico/ca *adj* medical:—*m/f* doctor.
medida *f* measure.
medio/dia *adj* half:—**a medias** partly:—*m* middle; average; way, means; medium.
mediodía *m* noon, midday.
medir *vt* to measure:—**~se** *vr* to be moderate.
medrar *vi* to grow, thrive, prosper; to improve.
médula *f* marrow; essence, substance; pith.
medusa *f* jellyfish.
mejilla *f* cheek.
mejillón *m* mussel.
mejor *adj*, *adv* better; best.
mejorar *vt* to improve, ameliorate; to enhance:—*vi* to improve; (*med*) to recover, get better:—**~se** *vr* to improve, get better.
melenudo/da *adj* long-haired.
melindroso/sa *adj* prudish, finicky.
mella *f* notch in edged tools; gap.
mellizo/za *adj*, *m/f* twin.
melocotón *m* peach.
meloso/sa *adj* honeyed; mellow.
membrete *m* letter head.
membrillo *m* quince; quince tree.
memoria *f* memory; report; record:—**~s** *fpl* memoirs *pl*.
mendigar *vt* to beg.
menear *vt* to move from place to place; (*fig*) to handle:—**~se** *vr* to move; to shake; to sway.
menguante *f* waning.
meñique *m* little finger.
menor *m/f* young person, juvenile:—*adj* less; smaller; minor:—**al por ~** retail.
menos *adv* less; least:—**a lo ~** *o* **por lo ~** at least:—*prep* except; minus.
menospreciar *vt* to undervalue; to despise, scorn.
mensaje *m* message.
mensual *adj* monthly.
menta *f* mint.
mente *f* mind; understanding.
mentecato/ta *adj* silly, stupid:—*m/f* idiot.
mentir *vt* to feign; to pretend:—*vi* to lie.
mentira *f* lie, falsehood.
menudo/da *adj* small; minute; petty, insignificant:—**a ~** frequently, often.
mercader *m* dealer, trader.
mercado *m* market; marketplace.
mercancía *f* commodity:—**~s** *fpl* goods *pl*, merchandise.
mercurio *m* mercury.
merecer *vt* to deserve, merit.
meridional *adj* southern.
merienda *f* (light) tea; afternoon snack; picnic.
merluza *f* hake.
mermelada *f* jam.
mero *m* pollack (fish):—**~/ra** *adj* mere, pure.
mes *m* month.
mesa *f* table; desk; plateau:—**~ redonda** round table.
mestizo/za *adj* of mixed race; crossbred:—*m/f* half-caste.
meta *f* goal; finish.
metal *m* metal; (*mus*) brass; timbre (of voice).
meter *vt* to place, put; to insert, put in; to involve; to make, cause:—**~se** *vr* to meddle, interfere.

método *m* method.
metro *m* meter; subway.
mezclar *vt* to mix:—**~se** *vr* to mix; to mingle.
mezquino/na *adj* mean; small-minded, petty; wretched.
mezquita *f* mosque.
mi *adj* my.
mí *pn* me; myself.
miedo *m* fear, dread.
miel *f* honey.
miembro *m* member.
mientras *adv* meanwhile:—*conj* while; as long as.
miércoles *m invar* Wednesday.
mierda *f* (*fam*) shit (*sl*).
miga *f* crumb:—**~s** *fpl* fried bread-crumbs *pl*.
mijo *m* (*bot*) millet.
mil *m* one thousand.
milagro *m* miracle, wonder.
milésimo/ma *adj*, *m* thousandth.
milímetro *m* millimeter.
milla *f* mile.
millión *m* million.
mimar *vt* to spoil, pamper.
mimbre *m* wicker.
mimo *m* caress; spoiling; mime.
mina *f* mine; underground passage.
minero/ra *m/f* miner.
minifalda *f* miniskirt.
mínimo/ma *adj* minimum.
minoría *f* minority.
minucioso/sa *adj* meticulous; very detailed.
minúsculo/la *adj* minute:—*f* small letter.
minusválido/da *adj* (physically) handicapped:—*m/f* (physically) handicapped person.
minuto *m* minute.
mío/mía *adj* mine.
miope *adj* short-sighted.
mirar *vt* to look at; to observe; to consider:—*vi* to look:—**~se** *vr* to look at oneself; to look at one another.
mirlo *m* blackbird.
misa *f* mass:—**~ del gallo** midnight mass.
miserable *adj* miserable; mean; squalid (place); (*fam*) despicable:—*m/f* rotter.
misericordia *f* mercy.
mismo/ma *adj* same; very.
mitad *f* half; middle.
mitin *m* (political) rally.
mixto/ta *adj* mixed.
mobiliario *m* furniture.
mochila *f* backpack.
mochuelo *m* red owl.
moco *m* snot (*sl*), mucus.
moda *f* fashion, style.
modales *mpl* manners *pl*.
modelo *m* model, pattern.
módico/ca *adj* moderate.
modificar *vt* to modify.
modisto/ta *m/f* dressmaker.
modo *m* mode, method, manner.
modorra *f* drowsiness.
mofarse *vr*:—**~ de** to mock, scoff at.
moflete *m* fat cheek.
moho *m* rust; mold, mildew.
mojar *vt* to wet, moisten:—**~se** *vr* to get wet.
mojón *m* landmark.
molde *m* mold; pattern; model.
moler *vt* to grind, pound; to tire out; to annoy, bore.
molestar *vt* to annoy, bother; to trouble:—*vi* to be a nuisance.
molino *m* mill.
momentáneo/nea *adj* momentary.
momento *m* moment.
momia *f* mummy.
mondadientes *m invar* toothpick.
mondar *vt* to clean; to cleanse; to peel:—**~se** *vr* **~ de risa** (*fam*) to split one's sides laughing.
mondo/da *adj* clean; pure:—**~ y lirondo** bare, plain; pure and simple.
moneda *f* money; currency; coin.
monja *f* nun.
mono/na *adj* lovely; pretty; nice:—*m/f* monkey; ape:—*mpl* dungarees *pl*; overalls *pl*.
monstruo *m* monster.
montaje *m* assembly; decor (of theater); montage.
montaña *f* mountain.
montar *vt* to mount, get on (a bicycle, horse, etc); to assemble, put together; to overlap; to set up (a business); to beat, whip (in cooking):—*vi* to mount; to ride:—**~ a** to amount to.
monte *m* mountain; woodland:—**~ alto** forest:—**~ bajo** scrub.
montón *m* heap, pile; mass:—**a ~ones**, abundantly, by the score.
montura *f* mount; saddle.
monzón *m* monsoon.
mora *f* blackberry.
morado/da *adj* violet, purple.
morcilla *f* blood sausage.
mordaz *adj* biting, scathing; pungent.
mordaza *f* gag; clamp.
morder *vt* to bite; to nibble; to corrode, eat away.
moreno/na *adj* brown; swarthy; dark-skinned.
morir *vi* to die; to expire; to die down: —**~se** *vr* to die; (*fig*) to be dying.
morisco/ca *adj* Moorish.
moroso/sa *adj* slow, sluggish; (*com*) slow to pay up.

morral *m* haversack.
morro *m* snout; nose (of plane, etc).
morsa *f* walrus.
mortal *adj* mortal; fatal, deadly.
mosca *f* fly.
mosquearse *vr* (*fam*) to get cross; (*fam*) to take offence.
mosquitero *m* mosquito net.
mosquito *m* gnat, mosquito.
mostaza *f* mustard.
mosto *m* must, grape juice.
mostrador *m* counter.
mostrar *vt* to show, exhibit; to explain: —**~se** *vr* to appear, show oneself.
mote *m* nickname.
motivo *m* motive, cause, reason.
moto (*fam*), **motocicleta** *f* motorcycle.
motor *m* engine, motor.
mover *vt* to move; to shake; to drive; (*fig*) to cause:—**~se** *vr* to move; (*fig*) to get a move on.
móvil *adj* mobile, movable; moving: —*m* motive.
mozo/za *adj* young:—*m/f* youth, young man/girl; waiter/waitress.
muchacho/a *m/f* boy/girl:—*f* maid, maidservant.
mucho/cha *adj* a lot of, much:—*adv* much, a lot; long.
mudar *vt* to change; to shed:—**~se** *vr* to change one's clothes; to change house:—*vi* to change;
mudo/da *adj* dumb; silent, mute.
mueble *m* piece of furniture:—**~s** *mpl* furniture.
mueca *f* grimace, funny face.
muela *f* tooth, molar.
muelle *m* spring; regulator; quay.
muérdago *m* (*bot*) mistletoe.
muerte *f* death.
mujer *f* woman.
mulato *adj* mulatto.
muleta *f* crutch.
mullido/da *adj* soft; springy.
mulo/la *m/f* mule.
multa *f* fine, penalty.
mundial *adj* worldwide; world *compd*.
mundo *m* world.
muñeca *f* wrist; child's doll.
municipio *m* town council; municipality.
murciélago *m* bat.
murmullo *m* murmur, mutter.
murmurar *vi* to murmur; to gossip.
muro *m* wall.
músculo *m* muscle.
museo *m* museum.
musgo *m* moss.
música *f* music.
muslo *m* thigh.
mustio/tia *adj* parched, withered; sad, sorrowful.
mutuo/tua *adj* mutual, reciprocal.
muy *adv* very; too; greatly:—**~ ilustre** most illustrious.

N

nabo *m* turnip.
nácar *m* mother-of-pearl, nacre.
nacer *vi* to be born; to bud, shoot (of plants); to rise; to grow.
nacimiento *m* birth; nativity.
nada *f* nothing:—*adv* no way, not at all, by no means.
nadar *vi* to swim.
nadie *pn* nobody, no one.
nafta *f* gas.
nalgas *fpl* buttocks *pl*.
naranja *f* orange.
nariz *f* nose.
narrar *vt* to narrate, tell.
nata *f* cream.
natillas *fpl* custard.
naturaleza *f* nature.
naufragar *vi* to be shipwrecked; to suffer ruin in one's affairs.
náutica *f* navigation.
navaja *f* penknife; razor.
nave *f* ship; nave; warehouse.
navegar *vt*, *vi* to navigate; to sail; to fly.
Navidad *f* Christmas.
nebuloso/sa *adj* misty; cloudy; nebulous; foggy; hazy; drizzling:—*f* nebula.
neceser *m* toilet bag; holdall.
necesitar *vt* to need:—*vi* to want, to need.
necio/cia *adj* ignorant; stupid, foolish; imprudent.
nefasto/ta *adj* unlucky.
negado/da *adj* incapable, unfit.
negar *vt* to deny; to refuse:—**~se** *vr* **~ a hacer** to refuse to do.
negocio *m* business, affair; transaction; firm; place of business.
negro/gra *adj* black:—*m* black:—*m/f* Black.
nene *m*, **nena** *f* baby.
neto/ta *adj* neat, pure; net.
neumático/ca *adj* pneumatic:—*m* tire.

neutro/tra *adj* neutral; neuter.
nevar *vi* to snow.
nevera *f* icebox.
ni *conj* neither, nor.
nido *m* nest; hiding place.
niebla *f* fog; mist.
nieta *f* granddaughter.
nieto *m* grandson.
nieve *f* snow.
niña *f* little girl; pupil, (of eye).
ningún, ninguno/na *adj* no:—*pn* nobody; none; not one; neither.
niño/ña *adj* childish:—*m/f* child; infant:—**desde ~** from infancy, from a child:—*m* boy.
nitidez *f* clarity; brightness; sharpness.
nivel *m* level; standard; height:—**a ~** perfectly level.
no *adv* no; not:—*excl* no!
no obstante *adv* nevertheless, notwithstanding.
noche *f* night; evening; darkness:—**~ buena** Christmas Eve:—**~ vieja** New Year's Eve:—**¡buenas ~s!** good night!
noción *f* notion, idea.
nocivo/va *adj* harmful.
nogal *m* walnut tree.
nombrar *vt* to name; to nominate; to appoint.
nombre *m* name; title; reputation.
nómina *f* list; (*com*) payroll.
non *adj* odd, uneven:—*m* odd number.
nor(d)este *adj* northeast, northeastern:—*m* northeast.
nórdico/ca *adj* northern; Nordic.
noria *f* water wheel; big wheel.
noroeste *adj* northwest, northwestern:—*m* northwest.
norte *adj* north, northern:—*m* north; (*fig*) rule, guide.
nos *pn* us; to us; for us; from us; to ourselves.
nosotros/tras *pn* we; us.
nostalgia *f* homesickness.
notar *vt* to note; to mark; to remark:—**~se** *vr* to be obvious.
noticia *f* information; note:—**~s** *fpl* news.
noticiario *m* newsreel; news bulletin.
notificar *vt* to notify, inform.
novato/ta *adj* inexperienced:—*m/f* beginner.
novecientos/tas *adj* nine hundred.
novedad *f* novelty; modernness; newness; piece of news; change.
noveno/na *adj* ninth.
noventa *adj*, *m* ninety.
novia *f* bride; girlfriend; fiancée.
noviembre *m* November.
novio *m* bridegroom; boyfriend; fiancé.
nube *f* cloud.
nublado/da *adj* cloudy:—*m* storm cloud.
nuca *f* nape (of the neck); scruff of the neck.
nudillo *m* knuckle.
nudo *m* knot.
nuera *f* daughter-in-law.
nuestro/tra *adj* our:—*pn* ours.
nueve *m*, *adj* nine.
nuevo/va *adj* new; modern; fresh:—*f* piece of news:—**¿que hay de ~?** is there any news?, what's new?
nuez *f* nut; walnut; Adam's apple:—**~ moscada** nutmeg.
número *m* number; cipher.
nunca *adv* never.
nutria *f* otter.
nutrir *vt* to nourish; to feed.

Ñ

ñato/ta *adj* snub-nosed.
ñoño/ña *adj* insipid; spineless; silly.
ñoñeria *f* insipidness.

O

o *conj* or; either.
obedecer *vt* to obey.
obeso/sa *adj* obese, fat.
objetar *vi* to object.
objeto *m* object; aim.
obligar *vt* to force:—**~se** *vr* to bind oneself.
obra *f* work; building, construction; play:—**por ~ de** thanks to.
obrero/ra *adj* working; labor *compd*:—*m/f* worker; laborer.

obsequiar *vt* to lavish attention on:— **~con** to present with.
observar *vt* to observe; to notice.
obstáculo *m* obstacle, impediment.
obstinarse *vr* to be obstinate:— **~ en** to persist in.
obstruir *vt* to obstruct:— **~se** *vr* to be blocked up, be obstructed.
obtener *vt* to obtain; to gain.
ocasión *f* occasion, opportunity.
ocasionar *vt* to cause, occasion.
occidente *m* occident, west.
océano *m* ocean.
ochenta *m, adj* eighty.
ocho *m, adj* eight.
ochocientos *m, adj* eight hundred.
ocio *m* leisure; pastime.
octavilla *f* pamphlet.
octavo/va *adj* eighth.
octubre *m* October.
ocultar *vt* to hide, conceal.
ocupar *vt* to occupy; to hold (office): —**~se** *vr* **~ de, ~ en** to concern oneself with; to look after.
ocurrencia *f* event; bright idea.
ocurrir *vi* to occur, happen.
odiar *vt* to hate:— **~se** *vr* to hate one another.
oeste *adj* west, western:—*m* west.
ofender *vt* to offend; to injure:— **~se** *vr* to be vexed; to take offence.
oficina *f* office.
oficio *m* employment, occupation; ministry; function; trade, business.
ofrecer *vt* to offer; to present; to exhibit:— **~se** *vr* to offer oneself; to occur, present itself.
oído *m* hearing; ear.
oír *vt, vi* to hear; to listen (to).
ojal *m* buttonhole.
ojalá *conj* if only!, would that!
ojear *vt* to eye, view; to glance.
ojera *f* bag under the eyes.
ojo *m* eye; sight; eye of a needle; arch of a bridge.
ola *f* wave.
oler *vt* to smell, scent:—*vi* to smell:— **~ a** to smack of.
olfato *m* sense of smell.
olivo *m* olive tree.
olla *f* pan; stew:— **~ exprés, ~ a presion** pressure cooker.
olmo *m* elm tree.
olor *m* smell, odor; scent.
olvidar *vt* to forget.
ombligo *m* navel.
once *m, adj* eleven.
onda *f* wave.
opaco/ca *adj* opaque; dark.
opinar *vt* to think:—*vi* to give one's opinion.
oponer *vt* to oppose:— **~se** *vr* to be opposed:— **~ a** to oppose.
oposición *f* opposition:— **~ones** *fpl* public examinations *pl*.
oprimir *vt* to oppress; to crush; to press; to squeeze.
optar *vt* to choose, elect.
optativo/va *adj* optional.
óptimo/ma *adj* best.
opuesto/ta *adj* opposite; contrary; adverse.
orar *vi* to pray.
ordenado/da *adj* methodical; tidy.
ordenador *m* computer.
ordenanza *f* order; statute, ordinance; ordination.
ordenar *vt* to arrange; to order; to ordain: —**~se** *vr* to take holy orders.
ordeñar *vt* to milk.
oreja *f* ear.
orgullo *m* pride, haughtiness.
oriental *adj* oriental, eastern.
orientar *vt* to orient; to point; to direct; to guide:— **~se** *vr* to get one's bearings; to decide on a course of action.
orificio *m* orifice; mouth; aperture.
orilla *f* limit, border, margin; edge (of cloth); shore.
orín *m* rust.
orina *f* urine.
orinal *m* chamber pot.
oro *m* gold; **~s** *mpl* diamonds *pl* (cards).
ortiga *f* (*bot*) nettle.
oruga *f* (*bot*) caterpillar.
orzuelo *m* (*med*) stye.
os *pn* you; to you.
osa *f* she-bear:—**O~ Mayor/Menor** Great/Little Bear.
osar *vi* to dare, venture.
oscuro/ra *adj* obscure; dark.
oso *m* bear:— **~ blanco** polar bear.
ostentar *vt* to show:—*vi* to boast, brag.
ostra *f* oyster.
otoño *m* fall, autumn.
otorgar *vt* to concede; to grant.
otorrino/na, otorrinolaringólogo/ga *m/f* ear, nose and throat specialist.
otro/tra *adj* another; other.
oveja *f* sheep.
ovillo *m* ball of wool.
óvulo *m* ovum.
oxidar *vt* to rust:— **~se** *vr* to go rusty.
oyente *m/f* listener, hearer.

P

pacificar *vt* to pacify, appease.
pacotilla *f*:—**de** ~ third-rate; cheap.
pactar *vt* to covenant; to contract; to stipulate.
padecer *vt* to suffer; to sustain (an injury); to put up with.
padrastro *m* stepfather.
padre *m* father:—~**s** *mpl* parents *pl*.
pagar *vt* to pay; to pay for; (*fig*) to repay:—*vi* to pay.
página *f* page.
pago *m* payment; reward.
país *m* country; region.
paisaje *m* landscape.
paisano/na *adj* of the same country: —*m/f* fellow countryman/woman.
paja *f* straw; (*fig*) trash.
pájaro *m* bird; sly, acute fellow.
pajita *f* (drinking) straw.
pala *f* spade, shovel.
palabra *f* word:—**de** ~ by word of mouth.
paladar *m* palate; taste, relish.
palanca *f* lever.
palangana *f* basin.
palco *m* box (in a theater).
paleto/ta *m/f* rustic.
pálido/da *adj* pallid, pale.
palillo *m* small stick; toothpick:—~**s** *mpl* chopsticks *pl*.
paliza *f* beating, thrashing.
palma *f* palm tree; palm of the hand; palm leaf.
palmada *f* slap, clap:—~**s** *fpl* clapping of hands, applause.
palmera *f* palm tree.
palo *m* stick; cudgel; blow given with a stick; post; mast; bat; suit (at cards):—~**s** *mpl* masting.
paloma *f* pigeon, dove:—~ **torcaz** ring dove:—~ **zorita** wood pigeon.
palomilla *f* moth; wing nut; angle iron.
palpar *vt* to feel, touch.
palta *f* avocado (pear).
pámpano *m* vine branch.
pan *m* bread; loaf; food in general.
pana *f* corduroy.
pañal *m* diaper, nappy.
pandereta *f* tambourine.
pandilla *f* group; gang; clique.
paño *m* cloth; piece of cloth; duster, rag.
pantalla *f* screen; lampshade.
pantalón *m*, **pantalones** *mpl* trousers, pants *pl*.
pantano *m* marsh; reservoir; obstacle, difficulty.
pantorrilla *f* calf (of the leg).
pañuelo *m* handkerchief.
panza *f* belly, paunch.
papá *m* (*fam*) dad, pop.
papada *f* double chin.
papel *m* paper; writing; part, role (in a play):—~ **de estraza** brown paper: —~ **sellado** stamped paper.
papeleo *m* red tape.
paperas *fpl* mumps.
paquete *m* packet; parcel; package tour.
par *adj* equal; alike; even:—*m* pair; couple; peer:—**sin** ~ matchless.
para *prep* for; to, in order to; towards.
parabrisas *m invar* windshield.
paracaídas *m invar* parachute.
parada *f* halt; suspension; pause; stop; shutdown; stopping place:—~ **de autobús** bus stop.
parado/da *adj* motionless; at a standstill; stopped; standing (up); unemployed.
paraguas *m invar* umbrella.
parar *vi* to stop, halt:—*vt* to stop, detain:—**sin** ~ instantly, without delay: —~**se** *vr* to stop, halt; to stand up.
parecer *m* opinion, advice, counsel; countenance, air, mien:—*vi* to appear; to seem:—~**se** *vr* ~ **a** to resemble.
parecido/da *adj* resembling, like.
pared *f* wall:—~ **medianera** party wall.
pareja *f* pair, couple, brace.
pariente/ta *m/f* relative, relation.
parir *vt* to give birth to:—*vi* to give birth.
paro *m* strike; unemployment.
párpado *m* eyelid.
parra *f* vine raised on stakes or nailed to a wall.
párrafo *m* paragraph.
parrilla *f* grill; grille.
parte *m* message; report:—*f* part; side; party:—**de ocho dias a esta** ~ within these last eight days:—**de** ~ **a** ~ from side to side, through and through.
partera *f* midwife.
particular *adj* particular, special:—*m* private individual; particular matter or subject treated upon.
partida *f* departure; party; item in an account; parcel; game.
partido *m* party; match; team.
partir *vt* to part; to divide, separate; to cut; to break:—*vi* to depart:—~**se** *vr* to break (in two, etc).
parvulario *m* nursery school.

pasa *f* raisin.
pasadizo *m* narrow passage; narrow, covered way.
pasado/da *adj* past; bad; overdone; out of date:—**~ mañana** the day after tomorrow:—**la semana pasada** last week:—*m* past.
pasaje *m* passage; fare; passengers *pl*.
pasajero/ra *adj* transient; transitory; fugitive:—*m/f* traveler; passenger.
pasamanos *m invar* (hand)rail; bannister.
pasar *vt* to pass; to surpass; to suffer; to strain; to dissemble:—*vi* to pass; to happen:—**~se** *vr* to go over (to another party); to go bad or off.
pasarela *f* footbridge; gangway.
pasatiempo *m* pastime, amusement.
Pascua *f* Passover; Easter.
pasear *vt* to walk:—*vi* **~se** *vr* to walk; to walk about.
pasmar *vt* to amaze; to numb; to chill:—**~se** *vr* to be astonished.
paso *m* pace, step; passage; manner of walking; flight of steps; accident:—(*ferro*) **~ a nivel** grade crossing:—**al ~** on the way, in passing.
pasta *f* paste; dough; pastry; (*fam*) dough:—**~s** *fpl* pastries *pl*; pasta:—**~ de dientes** toothpaste.
pastel *m* cake; pie; crayon (for drawing).
pastilla *f* bar (of soap); tablet, pill.
pastor *m* shepherd; pastor.
pata *f* leg (of animal or furniture); foot:—**meter la ~** to put one's foot in it.
patata *f* potato.
patear *vt* to kick; to stamp on.
patillas *fpl* sideburns *pl*.
patín *m* skate; runner.
patinar *vi* to skate; to skid; (*fam*) to blunder.
patio *m* courtyard; playground.
pato *m* duck.
patoso/sa *adj* (*fam*) clumsy.
patraña *f* lie.
patrocinar *vt* to sponsor; to back, support.
patrón/ona *m/f* boss, master/mistress; landlord/lady; patron saint:—*m* pattern.
patronal *adj*:—**la clase ~** management.
patrulla *f* patrol.
paulatino/na *adj* gradual, slow.
pausar *vi* to pause.
pauta *f* guideline.
pavo *m* turkey:—**~ real** peacock.
pavor *m* dread, terror.
payaso/sa *m/f* clown.
payo/ya *m/f* non-Gipsy (for a Gipsy).
paz *f* peace; tranquillity, ease.
peaje *m* toll.
peana *f* pedestal; footstool.
peatón *m* pedestrian.
peca *f* freckle; spot.
pecado *m* sin.
pecho *m* chest; breast(s) (*pl*); teat; (*fig*) courage, valor:—**dar el ~ a** to suckle:—**tomar a ~** to take to heart.
pechuga *f* breast of a fowl; (*fam*) bosom.
pedazo *m* piece, bit.
pedernal *m* flint.
pediatra *m/f* pediatrician.
pedicuro/ra *m/f* chiropodist.
pedir *vt* to ask for; to petition; to beg; to order; to need; to solicit:—*vi* to ask.
pedo *m* (*fam*) fart (*sl*):—**tirarse un ~** to fart (*sl*).
pegamento *m* glue.
pegar *vt* to cement; to join, unite; to beat:—**~ fuego a** to set fire to:—*vi* to stick; to match:—**~se** *vr* to intrude; to steal in.
pegatina *f* sticker.
peinar *vt* to comb; to style.
peine *m* comb.
pelar *vt* to cut (hair); to strip off (feathers); to peel:—**~se** *vr* to peel off; to have one's hair cut.
peldaño *m* step (of a flight of stairs).
pelear *vt* to fight, combat:—**~se** *vr* to scuffle.
pelele *m* dummy; man of straw.
película *f* film, thin covering; movie.
peligro *m* danger, peril; risk.
pelirrojo/ja *m/f* redhead:—*adj* red-haired.
pellejo *m* skin; hide, pelt; peel; wine skin; oilskin; drunkard.
pellizcar *vt* to pinch.
pelo *m* hair; pile; flaw (in precious stones).
pelota *f* ball.
peluca *f* wig.
peluquería *f* hairdresser's/barber's premises.
pelusa *f* bloom (on fruit); fluff.
pena *f* punishment, pain:—**a duras ~s** with great difficulty or trouble.
pendiente *f* slope, declivity:—*m* earring:—*adj* pending; unsettled.
pene *m* penis.
penetrante *adj* deep; sharp; piercing; searching; biting.
penique *m* penny.
penoso/sa *adj* painful.
pensar *vi* to think.
pensativo/va *adj* pensive, thoughtful.
pensión *f* guest-house; pension.
penúltimo/ma *adj* penultimate, last but one.
penumbra *f* half-light.
penuria *f* penury, poverty, neediness, extreme want.

peña *f* rock, large stone.
peón *m* (day) laborer; foot soldier; pawn (at chess).
peor *adj, adv* worse:—**~ que ~** worse and worse.
pepino *m* cucumber.
pepita *f* kernel; pip.
pequeño/ña *adj* little, small; young.
pera *f* pear.
percatarse *vr*:—**~ de** to notice.
percha *f* coat hook; coat hanger; perch.
percibir *vt* to receive; to perceive, comprehend.
perder *vt* to lose; to waste; to miss:—**~se** *vr* to go astray; to be lost; to be spoiled.
perdiz *f* partridge.
perdón *m* pardon; mercy:—**¡~!** sorry!
perdonar *vt* to pardon, forgive; to excuse.
perdurar *vi* to last; to still exist.
perecedero/ra *adj* perishable.
peregrino/na *adj* (*fig*) strange:—*m* pilgrim.
perejil *m* parsley.
pereza *f* laziness, idleness.
perfil *m* profile.
perforar *vt* to perforate; to drill; to punch a hole in:—*vi* to drill.
perfume *m* perfume.
pergamino *m* parchment.
periódico/ca *adj* periodical:—*m* newspaper.
periodista *m/f* journalist.
peripecia *f* vicissitude; sudden change.
periquito *m* budgie.
perito/ta *adj* skillful, experienced:—*m/f* expert; skilled worker; technician.
perjudicar *vt* to prejudice, damage; to injure, hurt.
perjurar *vi* to perjure, swear falsely; to swear.
perla *f* pearl:—**de ~s** fine.
permanecer *vi* to stay; to continue to be.
permiso *m* permission, leave, license.
permitir *vt* to permit, allow.
permutar *vt* to exchange, permute.
pernera *f* trouser leg.
perno *m* bolt.
pernoctar *vi* to spend the night.
pero *m* kind of apple:—*conj* but, yet.
perogrullada *f* truism, platitude.
perol *m* large metal pan.
perro *m* dog.
perseguir *vt* to pursue; to persecute; to chase after.
perseverar *vi* to persevere, persist.
persiana *f* (Venetian) blind.
persistir *vi* to persist.
persona *f* person:—**de ~ a ~** from person to person.
personaje *m* celebrity; character.
persuadir *vt* to persuade:—**~se** *vr* to be persuaded.
pertenecer *vi*:—**~ a** to belong to; to appertain, concern.
pértiga *f* long pole or rod.
pertinaz *adj* pertinacious; obstinate.
pertinente *adj* relevant; appropriate.
perturbar *vt* to perturb, disturb.
pervertir *vt* to pervert; to corrupt.
pesa *f* weight.
pesadez *f* heaviness, weight; gravity; slowness; peevishness, fretfulness; trouble; fatigue.
pesadilla *f* nightmare.
pesado/da *adj* peevish; troublesome; cumbersome; tedious; heavy, weighty.
pesar *m* sorrow, grief; repentance:—**a ~ de** in spite of, notwithstanding:—*vi* to weigh; to repent:—*vt* to weigh.
pescado *m* fish (in general).
pescar *vt* to fish for, catch (fish):—*vi* to fish.
pescuezo *m* neck.
pésimo/ma *adj* very bad.
peso *m* weight, heaviness; balance scales *pl*.
pesquisa *f* inquiry, examination.
pestaña *f* eyelash.
pestañear *vi* to blink.
pestillo *m* bolt.
petróleo *m* crude oil, petroleum.
pez *m* fish:—*f* pitch.
pezón *m* nipple.
pezuña *f* hoof.
piadoso/sa *adj* pious; mild; merciful; moderate.
piar *vi* to squeak; to chirp.
pibe/ba *m/f* boy/girl.
picado/da *adj* pricked; minced, chopped; bad (tooth); cross.
picante *adj* hot, spicy; racy.
picaporte *m* doorhandle; latch.
picar *vt* to prick; to sting; to mince; to nibble:—*vi* to prick; to sting; to itch:—**~se** *vr* to be piqued; to take offence; to be moth-eaten; to begin to rot.
pícaro/ra *adj* roguish; mischievous, malicious; sly:—*m/f* rogue, knave.
pico *m* beak; bill, nib; peak; pick-ax.
pie *m* foot; leg; basis; trunk (of trees); foundation; occasion:—**a ~** on foot.
piedad *f* piety; mercy, pity.
piedra *f* stone.
piel *f* skin; hide; peel.
pienso *m* fodder.
pierna *f* leg (human).
pieza *f* piece; room.

pila *f* battery; trough; font; sink; pile, heap:—**nombre de ~** first name.
píldora *f* pill.
pileta *f* basin; swimming pool.
pimentón *m* paprika.
pimienta *f* pepper.
pimiento *m* pepper, pimiento.
piña *f* pineapple; fir cone; group.
pincel *m* paintbrush.
pinchar *vt* to prick; to puncture.
pincho *m* thorn; snack.
ping-pong *m* table tennis.
pino *m* (*bot*) pine.
piñón *m* pine nut; pinion.
pintar *vt* to paint; to picture; to describe; to exaggerate:—*vi* to paint; (*fam*) to count, to be important:—**~se** *vr* to put on make-up.
pintura *f* painting.
pinza *f* claw; clothes pin; pincers *pl*: —**~s** *fpl* tweezers *pl*.
piojo *m* louse; troublesome hanger-on.
pipa *f* pipe; sunflower seed.
pipí *m* (*fam*):—**hacer ~** to have to go (wee-wee).
piquete *m* prick, jab; hole; (*mil*) squad.
piragua *f* canoe.
piropo *m* compliment; flattery.
pisar *vt* to tread, trample; to stamp on (the ground); to hammer down:—*vi* to tread, walk.
piscina *f* swimming pool.
piso *m* apartment; tread, trampling; floor, sidewalk; floor, story.
pisotear *vt* to trample, tread under foot.
pista *f* trace, footprint; clue.
pita *f* (*bot*) agave.
pitar *vt* to blow; to whistle at:—*vi* to whistle; to toot one's horn; to smoke.
pito *m* whistle; horn.
pizarra *f* slate.
pizca *f* mite; pinch.
placa *f* plate; badge.
placer *m* pleasure; delight:—*vt* to please.
plan *m* plan; design; plot; scheme.
plancha *f* plate; iron; gangway.
planear *vt* to plan:—*vi* to glide.
planicie *f* plain.
planificación *f* planning:—**~ familiar** family planning.
plano/na *adj* plain, level, flat:—*m* plan; ground plot, map:—**~ inclinado** (*ferro*) dead level.
plantación *f* plantation.
plantar *vt* to plant; to fix upright; to strike or hit (a blow); to found; to establish:—**~se** *vr* to stand upright.
plantilla *f* personnel; insole of a shoe.
plata *f* silver; plate (wrought silver); cash:—**en ~** briefly.
plátano *m* banana; plane tree.
plateado/da *adj* silvered; plated.
platicar *vi* to converse.
platillo *m* saucer:—**~s** *mpl* cymbals *pl*: —**~ volador/~ volante** flying saucer.
platino *m* platinum:—**~s** *mpl* contact points *pl*.
plato *m* dish; plate.
playa *f* beach.
playera *f* T-shirt:—**~s** *fpl* sneakers *pl*.
plaza *f* square; place; office, employment; room; seat.
plazo *m* term; installment; expiry date.
plegar *vt* to fold; to crease.
pleito *m* contract, bargain; dispute, controversy, debate; lawsuit.
plenilunio *m* full moon.
pleno/na *adj* full; complete:—*m* plenum.
pliego *m* sheet of paper.
pliegue *m* fold; pleat.
plisado/da *adj* pleated:—*m* pleating.
plomero *m* plumber.
plomo *m* lead:—**a ~** perpendicularly.
pluma *f* feather, plume.
población *f* population; town.
pobre *adj* poor.
poco/ca *adj* little, scanty; (*pl*) few:—*adv* little:—**~ a ~** gently; little by little:—*m* small part; little.
podar *vt* to prune.
poder *m* power, authority; command; force:—*vi* to be able to; to possess the power of doing or performing.
podrido/da *adj* rotten, bad; (*fig*) rotten.
poesía *f* poetry.
polea *f* pulley; (*mar*) tackle-block.
polideportivo *m* sports center.
polilla *f* moth.
pollera *f* skirt.
pollo *m* chicken.
polo *m* pole; ice lolly; polo; polo neck.
polvo *m* powder, dust.
pólvora *f* gunpowder.
pomada *f* cream, ointment.
pomelo *m* grapefruit.
pómez *f*:—**piedra ~** pumice stone.
pompa *f* pomp; bubble.
pómulo *m* cheekbone.
poner *vt* to put, place; to put on; to impose; to lay (eggs):—**~se** *vr* to oppose; to set (of stars); to become.
poniente *m* west; west wind.
ponzoña *f* poison.
popa *f* (*mar*) poop, stern.

por *prep* for; by; about; by means of; through; on account of.
porción *f* part, portion; lot.
porfiar *vt* to dispute obstinately; to persist in a pursuit.
pormenor *f* detail.
poro *m* pore.
porque *conj* because; since; so that.
porquería *f* nastiness, foulness; brutishness, rudeness; trifle; dirty action.
porrón *m* spouted wine jar.
portada *f* portal, porch; frontispiece.
portaequipajes *m invar* trunk (in car); baggage rack.
portarse *vr* to behave.
portátil *adj* portable.
portavoz *m/f* spokesman/woman.
porte *m* transportation (charges *pl*); deportment, demeanor, conduct.
portero *m* porter, gatekeeper.
porvenir *m* future.
posar *vi* to sit, pose:—*vt* to lay down (a burden):—**~se** *vr* to settle; to perch; to land.
posdata *f* postcript.
poseer *vt* to hold, possess.
posesivo/va *adj* possessive.
posibilitar *vt* to make possible; to make feasible.
poso *m* sediment, dregs *pl*.
posponer *vt* to postpone.
postal *adj* postal:—*f* postcard.
poste *m* post, pillar.
postergar *vt* to leave behind; to postpone.
posterioridad *f*:—**con ~** subsequently, later.
postigo *m* wicket; postern; shutter.
postizo/za *adj* artificial (not natural): —*m* wig.
postrar *vt* to humble, humiliate:—**~se** *vr* to prostrate oneself.
postre *m* dessert.
postura *f* posture, position; attitude; bet, wager; agreement, convention.
potable *adj* drinkable.
potaje *m* pottage; drink made up of several ingredients; medley of various useless things.
potro/ra *m/f* colt; foal.
pozo *m* well.
practicar *vt* to practice.
práctico/ca *adj* practical; skillful, experienced.
prado *m* lawn; meadow.
precaver *vt* to prevent; to guard against.
preceder *vt* to precede, go before.
preciado/da *adj* esteemed, valued.
precinto *m* seal.
precio *m* price; value.
precioso/sa *adj* precious; (*fam*) beautiful.
precisamente *adv* precisely; exactly.
precisar *vt* to compel, oblige; to need.
preciso/sa *adj* necessary, requisite; precise, accurate; abstracted.
precoz *adj* precocious.
precursor/ra *m/f* harbinger, forerunner.
predecir *vt* to foretell.
predicar *vt* to preach.
predilecto/ta *adj* darling, favorite.
predisponer *vt* to predispose; to prejudice.
predominar *vi* to predominate, prevail.
preferir *vt* to prefer.
pregón *m* proclamation; hue and cry.
preguntar *vt* to ask; to question; to demand; to inquire.
prejuicio *m* prejudgement; preconception; prejudice.
premiar *vt* to reward, remunerate.
premura *f* pressure, haste, hurry.
preñada *adj* pregnant.
prenda *f* pledge; garment; sweetheart; person or thing dearly loved: —**~s** *fpl* accomplishments, talents *pl*.
prender *vt* to seize, catch, lay hold of; to imprison:—**~se** *vr* to catch fire:—*vi* to take root.
prensar *vt* to press.
preocupar(se) *vt* (*vr*) to worry.
preparar *vt* to prepare:—**~se** *vr* to be prepared.
prepucio *m* foreskin.
presa *f* capture, seizure; dike, dam.
presagio *m* omen.
prescindir *vi*:—**~ de** to do without; to dispense with.
presenciar *vt* to attend; to be present at; to witness.
presentar *vt* to present; to introduce; to offer; to show:—**~se** *vr* to present oneself; to appear; to run (as candidate); to apply.
presentir *vt* to have a premonition of.
preservativo *m* condom, sheath.
presidiario *m* convict.
presilla *f* clip; loop (in clothes).
presión *f* pressure, pressing.
presionar *vt* to press; (*fig*) to put pressure on.
preso/sa *m/f* prisoner.
prestar *vt* to lend.
presto/ta *adj* quick; prompt; ready: —*adv* soon; quickly.
presumir *vt* to presume, conjecture: —*vi* to be conceited.
presunto/ta *adj* supposed; so-called.

presupuesto *m* presumed cost; budget.
pretender *vt* to claim; to try, attempt.
pretendiente *m* pretender; suitor.
pretexto *m* pretext; pretence, excuse.
prevalacer *vi* to prevail; to triumph; to take root.
prevenir *vt* to prepare; to foresee, know in advance; to prevent; to warn:—**~se** *vr* to be prepared; to be predisposed.
prever *vt* to foresee, forecast.
previo/via *adj* previous.
previsión *f* foresight, prevision; forecast.
prima *f* bonus; (female) cousin.
primario/ria *adj* primary.
primavera *f* spring (the season).
primer(o)/ra *adj* first; prior; former:—*adv* first; rather, sooner.
primicias *f* first fruits *pl*.
primo/ma *m* cousin.
primogénito/ta *adj*, *m/f* first-born.
príncipe *m* prince.
principiante *m* beginner, learner.
principio *m* beginning, commencement; principle.
pringoso/sa *adj* greasy; sticky.
prisa *f* speed; hurry; urgency; promptness.
prismáticos *mpl* binoculars *pl*.
privación *f* deprivation, want.
privado/da *adj* private; particular.
proa *f* (*mar*) prow.
probador *m* fitting room.
probar *vt* to try; to prove; to taste:—*vi* to try.
probeta *f* test tube.
procedente *adj* reasonable; proper:—**~ de** coming from.
procesador *m*:—**~ de textos** word processor.
procesar *vt* to put on trial.
procurar *vt* to try; to obtain; to produce.
prodigar *vt* to waste, lavish.
producir *vt* to produce; (*jur*) to produce as evidence:—**~se** *vr* to come about; to arise; to be made; to break out.
proeza *f* prowess, valor, bravery.
profanar *vt* to profane, desecrate.
profesor/ra *m/f* teacher.
prófugo *m* fugitive.
profundo/da *adj* profound.
programa *m* program(me).
prohibir *vt* to prohibit, forbid; to hinder.
prójimo *m* fellow creature; neighbor.
prole *f* offspring, progeny; race.
prolijidad *f* prolixity; minute attention to detail.
prólogo *m* prolog.
promedio *m* average; middle.
prometer *vt* to promise; to assure:—**~se** *vr* to become engaged.
promiscuo/cua *adj* promiscuous; confusedly mingled.
promover *vt* to promote, advance; to stir up.
promulgar *vt* to promulgate, publish.
pronosticar *vt* to predict, foretell; to conjecture.
pronto/ta *adj* prompt; ready:—*adv* promptly.
pronunciamiento *m* (*jur*) publication; insurrection, sedition.
pronunciar *vt* to pronounce; to deliver: —**~se** *vr* to rebel.
propaganda *f* propaganda; advertising.
propagar *vt* to propagate.
propasar *vt* to go beyond, exceed.
propenso/sa *adj* prone, inclined.
propiamente *adv* properly; really.
propiciar *vt* to favor; to cause.
propiedad *f* property, possessions *pl*; right of property; propriety.
propina *f* tip.
propio/pia *adj* proper; own; typical; very.
proponer *vt* to propose.
proporcionar *vt* to provide.
propósito *m* aim, purpose:—**a ~** on purpose.
propuesta *f* proposal, offer; representation.
propulsar *vt* to propel; (*fig*) to promote.
prórroga *f* prolongation; extension; extra time.
prorrumpir *vi* to break forth, burst forth.
prosa *f* prose.
proscrito/ta *adj* banned.
proseguir *vt* to continue:—*vi* to continue, go on.
prospección *f* exploration; prospecting.
prosperar *vi* to prosper, thrive.
proteger *vt* protector.
protestar *vt* to protest; to make public declaration (of faith):—*vi* to protest.
provecho *m* profit; advantage.
proveedor/ra *m/f* purveyor, supplier.
provenir *vi* to arise, originate; to issue.
provocar *vt* to provoke; to lead to; to excite.
próximamente *adv* soon.
próximo/ma *adj* next; neighboring; close, nearby.
proyectar *vt* to throw; to cast; to screen; to plan.
prueba *f* proof; reason; argument; token; experiment; essay; attempt; relish, taste.
púa *f* sharp point, prickle; shoot; pick.
pubertad *f* puberty.
publicar *vt* to publish; to make public.
publicidad *f* publicity; advertising.
público/ca *adj* public:—*m* public; audience; crowd.
puchero *m* pot; stew.
púdico/ca *adj* chaste, pure.

pudiente *adj* rich, opulent.
pudor *m* bashfulness.
pudrir *vt* to rot, putrefy:—**~se** *vr* to decay, rot.
pueblo *m* people *pl*; town, village; population; populace.
puente *m* bridge.
puerco/ca *adj* nasty; filthy, dirty; rude, coarse:—*m* pig, hog:—**~ espín** porcupine.
pueril *adj* childish; puerile.
puerro *m* leek.
puerta *f* door; doorway; gateway:—**~ trasera** back door.
puerto *m* port, harbor; haven; pass.
pues *adv* then; therefore; well:—**¡~!** well, then.
puesto *m* place; particular spot; post, employment; barracks *pl*; stand.
púgil *m* boxer.
pujante *adj* powerful, strong; robust; stout, strapping.
pulga *f* flea:—**tener malas ~s** to be easily piqued; to be ill-tempered.
pulgada *f* inch.
pulgar *m* thumb.
pulir *vt* to polish; to put the last touches to.
pulmón *m* lung.
pulpa *f* pulp; soft part (of fruit).
pulpería *f* small grocery store.
pulpo *m* octopus.
pulsar *vt* to touch; to play; to press.
pulsera *f* bracelet.
pulso *m* pulse; wrist; firmness or steadiness of the hand.
pulular *vi* to swarm.
pulverizador *m* spray gun.
puna *f* (*med*) mountain sickness.
puñado *m* handful.
puñal *m* dagger.
puño *m* fist; handful; wrist-band; cuff; handle.
punta *f* point; end; trace.
puntada *f* stitch.
puntal *m* prop, stay; buttress.
puntapié *m* kick.
puntería *f* aiming.
puntiagudo/da *adj* sharp-pointed.
puntilla *f* narrow lace edging:—**de ~s** on tiptoe.
punto *m* point; end; spot; stitch; full stop.
puntual *adj* punctual; exact; reliable.
punzada *f* prick; sting; pain; compunction.
punzante *adj* sharp.
pupila *f* pupil (of eye).
puro/ra *adj* pure; mere; clear; genuine.
púrpura *f* purple.
purulento/ta *adj* purulent.
puta *f* whore.

Q

que *pn* that; who; which; what:—*conj* that; than.
¿qué? *adj* what?; which?:—*pn* what?; which?.
quebrantar *vt* to break; to crack; to burst; to pound, grind; to violate; to fatigue; to weaken.
quedar *vi* to stay:—**~se** *vr* to remain.
quedo/da *adj* quiet, still:—*adv* softly, gently.
quejarse *vr* to complain of.
quemar *vt* to burn; to kindle:—**~se** *vr* to be parched with heat; to burn oneself:—*vi* to be too hot.
querella *f* charge; dispute; complaint.
querer *vt* to want; to desire; to will; to love:—*m* will, desire.
querido/da *adj* dear, beloved:—*m/f* darling; lover:—**~ mio, ~da mia** my dear, my love, my darling.
queso *m* cheese.
quicio *m* hook, hinge (of a door).
quien *pn* who; whom.
¿quién? *pn* who?; whom?.
quienquiera *adj* whoever.
quieto/ta *adj* still, peaceable.
quilla *f* keel.
química *f* chemistry.
quina *f* Peruvian bark, quinine.
quince *adj*, *m* fifteen; fifteenth.
quincena *f* fortnight.
quinientos/tas *adj* five hundred.
quinta *f* country house; levy, drafting of soldiers.
quinto *adj* fifth:—*m* fifth; drafted soldier.
quiosco *m* bandstand; news stand.
quirúrgico/ca *adj* surgical.
quiste *m* cyst.
quitamanchas *m invar* stain remover.
quitanieves *m invar* snowplough.
quitar *vt* to take away, remove; to take off; to relieve; to annul:—**~se** *vr* to take off (clothes, etc); to withdraw.
quitasol *m* parasol.
quizá/quizás *adv* perhaps.

R

rábano *m* radish.
rabia *f* rage, fury.
rabo *m* tail.
racha *f* gust of wind:—**buena/mala ~** spell of good/bad luck.
racimo *m* bunch of grapes.
radiografía *f* x-ray.
ráfaga *f* gust; flash; burst.
raído/da *adj* scraped; worn-out; impudent.
raíz *f* root; base, basis; origin:—**bienes raices** *mpl* landed property.
raja *f* splinter, chip (of wood); chink, fissure.
rajatabla *f*:—**a ~** *adv* strictly.
rallar *vt* to grate.
rama *f* branch (of tree, of family).
ramo *m* branch (of tree).
rampa *f* ramp.
rana *f* frog.
rancho *m* grub; ranch; small farm.
rancio/cia *adj* rank; rancid.
ranura *f* groove; slot.
rapar *vt* to shave; to plunder.
rapaz/za *adj* rapacious:—*m/f* young boy/girl.
rápido/da *adj* quick, rapid, swift.
rapiña *f* robbery.
raptar *vt* to kidnap.
raquítico/ca *adj* stunted; (*fig*) inadequate.
raro/ra *adj* rare, scarce; extraordinary.
ras *m*:—**a ~ de** level with:—**a ~ de tierra** at ground level.
rascacielos *m invar* skyscraper.
rascar *vt* to scratch, scrape.
rasgar *vt* to tear, rip.
rasgo *m* dash, stroke; grand or magnanimous action:—**~s** *mpl* features *pl*.
rasguño *m* scratch.
raso *m* satin; glade:—**~/sa** *adj* plain; flat:—**al ~** in the open air.
raspa *f* beard (of an ear of corn); backbone (of fish); stalk (of grapes); rasp.
raspar *vt* to scrape, rasp.
rastrear *vt* to trace; to inquire into:—*vi* to skim along close to the ground (of birds).
rastrillo *m* rake.
rastro *m* track; rake; trace.
rata *f* rat.
ratificar *vt* to ratify, confirm.
rato *m* moment:—**a ~s perdidos** in leisure time.
ratón *m* mouse.
raya *f* stroke; line; part; frontier; ray (fish); roach (fish).
rayar *vt* to draw lines on; to cross out; to underline; to cross; to rifle.
rayo *m* ray, beam (of light).
raza *f* race, lineage; quality; crack, fissure.
razonar *vi* to reason; to discourse, talk.
reaccionar *vi* to react.
real *adj* real, actual; royal:—*m* (*mil*) camp.
realidad *f* reality; sincerity.
realizador/ra *m/f* producer (in TV, etc).
realzar *vt* to raise, elevate; to emboss; to heighten.
reanimar *vt* to cheer, encourage; to reanimate.
reanudar *vt* to resume.
rebaja *f* abatement; deduction:—**~s** *fpl* sale.
rebanada *f* slice.
rebaño *m* flock (of sheep), herd (of cattle).
rebasar *vt* to exceed.
rebatir *vt* to resist; to parry, ward off; to refute; to repress.
rebeca *f* cardigan.
rebelarse *vr* to revolt; to rebel; to resist.
rebosar *vi* to run over, overflow; to abound.
rebotar *vt* to bounce; to clinch; to repel:—*vi* to rebound.
rebozar *vt* to wrap up; to fry in batter or breadcrumbs.
rebuznar *vi* to bray.
recado *m* message; errand.
recaída *f* relapse.
recalcar *vt* to stress, emphasize.
recalentar *vt* to heat again; to overheat.
recambio *m* spare; refill.
recapacitar *vt* to reflect.
recargar *vt* to overload; to recharge; to charge again.
recatado/da *adj* prudent; circumspect; modest.
recaudar *vt* to gather; to obtain; to recover.
recelo *m* dread; suspicion, mistrust.
receta *f* recipe; prescription.
rechazar *vt* to refuse; to repulse; to contradict.
recibir *vt* to receive, accept; to let in; to go to meet:—**~se** *vr* **~ de** to qualify as.
recibo *m* receipt.
recién *adv* recently, lately.
reciente *adj* recent; new, fresh; modern.
recio/cia *adj* stout; strong, robust; coarse, thick; rude; arduous, rigid:—*adv* strongly, stoutly:—**hablar ~** to talk loud.
recipiente *m* container.
reclamación *f* claim; reclamation; protest.
recluir *vt* to shut up.
reclutar *vt* to recruit.

recobrar *vt* to recover:—**~se** *vr* to recover (from sickness).
recodo *m* corner or angle jutting out.
recoger *vt* to collect; to take back; to get; to gather; to shelter; to compile: —**~se** *vr* to take shelter or refuge; to retire; to withdraw from the world.
recompensa *f* compensation; recompense, reward.
reconfortar *vt* to comfort.
reconocer *vt* to recognize; to examine closely; to acknowledge; to consider; (*mil*) to reconnoiter.
reconstituyente *m* tonic.
reconversión *f*:—**~ industrial** industrial rationalization.
recopilar *vt* to compile.
recordar *vt* to remember; to remind: —*vi* to remember.
recorrer *vt* to run over, peruse; to cover.
recortar *vt* to cut out.
recostar *vt* to lean, recline:—**~se** *vr* to lie down.
recoveco *m* cubby hole; bend.
recreo *m* recreation; playtime (school).
recta *f* straight line.
rectángulo/la *adj* rectangular:—*m* rectangle.
rectitud *f* straightness; rectitude; justness, honesty; exactitude.
recto/ta *adj* straight; right; just, honest:—*m* rectum.
rector/ra *m/f* superior of a community or establishment; rector (of a university); curate, rector:—*adj* governing.
recuadro *m* box; inset.
recuento *m* inventory.
recuerdo *m* souvenir; memory.
recuperar *vt* to recover:—**~se** *vr* to recover (from sickness).
recurrir *vi*:—**~ a** to resort to.
red *f* net; network; snare.
redactar *vt* to draft; to edit.
redada *f*:—**~ policial** police raid.
redimir *vt* to redeem; to ransom.
redoblar *vt* to redouble; to rivet.
redondo/da *adj* round; complete.
reducir *adj* to reduce; to limit:—**~se** *vr* to diminish.
redundancia *f* superfluity, redundancy, excess.
reembolso *m* reimbursement; refund: —**contra ~** C.O.D.
referir *vt* to refer, relate, report:—**~se** *vr* to refer or relate to.
refinado/da *adj* refined; subtle, artful.
reflejar *vt* to reflect.
reflejo *m* reflex; reflection.
reflujo *m* reflux, ebb:—**flujo y ~** the tides *pl*.
reformar *vt* to reform; to correct; to restore:—**~se** *vr* to mend; to have one's manners reformed or corrected.
reforzar *vt* to strengthen, fortify; to encourage.
refrán *m* proverb.
refrescar *vt* to refresh:—**~se** *vr* to get cooler; to go out for a breath of fresh air:—*vi* to cool down.
refriega *f* affray, skirmish, fray.
refrigerador *m*, **refrigeradora** *f* refrigerator, fridge.
refuerzo *m* reinforcement.
refugiar *vt* to shelter:—**~se** *vr* to take refuge.
refunfuñar *vi* to snarl; to growl; to grumble.
regadera *f* watering can.
regalar *vt* to give (as present); to give away; to pamper; to caress.
regaliz *m* licorice.
regalo *m* present, gift; pleasure; comfort.
regañadientes: —**a ~** *adv* reluctantly.
regañar *vt* to scold:—*vi* to growl; to grumble; to quarrel.
regar *vt* to water, irrigate.
regata *f* irrigation ditch; regatta.
regatear *vt* (*com*) to bargain over; to be mean with:—*vi* to haggle; to dribble (in sport).
regazo *m* lap.
regentar *vt* to rule; to govern.
régimen *m* regime, management; diet; (*gr*) rules *pl* of verbs.
registrar *vt* to survey; to inspect, examine; to record, enter in a register: —**~se** *vr* to register; to happen.
regla *f* rule, ruler; period.
reglamentar *vt* to regulate.
regocijar *vt* to gladden:—**~se** *vr* to rejoice.
regordete *adj* chubby, plump.
regresar *vi* to return, go back.
reguero *m* small rivulet; trickle of spilt liquid; drain, gutter.
regular *vt* to regulate, adjust:—*adj* regular; ordinary.
rehén *m* hostage.
rehuir *vt* to avoid.
rehusar *vt* to refuse, decline.
reimpresión *f* reprint.
reina *f* queen.
reincidir *vi*:—**~ en** to relapse into, fall back into.
reino *m* kingdom, reign.
reintegrar *vt* to reintegrate, restore:—**~se** *vr* to be reinstated or restored.
reír(se) *vi* (*vr*) to laugh.

reiterar *vt* to reiterate, repeat.
reivindicar *vt* to claim.
reja *f* ploughshare; lattice, grating.
rejoneador *m* mounted bullfighter.
relación *f* relation; relationship; report; account.
relajar *vt* to relax, slacken:—**~se** *vr* to relax.
relamerse *vr* to lick one's lips; to relish.
relámpago *m* flash of lightning.
relatar *vt* to relate, tell.
relato *m* story; recital.
relegar *vt* to relegate; to banish, exile.
relente *m* evening dew.
relieve *m* relief; (*fig*) prominence.
relinchar *vi* to neigh.
reliquia *f* residue, remains *pl*; (saintly) relic.
rellano *m* landing (of stairs).
rellenar *vt* to fill up; to stuff.
reloj *m* clock; watch.
relucir *vi* to shine, glitter; to excel, be brilliant.
relumbrar *vi* to sparkle, shine.
remachar *vt* to rivet; (*fig*) to drive home.
remache *m* rivet; clinch; obstinacy.
remanente *m* remainder; (*com*) balance; surplus.
remanso *m* stagnant water; quiet place.
remar *vi* to row.
rematar *vt* to terminate, finish; to sell off cheaply:—*vi* to end.
remedar *vt* to copy, imitate; to mimic.
remediar *vt* to remedy; to assist, help; to free from danger; to avoid.
remesa *f* shipment; remittance.
remilgado/da *adj* prim; affected.
remitente *m* sender.
remojar *vt* to steep; to dunk.
remolacha *f* beet.
remolcar *vt* to tow.
remordimiento *m* remorse.
remoto/ta *adj* remote, distant; far.
remover *vt* to stir; to move around.
remozar *vt* to rejuvenate; to renovate.
renacer *vi* to be born again; to revive.
renacuajo *m* tadpole.
rendija *f* crevice, crack, cleft.
rendir *vt* to subject, subdue:—**~se** *vr* to yield; to surrender; to be tired out.
renegar *vt* to deny; to disown; to detest, abhor:—*vi* to apostatize; to blaspheme, curse.
renglón *m* line; item.
reñir *vt*, *vi* to wrangle, quarrel; to scold, chide.
renombre *m* renown.
renovar *vt* to renew; to renovate; to reform.
renta *f* income; rent; profit.
reo *m* offender, criminal.
reparar *vt* to repair; to consider, observe; to parry:—*vi* **~ en** to notice; to pass (at cards).
repartir *vt* to distribute; to deliver.
repasar *vt* to revise; to check; to mend.
repente:—de ~ *adv* suddenly.
repercutir *vi* to reverberate; to rebound.
repetir *vt*, *vi* to repeat.
repiquetear *vt* to ring merrily.
repisa *f* pedestal, stand; shelf; windowsill.
repleto/ta *adj* replete, very full.
replicar *vi* to reply.
repoblar *vt* to repopulate; to reafforest.
repollo *m* cabbage.
reponer *vt* to replace; to restore:—**~se** *vr* to recover lost health or property.
reportaje *m* report, article.
reposar *vi* to rest, repose.
repostería *f* confectioner's (store).
reprender *vt* to reprimand.
represa *f* dam; lake.
representar *vt* to represent; to play on the stage; to look (age).
reprimir *vt* to repress; to check; to contain.
reprobable *adj* reprehensible.
reprochar *vt* to reproach.
repuesto *m* supply; spare part.
repugnancia *f* reluctance; repugnance; disgust.
requerir *vt* to intimate, notify; to request; to require, need; to summon.
requesón *m* cottage cheese.
requiebro *m* endearing expression.
res *f* head of cattle.
resabio *m* (unpleasant) aftertaste; vicious habit, bad custom.
resaca *f* surge, surf; (*fig*) backlash; (*fam*) hangover.
resaltar *vi* to rebound; to jut out; to be evident; to stand out.
resbaladizo/za *adj* slippery.
resbalar(se) *vi* (*vr*) to slip, slide.
rescindir *vt* to rescind, annul.
rescoldo *m* embers *pl*, cinders *pl*.
resecarse *vr* to dry up.
reseña *f* review; account.
resentirse *vr*:—**~ de** to suffer:—**~ con** to resent.
reservar *vt* to keep; to reserve:—**~se** *vr* to preserve oneself; to keep to oneself.
resfriado *m* cold.
resguardar *vt* to preserve, defend:—**~se** *vr* to be on one's guard.
residir *vi* to reside, dwell.
residuo *m* residue, remainder.

resistir *vt* to resist, oppose; to put up with:—*vi* to resist; to hold out.
resol *m* glare (of the sun).
resollar *vi* to wheeze; to take breath.
resolver *vt* to resolve, decide; to analyse:—**~se** *vr* to resolve, determine.
resoplar *vi* to snore; to snort.
resorte *m* spring.
respaldo *m* backing; endorsement; back of a seat.
respetar *vt* to respect; to revere.
respingo *m* start; jump.
respiradero *m* vent, breathing hole; rest, repose.
respirar *vi* to breathe.
resplandecer *vi* to shine; to glisten.
resplandor *m* splendor, brilliance.
responder *vt* to answer:—*vi* to answer; to correspond:—**~ de** to be responsible for.
responso *m* prayer for the dead.
respuesta *f* answer, reply.
resquemor *m* resentment.
restablecer *vt* to re-establish:—**~se** *vr* to recover.
restallar *vi* to crack; to click.
restar *vt* to subtract, take away:—*vi* to be left.
restaurar *vt* to restore.
restituir *vt* to restore; to return.
resto *m* remainder, rest.
restregar *vt* to scrub, rub.
restringir *vt* to restrict, limit; to restrain.
resuelto/ta *adj* resolute, determined; prompt.
resultar *vi* to be; to turn out; to amount to.
resumir *vt* to abridge; to summarize.
retahíla *f* range, series.
retal *m* remnant.
retar *vt* to challenge.
retener *vt* to retain, keep back.
retentiva *f* memory.
retirar *vt* to withdraw, retire; to remove:—**~se** *vr* to retire, retreat; to go to bed.
reto *m* challenge; threat, menace.
retocar *vt* to retouch; to mend; to finish off (work).
retoñar *vi* to sprout.
retorcer *vt* to twist; to wring.
retozar *vi* to frisk, skip.
retraído/da *adj* shy.
retransmitir *vt* to broadcast; to relay; to retransmit.
retraso *m* delay; slowness; backwardness; lateness:—(*ferro*) **el tren ha tenido ~** the train is overdue or late.
retrato *m* portrait, effigy.
retrete *m* lavatory.
retribuir *vt* to repay.
retroceder *vi* to go backwards, fly back; to back down.
retrovisor *m* rear-view mirror.
retumbar *vi* to resound, jingle.
reúma *f* rheumatism.
reunir *vt* to reunite; to unite:—**~se** *vr* to gather, meet.
revancha *f* revenge.
revelar *vt* to reveal; to develop (photographs).
reventar *vi* to burst, crack; to explode; to toil, drudge.
reverdecer *vi* to grow green again; to revive.
revés *m* back; wrong side; disappointment, setback.
revisar *vt* to revise, review.
revisor *m* inspector; ticket collector.
revista *f* review, revision; magazine.
revolcarse *vr* to wallow.
revolotear *vi* to flutter.
revoltijo *m* confusion, disorder.
revoltoso/sa *adj* rebellious, unruly.
revolver *vt* to move about; to turn around; to mess up; to revolve; **~se** *vr* to turn round; to change (of the weather).
revuelta *f* turn; disturbance, revolt.
rey *m* king; king (in cards or chess).
rezagar *vt* to leave behind; to defer: —**~se** *vr* to remain behind.
rezar *vi* to pray, say one's prayers.
rezumar *vt* to ooze, leak.
ría *f* estuary.
riada *f* flood.
ribera *f* shore, bank.
rico/ca *adj* rich; delicious; lovely; cute.
riego *m* irrigation.
rienda *f* rein of a bridle:—**dar ~ suelta** to give free rein to.
riesgo *m* risk, danger.
rifa *f* raffle, lottery.
rígido/da *adj* rigid, inflexible; severe.
riguroso/sa *adj* rigorous.
rimar *vi* to rhyme.
rímel, rimmel *m* mascara.
riña *f* quarrel, dispute.
rincón *m* (inside) corner.
rinoceronte *m* rhinoceros.
riñón *m* kidney.
río *m* river, stream.
riqueza *f* riches *pl*, wealth.
risa *f* laugh, laughter.
risco *m* steep rock.
ritmo *m* rhythm.
rizo *m* curl; ripple (on water).
robar *vt* to rob; to steal; to break into.
roble *m* oak tree.

robusto/ta *adj* robust, strong.
roca *f* rock.
rociar *vt* to sprinkle; to spray.
rocío *m* dew.
rodaja *f* slice.
rodaje *m* filming:—**en ~** (*auto*) running in.
rodear *vi* to make a detour:—*vt* to surround, enclose.
rodilla *f* knee:—**de ~s** on one's knees.
rodillo *m* roller; rolling pin.
roer *vt* to gnaw; to corrode.
rogar *vt*, *vi* to ask for; to beg, entreat; to pray.
rojizo/za *adj* reddish.
rojo/ja *adj* red; ruddy.
rol *m* list, roll, catalog; role.
rollo *m* roll; coil.
romería *f* pilgrimage.
romero *m* (*bot*) rosemary.
rompecabezas *m invar* riddle; jigsaw.
romper *vt* to break; to tear up; to wear out; to break up (land):—*vi* to break (of waves); to break through.
ron *m* rum.
roña *f* scab, mange; grime; rust.
roncar *vi* to snore; to roar.
ronco/ca *adj* hoarse; husky; raucous.
ronda *f* night patrol; round (of drinks, cards, etc).
ronronear *vi* to purr.
ropa *f* clothes *pl*; clothing; dress.
rosa *f* rose; birthmark.
rosado/da *adj* pink; rosy.
rosca *f* thread (of a screw); coil, spiral.
rosquilla *f* doughnut.
rostro *m* face.
roto/ta *adj* broken, destroyed; debauched.
rótula *f* kneecap; ball-and-socket joint.
rotulador *m* felt-tip pen.
rótulo *m* inscription; label, ticket; placard, poster.
rotundo/da *adj* round; emphatic.
rozar *vt* to rub; to chafe; to nibble (the grass); to scrape; to touch lightly.
rubio/bia *adj* fair-haired, blond(e): —*m/f* blond/blonde.
rudimento *m* principle; beginning:—**~s** *mpl* rudiments *pl*.
rudo/da *adj* rough, coarse; plain, simple; stupid.
rueda *f* wheel; circle; slice, round.
ruedo *m* rotation; border, selvage; arena, bullring.
ruego *m* request, entreaty.
rufián *m* pimp, pander; lout.
rugir *vi* to roar, bellow.
rugoso/sa *adj* wrinkled.
ruido *m* noise, sound; din, row; fuss.
ruin *adj* mean, despicable; stingy.
ruina *f* ruin, collapse; downfall, destruction: —**~s** *fpl* ruins *pl*.
ruiseñor *m* nightingale.
rulo *m* curler.
rumbo *m* (*mar*) course, bearing; road, route, way; course of events, pomp, ostentation.
rumboso/sa *adj* generous, lavish.
rústico/ca *adj* rustic:—*m/f* peasant.
ruta *f* route, itinerary.
rutina *f* routine; habit.

S

sábado *m* Saturday; (*Jewish*) Sabbath.
sábana *f* sheet; altar cloth.
sabañón *m* chilblain.
sabelotodo *m/f invar* know-all.
saber *vt* to know; to be able to; to find out, learn; to experience:—*vi* **~ a** to taste of: —*m* learning, knowledge.
sabiduría *f* learning, knowledge; wisdom.
sabio/bia *adj* sage, wise:—*m/f* sage, wise person.
sablazo *m* sword wound; (*fam*) sponging, scrounging.
sabor *m* taste, savor, flavor.
sabroso/sa *adj* tasty, delicious; pleasant; salted.
sabueso *m* bloodhound.
sacacorchos *m invar* corkscrew.
sacapuntas *m invar* pencil sharpener.
sacar *vt* to take out, extract; to get out; to bring out (a book etc); to take off (clothes); to receive, get; (*dep*) to serve.
sacerdote *m* priest.
saco *m* bag, sack; jacket.
sacudir *vt* to shake, jerk; to beat, hit.
sagaz *adj* shrewd, clever, sagacious.
sagrado/da *adj* sacred, holy.
sal *f* salt.
sala *f* large room; (*teat*) house, auditorium; public hall; (*jur*) court; (*med*) ward.
salado/da *adj* salted; witty, amusing.

salario *m* salary.
salchicha *f* sausage.
salchichón *m* (salami-type) sausage.
saldo *m* settlement; balance; remainder:—**~s** *mpl* sale.
salida *f* exit, way out; leaving, departure; production, output; (*com*) sale; sales outlet.
saliente *adj* projecting; rising; (*fig*) outstanding.
salir *vi* to go out, leave; to depart, set out; to appear; to turn out, prove:—**~se** *vr* to escape, leak.
salmo *m* psalm.
salmonete *m* red mullet.
salmuera *f* brine.
salón *m* living room, lounge; public hall.
salpicadero *m* dashboard.
salpicar *vt* to sprinkle, splash, spatter.
salsa *f* sauce.
saltamontes *m invar* grasshopper.
saltar *vt* to jump, leap; to skip, miss out:—*vi* to leap, jump; to bounce; (*fig*) to explode, blow up.
saltimbanqui *m/f* acrobat.
salubre *adj* healthy.
salud *f* health.
saludar *vt* to greet; (*mil*) to salute.
salvado *m* bran.
salvaguardar *vt* to safeguard.
salvaje *adj* savage.
salvar *vt* to save; to rescue; to overcome; to cross, jump across; to cover, travel; to exclude:—**~se** *vr* to escape from danger.
salvavidas *adj invar*:—**bote/chaleco/cinturón ~** lifeboat/life preserver/life belt.
salvia *f* (*bot*) sage.
salvo/va *adj* safe:—*adv* save, except (for).
San *adj* Saint (as title).
saña *f* anger, passion.
sanar *vt*, *vi* to heal.
sandalia *f* sandal.
sandez *f* folly, stupidity.
sandía *f* watermelon.
sangre *f* blood:—**a ~ fria** in cold blood:—**a ~ y fuego** without mercy.
sangriento/ta *adj* bloody, blood-stained, gory; cruel.
sano/na *adj* healthy, fit; intact, sound.
sapo *m* toad.
saquear *vt* to ransack, plunder.
sarampión *m* measles.
sarna *f* itch; mange; (*med*) scabies.
sarpullido *m* (*med*) rash.
sarro *m* (*med*) tartar.
sarta *f* string of beads, etc; string, row.
sartén *f* frying pan.
sastre *m* tailor.
satisfacer *vt* to satisfy; to pay (a debt):—**~se** *vr* to satisfy oneself; to take revenge.
sauce *m* (*bot*) willow.
saúco *m* (*bot*) elder.
savia *f* sap.
sazonar *vt* to ripen; to season.
se *pn reflexivo* himself; herself; itself; yourself; themselves; yourselves; each other; one another; oneself.
se(p)tiembre *m* September.
sebo *m* fat, grease.
secano *m* dry, arable land which is not irrigated.
secar *vt* to dry:—**~se** *vr* to dry up; to dry oneself.
seco/ca *adj* dry; dried up; skinny; cold (of character); brusque, sharp; bare.
secuestrar *vt* to kidnap; to confiscate.
sed *f* thirst:—**tener ~** to be thirsty.
seda *f* silk.
sedal *m* fishing line.
sede *f* see; seat; headquarters.
sediento/ta *adj* thirsty; eager.
seducir *vt* to seduce; to bribe; to charm, attract.
segar *vt* to reap, harvest; to mow.
seguido/da *adj* continuous; successive; long-lasting:—*adv* straight (on); after; often.
seguir *vt* to follow, pursue; to continue:—*vi* to follow; to carry on:—**~se** *vr* to follow, ensue.
según *prep* according to.
segundo/da *adj* second:—*m* second (of time).
seguro/ra *adj* safe, secure; sure, certain; firm, constant:—*adv* for sure: —*m* safety device; insurance; safety, certainty.
seis *adj*, *m* six; sixth.
seiscientos/tas *adj* six hundred.
seísmo *m* earthquake.
sello *m* seal; stamp.
seleccionar *vt* to select, chose, pick.
selectivo *adj* selective.
selva *f* forest.
semáforo *m* traffic lights *pl*; signal.
semana *f* week.
sembrar *vt* to sow; to sprinkle, scatter.
semejante *adj* similar, like:—*m* fellow man.
semestral *adj* half-yearly.
semilla *f* seed.
sémola *f* semolina.
sempiterno/na *adj* everlasting.
seña *f* sign, mark, token; signal; (*mil*) password:—**~s** *fpl* address.

señal *f* sign, token; symptom; signal; landmark; (*com*) deposit.
señalar *vt* to stamp, mark; to signpost; to point out; to fix, settle:—**~se** *vr* to distinguish oneself, excel.
sencillo/lla *adj* simple; natural; unaffected; single.
senda *f*, **sendero** *m* path, trail.
seno *m* bosom; lap; womb; hole, cavity; sinus:—**~s** *mpl* breasts *pl*.
señor *m* man; gentleman; master; Mr; sir.
señora *f* lady; Mrs; madam; wife.
señorita *f* Miss; young lady.
señorito *m* young gentleman; rich kid.
sensación *f* sensation, feeling; sense.
sensato/ta *adj* sensible.
sensible *adj* sensitive; perceptible, appreciable; regrettable.
sentado/da *adj* sitting, seated; sedate; settled.
sentar *vt* to seat; (*fig*) to establish:—*vi* to suit:—**~se** *vr* to sit down.
sentido *m* sense; feeling; meaning:—**~/da** *adj* regrettable; sensitive.
sentir *vt* to feel; to hear; to perceive; to sense; to suffer from; to regret, be sorry for:—**~se** *vr* to feel; to feel pain; to crack (of walls, etc):—*m* opinion, judgement.
separar *vt* to separate:—**~se** *vr* to separate; to come away, come apart; to withdraw.
septentrional *adj* north, northern.
séptimo/ma *adj* seventh.
sepultar *vt* to bury, inter.
sequía *f* dryness; thirst; drought.
séquito *m* retinue, suite; group of supporters; aftermath.
ser *vi* to be; to exist:—**~ de** to come from; to be made of; to belong to:—*m* being.
serenata *f* (*mus*) serenade.
sereno *m* night watchman:—**~/na** *adj* serene, calm, quiet.
serie *f* series; sequence.
serio/ria *adj* serious; grave; reliable.
serpentear *vi* to wriggle; to wind, snake.
serpiente *f* snake.
serranía *f* range of mountains; mountainous country.
serrar *vt* to saw.
serrín *m* sawdust.
servicial *adj* helpful, obliging.
servilleta *f* napkin, serviette.
servir *vt* to serve; to wait on:—*vi* to serve; to be of use; to be in service: —**~se** *vr* to serve oneself, help oneself; to deign, please; to make use of.
sesenta *m*, *adj* sixty; sixtieth.
seso *m* brain.
sestear *vi* to take a nap.
seta *f* mushroom.
setecientos/tas *adj* seven hundred.
setenta *adj*, *m* seventy.
setiembre *m* September.
seto *m* fence; enclosure; hedge.
severo/ra *adj* severe, strict; grave, serious.
sexto/ta *adj*, *m* sixth.
si *conj* whether; if.
sí *adv* yes; certainly; indeed:—*pn* oneself; himself; herself; itself; yourself; themselves; yourselves; each other; one another.
siderúrgico/ca *adj* iron and steel *compd*:—*f* **la siderúrgica** the iron and steel industry.
sidra *f* cider.
siempre *adv* always; all the time; ever; still:—**~ jamás** for ever and ever.
sien *f* temple (of the head).
sierra *f* saw; range of mountains.
siete *adj*, *m* seven.
sigilo *m* secrecy.
sigla *f* acronym; abbreviation.
siglo *m* century.
significado *m* significance, meaning.
significativo/va *adj* significant.
signo *m* sign, mark.
siguiente *adj* following, successive, next.
silbar *vt*, *vi* to hiss; to whistle.
silencio *m* silence:—**¡~!** silence! quiet!
silla *f* chair; saddle; seat:—**~ de ruedas** wheelchair.
silo *m* silo; underground wheat store.
silueta *f* silhouette; outline; figure.
silvestre *adj* wild, uncultivated; rustic.
símbolo *m* symbol.
simio *m* ape.
simpático/ca *adj* pleasant; kind.
simpatizar *vi*:—**~ con** to get on well with.
simular *vt* to simulate.
sin *prep* without.
sindicato *m* trade(s) union; syndicate.
sinfín *m*:—**un ~ de** a great many.
singular *adj* singular; exceptional; peculiar, odd.
siniestro/tra *adj* left; (*fig*) sinister:—*m* accident.
sino *conj* but; except; save; only:—*m* fate.
sinsabor *m* unpleasantness; disgust.
sinuoso/sa *adj* sinuous; wavy; winding.
sinvergüenza *m/f* rogue.
siquiera *conj* even if, even though:—*adv* at least.
sitio *m* place; spot; site, location; room, space; job, post; (*mil*) siege, blockade.
situar *vt* to place, situate; to invest:—**~se** *vr* to be established in place or business.
smoking *m* tuxedo.
sobaco *m* armpit, armhole.

sobar *vt* to handle, soften; to knead; to massage, rub hard; to rumple (clothes); to fondle.
soberbia *f* pride, haughtiness; magnificence.
sobornar *vt* to suborn, bribe.
sobrante *adj* remaining:—*m* surplus, remainder.
sobrar *vt* to exceed, surpass:—*vi* to be more than enough; to remain, be left.
sobre *prep* on; on top of; above, over; more than; besides:—*m* envelope.
sobrecargar *vt* to overload; (*com*) to surcharge.
sobredosis *f* overdose.
sobreentender *vt* to deduce:—**~se** *vr* **se sobreentiende que** . . . it is implied that.
sobrellevar *vt* to carry; to tolerate.
sobremesa *f*:—**de ~** immediately after dinner.
sobrenombre *m* nickname.
sobrepasar *vt* to surpass.
sobresalto *m* start, scare; sudden shock.
sobrevenir *vi* to happen, come unexpectedly; to supervene.
sobrevivir *vi* to survive.
sobrevolar *vt* to fly over.
sobrino/na *m/f* nephew/niece.
sobrio/ria *adj* sober, frugal.
socarrón/ona *adj* sarcastic; ironic(al).
socavar *vt* to undermine.
socio/cia *m/f* associate, member.
socorrista *m/f* first aider; lifeguard.
socorro *m* help, aid, assistance, relief.
soez *adj* dirty, obscene.
sofá *m* sofa.
soga *f* rope.
soja *f* soya.
sol *m* sun; sunshine, sunlight.
solamente *adv* only, solely.
solapa *f* lapel.
solar *m* building site; piece of land; ancestral home of a family:—*adj* solar.
soldado *m/f* soldier:—**~ raso** private.
soldar *vt* to solder; to weld; to unite.
soledad *f* solitude; loneliness.
soler *vi* to be accustomed to, be in the habit of.
solicitar *vt* to ask for, seek; to apply for (a job); to canvass for; to chase after, pursue.
solidario/ria *adj* joint; mutually binding.
soliloquio *m* soliloquy, monologue.
solista *m/f* soloist.
solitario/ria *adj* solitary:—*m* solitaire:—*m/f* hermit.
sollozar *vi* to sob.
solo *m* (*mus*) solo:—**~la** *adj* alone, single: —**a solas** alone, unaided.
sólo *adv* only.
solomillo *m* sirloin.
soltar *vt* to untie, loosen; to set free, let out:—**~se** *vr* to get loose; to come undone.
soltero/ra *m/f* bachelor/single woman: —*adj* single, unmarried.
soltura *f* looseness, slackness; agility, activity; fluency.
solucionar *vt* to solve; to resolve.
sombra *f* shade; shadow.
sombrero *m* hat.
sombrilla *f* parasol.
sombrío/bría *adj* shady, gloomy; sad.
somero/ra *adj* superficial.
someter *vt* to conquer (a country); to subject to one's will; to submit; to subdue:—**~se** *vr* to give in, submit.
somnífero *m* sleeping pill.
sonar *vt* to ring:—*vi* to sound; to make a noise; to be pronounced; to be talked of; to sound familiar:—**~se** *vr* to blow one's nose.
soñar *vt*, *vi* to dream.
sondeo *m* sounding; boring; (*fig*) poll.
soneto *m* sonnet.
sonido *m* sound.
sonreír(se) *vi* (*vr*) to smile.
sonrisa *f* smile.
sonrojarse *vr* to blush.
sonsacar *vt* to wheedle; to cajole; to obtain by cunning.
sopa *f* soup; sop.
sopetón *m*:—**de ~** suddenly.
soplar *vt* to blow away, blow off; to blow up, inflate:—*vi* to blow, puff.
soplón/ona *m/f* telltale.
soportal *m* portico.
soportar *vt* to suffer, tolerate; to support.
sorber *vt* to sip; to inhale; to swallow; to absorb.
sorbete *m* sherbet; iced fruit drink.
sordo/da *adj* deaf; silent, quiet:—*m/f* deaf person.
sorprender *vt* to surprise.
sorteo *m* draw; raffle.
sortija *f* ring; ringlet, curl.
sortilegio *m* sorcery.
sosegar *vt* to appease, calm:—*vi* to rest.
soso/sa *adj* insipid, tasteless; dull.
sospechar *vt* to suspect.
sostén *m* support; bra; sustenance.
sostener *vt* to sustain, maintain:—**~se** *vr* to support or maintain oneself; to contrive, remain.
sota *f* knave (at cards).
sótano *m* basement, cellar.
su *pn* his, her, its, one's; their; your.

suave *adj* smooth, soft, delicate; gentle; mild, meek.
subalterno/na *adj* secondary; auxiliary.
subasta *f* auction.
subcampeón/ona *m/f* runner-up.
subestimar *vt* to underestimate.
subir *vt, vi* to raise, lift up; to go up; to climb, ascend, mount; to increase, swell; to get in, get on, board; to rise (in price).
súbito/ta *adj* sudden, hasty; unforeseen.
sublevar *vt* to excite (a rebellion); to incite (a revolt):—**~se** *vr* to revolt.
submarino/na *adj* underwater:—*m* submarine.
subrayar *vt* to underline.
subsanar *vt* to excuse; to mend, repair; to overcome.
subsidio *m* subsidy, aid; benefit, allowance.
su(b)stancia *f* substance.
su(b)straer *vt* to remove; (*mat*) to subtract:—**~se** *vr* to avoid; to withdraw.
subterráneo/nea *adj* subterranean; underground:—*m* underground passage; (*ferro*) underground (railway).
suburbio *m* slum quarter; suburbs *pl*.
subvencionar *vt* to subsidize.
sucedáneo/nea *adj* substitute:—*m* substitute (food).
suceder *vt* to succeed, inherit:—*vi* to happen.
suceso *m* event; incident.
sucesor/ra *m/f* successor; heir.
sucio/cia *adj* dirty, filthy; obscene; dishonest.
sucursal *f* branch (office).
sudar *vt, vi* to sweat.
sudeste *adj* southeast, southeastern: —*m* southeast.
sudoeste *adj* southwest, southwestern:—*m* southwest.
suegra *f* mother-in-law.
suegro *m* father-in-law.
suela *f* sole of the shoe.
sueldo *m* wages *pl*, salary.
suelo *m* ground; floor; soil, surface.
suelto/ta *adj* loose; free; detached; swift:—*m* loose change.
sueño *m* sleep; dream.
suero *m* (*med*) serum; whey.
suerte *f* fate, destiny, chance, lot, fortune, good luck; kind, sort.
sufrir *vt* to suffer; to bear, put up with; to support.
sugerir *vt* to suggest.
sujetador *m* fastener; bra.
sujetar *vt* to fasten, hold down; to subdue; to subject:—**~se** *vr* to subject oneself.
sujeto/ta *adj* fastened, secure; subject, liable:—*m* subject; individual.
sumamente *adv* extremely.
sumar *vt* to add, add up; to collect, gather: —*vi* to add up.
sumergir *vt* to submerge, sink; to immerse.
sumidero *m* sewer, drain.
suministrar *vt* to supply, furnish.
sumiso/sa *adj* submissive, docile.
sumo/ma *adj* great, extreme; highest, greatest:—**a lo ~** at most.
súper *f* four-star (gas).
superar *vt* to surpass; to overcome; to exceed, go beyond.
superficial *adj* superficial; shallow.
superficie *f* surface; area.
superintendente *m/f* superintendent, supervisor; floorwalker.
superior *adj* superior; upper; higher; better: —*m/f* superior.
supermercado *m* supermarket.
superviviente *m/f* survivor:—*adj* surviving.
suplente *m/f* substitute.
suplicar *vt* to beg (for), plead (for); to beg; to plead with.
suplicio *m* torture.
suplir *vt* to supply; to make good, make up for; to replace.
suponer *vt* to suppose:—*vi* to have authority.
suprimir *vt* to suppress; to abolish; to remove; to delete.
supuesto *m* assumption:—**~/ta** *adj* supposed:—**~ que** *conj* since, granted that.
sur *adj* south, southern:—*m* south; south wind.
surco *m* furrow; groove.
surgir *vi* to emerge; to crop up.
surtido *m* assortment, supply.
surtir *vt* to supply, furnish, provide: —*vi* to spout, spurt.
suscitar *vt* to excite, stir up.
susodicho/cha *adj* above-mentioned.
suspender *vt* to suspend, hang up; to stop; to fail (an exam etc).
suspicaz *adj* suspicious, mistrustful.
suspirar *vi* to sigh.
sustentar *vt* to sustain; to support, nourish.
susto *m* fright, scare.
sustraer *vt* to take away; to subtract.
susurrar *vi* to whisper; to murmur; to rustle: —**~se** *vr* to be whispered about.
sutil *adj* subtle; thin; delicate; very soft; keen, observant.
suyo/ya *adj* his; hers; theirs; one's; his; her; its own; one's own; their own:—**de ~** per se:—**los ~s** *mpl* his own, near friends, relations, family, supporters.

T

tabaco *m* tobacco; (*fam*) cigarettes *pl*.
tabique *m* thin wall; partition wall.
tabla *f* board; shelf; plank; slab; index of a book; bed of earth in a garden.
tablero *m* plank, board; chessboard; dashboard; bulletin board; gambling den.
taburete *m* stool.
tacaño/ña *adj* mean, stingy; crafty.
tachar *vt* to find fault with; to erase.
tachuela *f* tack, nail.
tácito/ta *adj* tacit, silent; implied.
taco *m* stopper, plug; heel (of a shoe); wad; book of coupons; billiard cue.
tacón *m* heel.
tacto *m* touch, feeling; tact.
tahona *f* bakery.
taimado/da *adj* sly, cunning, crafty.
tajo *m* cut, incision; cleft, sheer drop; working area; chopping block.
tal *adj* such:—**con ~ que** provided that:—**no hay ~** no such thing.
taladro *m* drill; borer, gimlet.
talante *m* mood; appearance; aspect; will.
talar *vt* to fell (trees); to desolate.
talega *f*, **talego** *m* bag; bagful.
talla *f* raised work; sculpture; stature, size; measure (of anything); hand, draw, turn (at cards).
tallar *vt* to cut, chop; to carve in wood; to engrave; to measure.
taller *m* workshop, laboratory.
tallo *m* shoot, sprout.
talón *m* heel; receipt; cheque.
tamaño *m* size, shape, bulk.
tambalearse *vr* to stagger, waver.
también *adv* also, as well; likewise; besides.
tambor *m* drum; drummer; eardrum.
tamiz *m* fine sieve.
tampoco *adv* neither, nor.
tan *adv* so.
tanto *m* certain sum or quantity; point; goal:—**~/ta** *adj* so much, as much; very great:—*adv* so much, as much; so long, as long.
tapar *vt* to stop up, cover; to conceal, hide.
tapia *f* wall.
tapicería *f* tapestry; upholstery; upholsterer's (store).
tapiz *m* tapestry; carpet.
tapón *m* cork, plug, bung.
taquigrafía *f* shorthand.
taquilla *f* booking office; takings *pl*.
tardar *vi* to delay; to take a long time; to be late.
tarde *f* afternoon; evening:—*adv* late.
tarea *f* task.
tarima *f* platform; step.
tarjeta *f* card; visiting card:—**~ postal** postcard.
tarro *m* pot.
tarta *f* cake.
tartamudear *vi* to stutter, stammer.
tarugo *m* wooden peg or pin.
tasar *vt* to appraise, value.
tatarabuelo/la *m/f* great-great-grandfather/mother.
tataranieto/ta *m/f* great-great-grandson/daughter.
tatuaje *m* tattoo; tattooing.
taurino/na *adj* bullfighting *compd*.
taza *f* cup; basin of a fountain.
te *pn* you.
té *m* (*bot*) tea.
teatro *m* theater, playhouse.
tebeo *m* comic.
techo *m* roof; ceiling.
tecla *f* key (of an organ, piano, etc).
técnico/ca *adj* technical.
tedio *m* boredom; dislike, abhorrence.
tejado *m* roof covered with tiles.
tejer *vt* to weave.
tejo *m* quoit; yew tree.
tejón *m* badger.
tela *f* cloth; material.
telaraña *f* cobweb.
telefax *m invar* fax; fax (machine).
televisor *m* television set.
telón *m* curtain, drape.
tema *m* theme.
temblar *vi* to tremble.
temer *vt* to fear, doubt:—*vi* to be afraid.
temerario/ria *adj* rash.
temible *adj* dreadful, terrible.
témpano *m* ice-floe.
templado/da *adj* temperate, tempered.
templar *vt* to temper, moderate, cool; to tune:—**~se** *vr* to be moderate.
temple *m* temperature; tempera; temperament; tuning:—**al ~** painted in distemper.
temporada *f* time, season; epoch, period.
temprano/na *adj* early, anticipated: —*adv* early; very early, prematurely.
tenaz *adj* tenacious; stubborn.
tenaza(s) *f* (*pl*) tongs *pl*, pincers *pl*.
tender *vt* to stretch out; to expand; to extend; to hang out; to lay:—**~se** *vr* to stretch oneself out.
tendero/ra *m/f* shop-keeper.

tendón *m* tendon, sinew.
tenebroso/sa *adj* dark, obscure.
tenedor *m* holder, keeper, tenant; fork.
tener *vt* to have; to take; to hold; to possess: —**~se** *vr* to stand upright; to stop, halt; to resist; to adhere.
tenia *f* tapeworm.
teñir *vt* to tinge, dye.
tensar *vt* to tauten; to draw.
tentar *vt* to touch; to try; to tempt; to attempt.
tentempié *m* (*fam*) snack.
tenue *adj* thin; tenuous, slender.
terapia *f* therapy.
tercer(o)/ra *adj* third:—*m* (*jur*) third party.
tercio/cia *adj* third:—*m* third part.
terciopelo *m* velvet.
terco/ca *adj* obstinate.
tergiversar *vt* to distort.
terminante *adj* decisive; categorical.
terminar *vt* to finish; to end; to terminate: —*vi* to end; to stop.
termo *m* flask.
ternero/ra *m/f* calf; veal; heifer.
ternilla *f* gristle.
ternura *f* tenderness.
terrado *m* terrace.
terrateniente *m/f* landowner.
terraza *f* balcony; (flat) roof; terrace (in fields).
terremoto *m* earthquake.
terreno/na *adj* earthly, terrestrial:—*m* land, ground, field.
terrón *m* clod of earth; lump:—**~ones** *mpl* landed property.
terror *m* terror, dread.
terso/sa *adj* smooth, glossy.
tertulia *f* club, assembly, circle.
tesorero *m* treasurer.
tesoro *m* treasure; exchequer.
testamento *m* will, testament.
testar *vt*, *vi* to make one's will.
testarudo/da *adj* obstinate.
testificar *vt* to attest, witness.
testigo *m* witness, deponent.
teta *f* breast.
tetera *f* teapot.
tetilla *f* nipple; teat (of a bottle).
tétrico/ca *adj* gloomy, sullen, surly.
tez *f* complexion, hue.
ti *pn* you; yourself.
tía *f* aunt; (*fam*) bird.
tibio/bia *adj* lukewarm.
tiburón *m* shark.
tiempo *m* time; term; weather; (*gr*) tense; occasion, opportunity; season.
tienda *f* tent; awning; tilt; shop.
tierno/na *adj* tender.
tierra *f* earth; land, ground; native country.
tieso/sa *adj* stiff, hard, firm; robust; valiant; stubborn.
tiesto *m* earthen pot.
tigre *m* tiger.
tijeras *fpl* scissors *pl*.
tilde *f* tilde (ñ).
tilo *m* lime tree.
timar *vt* to con; to swindle.
timbre *m* stamp; bell; timbre; stamp duty.
tímido/da *adj* timid; cowardly.
timón *m* helm, rudder.
tímpano *m* ear-drum; small drum.
tina *f* tub; bath (tub).
tinieblas *fpl* darkness; shadows *pl*.
tino *m* skill; judgement, prudence.
tinta *f* ink; tint, dye; color.
tinte *m* tint, dye; dry cleaner's.
tinto/ta *adj* dyed:—*m* red wine.
tío *m* uncle; (*fam*) guy.
tiovivo *m* merry-go-round.
tipico/ca *adj* typical; characteristic; picturesque; traditional; regional.
tipo *m* type; norm; pattern; guy.
tiquismiquis *m invar* fussy person.
tira *f* abundance; strip.
tirachinas *m invar* slingshot.
tirado/da *adj* dirt-cheap; (*fam*) very easy:—*f* cast; distance; series; edition.
tirano/na *m/f* tyrant.
tirante *m* joist; stay; strap; brace:—*adj* taut, extended, drawn.
tirar *vt* to throw; to pull; to draw; to drop; to tend, aim at:—*vi* to shoot; to pull; to go; to tend to.
tirita *f* (sticking) plaster.
tiritar *vi* to shiver.
títere *m* puppet; ridiculous little fellow.
titubear *vi* to stammer; to stagger; to hesitate.
titular *adj* titular:—*m/f* occupant:—*m* headline:—*vt* to title:—**~se** *vr* to obtain a title.
tiza *f* chalk.
tiznar *vt* to stain; to tarnish.
tizón *m* half-burnt wood.
toalla *f* towel.
tobillo *m* ankle.
tobogán *m* toboggan; roller-coaster; slide.
tocadiscos *m invar* record player.
tocado *m* headdress, headgear.
tocar *vt* to touch; to strike; (*mus*) to play; to ring (a bell):—*vi* to belong; to concern; to knock; to call; to be a duty or obligation.
tocino *m* bacon.
todavía *adv* even; yet, still.

todo/da *adj* all, entire; every:—*pn* everything, all:—*m* whole.
todopoderoso/sa *adj* almighty.
toldo *m* awning; parasol.
tomar *vt* to take; to seize, grasp; to understand; to interpret, perceive; to drink; to acquire:—*vi* to drink; to take.
tomavistas *m invar* cine-camera.
tomillo *m* thyme.
tomo *m* bulk; tome; volume.
tonada *f* tune, melody.
tonel *m* cask, barrel.
tonelada *f* ton; (*mar*) tonnage duty.
tónico/ca *adj* tonic, strengthening:—*m* tonic:—*f* tonic (water); (*mus*) tonic; (*fig*) keynote.
tontería *f* foolery, nonsense.
tonto/ta *adj* stupid, foolish.
topar *vt* to run into; to find.
topo *m* mole; stumbler.
toquilla *f* head-scarf; shawl.
tórax *m* thorax.
torbellino *m* whirlwind.
torcer *vt* to twist, curve; to turn; to sprain: —**~se** *vr* to bend; to go wrong:—*vi* to turn off.
torcido/da *adj* oblique; crooked.
tordo *m* thrush:—**~/da** *adj* speckled black and white.
torear *vt* to avoid; to tease:—*vi* to fight bulls.
tormenta *f* storm, tempest.
tornar *vt* to return; to restore:—**~se** *vr* to become:—*vi* to return:—**~ a hacer** to do again.
tornasolado *adj* iridescent; shimmering.
torneo *m* tournament.
tornillo *m* screw.
torno *m* winch; revolution.
toro *m* bull.
toronja *f* grapefruit.
torpe *adj* dull, heavy; stupid.
torre *f* tower; turret; steeple.
torrefacto/ta *adj* roasted.
torta *f* cake; (*fam*) slap.
tortilla *f* omelet; pancake.
tortuga *f* tortoise; turtle.
tos *f* cough.
tosco/ca *adj* coarse, ill-bred, clumsy.
toser *vi* to cough.
tostado/da *adj* parched; sunburnt; light-yellow; light-brown.
tostar *vt* to toast, roast.
total *m* whole, totality:—*adj* total, entire: —*adv* in short.
tóxico/ca *adj* toxic:—*m* poison.
trabajar *vt* to work, labor; to persuade; to push:—*vi* to strive.
trabalenguas *m invar* tongue twister.
trabar *vt* to join, unite; to take hold of; to fetter, shackle.
tracción *f* traction:—**~ delantera/trasera** front-wheel/rear-wheel drive.
traducir *vt* to translate.
traer *vt* to bring, carry; to attract; to persuade; to wear; to cause.
traficar *vi* to trade, do business, deal.
tragaluz *m* skylight.
tragaperras *m* o *f invar* slot machine.
tragar *vt* to swallow; to swallow up.
trago *m* drink; gulp; adversity, misfortune.
traicionar *vt* to betray.
traje *m* suit; dress; costume.
trajinar *vt* to carry:—*vi* to bustle about; to travel around.
trama *f* plot; weft, woof.
tramitar *vt* to transact; to negotiate; to handle.
tramo *m* section; piece of ground; flight of stairs.
tramoya *f* scene, theatrical decoration; trick.
trampa *f* trap, snare; trapdoor; fraud.
trampolín *m* trampoline; diving board.
tramposo/sa *adj* deceitful, swindling.
tranca *f* bar, crossbeam.
trance *m* danger; last stage of life; trance.
tranquilizar *vt* to calm; to reassure.
tranquilo/la *adj* tranquil, calm, quiet.
transbordador *m* ferry.
transbordo *m* transfer:—**hacer ~** to change (trains).
transcurrir *vi* to pass; to turn out.
transeúnte *adj* transitory:—*m* passer-by.
transigir *vi* to compromise.
tránsito *m* passage; transition; road, way; change; removal; death of holy or virtuous persons.
transmitir *vt* to transmit; to broadcast.
transparente *adj* transparent; see-through.
transpirar *vt* to perspire; to transpire.
tranvía *m* tram.
trapo *m* rag, tatter.
tráquea *f* windpipe.
tras *prep* after, behind.
trascender *vi* to smell; to come out: —**~ de** to go beyond.
trasegar *vt* to move about; to decant.
trasero/ra *adj* back:—*m* bottom.
trasfondo *m* background.
trasgredir *vt* to contravene.
trashumante *adj* migrating.
trasladar *vt* to transport; to transfer; to postpone; to transcribe, copy:—**~se** *vr* to move.
trasnochar *vi* to watch, sit up the whole night.

traspasar *vt* to remove, transport; to transfix, pierce; to return; to exceed (the proper bounds); to transfer.
traste *m* fret (of a guitar):—**dar al ~ con algo** to ruin something.
trastero *m* lumber room.
trastienda *f* back room behind a shop.
trasto *m* piece of junk; useless person.
trastornar *vt* to overthrow, overturn; to confuse:—**~se** *vr* to go crazy.
trastrocar *vt* to invert (the order of).
tratar *vt* to traffic, trade; to use; to treat; to handle; to address; **~se** *vr* to treat each other.
trato *m* treatment; manner, address; trade, traffic; conversation; (*com*) agreement.
través *m* (*fig*) reverse:—**de** *o* **al ~** across, crossways:—**a ~ de** *prep* across; over; through.
travesía *f* crossing; cross-street; trajectory; (*mar*) side wind.
travieso/sa *adj* restless, uneasy, fidgety; lively; naughty.
trayecto *m* road; journey, stretch; course.
trazar *vt* to plan out; to project; to trace.
trébedes *fpl* trivet, tripod.
trébol *m* trefoil, clover.
trece *adj*, *m* thirteen; thirteenth.
trecho *m* space, distance of time or place:—**a ~s** at intervals.
tregua *f* truce, cessation of hostilities.
treinta *adj*, *m* thirty.
tremendo/da *adj* terrible, formidable; awful, grand.
tren *m* train, retinue; show, osten-tation; (*ferro*) train:—**~ de gran velocidad** fast *or* express train:—**~ de mercancias** freight train.
trenza *f* braid (in hair), plaited silk.
trepar *vi* to climb; to crawl.
tres *adj*, *m* three.
tresillo *m* three-piece suite; (*mus*) triplet.
tricotar *vi* to knit.
trigésimo/ma *adj*, *m* thirtieth.
trigo *m* wheat.
trillado/da *adj* beaten; trite, hackneyed:—**camino ~** common routine.
trinar *vi* to trill, quaver; to be angry.
trinchar *vt* to carve, divide (meat).
trineo *m* sled.
trino *m* trill.
tripa *f* gut, intestine:—**~s** *fpl* guts; tripe.
tripulación *f* crew.
tripular *vt* to man; to drive.
tris *m invar*:—**estar en un ~ de** to be on the point of.
triste *adj* sad, mournful, melancholy.
triturar *vt* to reduce to powder; to grind, pound.
triza *f*:—**hacer ~s** to smash to bits; to tear to shreds.
trocar *vt* to exchange.
trompa *f* trumpet; proboscis; large top.
trompazo *m* heavy blow; accident.
trompeta *f* trumpet:—*m* trumpeter.
tronar *vi* to thunder; to rage.
tronco *m* trunk; log of wood; stock.
tropel *m* confused noise; hurry; bustle, confusion; heap; crowd:—**en ~** in a tumultuous and confused way.
tropezar *vi* to stumble:—*vt* to meet accidentally.
trotamundos *m invar* globetrotter.
trotar *vi* to trot.
trozo *m* piece.
trucha *f* trout.
truco *m* knack; trick.
trueno *m* thunderclap.
trueque *m* exchange.
truncar *vt* to truncate, maim.
tu *adj* your.
tú *pn* you.
tubería *f* pipe; pipeline.
tubo *m* tube.
tuerca *f* nut.
tumba *f* tomb.
tumbar *vt* to knock down:—*vi* to fall down:—**~se** *vr* to lie down to sleep.
tumbona *f* easy chair; beach chair.
tunda *f* beating.
tupido/da *adj* dense.
turbar *vt* to disturb, trouble:—**~se** *vr* to be disturbed.
turbio/bia *adj* muddy; troubled.
turno *m* turn; shift; opportunity.
turrón *m* nougat (almond cake).
tutear *vt* to address as 'tu'.
tutor *m* guardian, tutor.
tuyo/ya *adj* yours:—**~s** *pl* friends and relations of the party addressed.

U

u *conj* or (instead of *o* before an *o* or *ho*).
ubicar *vt* to place:—**~se** to be located.
ufanarse *vr* to boast.
últimamente *adv* lately.

ultimar *vt* to finalize; to finish.
último/ma *adj* last; latest; bottom; top.
ultrajar *vt* to outrage; to despise; to abuse.
ultramar *adj*, *m* overseas.
ultramarinos *mpl* groceries.
umbral *m* threshold.
un/una *art* a, an:—*adj*, *m* one (for **uno**).
uña *f* nail; hoof; claw, talon.
ungir *vt* to anoint.
ungüento *m* ointment.
únicamente *adv* only, simply.
único/ca *adj* only; singular, unique.
unidad *f* unity; unit; conformity; union.
unificar *vt* to unite.
unir *vt* to join, unite; to mingle; to bind, tie:—**~se** *vr* to associate.
uno *m* one:—**~/una** *adj* one; sole, only:—**~ a otro** one another:—**~ a ~** one by one:—**a una** jointly together.
untar *vt* to anoint; to grease; (*fam*) to bribe.
urbanidad *f* urbanity, politeness.
urbanismo *m* town planning.
urbanización *f* housing estate.
urdir *vt* to warp; to contrive.
urgencia *f* urgency; emergency; need, necessity.
urinario/ria *adj* urinary:—*m* urinal.
urna *f* urn; ballot box.
urraca *f* magpie.
usado/da *adj* used; experienced; worn.
usar *vt* to use, make use of; to wear: —**~se** *vr* to be used.
usted *pn* you.
usuario *m* user.
útero *m* uterus, womb.
util *adj* useful, profitable:—*m* utility.
utilizar *vt* to use; to make useful.
uva *f* grape.

V

vaca *f* cow; beef.
vacaciones *fpl* vacation; holidays *pl*.
vacante *adj* vacant:—*f* vacancy.
vaciar *vt* to empty, clear; to mold:—*vi* to fall, decrease (of waters):—**~se** *vr* to empty.
vacilar *vi* to hesitate; to falter; to fail.
vacío/cía *adj* void, empty; unoccupied; concave; vain; presumptuous: —*m* vacuum; emptiness.
vacuna *f* vaccine.
vacuno/na *adj* bovine, cow *compd*.
vagar *vi* to rove or loiter about; to wander.
vago/ga *adj* vagrant; restless; vague.
vagón *m* (*ferro*) wagon; carriage:—**~ de mercancias** goods wagon.
vaho *m* steam, vapor.
vaina *f* pod, husk.
vaivén *m* fluctuation, instability; giddiness.
vajilla *f* crockery.
vale *m* OK; promissory note, IOU.
valer *vi* to be valuable; to be deserving; to cost; to be valid; to be worth; to produce; to be current:—*vt* to protect, favor; to be worth; to be equivalent to:—**~se** *vr* to employ, make use of; to have recourse to.
valiente *adj* robust, vigorous; valiant, brave; boasting.
valija *f* suitcase.
valioso/sa *adj* valuable.
valla *f* fence; hurdle; barricade.
valle *m* valley.
valor *m* value; price; validity; force; power; courage, valor.
valorar *vt* to value; to evaluate.
vals *m invar* waltz.
valsar *vi* to waltz
válvula *f* valve.
vanidoso/sa *adj* vain, showy; haughty; conceited.
vano/na *adj* vain; useless, frivolous; arrogant; futile:—**en ~** in vain.
vapor *m* vapor, steam; breath.
vaquero *m* cow-herd:—**~/ra** *adj* belonging to a cowman:—**~s** *mpl* jeans *pl*.
vara *f* rod; pole, staff; stick.
variar *vt* to vary; to modify; to change: —*vi* to vary.
varices *fpl* varicose veins *pl*.
varilla *f* small rod; curtain rod; spindle, pivot.
vario/ria *adj* varied, different; vague; variegated:—**~s** *pl* some; several.
varón *m* man, male.
vasco/ca *adj*, *m/f* Basque.
vasija *f* vessel.
vaso *m* glass; vessel; vase.
vástago *m* bud, shoot; offspring.
vasto/ta *adj* vast, huge.
vaticinar *vt* to divine, foretell.
vatio *m* watt.
vecindad *f* inhabitants of a place; neighborhood.
vecino/na *adj* neighboring; near:—*m* neighbor, inhabitant.
veinte *adj*, *m* twenty.
veintena *f* twentieth part; score.

vejar *vt* to vex; to humiliate.
vejez *f* old age.
vejiga *f* bladder.
vela *f* watch; watchfulness; night-guard; candle; sail:—**hacerse a la ~** to set sail.
velar *vi* to stay awake; to be attentive: —*vt* to guard, watch.
velero/ra *adj* swift-sailing.
veleta *f* weather cock.
vello *m* down; gossamer; short downy hair.
velo *m* veil; pretext.
velocidad *f* speed; velocity.
vena *f* vein.
venado *m* deer; venison.
vencer *vt* to defeat; to conquer, vanquish:—*vi* to win; to expire.
vendaje *m* bandage, dressing for wounds.
vendaval *m* gale.
vender *vt* to sell.
vendimia *f* grape harvest; vintage.
vendimiar *vt* to harvest, gather; to profit from (something).
veneno *m* poison, venom.
venerar *vt* to venerate, worship.
vengar *vt* to revenge, avenge:—**~se** *vr* to take revenge.
venida *f* arrival; return; overflow of a river.
venidero/ra *adj* future:—**~s** *mpl* posterity.
venir *vi* to come, arrive; to follow, succeed; to happen; to spring from: —**~se** *vr* to ferment.
venta *f* sale.
ventaja *f* advantage.
ventana *f* window; window shutter; nostril.
ventilar *vt* to ventilate; to fan; to discuss.
ventisca *f*, **ventisco** *m* snowstorm.
ventosidad *f* flatulence.
ventura *f* happiness; luck, chance, fortune: —**por ~** by chance.
ver *vt* to see, look at; to observe; to visit:—*vi* to understand; to see:—**~se** *vr* to be seen; to be conspicuous; to find oneself: —**~se con uno** to have a bone to pick with someone: —*m* sense of sight; appearance.
veraneo *m* summer vacation.
verano *m* summer.
veras *fpl* truth, sincerity:—**de ~** in truth, really.
veraz *adj* truthful.
verbena *f* fair; dance.
verdad *f* truth, veracity; reality; reliability.
verdadero/ra *adj* true; real; sincere.
verde *m*, *adj* green.
verdura *f* verdure; vegetables *pl*, greens *pl*.
vereda *f* path, trail; sidewalk.
vergüenza *f* shame; bashfulness; confusion.
verificar *vt* to check, verify:—**~se** *vr* to happen.
verruga *f* wart.
vertedero *m* sewer, drain; tip.
verter *vt* to pour; to spill; to empty:—*vi* to flow.
vértice *m* vertex, zenith; crown (head).
vertiente *f* slope; waterfall, cascade.
vertiginoso/sa *adj* giddy.
vespertino/na *adj* evening *compd*.
vestíbulo *m* vestibule, lobby.
vestido *m* dress; clothes *pl*.
vestir *vt* to put on; to wear; to dress; to adorn; to cloak, disguise:—*vi* to dress: —**~se** to get dressed.
vestuario *m* clothes *pl*; uniform; vestry; changing room.
veta *f* vein (in mines, wood, etc); streak; grain.
veteado/da *adj* veined; striped:—*m* veining; streaks.
veterano/na *adj* experienced, practiced: —*m* veteran, old soldier.
veterinaría *f* veterinary medicine.
veterinario/ria *m/f* veterinary surgeon.
vez *f* time; turn; return:—**cada ~** each time: —**una ~** once:—**a veces** sometimes, by turns.
veza *f* (*bot*) vetch.
vía *f* way; road, route; mode, manner, method; (*ferro*) railway line.
viajante *m* sales representative.
viajar *vi* to travel.
víbora *f* viper.
vibrar *vt*, *vi* to vibrate.
vicio *m* vice.
vid *f* (*bot*) vine.
vida *f* life.
vídeo *m* video.
vidriera *f* stained-glass window; shop window.
vidrio *m* glass.
vieira *f* scallop.
viejo/ja *adj* old; ancient, antiquated.
viento *m* wind; air.
vientre *m* belly.
viernes *m invar* Friday:—**V ~ Santo** Good Friday.
viga *f* beam; girder.
vigente *adj* in force.
vigésimo/ma *adj*, *m* twentieth.
vigía *f* (*mar*) lookout:—*m* watchman.
vigilar *vt* to watch over:—*vi* to keep watch.
vil *adj* mean, sordid, low; worthless; infamous; ungrateful.
vilipendiar *vt* to despise, revile.
villancico *m* Christmas carol.

vilo: —**en ~** *adv* in the air; in suspense.
vinagre *m* vinegar.
vincular *vt* to link.
viñedo *m* vineyard.
vino *m* wine:—**~ tinto** red wine.
violar *vt* to rape; to violate; to profane.
violentar *vt* to force.
violento/ta *adj* violent; forced; absurd; embarrassing.
violeta *f* violet.
violón *m* double bass.
virar *vi* to swerve.
viril *adj* virile, manly.
virtud *f* virtue.
viruela *f* smallpox.
visa *f*, **visado** *m* visa.
viscoso/sa *adj* viscous, glutinous.
visillos *mpl* net curtains *pl*.
visión *f* sight, vision; fantasy.
visitar *vt* to visit.
vislumbrar *vt* to catch a glimpse of; to perceive indistinctly.
visón *m* mink.
víspera *f* eve; evening before:—**~s** *pl* vespers.
vista *f* sight, view; vision; eyesight; appearance; looks *pl*; prospect; intention; (*jur*) trial:—*m* customs officer.
vistazo *m* glance.
vistoso/sa *adj* colorful, attractive, lively.
vitalicio/cia *adj* for life.
vitorear *vt* to shout, applaud.
vitrina *f* showcase.
viudo/a *f* widower, widow.
vivaz *adj* lively.
víveres *mpl* provisions.
vivero *m* nursery (for plants); fish farm.
vivienda *f* housing; flat, apartment.
viviente *adj* living.
vivir *vt* to live through; to go through: —*vi* to live; to last.
vivo/va *adj* alive; lively:—**al ~** to the life; very realistically.
vocablo *m* word, term.
vocal *f* vowel:—*m/f* member (of a committee):—*adj* vocal, oral.
vociferar *vt* to shout; to proclaim in a loud voice:—*vi* to yell.
volante *adj* flying:—*m* (*auto*) steering wheel; note; pamphlet; shuttlecock.
volar *vi* to fly; to pass swiftly (of time); to rush, hurry:—*vt* to blow up, explode.
volcán *m* volcano.
volcar *vt* to upset, overturn; to make giddy; to empty out; to exasperate:—**~se** *vr* to tip over.
volquete *m* tipcart; dump truck.
voltear *vt* to turn over; to overturn:—*vi* to roll over, tumble.
voltereta *f* tumble; somersault.
voluble *adj* unpredictable; fickle.
volumen *m* volume; size.
voluntad *f* will, willpower; wish, desire.
volver *vt* to turn (over); to turn upside down; to turn inside out:—*vi* to return, go back:—**~se** *vr* to turn around.
vórtice *m* whirlpool.
vos *pn* you.
vosotros/tras *pn pl* you.
votar *vi* to vow; to vote.
voz *f* voice; shout; rumor; word, term.
vuelo *m* flight; wing; projection of a building; ruffle, frill:—**cazar al ~** to catch in flight:—**~ chárter** charter flight.
vuelta *f* turn; circuit; return; row of stitches; cuff; change; bend, curve; reverse, other side; return journey.
vuestro/tra *adj* your:—*pn* yours.

WXYZ

xenofobia *f* xenophobia.
xilófono *m* xylophone.
y *conj* and.
ya *adv* already; now; immediately; at once; soon:—*conj* **~ que** since, seeing that:—**¡~!** of course!, sure!
yacimiento *m* deposit.
yate *m* yacht, sailing boat.
yedra *f* ivy.
yegua *f* mare.
yema *f* bud; leaf; yolk:—**~ del dedo** tip of the finger.
yerno *m* son-in-law.
yeso *m* gypsum; plaster:—**~ mate** plaster of Paris.
yo *pn* I:—**~ mismo** I myself.
yodo *m* iodine.
yogur *m* yogurt.
yunque *m* anvil.
yute *m* jute.
zafiro *m* sapphire.
zaguán *m* porch, hall.
zalamero/ra *adj* flattering:—*m/f* wheedler.
zamarra *f* sheepskin (jacket).

zambullirse *vr* to plunge into water, dive.
zampar *vt* to gobble down; to put away hurriedly:—**~se** *vr* to thrust oneself suddenly into any place; to crash, hurtle.
zanahoria *f* carrot.
zancada *f* stride.
zancudo/da *adj* long legged:—*m* mosquito.
zángano *m* drone; idler, slacker.
zanja *f* ditch, trench.
zapata *f* boot:—**~ de freno** (*auto*) brake shoe.
zapatilla *f* slipper; pump (shoe); (*dep*) trainer, training shoe.
zapato *m* shoe.
zarandear *vt* to shake vigorously.
zarcillo *m* earring; tendril.
zarpar *vi* to weigh anchor.
zarza *f* bramble.
zarzuela *f* Spanish light opera.
zócalo *m* plinth, base; baseboard.
zona *f* zone; area, belt.
zopenco/ca *adj* dull, very stupid.
zoquete *m* block; crust of bread; (*fam*) blockhead.
zorro/a *m* fox; cunning person.
zozobrar *vi* (*mar*) to founder; to capsize; (*fig*) to fail; to be anxious.
zueco *m* wooden shoe; clog.
zumbar *vt* to hit:—**~se** *vr* to hit each other:—*vi* to buzz.
zumo *m* juice.
zurcir *vt* to darn; (*fig*) to join, unite; to hatch (lies).
zurdo/da *adj* left; left-handed.
zurrar *vt* (*fam*) to flog, lay into; (*fig*) to criticize harshly.

English–Spanish

A

a *art* un, uno, una:—*prep* a, al, en.
abandon *vt* abandonar, dejar.
abash *vt* avergonzar, causar confusión,
abbey *n* abadía *f*.
abbot *n* abad *m*.
abbreviate *vt* abreviar, acortar.
abbreviation *n* abreviatura *f*.
abdicate *vt* abdicar; renunciar.
abdication *n* abdicación *f*; renuncia *f*.
abdomen *n* abdomen, bajo vientre *m*.
abduct *vt* secuestrar.
aberration *n* error *m*; aberración *f*.
abet *vt*:—**to aid and ~** ser cómplice de.
abide *vt* soportar, sufrir.
ability *n* habilidad, capacidad.
ablaze *adj* en llamas.
able *adj* capaz, hábil.
able-bodied *adj* robusto/ta, vigoroso/sa.
ably *adv* con habilidad.
abnormal *adj* anormal.
abnormality *n* anormalidad *f*.
aboard *adv* a bordo.
abode *n* domicilio *m*.
abolish *vt* abolir, anular.
abolition *n* abolición, anulación *f*.
abominable *adj* abominable.
abomination *n* abominación *f*.
aboriginal *adj* aborigen.
abort *vi* abortar.
abortion *n* aborto *m*.
abound *vi* abundar.
about *prep* acerca de, acerca.
above *prep* encima.
aboveboard *adj* legitimo/ma.
abrasion *n* abrasión *f*.
abrasive *adj* abrasivo/va.
abroad *adv* en el extranjero.
abrupt *adj* brusco/ca.
abscess *n* absceso *m*.
abscond *vi* esconderse; huirse.
absence *n* ausencia *f*.
absent *adj* ausente.
absentee *n* ausente *m*.
absent-minded *adj* distraído/da.
absolute *adj* absoluto/ta.
absorb *vt* absorber.
abstain *vi* abstenerse.
abstinence *n* abstinencia *f*.
abstinent *adj* abstinente.
abstract *adj* abstracto/ta:—*n* extracto *m*.
abstraction *n* abstracción *f*.
absurd *adj* absurdo/da.
abundance *n* abundancia *f*.
abundant *adj* abundante.
abuse *vt* abusar; maltratar.
abusive *adj* abusivo/va, ofensivo/va.
abysmal *adj* abismal.
abyss *n* abismo *m*.
acacia *n* acacia *f*.
academic *adj* académico/ca.
academy *n* academia *f*.
accede *vi* acceder.
accelerate *vt* acelerar.
accelerator *n* acelerador *m*.
accent *n* acento *m*; tono *m*.
accentuate *vt* acentuar.
accept *vt* aceptar; admitir.
acceptable *adj* aceptable.
acceptance *n* aceptación *f*.
access *n* acceso *m*; entrada *f*.
accessible *adj* accesible.
accession *n* aumento.
accessory *n* accesorio *m*.
accident *n* accidente *m*; casualidad *f*.
acclaim *vt* aclamar, aplaudir.
accommodate *vt* alojar; complacer.
accommodation *n* alojamiento *m*.
accompany *vt* acompañar.
accomplice *n* cómplice *m*.
accomplish *vt* efectuar, completar.
accord *n* acuerdo, convenio *m*.
accordance *n*:—**in ~ with** de acuerdo con.
according *prep* segun, conforme.
accordion *n* (*mus*) acordeón *m*.
account *n* cuenta *f*.
accountability *n* responsabilidad *f*.
accountancy *n* contabilidad *f*.
accountant *n* contable, contador *m*.
accrue *vi* resultar, provenir.
accumulate *vt* acumular; amontonar.
accuracy *n* exactitud *f*.
accurate *adj* exacto/ta.
accursed *adj* maldito/ta.
accuse *vt* acusar; culpar.
accustom *vt* acostumbrar.
ache *n* dolor *m*:—*vi* doler.
achieve *vt* realizar; obtener.
achievement *n* realización *f*.
acid *adj* ácido/da; agrio/ria:—*n* ácido *m*.
acknowledge *vt* reconocer, confesar.
acne *n* acne *m*.
acorn *n* bellota *f*.
acoustics *n* acústica *f*.
acquaint *vt* informar, avisar.
acquaintance *n* conocimiento *m*; conocido *m*.
acquire *vt* adquirir.
acquisition *n* adquisición
acquit *vt* absolver.

acquittal *n* absolución *f*.
acre *n* acre *m*.
acrid *adj* acre.
acrimony *n* acrimonio *m*.
across *adv* de través.
action *n* acción *f*.
activate *vt* activar.
active *adj* activo/va.
activity *n* actividad *f*.
actor *n* actor *m*.
actress *n* actriz *f*.
actual *adj* real; efectivo/va.
actuary *n* actuario de seguros *m*.
acumen *n* agudeza *f*.
acute *adj* agudo/da; ingenioso/sa.
ad *n* aviso *m*.
adage *n* proverbio *m*.
adamant *adj* inflexible.
adapt *vt* adaptar.
adaptor *n* adaptador *m*.
add *vt* añadir, agregar:—**to ~ up** sumar.
adder *n* culebra *f*; víbora *f*.
addict *n* drogadicto *m*.
addiction *n* dependencia *f*.
addition *n* adición *f*.
additional *adj* adicional.
additive *n* aditivo *m*.
address *vt* dirigir:—*n* dirección *f*.
adenoids *npl* vegetaciones adenoideas *fpl*.
adept *adj* hábil.
adequacy *n* suficiencia *f*.
adequate *adj* adecuado/da; suficiente.
adhere *vi* adherir.
adhesion *n* adhesión *f*.
adhesive *adj* pegajoso/sa.
adhesiveness *n* adhesividad *f*.
adieu *adv* adiós:—*n* despedida *f*.
adjacent *adj* adyacente, contiguo/gua.
adjective *n* adjetivo *m*.
adjoining *adj* contiguo/gua.
adjournment *n* prorroga *f*.
adjudicate *vt* adjudicar.
adjust *vt* ajustar, acomodar.
adjustable *adj* ajustable.
adjustment *n* ajustamiento *m*.
ad lib *vt* improvisar.
administer *vt* administrar.
administration *n* administración *f*.
administrative *adj* administrativo/va.
admirable *adj* admirable.
admiral *n* almirante *m*.
admire *vt* admirar.
admirer *n* admira/a *m/f*.
admission *adj* entrada *f*.
admit *vt* admitir.
admittance *n* entrada *f*.
admittedly *adj* de acuerdo que.
admonish *vt* amonestar.
ad nauseam *adv* hasta el cansancio.
adolescence *n* adolescencia *f*.
adopt *vt* adoptar.
adorable *adj* adorable.
adore *vt* adorar.
adorn *vt* adornar.
adrift *adv* a la deriva.
adult *adj* adulto/ta.
adulterate *vt* adulterar, corromper.
adulterer *n* adultero *m*.
adultery *n* adulterio *m*.
advance *vt* avanzar; promover.
advantage *n* ventaja *f*.
advantageous *adj* ventajoso/sa.
adventure *n* aventura *f*.
adventurous *adj* intrépido/da.
adverb *n* adverbio *m*.
adversary *n* adversario enemigo *m*.
adversity *n* calamidad *f*; infortunio *m*.
advertise *vt* anunciar.
advertisement *n* aviso *m*.
advice *n* consejo *m*; aviso *m*.
advisability *n* prudencia *f*.
advise *vt* aconsejar; avisar.
advocacy *n* defensa *f*.
advocate *n* abogado *m*; protector *m*.
aerial *n* antena *f*.
aerobics *npl* aerobic *m*.
aerometer *n* areómetro *m*.
aerosol *n* aerosol *m*.
afar *adv* lejos, distante.
affair *n* asunto *m*; negocio *m*.
affect *vt* conmover; afectar.
affection *n* cariño *m*.
affidavit *n* declaración jurada *f*.
affiliate *vt* afiliar.
affiliation *n* afiliación *f*.
affinity *n* afinidad *f*.
affirm *vt* afirmar, declarar.
affirmation *n* afirmación *f*.
affirmative *adj* afirmativo/va.
affix *vt* pegar:—*n* (*gr*) afijo *m*.
afflict *vt* afligir.
affliction *n* aflicción *f*; dolor *m*.
affluence *n* opulencia *f*.
affluent *adj* opulento/ta.
affray *n* asalto *m*; tumulto *m*.
aflame *adv* en llamas.
afloat *adv* flotante, a flote.
afore *prep* antes:—*adv* primero.
afraid *adj* espantado/da.
afresh *adv* de nuevo, otra vez.
after *prep* después.
afterbirth *n* secundinas *fpl*.
after-effects *npl* consecuencias *fpl*.
afterlife *n* vida venidera *f*.

aftermath *n* consecuencias *fpl*.
afternoon *n* tarde *f*.
aftershave *n* aftershave *m*.
aftertaste *n* resabio *m*.
afterwards *adv* después.
again *adv* otra vez.
against *prep* contra.
agate *n* ágata *f*.
age *n* edad *f*; vejez *f*.
agency *n* agencia *f*.
agenda *n* orden del día *m*.
agent *n* agente *m*.
aggrandizement *n* engrandecimiento *m*.
aggravate *vt* agravar, exagerar.
aggregate *n* agregado *m*.
aggregation *n* agregación *f*.
aggression *n* agresión *f*.
aggressor *n* agresor *m*.
aggrieved *adj* ofendido/da.
aghast *adj* horrorizado/da.
agile *adj* ágil; diestro/tra.
agitate *vt* agitar.
ago *adv* pasado.
agonizing *adj* atngustioso.
agony *n* agonía *f*.
agree *vt* convenir:—*vi* estar de acuerdo/da.
agreeable *adj* agradable; amable.
agreement *n* acuerdo *m*.
agriculture *n* agricultura *f*.
ah! *excl* ¡ah! ¡ay!
ahead *adv* más allá, delante de otro.
aid *vt* ayudar, socorrer.
AIDS *n* SIDA *m*.
ail *vt* afligir, molestar.
ailment *n* dolencia, indisposición *f*.
aim *vt* apuntar aspirar a; intentar.
air *n* aire *m*:—*vt* airear; ventilar.
air balloon *n* globo aerostático *m*.
airborne *adj* aerotransportado/da.
air-conditioning *n* climatización *f*.
aircraft *n* avión *m*.
air force *n* fuerzas aéreas *fpl*.
airline *n* línea aérea *f*.
airmail *n*:—**by ~** por avión,
airplane *n* avión *m*.
airport *n* aeropuerto *m*.
airstrip *n* pista de aterrizaje *f*.
airy *adj* bien ventilado/da.
aisle *n* nave de una iglesia *f*.
akin *adj* parecido/da.
alabaster *n* alabastro *m*.
alarm *n* alarma *f*:—*vt* alarmar; inquietar.
alas *adv* desgraciadamente.
albeit *conj* aunque.
album *n* album *m*.
alchemy *n* alquimia *f*.
alcohol *n* alcohol *m*.
alcoholic *adj* alcohólico/ca:—*n* alcoholizado *m*.
alcove *n* nicho *m*.
alder *n* aliso *m*.
ale *n* cerveza *f*.
alert *adj* vigilante; alerto/ta.
algae *npl* alga *f*.
algebra *n* álgebra *f*.
alias *adj* alias.
alibi *n* (*law*) coartada *f*.
alien *adj* ajeno/na.
alienate *vt* enajenar.
alight *vi* apearse.
align *vt* alinear.
alike *adj* semejante, igual.
alive *adj* vivo/va, viviente; activo/va.
alkali *n* álcali *m*.
alkaline *adj* alcalino/na.
all *adj* todo/da.
allay *vt* aliviar.
allegation *n* alegación *f*.
allege *vt* alegar; declarar.
allegiance *n* lealtad, fidelidad *f*.
allegorical *adj* alegórico/ca.
allegory *n* alegoría *f*.
allergy *n* alergia *f*.
alley *n* callejuela *f*.
alliance *n* alianza *f*.
allied *adj* aliado/da.
alligator *n* caimán *m*.
allocate *vt* repartir.
allot *vt* asignar.
allow *vt* conceder; permitir; dar.
allowance *n* concesión *f*.
alloy *n* liga, mezcla *f*.
allspice *n* pimienta de Jamaica *f*.
allude *vt* aludir.
allure *n* fascinación *f*.
allusion *n* alusión *f*.
allusive *adj* alusivo/va.
alluvial *adj* aluvial.
ally *n* aliado *m*:—*vt* aliar.
almanac *n* almanaque *m*.
almighty *adj* omnipotente, todopoderoso/sa.
almond *n* almendra *f*.
almost *adv* casi; cerca de.
aloft *prep* arriba.
alone *adj* solo.
along *adv* a lo largo.
aloof *adv* lejos.
alphabet *n* alfabeto *m*.
alphabetical *adj* alfabético/ca.
alpine *adj* alpino/na.
already *adv* ya.
also *adv* también, además.
altar *n* altar *m*.
altarpiece *n* retablo *m*.

alter *vt* modificar.
alteration *n* alteración *f.*
alternate *adj* alterno/na:—*vt* alternar, variar.
alternator *n* alternador *m.*
alternative *n* alternativa *f.*
although *conj* aunque, no obstante.
altitude *n* altitud, altura *f.*
altogether *adv* del todo.
aluminum *n* aluminio *m.*
always *adv* siempre, constantemente.
a.m. *adv* de la mañana.
amalgam *n* amalgama *f.*
amalgamate *vt vi* amalgamar(se).
amaryllis *n* (*bot*) amarillas *f.*
amass *vt* acumular, amontonar.
amateur *n* aficionado *m.*
amateurish *adj* torpe.
amaze *vt* asombrar.
amazon *n* amazona *f.*
ambassador *n* embajador *m.*
amber *n* ámbar *m.*
ambidextrous *adj* ambidextro/tra.
ambiguity *n* ambigüedad, duda *f.*
ambiguous *adj* ambiguo:—**~ly** *adv* ambiguamente.
ambition *n* ambición *f.*
amble *vi* andar sin prisa.
ambulance *n* ambulancia *f.*
ambush *n* emboscada *f.*
amenable *adj* sensible.
amend *vt* enmendar.
amendment *n* enmienda *f.*
amends *npl* compensación *f.*
amenities *npl* comodidades *fpl.*
America *n* América *f.*
amethyst *n* amatista *f.*
amiable *adj* amable.
amiableness *n* amabilidad *f.*
amiably *adv* amablemente.
amicable *adj* amigable.
amid(st) *prep* entre, en medio de.
amiss *adv*:—**something's ~** pasa algo malo.
ammonia *n* amoníaco *m.*
ammunition *n* municiones *fpl.*
amnesia *n* amnesia *f.*
amnesty *n* amnistía *f.*
amoral *adv* amoral.
amorous *adj* amoroso/sa.
amount *n* importe *m*; cantidad *f.*
amp(ere) *n* amperio *m.*
amphibian *n* anfibio *m.*
amphibious *adj* anfibio/bia.
amphitheater *n* anfiteatro *m.*
ample *adj* amplio/lia.
ampleness *n* amplitud, abundancia *f.*
amplifier *n* amplificador *m*
amplify *vt* ampliar, extender.
amplitude *n* amplitud, extensión *f.*
amputate *vt* amputar.
amuse *vt* entretener, divertir.
amusement *n* diversión *f.*
amusing *adj* divertido/da.
an *art* un, uno, una.
anachronism *n* anacronismo *m.*
anemia *n* anemia *f.*
anesthetic *n* anestesia *f.*
analogy *n* analogía *f.*
analyse *vt* analizar.
anarchy *n* anarquía *f.*
anatomical *adj* anatómico/ca.
anatomy *n* anatomía *f*
ancestor *n*:—**~s** *pl* antepasados *mpl.*
ancestral *adj* hereditario/ria.
ancestry *n* raza, alcurnia *f.*
anchor *n* ancla *f*:—*vi* anclar.
anchovy *n* anchoa *f.*
ancient *adj* antiguo.
and *conj* y, e.
anecdote *n* anécdota *f*
anemone *n* (*bot*) anémona *f*
angel *n* ángel *m*
anger *n* cólera *f*:—*vt* enojar, irritar.
angle *n* ángulo *m*:—*vt* pescar con cana.
anglicism *n* anglicismo *m.*
angry *adj* enojado/da.
anguish *n* ansia, angustia *f*
angular *adj* angular.
animal *n adj* animal *m.*
animation *n* animación *f*
aniseed *n* anís *m*
ankle *n* tobillo *m.*
annals *n* anales *mpl.*
annex *vt* anejar:—*n* anejo *m.*
annihilate *vt* aniquilar.
annihilation *n* aniquilación *f.*
anniversary *n* aniversario *m.*
annotate *vi* anotar.
announce *vt* anunciar, publicar.
announcement *n* anuncio *m.*
annoy *vt* molestar.
annual *adj* anual.
annunciation *n* anunciación *f*
anoint *vt* untar, ungir.
anomaly *n* anomalía, irregularidad *f.*
anon *adv* más tarde.
anonymity *n* anonimato *m.*
anonymous *adj* anónimo/ma.
anorexia *n* anorexia *f.*
another *adj* otro/tra.
answer *vt* responder.
answering machine *n* contestador automático *m.*
ant *n* hormiga *f.*
antagonize *vt* provocar.

antarctic *adj* antártico/ca.
antelope *n* antílope *m*.
antenna *npl* antena *f*.
anterior *adj* anterior, precedente.
anthem *n* himno *m*.
anthology *n* antología *f*.
anthropology *n* antropología *f*
antibiotic *n* antibiótico *m*.
antibody *n* anticuerpo *m*.
Antichrist *n* Anticristo *m*.
anticipate *vt* anticipar, prevenir.
anticipation *n* anticipación *f*.
antidote *n* antídoto *m*.
antipodes *npl* antípodas *fpl*
antiquarian *n* anticuario *m*.
antiquated *adj* antiguo/gua.
antiquity *n* antigüedad *f*.
antiseptic *adj* antiséptico/ca.
antler *n* cuerna *f*.
anvil *n* yunque *m*.
anxiety *n* ansiedad, ansia *f*.
anxious *adj* ansioso/sa.
any *adj pn* cualquier, cualquiera; alguno, alguna
apart *adv* aparte, separadamente.
apartment *n* departamento *m*.
apathy *n* apatía *f*.
ape *n* mono *m*.
apologize *vt* disculpar.
apology *n* apología, defensa *f*.
apostrophe *n* apóstrofe *m*.
appall *vt* espantar, aterrar.
apparatus *n* aparato *m*.
apparent *adj* evidente, aparente.
apparition *n* aparición, visión *f*.
appeal *vi* apelar.
appear *vi* aparecer.
appease *vt* aplacar.
append *vt* anejar.
appendicitis *n* apendicitis *f*.
appendix *n* apéndice *m*.
appetite *n* apetito *m*.
applaud *vi* aplaudir.
apple *n* manzana *f*.
appliance *n* aparato *m*.
applicable *adj* aplicable.
applicant *n* aspirante, candidato *m*.
application *n* aplicación *f*; solicitud *f*.
applied *adj* aplicado/da.
apply *vt* aplicar.
appoint *vt* nombrar.
appointment *n* cita *f*; nombramiento *m*.
apportion *vt* repartir.
appraisal *n* estimación *f*.
appraise *vt* tasar; estimar.
appreciate *vt* apreciar; agradecer.
apprehend *vt* arrestar.
apprehension *n* aprensión *f*.
apprehensive *adj* aprensivo/va.
apprentice *n* aprendiz *m*.
approach *vt vi* aproximar(se).
appropriate *vt* apropiarse de:—*adj* apropiado/da.
approve (of) *vt* aprobar.
April *n* abril *m*.
apron *n* delantal *m*.
apse *n* ábside *m*.
apt *adj* apto/ta, idóneo/nea.
aptitude *n* aptitud *f*.
aquarium *n* acuario *m*.
Aquarius *n* Acuario *m*.
aqueduct *n* acueducto *m*.
arable *adj* labrantío/tía.
arbitrate *vt* arbitrar.
arcade *n* galería *f*.
arch *n* arco *m*.
archeology *n* arqueología *f*.
archaic *adj* arcaico/ca.
archbishop *n* arzobispo *m*.
archer *n* arquero *m*.
architect *n* arquitecto/ta *m/f*.
architecture *n* arquitectura *f*.
archives *npl* archivos *mpl*.
arctic *adj* ártico/ca.
area *n* área *f*; espacio *m*.
arena *n* arena *f*.
arguably *adv* posiblemente.
argue *vi* discutir.
argument *n* argumento *m*, controversia *f*.
arid *adj* árido/da, estéril.
aridity *n* sequedad *f*.
Aries *n* Aries *m*.
arise *vi* levantarse.
aristocracy *n* aristocracia *f*.
arithmetic *n* aritmética *f*.
ark *n* arca *f*.
arm *n* brazo *m*; arma *f*.
armament *n* armamento *m*.
armchair *n* sillón *m*.
armor *n* armadura *f*.
armpit *n* sobaco *m*.
army *n* ejercito *m*.
aroma *n* aroma *m*.
around *prep* alrededor de.
arouse *vt* despertar; excitar.
arraign *vt* acusar.
arraignment *n* acusación *f*; proceso criminal *m*.
arrange *vt* organizar.
arrangement *n* colocación *f*; arreglo.
arrant *adj* consumado/da.
array *n* serie *f*.
arrears *npl* resto de una deuda *m*; atraso *m*.
arrest *n* arresto *m*:—*vt* detener, arrestar.

arrival *n* llegada *f*.
arrive *vi* llegar.
arrogance *n* arrogancia, presunción *f*.
arrogant *adj* arrogante, presuntuoso/sa:—~**ly** *adv* arrogantemente.
arrogate *vt* arrogarse.
arrogation *n* arrogación *f*.
arrow *n* flecha *f*.
arsenal *n* (*mil*) arsenal *m*; (*mar*) atarazana, armería *f*.
arsenic *n* arsénico *m*.
art *n* arte *m*.
arterial *adj* arterial.
artery *n* arteria *f*.
artful *adj* ingenioso/sa.
art gallery *n* pinacoteca *f*.
arthritis *n* artritis *f*.
artichoke *n* alcachofa *f*.
article *n* articulo *m*.
articulate *vt* articular.
artifice *n* artificio *m*.
artillery *n* artillería *f*.
artisan *n* artesano/na *m/f*.
artist *n* artista *m*.
artistry *n* habilidad *f*.
artless *adj* sencillo, simple.
artlessness *n* sencillez *f*.
as *conj* como; mientras.
asbestos *n* asbesto *m*.
ascend *vi* ascender, subir.
ascribe *vt* atribuir.
ash *n* (*bot*) fresno *m*; ceniza *f*
ashamed *adj* avergonzado/da.
ashtray *n* cenicero *m*.
Ash Wednesday *n* miércoles de ceniza *m*.
ask *vt* pedir, rogar, preguntar por.
askew *adv* de lado.
asleep *adj* dormido/da.
asparagus *n* espárrago *m*.
aspect *n* aspecto *m*.
aspen *n* álamo temblón *m*.
asphalt *n* asfalto *m*.
asphyxia *n* (*med*) asfixia *f*.
asphyxiate *vt* asfixiar.
asphyxiation *n* asfixia *f*.
aspiration *n* aspiración *f*.
aspire *vi* aspirar, desear.
aspirin *n* aspirina *f*.
ass *n* asno *m*:—**she** ~ burra *f*.
assassin *n* asesino *m*.
assassinate *vt* asesinar.
assault *n* asalto *m*.
assemble *vt* reunir, convocar.
assembly *n* asamblea *f*.
assert *vt* sostener, mantener.
assess *vt* valorar.
assessment *n* valoración *f*.
assets *npl* bienes *mpl*.
assign *vt* asignar.
assimilate *vt* asimilar.
assist *vt* asistir, ayudar.
assistance *n* asistencia *f*.
assistant *n* asistente, ayudante *m*.
associate *vt* asociar.
association *n* asociación, sociedad *f*.
assortment *n* surtido *m*.
assume *vt* asumir; suponer.
assurance *n* seguro *m*.
assure *vt* asegurar.
asterisk *n* asterisco *m*.
asthma *n* asma *f*.
asthmatic *adj* asmático/ca.
astonish *vt* pasmar, sorprender.
astringent *adj* astringente.
astrologer *n* astrólogo/ga *m/f*.
astrology *n* astrología *f*.
astronaut *n* astronauta *m/f*.
astronomer *n* astrónomo *m*.
astronomy *n* astronomía *f*.
astute *adj* astuto/ta.
asylum *n* asilo, refugio *m*.
at *prep* a; en.
atheism *n* ateísmo *m*.
atheist *n* ateo *m*, atea *f*.
athlete *n* atleta *m/f*.
atlas *n* atlas *m*.
atmosphere *n* atmósfera *f*.
atom *n* átomo *m*.
atomic *adj* atómico/ca.
atrocious *adj* atroz.
atrocity *n* atrocidad, enormidad *f*.
attach *vt* adjuntar.
attaché *n* agregado *m*.
attack *vt* atacar; acometer.
attempt *vt* intentar; probar, experimentar.
attend *vt* servir; asistir.
attendant *n* sirviente *m*.
attention *n* atención *f*; cuidado *m*.
attentive *adj* atento/ta; cuidadoso/sa.
attest *vt* atestiguar.
attic *n* desván *m*; guardilla *f*.
attorney *n* abogado *m*.
attract *vt* atraer.
attraction *n* atracción *f*; atractivo *m*.
auburn *adj* moreno/na, castaño/ña.
auction *n* subasta *f*.
auctioneer *n* subastador/a.
audacious *adj* audaz.
audible *adj* perceptible al oído.
audience *n* audiencia *f*.
audit *n* auditoría *f*.
augment *vt* aumentar, acrecentar.
August *n* agosto *m*.
august *adj* augusto/a.

aunt *n* tia *f*.
au pair *n* au pair *f*.
aura *n* aura *f*.
auspicious *adj* propicio/cia.
austere *adj* austero/ra, severo/ra;
authentic *adj* auténtico/ca.
authenticate *vt* autenticar.
authenticity *n* autenticidad *f*.
author *n* autor *m*; escritor *m*.
authorization *n* autorización *f*.
authorize *vt* autorizar.
authority *n* autoridad *f*.
auto *n* carro, coche *m*.
autograph *n* autógrafo *m*.
automatic *adj* automático/ca.
autonomy *n* autonomía *f*.
autopsy *n* autopsia *f*.
auxiliary *adj* auxiliar, asistente.
available *adj* disponible.
avalanche *n* alud *m*.
avarice *n* avaricia *f*.
avenue *n* avenida *f*.
avert *vt* desviar, apartar.
aviary *n* pajarera *f*.
avoid *vt* evitar, escapar.
await *vt* aguardar.
awake *vt* despertar.
award *vt* otorgar:—*n* premio *m*.
aware *adj* consciente; vigilante.
away *adv* ausente, fuera.
awe *n* miedo, temor *m*.
awful *adj* tremendo/da; horroroso/sa.
awhile *adv* un rato, algún tiempo.
awkward *adj* torpe, rudo/da.
awning *n* (*mar*) toldo *m*.
awry *adv* oblicuamente, torcidamente.
axe *n* hacha *f*.
axiom *n* axioma *m*.
axis *n* eje *m*.
axle *n* eje *m*.

B

baboon *n* cinocéfalo *m*.
baby *n* niño pequeño *m*.
bachelor *n* soltero *m*; bachiller *m*.
back *n* dorso *m*.
backbone *n* hueso dorsal, espinazo *m*.
backer *n* partidario/ria *m*.
backgammon *n* juego de chaquete o tablas *m*.
background *n* fondo *m*.
backlash *n* reacción *f*.
backpack *n* mochila *f*.
backside *n* trasero *m*.
backward *adj* tardo/da, lento/ta.
bacon *n* tocino *m*.
bad *adj* mal, malo.
badge *n* señal *f*; símbolo *m*.
badger *n* tejón *m*.
badminton *n* bádminton *m*.
baffle *vt* confundir.
bag *n* saco *m*; bolsa *f*.
baggage *n* bagaje, equipaje *m*.
bail *n* fianza, caución (juratoria) *f*.
bailiff *n* alguacil *m*.
bake *vt* cocer en horno.
bakery *n* panadería *f*.
baking powder *n* levadura *f*.
balance *n* balanza *f*; equilibrio *m*.
balcony *n* balcón *m*.
bald *adj* calvo/va.
ball *n* bola *f*; pelota *f*; baile *m*.
ballad *n* balada *f*.
ballerina *n* bailarina *f*.
ballet *n* ballet *m*.
balloon *n* globo *m*.
ballpoint (pen) *n* bolígrafo *m*.
balm, balsam *n* bálsamo *m*.
balustrade *n* balaustrada *f*.
bamboo *n* bambú *m*.
ban *n* prohibición *f*.
banal *adj* vulgar.
banana *n* plátano *m*.
band *n* faja *f*; cuadrilla *f*.
bandage *n* venda *f*.
bandit *n* bandido/da *m/f*.
bang *n* golpe *m*.
bangle *n* brazalete *m*.
banister(s) *n*(*pl*) pasamanos *m*.
banjo *n* banjo *m*.
bank *n* orilla (de rió) *f*; montón de tierra *m*; banco *m*.
bank account *n* cuenta de banco *f*.
bankrupt *adj* insolvente.
banner *n* bandera *f*.
banquet *n* banquete *m*.
baptize *vt* bautizar.
bar *n* bar *m*; barra *f*.
barbecue *n* barbacoa *f*.
barber *n* peluquero *m*.
bare *adj* desnudo/da, descubierto/ta.
barely *adv* apenas.
bargain *n* ganga *f*.
barge *n* barcaza *f*.
bark *n* corteza *f*.
barley *n* cebada *f*.
barn *n* granero.
barometer *n* barómetro *m*.
baron *n* barón *m*.

barracks *npl* cuartel *m*.
barrel *n* barril *m*.
barren *adj* estéril, infructuoso/sa.
barrier *n* barrera *f*; obstáculo *m*.
barter *vi* baratar.
base *n* fondo *m*; base *f*; basa *f*.
baseball *n* béisbol *m*.
basement *n* sótano *m*.
basic *adj* básico/ca.
basin *n* jofaina, bacía *f*.
basis *n* base *f*; fundamento *m*.
basket *n* cesta, canasta *f*.
basketball *n* baloncesto *m*.
bastard *n*, *adj* bastardo/da *m/f*.
bat *n* murciélago *m*.
batch *n* serie *f*.
bath *n* baño *m*.
bathe *vt* (*vi*) bañar(se).
bathing suit *n* traje de baño *m*.
bathroom *n* (cuarto de) baño *m*.
baths *npl* piscina *f*.
battery *n* batería *f*.
battle *n* combate *m*.
bawdy *adj* indecente.
bay *n* bahía *f*; laurel.
bazaar *n* bazar *m*.
be *vi* ser; estar.
beach *n* playa, orilla *f*.
beacon *n* almenara *f*.
beagle *n* sabueso *m*.
beak *n* pico *m*.
beam *n* rayo de luz *m*; travesaño *m*.
bean *n* haba *f*.
beansprouts *npl* brotes de soja *mpl*.
bear *vt* llevar alguna cosa como carga; sostener; soportar.
bear *n* oso *m*.
beard *n* barba *f*.
bearer *n* portador/a *m/f*.
beast *n* bestia *f*.
beat *vt* golpear; tocar (un tambor).
beatify *vt* beatificar, santificar.
beautiful *adj* hermoso/sa, bello.
beauty *n* hermosura, belleza *f*.
because *conj* porque, a causa de.
bed *n* cama *f*.
bedroom *n* dormitorio *m*.
bee *n* abeja *f*.
beech *n* haya *f*.
beef *n* carne de vaca *f*.
beefburger *n* hamburguesa *f*.
beefsteak *n* bistec *m*.
beeline *n* línea recta *f*.
beer *n* cerveza *f*.
beetle *n* escarabajo *m*.
befall *vi* suceder, acontecer.
before *adv*, *prep* antes de; delante.
beg *vt* mendigar.
beggar *n* mendigo/ga *m/f*.
begin *vt vi* comenzar, empezar.
beginning *n* principio *m*.
begrudge *vt* envidiar.
behave *vi* comportarse.
behind *prep* detrás; atrás.
beige *adj* color beige.
belch *vi* eructar.
belief *n* fe, creencia *f*.
believe *vt* creer.
believer *n* creyente, fiel.
bell *n* campana *f*.
bellows *npl* fuelle *m*.
belly *n* vientre *m*; panza *f*.
belong *vi* pertenecer.
beloved *adj* querido/da, amado/da.
below *adv*, *prep* debajo, inferior; abajo.
belt *n* cinturón, cinto *m*.
bench *n* banco *m*.
bend *vt* encorvar, inclinar, plegar.
beneath *adv*, *prep* debajo, abajo.
benefit *n* beneficio *m*; utilidad *f*; provecho *m*.
benevolence *n* benevolencia *f*.
benevolent *adj* benévolo.
benign *adj* benigno/na.
bent *n* inclinación *f*.
bereave *vt* privar.
bereavement *n* perdida *f*.
beret *n* boina *f*.
berry *n* baya *f*.
beset *vt* acosar.
beside(s) *prep* al lado de; excepto.
best *adj* mejor.
bestial *adj* bestial, brutal.
bestow *vt* dar, conferir.
bestseller *n* bestseller *m*.
bet *n* apuesta *f*.
betray *vt* traicionar.
betroth *vt* contraer esponsales.
betting *n* juego *m*.
between *prep* entre, en medio de.
beverage *n* bebida *f*.
beware *vi* guardarse.
bewitch *vt* encantar, hechizar.
beyond *prep* más allá.
bias *n* propensión.
bib *n* babador *m*.
Bible *n* Biblia *f*.
bibliography *n* bibliografía *f*.
bicycle *n* bicicleta *f*.
bid *vt* mandar, ordenar; ofrecer.
biennial *adj* bienal.
bifocals *npl* anteojos bifocales *mpl*.
big *adj* grande, lleno/na.
bigamist *n* bígamo/ma *m/f*.
bigamy *n* bigamia *f*.

bigot *n* fanático/ca *m/f*.
bike *n* bici *f*.
bikini *n* bikini *m*.
bile *n* bilis *f*.
bilingual *adj* bilingüe.
bill *n* pico de ave *m*; billete.
billboard *n* cartelera *f*.
billet *n* alojamiento *m*.
billfold *n* cartera.
billiards *npl* billar *m*.
billion *n* billón *f*.
bin *n* cubo de la basura *m*.
binder *n* encuadernador/a *m/f*.
bingo *n* bingo *m*.
binoculars *npl* prismáticos *mpl*.
biographer *n* biógrafo/fa *m/f*.
biography *n* biografía *f*.
biological *adj* biológico/ca.
biology *n* biología *f*.
birch *n* abedul *m*.
bird *n* ave *f*; pájaro *m*.
birth *n* nacimiento *m*.
birthday *n* cumpleaños *m invar*.
biscuit *n* bizcocho *m*.
bishop *n* obispo *m*.
bit *n* bocado *m*; pedacito *m*.
bitch *n* perra *f*.
bite *vt* morder; picar.
bitter *adj* amargo/ga.
bitumen *n* betún *m*.
bizarre *adj* raro/ra.
blab *vi* chismear.
black *adj* negro/gra, oscuro/ra.
blackberry *n* zarzamora *f*.
blackbird *n* mirlo *m*.
blackboard *n* pizarra *f*.
blackmail *n* chantaje *m*:—*vt* chantajear.
blacksmith *n* herrero *m*.
bladder *n* vejiga *f*.
blade *n* hoja *f*; filo *m*.
blame *vt* culpar.
blameless *adj* inocente.
blank *adj* blanco/ca.
blanket *n* manta *f*.
blaspheme *vt* blasfemar, jurar.
blasphemy *n* blasfemia *f*.
blatant *adj* obvio.
blaze *n* llama *f*.
bleed *vi*, *vt* sangrar.
blemish *vt* manchar.
bless *vt* bendecir.
blessing *n* bendición *f*.
blight *vt* arruinar.
blind *adj* ciego/ga.
blink *vi* parpadear.
bliss *n* felicidad (eterna) *f*.
blister *n* ampolla *f*.
blitz *n* bombardeo aéreo *m*.
blizzard *n* huracán *m*.
bloated *adj* hinchado/da.
blob *n* gota *f*.
bloc *n* bloque *m*.
block *n* bloque *m*; obstáculo *m*.
blockade *n* bloqueo *m*:—*vt* bloquear.
blond *adj* rubio/bia.
blood *n* sangre *f*.
blood group *n* grupo sanguíneo *m*.
blood poisoning *n* envenenamiento de la sangre. *m*.
blood pressure *n* presión de sangre *f*.
blood sausage *n* morcilla *f*.
blood test *n* análisis de sangre *m*.
blood transfusion *n* transfusion de sangre *f*.
bloom *n* flor *f*; (*also fig*):—*vi* florecer.
blossom *n* flor *f*.
blot *vt* manchar.
blotchy *adj* muy manchado/da.
blouse *n* blusa *f*.
blow *vi* soplar; sonar.
blubber *n* grasa de ballena *f*.
blue *adj* azul.
bluebell *n* campanilla *f*.
blueprint *n* (*fig*) anteproyecto *m*.
blunder *n* desatino *m*.
blunt *adj* obtuso/sa; grosero/ra.
blush *n* rubor *m*; sonrojo *m*.
boar *n* verraco *m*:—**wild ~** jabalí *m*.
board *n* tabla *f*; mesa *f*.
boarder *n* pensionista *m*.
boarding card *n* tarjeta de embarque *f*.
boast *vi* jactarse.
boat *n* barco *m*.
bobsleigh *n* bob *m*.
bodice *n* corsé *m*.
body *n* cuerpo *m*; individuo *m*; gremio *m*.
body-building *n* culturismo *m*.
bodyguard *n* guardaespaldas *m*.
boil *vi* hervir; bullir.
bold *adj* ardiente, valiente; audaz.
bolt *n* cerrojo *m*.
bomb *n* bomba *f*.
bond *n* ligadura *f*; vinculo *m*.
bondage *n* esclavitud, servidumbre *f*.
bone *n* hueso *m*.
bonfire *n* hoguera *f*.
bonny *adj* bonito/ta.
bonus *n* cuota, prima *f*.
book *n* libro *m*.
bookcase *n* armario para libros *m*.
bookmarker *n* registro *m*.
bookstore *n* librería *f*.
boom *n* trueno *m*.
boon *n* presente, regalo *m*.
booth *n* barraca, cabaña *f*.

booty *n* botín *m*; presa *f*; saqueo *m*.
border *n* orilla *f*; borde *m*.
borderline *n* frontera *f*.
bore *vt* taladrar; barrenar; fastidiar.
boredom *n* aburrimiento *m*.
borrow *vt* pedir prestado/da.
bosom *n* seno, pecho *m*.
boss *n* jefe *m*; patrón/ona *m/f*.
botany *n* botánica *f*.
botch *vt* chapuzar.
both *adj* ambos.
bother *vt* preocupar; fastidiar.
bottle *n* botella *f*.
bottom *n* fondo *m*.
bough *n* brazo del árbol *m*; ramo *m*.
boulder *n* canto rodado *m*.
bounce *vi* rebotar.
bound *n* limite *m*; salto *m*.
boundary *n* limite *m*; frontera *f*.
bouquet *n* ramillete de flores *m*.
bourgeois *adj* burgués.
bout *n* ataque *m*.
bow *vt* encorvar, doblar.
bow *n* arco *m*.
bowels *npl* intestinos *mpl*.
bowl *n* taza; bola *f*.
bow tie *n* pajarita *f*.
box *n* caja, cajita *f*.
boxer *n* boxeador *m*.
boxing *n* boxeo *m*.
box office *n* taquilla *f*.
boy *n* muchacho *m*; niño *m*.
boycott *vt* boicotear:—*n* boicot *m*.
boyfriend *n* novio *m*.
bra *n* sujetador *m*.
bracelet *n* brazalete *m*.
bracket *n* puntal *m*; paréntesis *m*.
brag *n* jactancia *f*:—*vi* jactarse.
braid *n* pliegue *m*, trenza *f*:—*vt* trenzar.
brain *n* cerebro *m*.
brake *n* freno *m*:—*vt vi* frenar.
bran *n* salvado *m*.
branch *n* ramo *m*; rama *f*.
brand *n* marca *f*.
brandy *n* coñac *m*.
brass *n* latón *m*.
brassiere *n* sujetador *m*.
brave *adj* bravo/va, valiente.
bravery *n* valor *m*.
brawl *n* pelea *f*.
brazier *n* brasero *m*.
breach *n* rotura *f*.
bread *n* pan *m*.
breadth *n* anchura *f*.
break *vt* romper; quebrantar.
breakage *n* rotura *f*.
breakfast *n* desayuno *m*:—*vi* desayunar.
breast *n* pecho, seno *m*.
breastbone *n* esternón *m*.
breath *n* aliento *m*, respiración *f*; soplo de aire *m*.
breathe *vt vi* respirar; exhalar.
breathtaking *adj* pasmoso/sa.
breed *n* casta, raza *f*.
breeze *n* brisa *f*.
brevity *n* brevedad, concisión *f*.
brew *vt* hacer; tramar, mezclar.
bribe *n* cohecho, soborno *m*.
bribery *n* cohecho, soborno *m*.
bric-a-brac *n* baratijas *fpl*.
brick *n* ladrillo *m*.
bricklayer *n* albañil *m*.
bride *n* novia *f*.
bridegroom *n* novio *m*.
bridesmaid *n* madrina de boda *f*.
bridge *n* puente *m/f*.
brief *adj* breve, conciso/sa, sucinto/ta.
briefcase *n* cartera *f*.
brigade *n* (*mil*) brigada *f*.
bright *adj* claro/ra, luciente, brillante.
brighten *vt* pulir, dar lustre.
brilliant *adj* brillante.
bring *vt* llevar, traer.
brisk *adj* vivo/va, alegre, jovial; fresco/ca.
brisket *n* pecho (de un animal) *m*.
briskly *adj* vigorosamente.
bristle *n* cerda, seta *f*:—*vi* erizarse.
bristly *adj* cerdoso/sa, lleno/na de cerdas.
brittle *adj* quebradizo, frágil.
broach *vt* comenzar a hablar de.
broad *adj* ancho.
broadcast *n* emisión *f*.
broadcasting *n* radiodifusión *f*.
broaden *vt vi* ensanchar(se).
broadly *adv* anchamente.
broad-minded *adj* tolerante.
brocade *n* brocado *m*.
broccoli *n* brécol *m*.
brochure *n* folleto *m*.
broil *vt* asar a la parrilla.
broken *adj* roto/ta.
broker *n* corredor/a *m/f*.
bronchial *adj* bronquial.
bronchitis *n* bronquitis *f*.
bronze *n* bronce *m*.
brooch *n* broche *m*.
brook *n* arroyo *m*.
broom *n* hiniesta *f*; escoba *f*.
broth *n* caldo *m*.
brothel *n* burdel *m*.
brother *n* hermano *m*.
brother-in-law *n* cuñado *m*.
brow *n* caja *f*; frente *f*; cima *f*.
browbeat *vt* intimidar.

brown *adj* moreno/na; castaño/ña.
browse *vt* ramonear.
bruise *vt* magullar.
brunette *n* morena *f*.
brunt *n* choque *m*.
brush *n* cepillo *m*; escobilla *f*.
brusque *adj* brusco/ca.
Brussels sprout *n* col de Bruselas *f*.
brutal *adj* brutal.
brutality *n* brutalidad *f*.
brute *n* bruto *m*.
bubble *n* burbuja *f*.
bubblegum *n* chicle *m*.
bucket *n* cubo, pozal *m*.
buckle *n* hebilla *f*.
bucolic *adj* bucólico/ca.
bud *n* pimpollo, botón *m*:—*vi* brotar.
Buddhism *n* Budismo *m*.
buddy *n* compañero *m*.
budge *vi* moverse.
budgerigar *n* periquito *m*.
budget *n* presupuesto *m*.
buff *n* entusiasta *m*.
buffalo *n* búfalo *m*.
buffet *n* buffet *m*.
buffoon *n* bufón, chocarrero *m*.
bug *n* chinche *m*.
bugle(horn) *n* trompa de caza *f*.
build *vt* edificar; construir.
building *n* edificio *m*; construcción *f*.
bulb *n* bulbo *m*; cebolla *f*.
bulge *vi* combarse:—*n* bombeo *m*.
bulk *n* masa *f*; volumen *m*.
bulky *adj* grueso/sa, grande.
bull *n* toro *m*.
bulldog *n* dogo *m*.
bulldozer *n* aplanadora *f*.
bullet *n* bala *f*.
bullfight *n* corrida de toros *f*.
bullfighter *n* toreo *m*.
bullfighting *n* los toros *mpl*.
bullion *n* oro o plata en barras *m* o *f*.
bullock *n* novillo capado *m*.
bullring *n* plaza de toros *f*.
bully *n* valentón *m*:—*vt* tiranizar.
bumblebee *n* abejorro *m*.
bump *n* hinchazón *f*.
bun *n* bollo *m*; mono *m*.
bunch *n* ramo *m*.
bundle *n* fardo *m*, haz *m*.
bung *n* tapón *m*.
bungalow *n* bungalow *m*.
bunk *n* litera *f*.
bunker *n* refugio *m*; bunker *m*.
burden *n* carga *f*:—*vt* cargar.
bureau *n* armario *m*; escritorio *m*.
bureaucracy *n* burocracia *f*.
burglar *n* ladrón *m*.
burial *n* enterramiento *m*; exequias *fpl*.
burial place *n* cementerio *m*.
burly *adj* corpulento/ta, fornido/da.
burn *vt* quemar, abrasar, incendiar:—*vi* arder: —*n* quema dura *f*.
burner *n* quemador *m*; mechero *m*.
burning *adj* ardiente.
burrow *n* conejera *f*.
bursar *n* tesorero *m*.
burse *n* bolsa, lonja *f*.
burst *vi* reventar; abrirse.
bury *vt* enterrar, sepultar; esconder.
bus *n* autobús *m*.
bush *n* arbusto, espinal *m*.
busily *adv* diligentemente, apresuradamente.
business *n* asunto *m*; negocios *mpl*.
businessman *n* hombre de negocios *m*.
bust *n* busto *m*.
bus-stop *n* parada de autobuses *f*.
bustle *vi* hacer ruido.
busy *adj* ocupado/da; entrometido/da.
busybody *n* entrometido *m*.
but *conj* pero; mas.
butcher *n* carnicero *m*.
butcher's (shop) *n* carnicería *f*.
butler *n* mayordomo *m*.
butter *n* mantequilla *f*.
buttercup *n* (*bot*) ranúnculo *m*.
butterfly *n* mariposa *f*.
buttocks *npl* posaderas *fpl*.
button *n* botón *m*.
buttonhole *n* ojal *m*.
buttress *n* estribo *m*; apoyo *m*.
buxom *adj* frescachona.
buy *vt* comprar.
buzz *n* susurro, zumbido *m*:—*vi* zumbar.
buzzard *n* ratonero común *m*.
buzzer *n* timbre *m*.
by *prep* por; a, en; de; cerca, al lado de.
bypass *n* carretera de circunvalación *f*.
by-product *n* derivado *m*.
bystander *n* mirador *m*.
byte *n* (*comput*) byte *m*.
byword *n* proverbio, refrán *m*.

C

cab *n* taxi *m*.
cabbage *n* berza, col *f*.
cabin *n* cabaña.
cabinet *n* consejo á ministros *m*; gabinete *m*.

cable *n* (*mar*) cable *m*.
cable car *n* teleférico *m*.
cactus *n* cacto *m*.
cadaver *n* cadáver *m*.
cadet *n* cadete *m*.
cadge *vt* mangar.
cafeteria *n* cantina *f*.
cage *n* jaula *f*.
cake *n* bollo *m*; tortita *f*.
calculate *vt* calcular.
calculator *n* calculadora *f*.
calendar *n* calendario *m*.
calf *n* ternero *m*.
call *vt* llamar, nombrar.
calligraphy *n* caligrafía *f*.
callous *adj* calloso/sa.
calm *n* calma, tranquilidad.
calorie *n* caloría *f*.
Calvinist *n* calvinista *m*.
camel *n* camello *m*.
cameo *n* camafeo *m*.
camera *n* máquina fotográfica *f*.
camomile *n* manzanilla *f*.
camouflage *n* camuflaje *m*.
camp *n* campo *m*.
campaign *n* campana *f*.
camping *n* camping *m*.
campsite *n* camping *m*.
can *vi* poder:—*n* lata *f*.
canal *n* estanque *m*; canal *m*.
cancel *vt* cancelar; anular.
cancer *n* cáncer *m*.
Cancer *n* Cáncer *m* (signo del zodiaco).
candid *adj* cándido/da, sencillo/lla.
candle *n* candela *f*; vela *f*.
candlestick *n* candelero *m*.
candy *n* caramelo *m*.
cane *n* cana *f*; bastón *m*.
cannabis *n* canabis *f*.
cannibal *n* caníbal *m*.
cannibalism *n* canibalismo *m*.
cannon *n* cañón *m*.
canoe *n* canoa *f*.
canon *n* canon *m*; regla *f*.
can opener *n* abrelatas *m invar*.
canopy *n* dosel, pabellón *m*.
canter *n* medio galope *m*.
canvas *n* cañamazo *m*.
canyon *n* cañón *m*.
cap *n* gorra *f*.
capability *n* capacidad *f*.
capable *adj* capaz.
cape *n* cabo, promontorio *m*.
capital *adj* capital; principal.
capitalism *n* capitalismo *m*.
Capitol *n* Capitolio *m*.
capitulate *vi* capitular.
Capricorn *n* Capricornio *m* (signo del zodiaco).
capsule *n* cápsula *f*.
captain *n* capitán *m*.
captivate *vt* cautivar.
capture *n* captura *f*; presa *f*.
car *n* coche, carro *m*; vagón *m*.
carafe *n* garrafa *f*.
caramel *n* caramelo *m*.
carat *n* quilate *m*.
carbohydrates *npl* hidratos de carbono *mpl*.
carcass *n* cadáver *m*.
card *n* naipe *m*; carta *f*.
cardboard *n* cartón *m*.
cardinal *adj* cardinal, principal.
care *n* cuidado *m*; solicitud *f*.
career *n* carrera *f*.
caress *n* caricia *f*.
caretaker *n* portero *m*.
cargo *n* cargamento de navío *m*.
caricature *n* caricatura *f*.
carnal *adj* carnal; sensual.
carnation *n* clavel *m*.
carnival *n* carnaval *m*.
carpenter *n* carpintero *m*.
carpentry *n* carpintería *f*.
carpet *n* alfombra *f*.
carrier *n* portador *m*.
carrot *n* zanahoria *f*.
carry *vt* llevar, conducir.
cart *n* carro *m*; carreta *f*.
cartilage *n* cartílago *m*.
carton *n* caja *f*.
cartoon *n* dibujo animado *m*.
carve *vt* cincelar.
carving *n* escultura *f*.
case *n* caja *f*; maleta *f*.
cash *n* dinero contante *m*.
cashmere *n* cachemira *f*.
cask *n* barril, tonel *m*.
casserole *n* cazuela *f*.
cassette *n* cassette *m*.
cassock *n* sotana *f*.
castanets *npl* castañetas *fpl*.
castaway *n* réprobo *m*.
caste *n* casta *f*.
castigate *vt* castigar.
castle *n* castillo *m*.
castrate *vt* castrar.
castration *n* capadura *f*.
casual *adj* casual.
cat *n* gato *m*; gata *f*.
catalog(ue) *n* catalogo *m*.
cataract *n* cascada *f*; catarata *f*.
catarrh *n* catarro *m*; reuma *f*.
catastrophe *n* catástrofe *f*.
catch *vt* coger.

catchphrase *n* lema *m*.
catechism *n* catecismo *m*.
categorize *vt* clasificar.
category *n* categoría *f*.
caterpillar *n* oruga *f*.
cathedral *n* catedral *f*.
catholic *adj*, *n* católico *m*.
Catholicism *n* catolicismo *m*.
cattle *n* ganado *m*.
cauliflower *n* coliflor *f*.
cause *n* causa *f*; razón *f*; motivo *m*.
causeway *n* arrecife *m*.
caustic *adj*, *n* cáustico *m*.
cauterize *vt* cauterizar.
caution *n* prudencia.
cavalry *n* caballería *f*.
cave *n* caverna *f*.
caviar *n* caviar *m*.
cease *vt* parar, suspender.
cedar *n* cedro *m*.
cede *vt* ceder.
ceiling *n* techo *m*.
celebrate *vt* celebrar.
celery *n* apio *m*.
celibacy *n* celibato *m*.
cell *n* celdilla *f*; célula *f*; cueva *f*.
cellar *n* sótano *m*.
cellophane *n* celofán *m*.
cement *n* cemento.
cemetery *n* cementerio *m*.
cenotaph *n* cenotafio *m*.
censor *n* censor *m*.
census *n* censo *m*.
cent *n* centavo *m*.
center *n* centro *m*.
centigrade *n* centígrado *m*.
centiliter *n* centilitro *m*.
centimeter *n* centímetro *m*.
centipede *n* escolopendra *f*.
central *adj* central.
centralize *vt* centralizar.
century *n* siglo *m*.
ceramic *adj* cerámico/ca.
ceremony *n* ceremonia *f*.
certain *adj* cierto/ta, evidente.
certificate *n* certificado, testimonio *m*.
certify *vt* certificar, afirmar.
cervical *adj* cervical.
chaffinch *n* pinzón *m*.
chain *n* cadena *f*.
chair *n* silla *f*.
chamber *n* cámara *f*.
chameleon *n* camaleón *m*.
champagne *n* champaña *m*.
championship *n* campeonato *m*.
chance *n* ventura, suerte *f*; oportunidad *f*.
chancellor *n* canciller *m*.
change *vt* cambiar.
channel *n* canal *m*.
chant *n* canto (llano) *m*.
chaos *n* caos *m*.
chapel *n* capilla *f*.
chaplain *n* capellán *m*.
chapter *n* capitulo *m*.
character *n* carácter *m*.
charcoal *n* carbón de leña *m*.
charge *vt* cargar; acusar, imputar.
charity *n* caridad.
charlatan *n* charlatán/tana *m/f*.
charm *n* encanto *m*.
charter flight *n* vuelo charter *m*.
chauffeur *n* chófer *m*.
chauvinist *n* machista *m*.
cheap *adj* barato/ta.
cheat *vt* engañar, defraudar.
check *n* cheque *m*.
checkmate *n* mate *m*.
checkout *n* caja *f*.
cheek *n* mejilla *f*.
cheese *n* queso *m*.
chef *n* jefe de cocina *m*.
chemical *adj* químico/ca.
chemist *n* químico *m*.
cheroot *n* puro *m*.
cherry *n* cereza *f*.
cherub *n* querubín *m*.
chess *n* ajedrez *m*.
chest *n* pecho *m*.
chestnut *n* castaña *f*.
chew *vt* mascar, masticar.
chewing gum *n* chicle *m*.
chicken *n* pollo *m*.
chickenpox *n* varicela *f*.
chickpea *n* garbanzo *m*.
chief *adj* principal.
chilblain *n* sabañón *m*.
child *n* niño *m*; niña *f*.
childhood *n* infancia, niñez *f*.
children *npl de* **child** niños *mpl*.
chimney *n* chimenea *f*.
chimpanzee *n* chimpancé *m*.
chin *n* barbilla *f*.
chiropodist *n* pedicuro *m*.
chirp *vi* chirriar.
chlorine *n* cloro *m*.
chloroform *n* cloroformo *m*.
chocolate *n* chocolate *m*.
choice *n* elección, preferencia *f*.
choir *n* coro *m*.
choke *vt* sofocar.
cholera *n* cólera *m*.
choose *vt* escoger, elegir.
chop *vt* tajar, cortar:—*n* chuleta *f*.
chore *n* faena *f*.

Christ *n* Cristo *m*.
christen *vt* bautizar.
Christianity *n* cristianismo *m*; cristiandad *f*.
Christmas *n* Navidad *f*.
chrome *n* cromo *m*.
chronicle *n* crónica *f*.
chronological *adj* cronológico/ca.
chubby *adj* gordo/da.
chunk *n* trozo *m*.
church *n* iglesia *f*.
churchyard *n* cementerio *m*.
cider *n* sidra *f*.
cigar *n* cigarro *m*.
cigarette *n* cigarrillo *m*.
cinder *n* carbonilla *f*.
cinema *n* cine *m*.
cinnamon *n* canela *f*.
circle *n* circulo *m*.
circumcize *vt* circuncidar.
circumcision *n* circuncisión *f*.
circumference *n* circunferencia *f*; circuito *m*.
circumflex *n* acento circunflejo *m*.
circumstance *n* circunstancia.
circus *n* circo *m*.
cistern *n* cisterna *f*.
cite *vt* citar.
citizen *n* ciudadano *m*.
city *n* ciudad *f*.
civic *adj* cívico/ca.
civil *adj* civil, cortés.
civilization *n* civilización *f*.
clairvoyant *n* clarividente *m/f*.
clam *n* almeja *f*.
clammy *adj* viscoso/sa.
clamor *n* clamor *m*.
clan *n* familia, tribu, raza *f*.
clandestine *adj* clandestino/na.
clap *vt* aplaudir.
claret *n* clarete *m*.
clarify *vt* clarificar, aclarar.
clarinet *n* clarinete *m*.
clarity *n* claridad *f*.
class *n* clase *f*; orden *f*.
classic(al) *adj* clásico/ca:—*n* autor clásico *m*.
classify *vt* clasificar.
classmate *n* compañero de clase *m*.
classroom *n* aula *f*.
clause *n* cláusula *f*.
claw *n* garra *f*.
clay *n* arcilla *f*.
clean *adj* limpio/pia; casto/ta:—*vt* limpiar.
cleanse *vt* limpiar, purificar; purgar.
clear *adj* claro/ra.
clemency *n* clemencia *f*.
clement *adj* clemente, benigno/na.
clergy *n* clero *m*.
clerical *adj* clerical, eclesiástico/ca.
clerk *n* dependiente *m*; oficinista *m*.
clever *adj* listo/ta; hábil.
client *n* cliente *m/f*.
cliff *n* acantilado *m*.
climate *n* clima *m*.
climax *n* clímax *m*.
climb *vt* escalar, trepar.
cling *vi* colgar, adherirse.
clinic *n* clínica *f*.
clip *vt* cortar.
clique *n* camarilla *f*.
cloak *n* capa *f*.
cloakroom *n* guardarropa *m*.
clock *n* reloj *m*.
clog *n* zueco *m*.
cloister *n* claustro, monasterio *m*.
close *vt* cerrar; concluir, terminar.
closet *n* armario *m*.
close-up *n* primer plano *m*.
clot *n* grumo *m*; embolia *f*.
cloth *n* paño *m*.
clothe *vt* vestir.
clothes *npl* ropa *f*.
clothes pin *n* pinza *f*.
cloud *n* nube *f*.
clout *n* tortazo *m*.
clove *n* clavo *m*.
clover *n* trébol *m*.
clown *n* payaso *m*.
coach *n* autocar, autobús *m*.
coagulate *vt* coagular, cuajar.
coal *n* carbón *m*.
coalition *n* coalición, confederación *f*.
coarse *adj* basto/ta; grosero/ra.
coast *n* costa *f*.
coastguard *n* guardacostas *m invar*.
coat *n* chaqueta *f*; abrigo *m*.
coat hanger *n* percha *f*.
cobbler *n* zapatero *m*.
cobweb *n* telaraña *f*.
cocaine *n* cocaína *f*.
cock *n* gallo *m*; macho *m*.
cockle *n* caracol de mar *m*.
cockpit *n* cabina *f*.
cockroach *n* cucaracha *f*.
cocktail *n* cóctel *m*.
cocoa *n* coco *m*; cacao *m*.
coconut *n* coco *m*.
cod *n* bacalao *m*.
code *n* código *m*.
cod-liver oil *n* aceite de hígado de bacalao *m*.
coffee *n* café *m*.
coffer *n* cofre *m*; caja *f*.
coffin *n* ataúd *m*.
cog *n* diente (de rueda) *m*.
cognac *n* coñac *m*.
cogwheel *n* rueda dentada *f*.

cohabit *vi* cohabitar.
coherence *n* coherencia *f*.
cohesion *n* coherencia *f*.
cohesive *adj* cohesivo.
coil *n* rollo *m*.
coin *n* moneda *f*.
coincide *vi* coincidir.
coke *n* coque *m*.
colander *n* colador, pasador *m*.
cold *adj* frío/ría.
cold sore *n* herpes labial *m*.
coleslaw *n* ensalada de col *f*.
colic *n* cólico *m*.
collaborate *vt* cooperar.
collapse *vi* hundirse.
collapsible *adj* plegable.
collar *n* cuello *m*.
collarbone *n* clavícula *f*.
collate *vt* comparar.
collateral *adj* colateral.
colleague *n* colega *m*.
collect *vt* recoger; coleccionar.
collection *n* colección *f*; compilación *f*.
college *n* colegio *m*.
collide *vi* chocar.
colloquial *adj* familiar.
collusion *n* colusión *f*.
colon *n* dos puntos *mpl*; (*med*) colon *m*.
colonel *n* (*mil*) coronel *m*.
colonial *adj* colonial.
colonize *vt* colonizar.
colony *n* colonia *f*.
color *n* color *m*.
colossal *adj* colosal.
colt *n* potro *m*.
column *n* columna *f*.
columnist *n* columnista *m*.
coma *n* coma *f*.
comatose *adj* comatoso/sa.
comb *n* peine *m*:—*vt* peinar.
combat *n* combate *m*.
combination *n* combinación *f*.
combine *vt* combinar.
combustion *n* combustión *f*.
come *vi* venir.
comedy *n* comedia *f*.
comet *n* cometa *f*.
comfort *n* confort *m*.
comfortable *adj* cómodo/da.
comma *n* (*gr*) coma *f*.
command *vt* comandar.
commemorate *vt* conmemorar; celebrar.
commence *vt*, *vi* comenzar.
commencement *n* principio *m*.
commend *vt* encomendar.
commensurate *adj* proporcionado/da.
comment *n* comentario *m*.
commentator *n* comentador *m*.
commerce *n* comercio *m*.
commercial *adj* comercial.
commiserate *vt* compadecer.
commission *n* comisión *f*.
commit *vt* cometer.
committee *n* comité *m*.
commodity *n* comodidad *f*.
common *adj* común.
commotion *n* tumulto *m*.
communicate *vt* comunicar.
communion *n* comunión *f*.
communism *n* comunismo *m*.
community *n* comunidad *f*.
commute *vt* conmutar.
compact *adj* compacto/ta.
compact disc *n* disco compacto *m*.
companion *n* compañero/ra.
company *n* compañía, sociedad *f*.
compare *vt* comparar.
compartment *n* compartimiento *m*.
compass *n* brújula *f*.
compassion *n* compasión *f*.
compatriot *n* compatriota *m*.
compensate *vt* compensar.
compensation *n* compensación *f*.
compère *n* presentador *m*.
compete *vi* concurrir.
competent *adj* competente.
competition *n* competencia *f*.
competitor *n* competidor, rival *m*.
compilation *n* compilación *f*.
complain *vi* quejarse, lamentarse.
complement *n* complemento *m*.
complex *adj* complejo/ja.
complexion *n* tez *f*; aspecto *m*.
complicate *vt* complicar.
component *adj* componente.
compose *vt* componer.
composer *n* autor *m*.
composite *adj* compuesto/ta.
composition *n* composición *f*.
comprehend *vt* comprender, contener; entender.
compress *vt* comprimir.
comprise *vt* comprender.
compromise *n* compromiso *m*.
compulsive *adj* compulsivo/va.
computer *n* ordenador *m*.
comrade *n* camarada.
con *vt* estafar:—*n* estafa *f*.
concave *adj* cóncavo/va.
conceal *vt* ocultar, esconder.
concede *vt* conceder.
conceit *n* concepto *m*, capricho *m*.
conceive *vt* concebir, comprender.
concentrate *vt* concentrar.

concept *n* concepto *m*.
conception *n* concepción *f*.
concern *vt* concernir, importar.
concert *n* concierto *m*.
concession *n* concesión *f*; privilegio *m*.
concise *adj* conciso/sa.
conclude *vt* concluir.
conclusion *n* conclusión.
concord *n* concordia, armonía *f*.
concrete *n* concreto *m*.
concussion *n* concusión *f*.
condemn *vt* condenar.
condensation *n* condensación *f*.
condiment *n* condimento *m*; salsa *f*.
condition *vt* condicionar.
conditional *adj* condicional.
condom *n* condón *m*.
conduct *n* conducta *f*.
conductor *n* conductor *m*.
conduit *n* conducto *m*.
cone *n* cono *m*.
confection *n* confitura *f*.
confectioner's (shop) *n* pastelería *f*.
conference *n* conferencia *f*.
confess *vt*, *vi* confesar(se).
confession *n* confesión *f*.
confessional *n* confesionario *m*.
confetti *n* confeti *m*.
confidant *n* confidente.
confide *vt*, *vi* confiar; fiarse.
confidence *n* confianza, seguridad *f*.
confident *adj* cierto/ta, seguro/ra; confiado/da.
confine *vt* limitar; aprisionar.
confirm *vt* confirmar; ratificar.
confiscate *vt* confiscar.
conflagration *n* conflagración *f*.
conflict *n* conflicto *m*; combate *m*; pelea *f*.
conflicting *adj* contradictorio/ria.
confluence *n* confluencia *f*.
conform *vt*, *vi* conformar(se).
conformity *n* conformidad.
confound *vt* turbar, confundir.
confront *vt* afrontar; confrontar.
confrontation *n* enfrentamiento *m*.
confuse *vt* confundir.
congeal *vt*, *vi* helar, congelar(se).
congenial *adj* congenial.
congenital *adj* congénito/ta.
congested *adj* atestado/da.
congestion *n* congestión *f*; acumulación *f*.
congratulate *vt* congratular, felicitar.
congratulations *npl* felicidades *fpl*.
congratulatory *adj* congratulatorio/ria.
congregate *vt* congregar.
congress *n* congreso *m*; conferencia *f*.
congruity *n* congruencia *f*.
coniferous *adj* (*bot*) conífero/ra.
conjecture *n* conjetura.
conjugal *adj* conyugal.
conjugate *vt* (*gr*) conjugar.
conjunction *n* conjunción *f*.
conjuncture *n* coyuntura *f*.
conjure *vi* conjurar.
con man *n* timador *m*.
connect *vt* juntar, unir.
connection *n* conexión *f*.
connivance *n* connivencia *f*.
connive *vi* tolerar.
connoisseur *n* conocedor/a *m/f*.
conquer *vt* conquistar; vencer.
conqueror *n* vencedor/a, conquistador/a *m/f*.
conquest *n* conquista *f*.
conscience *n* conciencia *f*.
consciousness *n* conciencia *f*.
conscript *n* conscripto *m*.
conscription *n* reclutamiento *m*.
consecrate *vt* consagrar.
consecration *n* consagración *f*.
consecutive *adj* consecutivo/va.
consensus *n* consenso *m*.
consent *n* consentimiento *m*; aprobación *f*.
consequence *n* consecuencia *f*.
consequent *adj* consecutivo/va.
conservation *n* conservación *f*.
conservative *adj* conservativo/va.
conservatory *n* conservatorio *m*.
conserve *vt* conservar.
consider *vt* considerar.
considerable *adj* considerable.
considerate *adj* considerado/da.
consideration *n* consideración *f*.
consign *vt* consignar.
consignment *n* consignación *f*.
consist *vi* consistir.
consistency *n* consistencia *f*.
consistent *adj* consistente.
consolation *n* consolación *f*; consuelo *m*.
console *vt* consolar.
consolidate *vt*, *vi* consolidar(se).
consolidation *n* consolidación *f*.
consonant *adj* consonante.
consort *n* consorte, socio *m*.
conspicuous *adj* conspicuo/cua.
conspiracy *n* conspiración *f*.
conspirator *n* conspirador/a *m/f*.
conspire *vi* conspirar.
constancy *n* constancia.
constant *adj* constante.
constellation *n* constelación *f*.
constipated *adj* estreñido/da.
constituency *n* junta electoral *f*.
constituent *n* constitutivo *m*.
constitute *vt* constituir.
constitution *n* constitución *f*.

constitutional *adj* constitucional.
constrict *vt* constreñir, estrechar.
construct *vt* construir, edificar.
construction *n* construcción *f*.
consul *n* cónsul *m*.
consulate, consulship *n* consulado *m*.
consult *vt, vi* consultar(se).
consultation *n* consulta *f*.
consume *vt* consumir.
consumer *n* consumidor/a *m/f*.
consumption *n* consumo *m*.
contact *n* contacto *m*.
contact lenses *npl* lentes de contacto *mpl*.
contagious *adj* contagioso/sa.
contain *vt* contener.
container *n* recipiente *m*.
contaminate *vt* contaminar.
contamination *n* contaminación *f*.
contemplate *vt* contemplar.
contemplation *n* contemplación *f*.
contempt *n* desprecio, desdén *m*.
contend *vi* contender.
content *adj* contento/ta, satisfecho/cha.
contention *n* contención, altercación *f*.
contest *vt* contestar, disputar, litigar.
contestant *n* concursante/ta *m/f*.
context *n* contexto *m*.
continent *adj* continente.
contingency *n* contingencia *f*.
contingent *n* contingente *m*; cuota *f*.
continue *vt* continuar.
contort *vt* torcer.
contortion *n* contorsión *f*.
contour *n* contorno *m*.
contraband *n* contrabando *m*.
contraception *n* contracepción *f*.
contraceptive *n* anticonceptivo *m*.
contract *vt* contraer; abreviar; contratar.
contraction *n* contracción *f*; abreviatura *f*.
contradict *vt* contradecir.
contradiction *n* contradicción, oposición *f*.
contraption *n* artilugio *m*.
contrary *adj* contrario/ria, opuesto/ta.
contrast *n* contraste *m*.
contrasting *adj* opuesto/ta.
contributary *adj* contributario/ria.
contribute *vt* contribuir, ayudar.
contrive *vt* inventar, trazar.
control *n* control *m*; inspección *f*:—*vt* controlar; manejar; restringir; gobernar.
controversial *adj* polémico/ca.
controversy *n* controversia *f*.
conurbation *n* urbanización *f*.
convalesce *vi* convalecer.
convalescence *n* convalecencia *f*.
convene *vt* convocar; juntar, unir.
convenient *adj* conveniente.
convent *n* convento *m*.
convention *n* convención *f*.
converge *vi* converger.
conversation *n* conversación *f*.
converse *vi* conversar; platicar.
conversely *adv* mutuamente, recíprocamente.
convert *vt, vi* convertir(se).
convertible *adj* convertible.
convex *adj* convexo/xa.
convey *vt* transportar; transmitir, transferir.
conveyance *n* transporte *m*.
conveyancer *n* notario *m*.
conviction *n* convicción *f*.
convince *vt* convencer.
convivial *adj* sociable; hospitalario/ria.
convoke *vt* convocar, reunir.
convoy *n* convoy *m*.
convulse *vt* conmover, convulsionar.
convulsion *n* convulsión *f*.
convulsive *adj* convulsivo/va.
cook *n* cocinero *m*; cocinera *f*:—*vt* cocinar.
cool *adj* fresco/ca; indiferente.
cooperate *vi* cooperar.
cooperation *n* cooperación *f*.
coordinate *vt* coordinar.
coordination *n* coordinación *f*.
cop *n* (*fam*) poli *m*.
copier *n* copiadora *f*.
copious *adj* copioso/sa, abundante.
copper *n* cobre *m*.
copulate *vi* copularse.
copy *n* copia *f*.
copying machine *n* copiadora *f*.
coral *n* coral *m*.
cord *n* cuerda *f*; cable *m*.
cordial *adj* cordial.
corduroy *n* pana *f*.
core *n* cuesco *m*; interior *m*.
cork *n* alcornoque *m*; corcho *m*.
corkscrew *n* tirabuzón *m*.
corn *n* maíz *m*; grano *m*; callo *m*.
corncob *n* mazorca *f*.
cornea *n* córnea *f*.
corner *n* rincón *m*; esquina *f*.
cornet *n* corneta *f*.
cornflakes *npl* copos de maíz *mpl*.
cornice *n* cornisa *f*.
coronary *n* infarto *m*.
coronation *n* coronación *f*.
coroner *n* oficial que hace la inspección jurídica de los cadáveres *m*.
corporation *n* corporación *f*.
corps *n* cuerpo (de ejercito) *m*.
correct *vt* corregir; enmendar.
correctness *n* exactitud *f*.
correspond *vi* corresponder.
correspondence *n* correspondencia *f*.

corridor *n* pasillo *m*.
corrode *vt* corroer.
corrosive *adj*, *n* corrosivo *m*.
corrupt *vt* corromper; sobornar.
corruption *n* corrupción *f*; depravación *f*.
corset *n* corsé *m*.
cosily *adv* cómodamente.
cosmetic *adj* cosmético/ca.
cosmic *adj* cósmico/ca.
cosmonaut *n* cosmonauta *m*.
cosmopolitan *adj* cosmopolita.
cosset *vt* mimar.
cost *n* coste, precio *m*:—*vi* costar.
costume *n* traje *m*.
cosy *adj* cómodo/da.
cottage *n* casita, casucha *f*.
cotton *n* algodón *m*.
cotton wool *n* algodón hidrófilo *m*.
couch *n* sofá *m*.
couchette *n* litera *f*.
cough *n* tos *f*:—*vi* toser.
council *n* concilio, consejo *m*.
counsel *n* consejo, aviso *m*.
count *vt* contar, numerar; calcular.
counter *n* mostrador *m*; ficha *f*.
counterfeit *vt* contrahacer, imitar, falsear.
counterpart *n* parte correspondiente *f*.
countersign *vt* refrendar.
countess *n* condesa *f*.
countless *adj* innumerable.
countrified *adj* rústico/ca.
country *n* país *m*; campo *m*; región *f*; patria *f*.
county *n* condado *m*.
coup *n* golpe *m*.
couple *n* par *m*.
couplet *n* copla *f*; par *m*.
coupon *n* cupón *m*.
courage *n* coraje, valor *f*.
courageous *adj* corajudo/da, valeroso/sa:—
~**ly** *adv* valerosamente.
courier *n* correo, mensajero/ra *m/f*, expreso *m*.
course *n* curso *m*; carrera *f*; camino *m*; ruta *f*.
court *n* corte *f*.
courteous *adj* cortés.
courtesy *n* cortesía *f*.
courthouse *n* palacio de justicia *m*.
courtyard *n* patio *m*.
cousin *n* primo *m*; prima *f*.
cove *n* (*mar*) ensenada, caleta *f*.
covenant *n* contrato *m*.
cover *n* cubierta *f*; abrigo *m*.
cover letter *n* carta de explicación *f*.
covert *adj* cubierto/ta; oculto/ta, secreto/ta.
cover-up *n* encubrimiento *m*.
covet *vt* codiciar.
cow *n* vaca *f*.
coward *n* cobarde *m/f*.
cowardice *n* cobardía, timidez *f*.
cowboy *n* vaquero *m*.
cower *vi* agacharse.
cowherd *n* vaquero *m*.
crab *n* cangrejo *m*.
crab apple *n* manzana silvestre *f*.
crack *n* crujido *m*; hendedura, quebraja *f*.
cracker *n* buscapiés *m invar*; galleta *f*.
crackle *vi* crujir, chillar.
cradle *n* cuna *f*.
craft *n* arte.
craftsman *n* artífice, artesano *m*.
craftsmanship *n* artesanía *f*.
crafty *adj* astuto/ta, artificioso/sa.
cramp *n* calambre *m*.
cranberry *n* arandilla *f*.
crane *n* grulla *f*; grua *f*.
crash *vi* estallar.
crash helmet *n* casco *m*.
crass *adj* craso/sa.
crater *n* cráter *m*; boca de volcán *f*.
cravat *n* pañuelo *m*.
crave *vt* rogar, suplicar.
craving *adj* insaciable.
crawl *vi* arrastrar.
crayfish *n* cangrejo de río *m*.
crayon *n* lápiz *m*.
craze *n* manía *f*.
craziness *n* locura *f*.
crazy *adj* loco/ca.
cream *n* crema *f*.
creamy *adj* cremoso.
crease *n* pliegue *m*.
create *vt* crear; causar.
creation *n* creación *f*; elección *f*.
creator *n* creador/a *m/f*.
creature *n* criatura *f*.
credence *n* creencia, fe *f*.
credibility *n* credibilidad *f*.
credible *adj* creíble.
credit *n* crédito *m*.
creditable *adj* estimable.
credit card *n* tarjeta de crédito *f*.
creed *n* credo *m*.
creek *n* arroyo, rio *m*.
creep *vi* arrastrar, serpear.
creeper *n* (*bot*) enredadera *f*.
cremate *vt* incinerar cadáveres.
cremation *n* cremación *f*.
crematorium *n* crematorio *m*.
crescent *adj* creciente.
cress *n* berro *m*.
crest *n* cresta *f*.
crevasse *n* grieta (de glaciar) *f*.
crevice *n* raja, hendedura *f*.
crew *n* banda, tropa *f*.
crib *n* cuna *f*; pesebre *m*.

cricket *n* grillo *m*; criquet *m*.
crime *n* crimen *m*.
criminal *adj* criminal.
crimson *adj*, *n* carmesí *m*.
cripple *n*, *adj* cojo/ja *m/f*.
crisis *n* crisis *f*.
crisp *adj* crujiente.
crispness *n* encrespadura *f*.
criss-cross *adj* entrelazado/da.
criterion *n* criterio *m*.
critic *n* crítico *m*; crítica *f*.
criticize *vt* criticar, censurar.
crochet *n* ganchillo *m*.
crockery *n* loza *fl*.
crocodile *n* cocodrilo *m*.
crook *n* (*fam*) ladrón *m*.
crooked *adj* torcido/da; perverso/sa.
cross *n* cruz *f*.
crossbar *n* travesaño *m*.
crossbreed *n* raza cruzada *f*.
cross-country *n* carrera a campo traviesa *f*.
crossing *n* cruce *m*; paso a nivel *m*.
cross-reference *n* contrarreferencia *f*.
crotch *n* entrepierna *f*.
crouch *vi* agacharse, bajarse.
crow *n* cuervo *m*.
crowd *n* publico *m*.
crown *n* corona *f*.
crown prince *n* príncipe real *m*.
crucial *adj* crucial.
crucible *n* crisol *m*.
crucifix *n* crucifijo *m*.
crucifixion *n* crucifixión *f*.
crude *adj* crudo/da, imperfecto/ta.
cruel *adj* cruel.
cruelty *n* crueldad *f*.
cruet *n* vinagrera *f*.
cruiser *n* crucero *m*.
crumb *n* miga *f*.
crumble *vt* desmigajar.
crumple *vt* arrugar.
crunchy *adj* crujiente.
crusade *n* cruzada *f*.
crush *vt* apretar, oprimir.
crust *n* costra *f*; corteza *f*.
crutch *n* muleta *f*.
crux *n* lo esencial.
cry *vt*, *vi* gritar; exclamar; llorar.
crypt *n* cripta (bóveda subterránea) *f*.
cryptic *adj* enigmático/ca.
crystal *n* cristal *m*.
cub *n* cachorro *m*.
cube *n* cubo *m*.
cuckoo *n* cuclillo, cuco *m*.
cucumber *n* pepino *m*.
cuddle *vt* abrazar.
cudgel *n* garrote, palo *m*.
cue *n* taco (de billar) *m*.
cuff *n* puñada *f*; vuelta *f*.
cull *vt* escoger, elegir.
culminate *vi* culminar.
culpable *adj* culpable.
cult *n* culto *f*.
cultivate *vi* cultivar.
cultivation *n* cultivación *f*.
cultural *adj* cultural.
culture *n* cultura *f*.
cumulative *adj* cumulativo/va.
cunning *adj* astuto/ta; intrigante.
cup *n* taza, jícara *f*; (*bot*) cáliz *m*.
cupboard *n* armario *m*.
curable *adj* curable.
curb *n* freno *m*; bordillo *m*.
curd *n* cuajada *f*.
cure *n* cura *f*; remedio *m*.
curiosity *n* curiosidad *f*; rareza *f*.
curious *adj* curioso/sa:—**~ly** *adv* curiosamente.
curl *n* rizo de pelo *m*.
curly *adj* rizado/da.
currant *n* pasa *f*.
currency *n* moneda *f*.
current *adj* corriente.
current affairs *npl* actualidades *fpl*.
currently *adv* corrientemente; actualmente.
curry *n* curry *m*.
curse *vt* maldecir.
cursor *n* cursor *m*.
curt *adj* sucinto/ta.
curtail *vt* acortar.
curtain *n* cortina *f*; telón (en los teatros) *m*.
curvature *n* curvatura *f*.
curve *vt* encorvar:—*n* curva *f*.
cushion *n* cojín *m*; almohada *f*.
custard *n* natillas *fpl*.
custodian *n* custodio *m*.
custody *n* custodia *f*; prisión *f*.
custom *n* costumbre *f*, uso *m*.
customary *adj* usual, acostumbrado/da, ordinario/ria.
customer *n* cliente *m/f*.
customs *npl* aduana *f*.
customs duty *n* derechos de aduana *mpl*.
customs officer *n* aduanero/ra *m/f*.
cut *vt* cortar; separar.
cutback *n* reducción *f*.
cute *adj* lindo/da.
cutlery *n* cuchillería *f*.
cutlet *n* chuleta *f*.
cut-rate *adj* a precio reducido.
cut-throat *n* asesino *m*:—*adj* encarnizado/da.
cutting *n* cortadura *f*:—*adj* cortante; mordaz.
cyanide *n* cianuro *m*.

cycle *n* ciclo *m*; bicicleta *f*:—*vi* ir en bicicleta.
cycling *n* ciclismo *m*.
cyclist *n* ciclista *m/f*.
cyclone *n* ciclón *m*.
cygnet *n* pollo del cisne *m*.
cylinder *n* cilindro *m*; rollo *m*.
cylindric(al) *adj* cilíndrico/ca.
cymbals *n* címbalo *m*.
cynic(al) *adj* cínico/ca; obsceno/na: —*n* cínico *m* (*filósofo*).
cynicism *n* cinismo *m*.
cypress *n* ciprés *m*.
cyst *n* quiste *m*.
czar *n* zar *m*.

D

dad(dy) *n* papa *m*.
daddy-long-legs *n* típula *m*.
daffodil *n* narciso *m*.
dagger *n* puñal *m*.
daily *adj* diario/ria.
dainty *adj* delicado/da.
dairy *n* lechería *f*.
dairy produce *n* productos lácteos *mpl*.
daisy *n* margarita *f*.
damage *n* daño *m*; perjuicio *m*.
damask *n* damasco *m*.
damn *vt* condenar.
damnation *n* perdición *f*.
damp *adj* húmedo/da.
dampen *vt* mojar.
dampness *n* humedad *f*.
dance *n* danza *f*; baile *m*.
dandelion *n* diente de león *m*.
dandruff *n* caspa *f*.
danger *n* peligro *m*.
dare *vi* atreverse.
daredevil *n* atrevido *m*.
dark *adj* oscuro/ra.
darling *n*, *adj* querido *m*.
darn *vt* zurcir.
dart *n* dardo *m*.
dartboard *n* diana *f*.
dash *vi* irse de prisa.
dashboard *n* tablero de instrumentos *m*.
data *n* datos *mpl*.
database *n* base de datos *f*.
date *n* fecha *f*; cita *f*.
daughter *n* hija *f*:—~ **in-law** nuera *f*.
dawn *n* alba *f*:—*vi* amanecer.
day *n* día *m*.
dazzle *vt* deslumbrar.
deacon *n* diácono *m*.
dead *adj* muerto/ta.
deadline *n* fecha tope *f*.
deadlock *n* punto muerto *m*.
deaf *adj* sordo/da.
deal *n* convenio *m*; transacción *f*.
dean *n* deán *m*.
dear *adj* querido/da. caro/ra.
dearness *n* carestía *f*.
death *n* muerte *f*.
debacle *n* desastre *m*.
debar *vt* excluir.
debase *vt* degradar.
debate *n* debate *m*; polémica *f*.
debilitate *vt* debilitar.
debt *n* deuda *f*.
decade *n* década *f*.
decadence *n* decadencia *f*.
decaffeinated *adj* descafeinado/da.
decay *vi* decaer; pudrirse.
deceit *n* engaño *m*.
deceive *vt* engañar.
December *n* diciembre *m*.
decent *adj* decente.
decide *vt*, *vi* decidir; resolver.
deciduous *adj* (*bot*) de hoja caduca.
decimal *adj* decimal.
decipher *vt* descifrar.
decision *n* decisión.
declare *vt* declarar.
decline *vt* (*gr*) declinar; evitar.
decompose *vt* descomponer.
decorate *vt* decorar, adornar.
decoration *n* decoración *f*.
decorum *n* decoro *m*.
decrease *vt* disminuir.
decree *n* decreto *m*.
dedicate *vt* dedicar; consagrar.
dedication *n* dedicación *f*.
deduce *vt* deducir.
deep *adj* profundo/da.
deep-freeze *n* congeladora *f*.
deer *n* ciervo *m*.
defamation *n* difamación *f*.
defeat *n* derrota *f*:—*vt* derrotar.
defect *n* defecto *m*.
defend *vt* defender.
defense *n* defensa *f*.
defensive *adj* defensivo/va.
defer *vt* aplazar.
deficient *adj* insuficiente.
deficit *n* déficit *m*.
define *vt* definir.
definition *n* definición *f*.
deflate *vt* desinflar.
deflect *vt* desviar.

deform *vt* desfigurar.
defraud *vt* estafar.
defuse *vt* desactivar.
degenerate *vi* degenerar.
degrade *vt* degradar.
degree *n* grado *m*; titulo *m*.
dehydrated *adj* deshidratado/da.
deity *n* deidad, divinidad *f*.
dejection *n* desaliento *m*.
delay *vt* demorar:—*n* retraso *m*.
delegate *vt* delegar:—*n* delegado *m*.
delete *vt* tachar; borrar.
delicacy *n* delicadeza *f*.
delicate *adj* delicado/da.
delicious *adj* delicioso/sa.
delight *n* delicia *f*.
delinquent *n* delincuente *m*.
delirium *n* delirio *m*.
deliver *vt* entregar.
delivery *n* entrega *f*; parto *m*.
delivery truck *n* camioneta *f*.
delude *vt* engañar.
deluge *n* diluvio *m*.
demagog(ue) *n* demagogo *m*.
demand *n* demanda *f*.
demean *vi* rebajarse.
demented *adj* demente.
demise *n* desaparición *f*.
democracy *n* democracia *f*.
democrat *n* demócrata *m/f*.
demolish *vt* demoler.
demon *n* demonio, diablo *m*.
demonstrate *vt* demostrar.
demoralize *vt* desmoralizar.
demote *vt* degradar.
demure *adj* modesto/ta.
den *n* guarida *f*.
denial *n* negación *f*.
denims *npl* vaqueros *mpl*.
denomination *n* valor *m*.
denote *vt* denotar.
denounce *vt* denunciar.
dense *adj* denso/sa.
density *n* densidad *f*.
dental *adj* dental.
dentist *n* dentista *m/f*.
denture *npl* dentadura postiza *f*.
denunciation *n* denuncia *f*.
deny *vt* negar.
deodorant *n* desodorante *m*.
depart *vi* partir(se).
department *n* departamento *m*.
department store *n* gran almacén *m*.
departure lounge *n* sala de embarque *f*.
depend *vi* depender.
depict *vt* pintar, retratar; describir.
deplore *vt* deplorar, lamentar.
deport *vt* deportar.
deposit *vt* depositar.
depositor *n* depositante *m*.
depot *n* depósito *m*.
deprave *vt* depravar.
depravity *n* depravación *f*.
deprecate *vt* lamentar.
depreciate *vi* depreciarse.
depreciation *n* depreciación *f*.
depress *vt* deprimir.
depressed *adj* deprimido/da.
depression *n* depresión *f*.
deprivation *n* privación *f*.
deprive *vt* privar.
depth *n* profundidad *f*.
deputation *n* diputación *f*.
deputize *vi* suplir a.
deputy *n* diputado *m*.
derelict *adj* abandonado/da.
deride *vt* burlar.
derision *n* mofa *f*.
derivative *n* derivado *m*.
derive *vt*, *vi* derivar(se).
derogatory *adj* despectivo/va.
descend *vi* descender.
descendant *n* descendiente *m*.
descent *n* descenso *m*.
describe *vt* describir.
description *n* descripción *f*.
descriptive *adj* descriptivo/va.
desecrate *vt* profanar.
desert *n* desierto *m*.
deserve *vt* merecer.
design *vt* diseñar.
designate *vt* nombrar.
designedly *adv* de propósito.
designer *n* diseñador *m*.
desirable *adj* deseable.
desire *n* deseo *m*.
desk *n* escritorio *m*.
desolate *adj* desierto/ta.
despair *n* desesperación *f*.
desperado *n* bandido *m*.
desperate *adj* desesperado/da.
despise *vt* despreciar.
despite *prep* a pesar de.
despoil *vt* despojar.
despondency *n* abatimiento *m*.
despot *n* déspota *m/f*.
dessert *n* postre *m*.
destination *n* destino *m*.
destine *vt* destinar.
destiny *n* destino *m*; suerte *f*.
destitute *adj* indigente.
destroy *vt* destruir.
destruction *n* destrucción.
detach *vt* separar.

detail *n* detalle *m*.
detain *vt* retener; detener.
detect *vt* detectar.
detection *n* descubrimiento *m*.
detective *n* detective *m/f*.
deter *vt* disuadir.
detergent *n* detergente *m*.
deteriorate *vt* deteriorar.
determination *n* resolución *f*.
determine *vt* determinar.
deterrent *n* fuerza de disuasión *f*.
detest *vt* detestar.
detonate *vi* detonar.
detonation *n* detonación *f*
detour *n* desviación *f*.
detriment *n* perjuicio *m*.
devaluation *n* devaluación *f*.
devastate *vt* devastar.
develop *vt* desarrollar.
development *n* desarrollo *m*.
deviate *vi* desviarse.
deviation *n* desviación *f*.
device *n* mecanismo *m*.
devil *n* diablo, demonio *m*.
devious *adj* taimado/da.
devise *vt* inventar.
devote *vt* dedicar.
devour *vt* devorar.
devout *adj* devoto/ta.
dew *n* rocío *m*.
dexterity *n* destreza *f*.
diabetes *n* diabetes *f*.
diabetic *n* diabético *m*.
diadem *n* diadema *f*.
diagnosis *n* (*med*) diagnosis *f*.
diagonal *adj*, *n* diagonal (*f*).
diagram *n* diagrama *m*.
dial *n* cuadrante *m*.
dialect *n* dialecto *m*.
dialog(ue) *n* dialogo *m*.
diameter *n* diámetro *m*.
diamond *n* diamante *m*.
diaper *n* pañal *m*.
diaphragm *n* diafragma *m*.
diarrhea *n* diarrea *f*.
diary *n* diario *m*.
dice *npl* dados *mpl*.
dictate *vt* dictar.
dictation *n* dictado *m*.
dictatorship *n* dictadura *f*.
diction *n* dicción *f*
dictionary *n* diccionario *m*.
didactic *adj* didáctico/ca.
die[1] *vi* morir.
die[2] *n* dado *m*.
diesel *n* diesel *m*.
diet *n* dieta *f*; régimen *m*.
differ *vi* diferenciarse.
difference *n* diferencia *f*.
different *adj* diferente.
difficult *adj* difícil.
dig *vt* cavar.
digest *vt* digerir.
digestion *n* digestión *f*.
digger *n* excavadora *f*.
digit *n* dígito *m*.
digital *adj* digital.
dignity *n* dignidad *f*.
dike *n* dique *m*.
dilate *vt*, *vi* dilatar(se).
dilemma *n* dilema *m*.
dilute *vt* diluir.
dim *adj* turbio/bia.
dimension *n* dimensión, extensión *f*.
diminish *vt*, *vi* disminuir(se).
dimple *n* hoyuelo *m*.
din *n* alboroto *m*.
dine *vi* cenar.
diner *n* café *m*, restaurante (económico) *m*.
dinghy *n* lancha neumática *f*.
dingy *adj* sombrío/ria.
dinner *n* cena *f*.
dinosaur *n* dinosaurio *m*.
diocese *n* diócesis *f*.
dip *vt* mojar.
diphtheria *n* difteria *f*.
diploma *n* diploma *m*.
diplomacy *n* diplomacia *f*.
diplomat *n* diplomático/ca *m/f*.
dire *adj* calamitoso/sa.
direct *adj* directo/ta:—*vt* dirigir.
direction *n* dirección *f*.
directly *adj* directamente.
director *n* director/a *m/f*.
directory *n* guía *f*.
dirt *n* suciedad *f*.
disability *n* incapacidad *f*.
disabled *adj* minusválido/da.
disadvantage *n* desventaja *f*:—*vt* perjudicar.
disagree *vi* no estar de acuerdo.
disappear *vi* desaparecer.
disappoint *vt* decepcionar.
disapprove *vt* desaprobar.
disaster *n* desastre *m*.
disbelieve *vt* desconfiar.
discard *vt* descartar.
discern *vt* discernir, percibir.
discharge *vt* descargar; pagar (una deuda).
disciple *n* discípulo *m*.
discipline *n* disciplina *f*:—*vt* disciplinar.
disclose *vi* revelar.
disco *n* discoteca *f*.
discomfort *n* incomodidad *f*.

discontent *n* descontento *m*:—*adj* malcontento/ta.
discontinue *vi* interrumpir.
discord *n* discordia *f*.
discount *n* descuento *m*; rebaja *f*.
discover *vt* descubrir.
discreet *adj* discreto/ta.
discriminate *vt* distinguir.
discuss *vt* discutir.
discussion *n* discusión *f*.
disease *n* enfermedad *f*.
disembark *vt*, *vi* desembarcar.
disentangle *vt* desenredar.
disfigure *vt* desfigurar.
disgrace *n* ignominia *f*.
disgruntled *adj* descontento/ta.
disguise *vt* disfrazar.
disgust *n* aversión *f*:—*vt* repugnar.
dish *n* fuente *f*; plato *m*.
disheveled *adj* desarreglado/da.
dishonest *adj* deshonesto/ta.
dishonesty *n* falta de honradez *f*.
dishonor *n* deshonra, ignominia *f*.
dishtowel *n* trapo de fregar *m*.
dishwasher *n* lavaplatos *m*.
disillusion *vt* desilusionar.
disillusioned *adj* desilusionado/da.
disincentive *n* freno *m*.
disinclination *n* aversión *f*.
disinclined *adj* reacio/cia.
disinfect *vt* desinfectar.
disinfectant *n* desinfectante *m*.
disinherit *vt* desheredar.
disintegrate *vi* disgregarse.
disinterested *adj* desinteresado/da.
disjointed *adj* inconexo/xa.
disk *n* disco, disquete *m*.
diskette *n* disco, disquete *m*.
dislike *n* aversión *f*.
dislocate *vt* dislocar.
dislocation *n* dislocación *f*.
dislodge *vt*, *vi* desalojar.
disloyal *adj* desleal.
disloyalty *n* deslealtad *f*.
dismal *adj* triste.
dismantle *vt* desmontar.
dismay *n* consternación *f*.
dismember *vt* despedazar.
dismiss *vt* despedir.
dismissal *n* despedida *f*.
disobedience *n* desobediencia *f*.
disobedient *adj* desobediente.
disobey *vt* desobedecer.
disorderly *adj* desarreglado/da.
disorganized *adj* desorganizado/da.
disorientated *adj* desorientado/da.
disown *vt* desconocer.
disparage *vt* despreciar.
disparaging *adj* despreciativo/va.
disparity *n* disparidad *f*.
dispassionate *adj* desapasionado/da.
dispatch *vt* enviar.
dispel *vt* disipar.
dispensary *n* dispensario *m*.
dispense *vt* dispensar; distribuir.
disperse *vt* disipersar.
dispirited *adj* desalentado/da.
displace *vt* desplazar.
display *vt* exponer.
displeased *adj* disgustado/da.
displeasure *n* disgusto *m*.
disposable *adj* desechable.
disposal *n* disposición *f*.
dispose *vt* disponer; arreglar.
disposition *n* disposición *f*.
dispossess *vt* desposeer.
disproportionate *adj* desproporcionado/da.
disprove *vt* refutar.
dispute *n* disputa, controversia *f*.
disqualify *vt* incapacitar.
disregard *vt* desatender:—*n* desdén *m*.
disreputable *adj* de mala fama.
disrespectful *adj* irreverente.
disrobe *vt* desnudar.
disrupt *vt* interrumpir.
disruption *n* interrupción *f*.
dissatisfaction *n* descontento/ta.
dissatisfied *adj* insatisfecho/cha.
dissect *vt* disecar.
dissection *n* disección.
dissent *vi* disentir.
dissertation *n* disertación *f*.
dissident *n* disidente *m*.
dissimilar *adj* distinto.
dissolution *n* disolución *f*.
dissolve *vt* disolver.
dissuade *vt* disuadir.
distance *n* distancia *f*:—**at a ~** de lejos:—*vt* apartar.
distant *adj* distante.
distillery *n* destilería *f*.
distinct *adj* distinto/ta.
distinction *n* distinción *f*.
distinctive *adj* distintivo/va.
distinguish *vt* distinguir.
distort *vt* retorcer.
distorted *adj* distorsionado/da.
distortion *n* distorción *f*.
distract *vt* distraer.
distracted *adj* distraído/da.
distraction *n* distracción *f*; confusión *f*.
distraught *adj* enloquecido/da.
distress *n* angustia *f*.
distribute *vt* distribuir, repartir.

distribution *n* distribución *f*.
district *n* distrito *m*.
disturb *vt* molestar.
disturbance *n* disturbio *m*.
disturbing *adj* inquietante.
disused *adj* abandonado/da.
ditch *n* zanja *f*.
ditto *adv* ídem.
diuretic *adj* (*med*) diurético/ca.
diver *n* buzo *m*.
diverge *vi* divergir.
diverse *adj* diverso/sa, diferente.
diversion *n* diversión *f*.
diversity *n* diversidad *f*.
divert *vt* desviar; divertir.
divide *vt* dividir:—*vi* dividirse.
divine *adj* divino/na.
divinity *n* divinidad *f*.
divorce *n* divorcio *m*.
DJ *n* pinchadiscos *m*.
do *vt* hacer, obrar.
docile *adj* dócil, apacible.
dockyard *n* (*mar*) astillero *m*.
doctor *n* médico/ca *m/f*.
doctrine *n* doctrina *f*.
document *n* documento *m*.
documentary *adj* documental.
doe *n* gama *f*:—~ **rabbit** coneja *f*.
dog(ue) *n* perro *m*.
do-it-yourself *n* bricolaje *m*.
doll *n* muñeca *f*.
dollar *n* dólar *m*.
dolphin *n* delfín *m*.
dome *n* cúpula *f*.
domestic *adj* doméstico/ca.
domesticity *n* domesticidad *f*.
domicile *n* domicilio *m*.
dominant *adj* dominante.
dominate *vi* dominar.
domineer *vi* dominar.
dominion *n* dominio *m*.
dominoes *npl* domino *m*.
donate *vt* donar.
donation *n* donación *f*.
donkey *n* asno, borrico *m*.
donor *n* donante *m*.
door *n* puerta *f*.
doorbell *n* timbre *m*.
doorman *n* portero *m*.
doormat *n* felpudo *m*.
dormouse *n* lirón *m*.
dose *n* dosis *f*.
dossier *n* expediente *m*.
dot *n* punto *m*.
dote *vi* adorar.
double *adj* doble.
doubly *adj* doblemente.
doubt *n* duda, sospecha *f*.
doubtful *adj* dudoso/sa.
doubtless *adv* sin duda.
dough *n* masa *f*.
douse *vt* apagar.
dove *n* paloma *f*.
dovecot *n* palomar *m*.
dowdy *adj* mal vestido/da.
down *n* plumón *m*; flojel *m*:—*prep* abajo.
downfall *n* ruina *f*.
downhearted *adj* desanimado/da.
downpour *n* aguacero *m*.
downtown *adv* al centro (de la ciudad).
dowry *n* dote *f*.
doze *vi* dormitar.
dozen *n* docena *f*.
dozy *adj* soñoliento/ta.
drab *adj* gris.
draft *n* borrador *m*; quinta *f*; corriente de aire *f*.
dragon *n* dragón *m*.
dragonfly *n* libélula *f*.
drain *vt* desaguar.
drake *n* ánade macho *m*.
drama *n* drama *m*.
dramatic *adj* dramático/ca.
dramatize *vt* dramatizar.
dramatist *n* dramaturgo/ga *m/f*.
drape *vt* cubrir.
drapes *npl* cortinas *fpl*.
drastic *adj* drástico/ca.
draw *vt* tirar; dibujar.
drawback *n* desventaja *f*.
drawer *n* cajón *m*.
drawing *n* dibujo *m*.
drawing room *n* salón *m*.
dread *n* terror, espanto *m*:—*vt* temer.
dreadful *adj* espantoso/sa.
dream *n* sueno *m*:—*vi* sonar.
drench *vt* empapar.
dress *vt* vestir:—*n* vestido *m*.
dresser *n* aparador *m*.
dressing gown *n* bata *f*.
dressing table *n* tocador *m*.
dressmaker *n* modista *f*.
dried *adj* seco/ca.
drill *n* taladro *m*.
drink *vt*, *vi* beber.
drinkable *adj* potable.
drip *vi* gotear.
drive *vt* manejar.
driver *n* conductor *m*.
driveway *n* entrada *f*.
drizzle *vi* lloviznar.
droop *vi* decaer.
drop *n* gota *f*.
drought *n* seguía *f*.

drown *vt* anegar.
drowsiness *n* somnolencia *f*.
drowsy *adj* soñoliento/ta.
drudgery *n* trabajo monótono *m*.
drug *n* droga *f*:—*vt* drogar.
drug addict *n* drogadicto *m*.
drug store *n* farmacia *f*.
drum *n* tambor *m*:—*vi* tocar el tambor.
drummer *n* batería *m*.
drumstick *n* palillo de tambor *m*.
drunk *adj* borracho/cha.
drunkard *n* borracho *m*.
drunkenness *n* borrachera *f*.
dry *adj* seco/ca. * *vt* secar.
dry goods store *n* mercería, camiseria *f*.
dry rot *n* podredumbre *f*.
dual *adj* doble.
dubbed *adj* doblado/da.
dubious *adj* dudoso/sa.
duck *n* pato *m*.
duckling *n* patito *m*.
dud *adj* estropeado/da.
due *adj* debido/da.
duel *n* duelo *m*.
duet *n* (*mus*) duo *m*.
dull *adj* lerdo/da. insípido/da.
duly *adv* debidamente; puntualmente.
dumb *adj* mudo/da.
dumbbell *n* pesa *f*.
dumbfounded *adj* pasmado/da.
dummy *n* maniquí *m*; imbécil *m*.
dumpling *n* bola de masa *f*.
dumpy *adj* gordito/ta.
dunce *n* zopenco *m*.
dune *n* duna *f*.
dung *n* estiércol *m*.
dungarees *npl* mono *m*.
dungeon *n* calabozo *m*.
dupe *n* bobo *m*.
duplicity *n* duplicidad *f*.
durability *n* durabilidad *f*.
durable *adj* duradero/ra.
duration *n* duración *f*.
during *prep* mientras, durante el tiempo que.
dusk *n* crepúsculo *m*.
dust *n* polvo *m*.
duster *n* plumero *m*.
dutch courage *n* valor fingido *m*.
duteous *adj* fiel, leal.
dutiful *adj* obediente.
duty *n* deber *m*; obligación *f*.
dwarf *n* enano *m*; enana *f*.
dwell *vi* habitar, morar.
dwelling *n* habitación *f*; domicilio *m*.
dwindle *vi* mermar, disminuirse.
dye *vt* teñir:—*n* tinte *m*.
dynamic *adj* dinámico/ca.
dynamite *n* dinamita *f*.
dynamo *n* dinamo *f*.
dynasty *n* dinastía *f*.
dysentery *n* disenteria *f*.
dyspepsia *n* (*med*) dispepsia *f*.

E

each *pn* cada uno, cada una.
eager *adj* entusiasmado/da.
eagle *n* águila *f*.
eaglet *n* aguilucho *m*.
ear *n* oreja *f*.
earache *n* dolor de oídos *m*.
eardrum *n* tímpano (del oído) *m*.
early *adj* temprano/na.
earn *vt* ganar; conseguir.
earnest *adj* serio/ria.
earth *n* tierra *f*.
earthenware *n* loza de barro *f*.
earthquake *n* terremoto *m*.
earthworm *n* lombriz *f*.
earthy *adj* sensual.
earwig *n* tijereta *f*.
ease *n* comodidad *f*; facilidad *f*.
easel *n* caballete *m*.
easily *adv* fácilmente.
east *n* este *m*; oriente *m*.
Easter *n* Pascua de Resurrección *f*.
easterly *adj* del este.
eastern *adj* del este, oriental.
easy *adj* fácil; cómodo/da.
easy chair *n* sillón *m*.
eat *vt* comer.
ebb *n* reflujo *m*.
ebony *n* ébano *m*.
eccentric *adj* excéntrico/ca.
echo *n* eco *m*.
eclectic *adj* ecléctico/ca.
eclipse *n* eclipse *m*.
ecology *n* ecología *f*.
economics *npl* economía *f*.
economy *n* economía *f*.
ecstasy *n* éxtasis *m*.
eczema *n* eczema *m*.
eddy *n* reflujo de agua *m*.
edge *n* filo *m*.
edict *n* edicto, mandato *m*.
edit *vt* dirigir; redactar.
edition *n* edición *f*.
editor *n* director *m*.
educate *vt* educar.

education *n* educación *f*.
eel *n* anguila *f*.
effect *n* efecto *m*.
effective *adj* eficaz..
effeminate *adj* afeminado/da.
effervescence *n* efervescencia *f*.
efficacy *n* eficacia *f*.
efficient *adj* eficaz.
effigy *n* efigie, imagen *f*.
effort *n* esfuerzo *m*.
egg *n* huevo *m*.
eggplant *n* berenjena *f*.
ego(t)ist *n* egoísta *m/f*.
eight *num* ocho.
eighteen *num* dieciocho.
eighth *adj* octavo.
eighty *num* ochenta.
either *pn* cualquiera.
eject *vt* expeler, desechar.
elastic *adj* elástico/ca.
elation *n* regocijo *m*.
elbow *n* codo *m*.
elder *n* saúco *m* (árbol):—*adj* mayor.
elect *vt* elegir.
election *n* elección *f*.
electrician *n* electricista *m/f*.
electricity *n* electricidad *f*.
elegance *n* elegancia *f*.
elegant *adj* elegante, delicado/da.
elegy *n* elegía *f*.
element *n* elemento *m*.
elephant *n* elefante *m*.
elevate *vt* elevar, alzar.
elevator *n* ascensor *m*.
eleven *num* once.
eleventh *adj* onceno, undécimo.
elf *n* duende *m*.
elicit *vt* sacar de.
eligible *adj* elegible.
eliminate *vt* eliminar, descartar.
elk *n* alce *m*.
elm *n* olmo *m*.
elocution *n* elocución *f*.
elongate *vt* alargar.
elope *vi* escapar, huir.
elopement *n* fuga *f*.
eloquence *n* elocuencia *f*.
else *pn* otro/ra.
elsewhere *adv* en otra parte.
elude *vt* eludir, evitar.
embargo *n* prohibición *f*.
embark *vt* embarcar.
embarrass *vt* avergonzar.
embarrassment *n* desconcierto *m*.
embassy *n* embajada *f*.
embed *vt* empotrar; clavar.
embellish *vt* hermosear.
embers *npl* rescoldo *m*.
embezzle *vt* desfalcar.
embitter *vt* amargar.
emblem *n* emblema *m*.
embrace *vt* abrazar.
embroider *vt* bordar.
embroil *vt* embrollar; confundir.
embryo *n* embrión *m*.
emerald *n* esmeralda *f*.
emerge *vi* salir, proceder.
emergency *n* emergencia *f*.
emery *n* esmeril *m*.
emigrant *n* emigrante *m*.
emigrate *vi* emigrar.
eminent *adj* eminente.
emission *n* emisión *f*.
emit *vt* emitir.
emotion *n* emoción *f*.
emperor *n* emperador *m*.
emphasis *n* énfasis *m*.
emphasize *vt* hablar con énfasis.
empire *n* imperio *m*.
employ *vt* emplear, ocupar.
employee *n* empleado *m*.
employer *n* patrón *m*; empresario *m*.
empress *n* emperatriz *f*.
empty *adj* vacío/cia.
emulate *vt* emular.
emulsion *n* emulsión *f*.
enable *vt* capacitar.
enact *vt* promulgar.
enamel *n* esmalte *m*.
enchant *vt* encantar.
enchanting *adj* encantador.
encircle *vt* cercar, circundar.
enclose *vt* cercar, circunvalar.
encore *adv* otra vez, de nuevo.
encounter *n* encuentro *m*.
encourage *vt* animar.
encouragement *n* estimulo, patrocinio *m*.
encroach *vt* usurpar.
encumber *vt* embarazar, cargar.
encyclopedia *n* enciclopedia *f*.
end *n* fin *m*.
endanger *vt* peligrar.
endear *vt* encarecer.
endeavor *vi* esforzarse; intentar.
endemic *adj* endémico/ca.
ending *n* conclusión.
endive *n* (*bot*) endibia *f*.
endless *adj* infinito/ta.
endorse *vt* endosar; aprobar.
endow *vt* dotar.
endure *vt* sufrir, soportar.
enemy *n* enemigo/ga.
energetic *adj* enérgico/ca.
energy *n* energía, fuerza *f*.

enforce *vt* hacer cumplir.
engine *n* motor *m*; locomotora *f*.
engineer *n* ingeniero *m*.
engrave *vt* grabar.
enhance *vt* aumentar.
enigma *n* enigma *m*.
enjoy *vt* gozar.
enjoyment *n* disfrute *m*; placer *m*.
enlarge *vt* engrandecer.
enlist *vt* alistar.
enliven *vt* animar.
enmity *n* enemistad *f*; odio *m*.
enormous *adj* enorme.
enough *adv* bastante; basta.
enrage *vt* enfurecer.
enrapture *vt* arrebatar.
enrich *vt* enriquecer.
enrol *vt* registrar.
enrolment *n* inscripción *f*.
ensign *n* (*mil*) bandera *f*.
enslave *vt* esclavizar.
ensue *vi* seguirse.
ensure *vt* asegurar.
entangle *vt* enmarañar.
enter *vt* entrar; admitir.
enterprise *n* empresa *f*.
entertain *vt* divertir; hospedar.
entertainer *n* artista *m/f*.
entertainment *n* entretenimiento, pasatiempo *m*.
enthralling *adj* cautivador.
enthusiasm *n* entusiasmo *m*.
entice *vt* tentar; seducir.
entire *adj* entero/ra, completo/ta.
entitle *vt* intitular; conferir algún derecho.
entity *n* entidad *f*.
entrance *n* entrada *f*.
entreat *vt* rogar, suplicar.
entrepreneur *n* empresario *m*.
entrust *vt* confiar.
entry *n* entrada *f*.
entwine *vt* entrelazar.
envelop *n* envolver.
envelope *vt* sobre *m*.
enviable *adj* envidiable.
environment *n* medio ambiente *m*.
environs *npl* vecindad *f*.
envisage *vt* prever; concebir.
envoy *n* enviado *m*.
envy *n* envidia.
ephemeral *adj* efímero/ra.
epic *adj* épico/ca.
epidemic *adj* epidémico/ca.
epilogue *n* epílogo *m*.
Epiphany *n* Epifanía *f*.
episcopacy *n* episcopado *m*.
episcopal *adj* episcopal.
episcopalian *n* anglicano *m*.
episode *n* episodio *m*.
epistle *n* epístola *f*.
epithet *n* epíteto *m*.
epoch *n* época *f*.
equal *adj* igual.
equalize *vt* igualar.
equality *n* igualdad, uniformidad *f*.
equally *adv* igualmente.
equate *vt* equiparar (con).
equation *n* ecuación *f*.
equator *n* ecuador *m*.
equatorial *adj* ecuatorial.
equestrian *adj* ecuestre.
equilibrium *n* equilibrio *m*.
equinox *n* equinoccio *m*.
equip *vt* equipar.
equipment *n* equipaje *m*.
equitable *adj* equitativo/va.
equity *n* equidad *f*.
equivalent *adj*, *n* equivalente *m*.
era *n* era *f*.
eradicate *vt* desarraigar.
eradication *n* extirpación *f*.
erase *vt* borrar.
eraser *n* goma de borrar *f*.
erect *vt* erigir; establecer.
ermine *n* armiño *m*.
erode *vt* erosionar.
erotic *adj* erótico/ca.
err *vi* vagar, errar.
errand *n* recado.
erratic *adj* errático/ca.
erroneous *adj* erróneo/nea.
error *n* error *m*.
erudite *adj* erudito/ta.
erupt *vi* entrar en erupción; hacer erupción.
eruption *n* erupción *f*.
escalate *vi* extenderse.
escalator *n* escalera móvil *f*.
escapade *n* travesura *f*.
escape *vt* evitar; escapar.
escapism *n* escapismo *m*.
escort *n* escolta *f*:—*vt* escoltar.
esoteric *adj* esotérico/ca.
especial *adj* especial.
essay *n* ensayo *m*.
essence *n* esencia *f*.
essential *n* esencia *f*:—*adj* esencial.
establish *vt* establecer.
establishment *n* establecimiento *m*.
estate *n* estado *m*.
esteem *vt* estimar, apreciar.
estimate *vt* estimar, apreciar.
estuary *n* estuario.
etch *vt* grabar al aguafuerte.
eternal *adj* eterno/na.

eternity *n* eternidad *f*.
ether *n* éter *m*.
ethical *adj* ético/ca.
ethics *npl* ética *f*.
ethnic *adj* étnico/ca.
ethos *n* genio *m*.
etiquette *n* etiqueta *f*.
etymology *n* etimología *f*.
Eucharist *n* Eucaristía *f*.
eulogy *n* elogio.
eunuch *n* eunuco *m*.
euphemism *n* eufemismo *m*.
evacuate *vt* evacuar.
evacuation *n* evacuación *f*.
evade *vt* evadir.
evaluate *vt* evaluar.
evangelical *adj* evangélico/ca.
evaporate *vt* evaporar.
evasion *n* evasión *f*.
evasive *adj* evasivo/va.
eve *n* víspera *f*.
even *adj* llano/na, igual; par, semejante:—*adv* aun; aun cuando, supuesto que; no obstante.
evening *n* tarde *f*.
event *n* acontecimiento, evento *m*.
eventuality *n* eventualidad *f*.
ever *adv* siempre.
every *adj* cada uno o cada una.
evict *vt* desahuciar.
eviction *n* desahucio *m*.
evidence *n* evidencia *f*.
evil *adj* malo/la, depravado/da.
evocative *adj* sugestivo/va.
evoke *vt* evocar.
evolution *n* evolución *f*.
evolve *vt*, *vi* evolucionar.
ewe *n* oveja *f*.
exacerbate *vt* exacerbar.
exact *adj* exacto/ta.
exacting *adj* exigente.
exaggerate *vt* exagerar.
exaggeration *n* exageración *f*.
exalt *vt* exaltar.
exaltation *n* exaltación.
examination *n* examen *m*.
examine *vt* examinar.
examiner *n* inspector/a *m/f*.
example *n* ejemplar *m*; ejemplo *m*.
excavate *vt* excavar.
excavation *n* excavación *f*.
exceed *vt* exceder.
exceedingly *adv* extremamente, en sumo grado.
excel *vt* sobresalir.
excellence *n* excelencia *f*.
excellent *adj* excelente.
except *vt* exceptuar, excluir:—**~(ing)** *prep* excepto, a excepción de.
exception *n* excepción, exclusión *f*.
exceptional *adj* excepcional.
excerpt *n* extracto *m*.
excess *n* exceso *m*.
excessive *adj* excesivo/va.
exchange *vt* cambiar; trocar.
exchange rate *n* tipo de cambio *m*.
excitability *n* excitabilidad *f*.
excitable *adj* excitable.
excite *vt* excitar; estimular.
excited *adj* emocionado/da.
excitement *n* estímulo *m*, excitación *f*.
exclaim *vi* exclamar.
exclamation *n* exclamación *f*.
exclamation mark *n* punto de admiración *m*.
exclamatory *adj* exclamatorio/ria.
exclude *vt* excluir; exceptuar.
exclusion *n* exclusión, *f*.
exclusive *adj* exclusivo/va.
excommunicate *vt* excomulgar.
excommunication *n* excomunión *f*.
excrement *n* excremento *m*.
excruciating *adj* atroz.
excursion *n* excursión *f*.
excusable *adj* excusable.
excuse *vt* disculpar.
execute *vt* ejecutar.
execution *n* ejecución *f*.
executioner *n* ejecutor/a.
executive *adj* ejecutivo/va.
executor *n* testamentario/ria, albacea *m/f*.
exemplary *adj* ejemplar.
exemplify *vt* ejemplificar.
exempt *adj* exento/ta.
exemption *n* exención *f*.
exercise *n* ejercicio *m*.
exercise book *n* cuaderno *m*.
exertion *n* esfuerzo *m*.
exhale *vt* exhalar.
exhaust *n* escape *m*.
exhausted *adj* agotado/da.
exhaustion *n* agotamiento *m*.
exhaustive *adj* comprensivo/va.
exhibit *vt* exhibir; mostrar.
exhibition *n* exposición *f*.
exhilarating *adj* estimulante.
exhort *vt* exhortar, excitar.
exhume *vt* exhumar.
exile *n* destierro *m*.
exist *vi* existir.
existence *n* existencia *f*.
exit *n* salida *f*:—*vi* hacer mutis.
exit ramp *n* vía de acceso *f*.
exodus *n* éxodo *m*.
exonerate *vt* exonerar.

exhorbitant *adj* exorbitante.
exorcize *vt* exorcizar, conjurar.
exorcism *n* exorcismo *m*.
exotic *adj* exótico/ca.
expand *vt* extender, dilatar.
expatriate *vt* expatriar.
expect *vt* esperar.
expectant mother *n* mujer encinta *f*.
expediency *n* conveniencia *f*.
expedition *n* expedición *f*.
expel *vt* expeler, desterrar.
expend *vt* expender.
expendable *adj* prescindible.
expenditure *n* gasto, desembolso *m*.
expense *n* gasto *m*; coste *m*.
experience *n* experiencia *f*; practica *f*.
experienced *adj* experimentado/da.
experiment *n* experimento *m*.
expert *adj* experto/ta.
expertise *n* pericia *f*.
expiration *n* expiración *f*.
expire *vi* expirar.
explain *vt* explanar, explicar.
explanation *n* explanación, explicación *f*.
expletive *adj* expletivo/va.
explicit *adj* explícito/ta.
explode *vt*, *vi* estallar, explotar.
exploit *vt* explotar.
exploitation *n* explotación *f*.
exploration *n* exploración *f*.
exploratory *adj* exploratorio/ria.
explore *vt* explorar.
explorer *n* explorador *m*.
explosion *n* explosión *f*.
explosive *adj*, *n* explosivo *m*.
exponent *n* (*math*) exponente *m*.
export *vt* exportar.
expose *vt* exponer; mostrar.
exposed *adj* expuesto/ta.
exposition *n* exposición *f*.
expostulate *vi* debatir, contender.
exposure *n* exposición *f*.
expound *vt* exponer.
express *vt* exprimir; representar.
expression *n* expresión *f*.
expressionless *adj* sin expresión (cara).
expressway *n* autopista *f*.
expulsion *n* explosión *f*.
expurgate *vt* expurgar.
exquisite *adj* exquisito/ta.
extend *vt* extender.
extension *n* extensión *f*.
extensive *adj* extenso/sa.
extent *n* extensión *f*.
extenuate *vt* extenuar.
exterior *adj*, *n* exterior *m*.
exterminate *vt* exterminar.
extermination *n* exterminación *f*.
external *adj* externo/na.
extinct *adj* extinto/ta.
extinction *n* extinción *f*.
extinguish *vt* extinguir.
extinguisher *n* extintor *m*.
extol *vt* alabar, magnificar.
extort *vt* sacar por fuerza.
extortion *n* extorsión *f*.
extortionate *adj* excesivo/va.
extra *adv* extra.
extract *vt* extraer.
extracurricular *adj* extraescolar.
extradition *n* (*law*) extradición *f*.
extramarital *adj* extramatrimonial.
extraneous *adj* extraño/ña.
extraordinary *adj* extraordinario/ria.
extravagance *n* extravagancia *f*.
extravagant *adj* extravagante.
extreme *adj* extremo/ma.
extremist *adj*, *n* extremista *m/f*.
extremity *n* extremidad *f*.
extrovert *adj*, *n* extrovertido *m*.
exuberance *n* exuberancia *f*.
exuberant *adj* exuberante.
exult *vt* exultar.
exultation *n* exultación *f*; regocijo *m*.
eye *n* ojo *m*:—*vt* ojear, contemplar, observar.
eyeball *n* globo del ojo *m*.
eyebrow *n* ceja *f*.
eyelash *n* pestaña *f*.
eyelid *n* párpado *m*.
eyesight *n* vista *f*.
eyewitness *n* testigo ocular *m*.
eyrie *n* aguilera *f*.

F

fabric *n* tejido *m*.
fabricate *vt* fabricar.
fabulous *adj* fabuloso/sa.
facade *n* fachada *f*.
face *n* cara, faz *f*; superficie *f*.
facet *n* faceta *f*.
facetious *adj* chistoso/sa.
facile *adj* fácil.
facilitate *vt* facilitar.
facility *n* facilidad *f*.
facsimile *n* facsímile *m*; telefax *m*.
fact *n* hecho *m*.
faction *n* facción *f*.
factor *n* factor *m*.

factory *n* fabrica *f*.
faculty *n* facultad *f*.
fad *n* moda , manía *f*.
fade *vi* decaer.
fail *vt* suspender, reprobar; fallar a.
failure *n* falta *f*; culpa *f*.
faint *vi* desmayarse, debilitarse.
faint-hearted *adj* cobarde.
fair *adj* hermoso/sa, bello/la; blanco/ca; rubio/bia; claro/ra, sereno/na; favorable; recto/ta, justo/ta; franco/ca:—*adv* limpio: —*n* feria *f*.
fairly *adv* justamente.
fairy *n* hada *f*.
faith *n* fe *f*; dogma de fe *m*.
faithfulness *n* fidelidad *f*.
fake *n* falsificación *f*.
falcon *n* halcón *m*.
fall[1] *n* otoño *m*.
fall[2] *vi* caer(se).
fallacy *n* falacia.
fallible *adj* falible.
false *adj* falso/sa.
falsify *vt* falsificar.
fame *n* fama *f*.
famed *adj* celebrado/da, famoso/sa.
familiar *adj* familiar.
family *n* familia *f*.
famine *n* hambre *f*; carestía *f*.
famous *adj* famoso/sa.
fan *n* abanico *m*; aficionado *m*.
fanatic *adj*, *n* fanático *m*.
fanciful *adj* imaginativo/va.
fancy *n* fantasía, imaginación *f*.
fanfare *n* (*mus*) fanfarria *f*.
fang *n* colmillo *m*.
fantastic *adj* fantástico/ca.
fantasy *n* fantasía *f*.
far *adv* lejos.
faraway *adj* remoto/ta.
farce *n* farsa *f*.
fare *n* precio *m*; tarifa *f*.
farm *n* finca *f*, granja *f*.
farmer *n* estanciero *m*; granjero *m*.
fascinate *vt* fascinar, encantar.
fascism *n* fascismo.
fashion *n* moda *f*; forma.
fashionable *adj* a la moda.
fashion show *n* desfile de modelos *m*.
fast *vi* ayunar; *adv* rápidamente.
fasten *vt* abrochar.
fastidious *adj* fastidioso/sa.
fat *adj* gordo/da.
fatal *adj* fatal.
fate *n* hado, destino *m*.
fateful *adj* fatídico/ca.
father *n* padre *m*.
father-in-law *n* suegro *m*.
fatherland *n* patria *f*.
fathom *n* braza (medida) *f*.
fatigue *n* fatiga *f*.
fatty *adj* graso/sa.
faucet *n* espita *f*.
fault *n* falta, culpa *f*.
fauna *n* fauna *f*.
faux pas *n* plancha *f*.
favor *n* favor.
favorite *n* favorito *m*.
fawn *n* cervato *m*.
fax *n* facsímil(e) *m*; telefax *m*.
fear *vi* temer:—*n* miedo *m*.
fearful *adj* medroso/sa, temeroso/sa.
feasible *adj* factible.
feast *n* banquete.
feat *n* hecho *m*.
feather *n* pluma *f*.
feature *n* característica *f*; rasgo *m*.
February *n* febrero *m*.
federal *adj* federal.
federalist *n* federalista *m/f*.
federation *n* federación *f*.
fed-up *adj* harto/ta.
fee *n* honorarios *mpl*.
feeble *adj* flaco/ca, débil.
feed *vt* nutrir; alimentar.
feedback *n* reacción *f*.
feel *vt* sentir; tocar.
feign *vt* inventar, fingir.
feline *adj* gatuno/na.
fellowship *n* compañerismo *m*.
felon *n* criminal *m/f*.
felony *n* crimen *m*.
felt *n* fieltro *m*.
female *n* hembra *f*:—*adj* femenino/na.
feminine *adj* femenino/na.
feminist *n* feminista *m/f*.
fence *n* cerca *f*; defensa *f*.
fennel *n* (*bot*) hinojo *m*.
fern *n* (*bot*) helecho *m*.
ferocious *adj* feroz.
ferret *n* hurón *m*.
ferry *n* barca de pasaje *f*.
fertile *adj* fértil, fecundo/da.
fester *vi* enconarse.
festival *n* fiesta *f*; festival *m*.
fetch *vt* ir a buscar.
fete *n* fiesta *f*.
fetus *n* feto *m*.
feud *n* riña, contienda *f*.
feudal *adj* feudal.
fever *n* fiebre *f*.
feverish *adj* febril.
few *adj* poco/ca.
fewer *adj* menor.

fewest *adj* los menos.
fiancé *n* novio *m*.
fiancée *n* novia *f*.
fib *n* mentira *f*.
fibre *n* fibra, hebra *f*.
fickle *adj* voluble.
fiction *n* ficción *f*.
fiddle *n* violín *m*; trampa *f*.
fidelity *n* fidelidad *f*.
field *n* campo *m*.
fieldmouse *n* ratón de campo *m*.
fierce *adj* fiero/ra, feroz.
fierceness *n* fiereza, ferocidad *f*.
fiery *adj* ardiente; apasionado/da.
fifteen *adj*, *n* quince.
fifteenth *adj*, *n* decimoquinto/ta.
fifth *adj*, *n* quinto/ta.
fiftieth *adj*, *n* quincuagésimo/ma.
fifty *adj*, *n* cincuenta.
fig *n* higo *m*.
fight *vt*, *vi* reñir; batallar; combatir.
fig-leaf *n* hoja de higuera *f*.
figurative *adj* figurativo/va.
figure *n* figura.
filament *n* filamento *m*.
fill *vt* llenar; hartar.
fillet *n* filete *m*.
filling station *n* estación de servicio *f*.
fillip *n* (*fig*) estimulo *m*.
filly *n* potra *f*.
film *n* película *f*; film *m*.
filter *n* filtro *m*.
filth(iness) *n* inmundicia, porquería *f*.
fin *n* aleta *f*.
final *adj* final, último/ma.
finalize *vt* concluir.
finance *n* fondos *mpl*.
financier *n* financiero *m*.
find *vt* hallar, descubrir.
finesse *n* sutileza *f*.
finger *n* dedo *m*.
fingernail *n* uña *f*.
finish *vt* acabar, terminar, concluir.
finite *adj* finito/ta.
fir *n* abeto *m*.
fire *n* fuego *m*; incendio *m*.
firearm *n* arma de fuego *f*.
firefly *n* luciérnaga *f*.
firewood *n* leña *f*.
fireworks *npl* fuegos artificiales *mpl*.
firm *adj* firme, estable.
firmament *n* firmamento *m*.
firmness *n* firmeza *f*.
first *adj* primero/ra.
fiscal *adj* fiscal.
fish *n* pez *m*.
fishbone *n* espina *f*.
fisherman *n* pescador *m*.
fishy *adj* (*fig*) sospechoso/sa.
fist *n* puño *m*.
fitness *n* salud *f*.
five *adj*, *n* cinco.
fix *vt* fijar.
fixation *n* obsesión *f*.
fizzy *adj* gaseoso/sa.
flabbergasted *adj* pasmado/da.
flabby *adj* blando/da.
flaccid *adj* flojo/ja.
flag *n* bandera *f*.
flagpole *n* asta de bandera *f*.
flagrant *adj* flagrante; notorio/ria.
flagship *n* navío almirante *m*.
flair *n* aptitud especial *f*.
flake *n* copo *m*.
flamboyant *adj* vistoso/sa.
flame *n* llama *f*.
flamingo *n* flamenco *m*.
flammable *adj* inflamable.
flank *n* ijada *f*.
flannel *n* franela *f*.
flare *vi* lucir, brillar.
flash *n* flash *m*.
flashlight *n* antorcha *f*.
flask *n* frasco *m*.
flat *adj* llano/na, plano/na.
flatness *n* llanura *f*.
flatten *vt* allanar.
flatter *vt* adular.
flattery *n* adulación *f*.
flatulence *n* (*med*) flatulencia *f*.
flaunt *vt* ostentar.
flavor *n* sabor *m*.
flavorless *adj* soso/sa.
flaw *n* falta *m*.
flawless *adj* sin defecto.
flax *n* lino *m*.
flea *n* pulga *f*.
fleck *n* mota *f*.
flee *vt* huir de.
fleece *n* vellón *m*.
fleet *n* flota *f*.
flesh *n* carne *f*.
flex *n* cordón *m*.
flexibility *n* flexibilidad *f*.
flexible *adj* flexible.
flight *n* vuelo *m*.
flight attendant *n* tripulante auxiliar *m*.
flimsy *adj* débil; fútil.
flinch *vi* encogerse.
fling *vt* lanzar.
flint *n* pedernal *m*.
flip *vt* arrojar.
flippant *adj* petulante.
flipper *n* aleta *f*.

flirt *vi* coquetear:—*n* coqueta *f*.
flirtation *n* coquetería *f*.
flock *n* manada *f*.
flog *vt* azotar.
flogging *n* tunda, zurra *f*.
flood *n* diluvio *m*; inundación *f*.
flooding *n* inundación *f*.
floodlight *n* foco *m*.
floor *n* suelo, piso *m*.
floorboard *n* tabla *f*.
flop *n* fracaso *m*.
floppy *adj* flojo/ja.
flora *n* flora *f*.
floral *adj* floral.
florescence *n* florescencia *f*.
florid *adj* florido/da.
florist *n* florista *m/f*.
florist's (shop) *n* florería *f*.
flotilla *n* (*mar*) flotilla *f*.
flounder *n* platija (pez de mar) *f*.
flour *n* harina *f*.
flourish *vi* florecer.
flout *vt* burlarse de.
flow *vi* fluir.
flower *n* flor *f*.
flowerbed *n* cuadro (en un jardín) *m*.
flowerpot *n* tiesto de flores *m*.
flowery *adj* florido/da.
fluctuate *vi* fluctuar.
fluctuation *n* fluctuación *f*.
fluency *n* fluidez *f*.
fluent *adj* fluido/da.
fluff *n* pelusa *f*.
fluid *adj*, *n* fluido/da *m*.
fluidity *n* fluidez *f*.
fluke *n* (*sl*) chiripa *f*.
fluoride *n* fluoruro *m*.
flurry *n* ráfaga *f*; agitación *f*.
flute *n* flauta *f*.
flutter *vi* revolotear; estar en agitación.
flux *n* flujo *m*.
fly *vt* pilotar; transportar:—*vi* volar.
flying saucer *n* platillo volante *m*.
foal *n* potro *m*.
foam *n* espuma *f*.
foamy *adj* espumoso/sa.
focus *n* foco.
fodder *n* forraje *m*.
foe *n* adversario/ria *m/f*, enemigo *m*.
fog *n* niebla *f*.
foggy *adj* nebuloso/sa.
fold *n* redil *m*; pliegue *m*.
folder *n* carpeta *f*.
folding *adj* plegable.
foliage *n* follaje *m*.
folio *n* folio *m*.
folk *n* gente *f*.
folklore *n* folklore *m*.
folk song *n* canción folklórica *f*.
follow *vt* seguir; acompañar.
follower *n* seguidor/a *m/f*.
following *adj* siguiente.
folly *n* extravagancia *f*.
foment *vt* fomentar.
fond *adj* cariñoso/sa.
fondle *vt* acariciar.
fondness *n* gusto *m*; cariño *m*.
font *n* pila bautismal *f*.
food *n* comida *f*.
food mixer *n* batidora *f*.
food poisoning *n* botulismo *m*.
fool *n* loco/ca, tonto/ta *m/f*.
foolish *adj* bobo/ba, tonto/ta.
foolscap *n* papel tamaño folio *m*.
foot *n* pie *m*; pata *f*.
footage *n* imágenes *fpl*.
footnote *n* nota de pie *f*.
footpath *n* senda *f*.
footprint *n* huella *f*.
for *prep* por, a causa de; para.
forbid *vt* prohibir.
force *n* fuerza *f*; poder, vigor *m*.
forced *adj* forzado/da.
forceful *adj* enérgico/ca.
forceps *n* fórceps *m*.
ford *n* vado *m*.
fore *n*:—**to the ~** en evidencia.
forearm *n* antebrazo *m*.
foreboding *n* presentimiento *m*.
forecast *vt* pronosticar.
forecourt *n* patio *m*.
forefather *n* abuelo, antecesor *m*.
forefinger *n* índice *m*.
forefront *n*:—**in the ~ of** en la vanguardia de.
forego *vt* ceder.
foreground *n* delantera *f*.
forehead *n* frente *f*.
foreign *adj* extranjero/ra; extraño/ña.
foreigner *n* extranjero/ra, forastero/ra *m/f*.
foreign exchange *n* divisas *fpl*.
foreleg *n* pata delantera *f*.
foreman *n* capataz *m*.
foremost *adj* principal.
forensic *adj* forense.
forerunner *n* precursor/a *m/f*.
foresee *vt* prever.
foresight *n* previsión *f*.
forest *n* bosque *m*; selva *f*.
forester *n* guardabosque *m*.
forestry *n* silvicultura *f*.
foretaste *n* muestra *f*.
foretell *vt* predecir, profetizar.
forethought *n* providencia *f*.
forever *adv* para siempre.

foreword *n* prefacio *m*.
forfeit *n* confiscación *f*.
forge *n* fragua *f*; fabrica de metales *f*.
forger *n* falsificador/a *m/f*.
forgery *n* falsificación *f*.
forget *vt* olvidar.
forgetful *adj* olvidadizo/za.
forget-me-not *n* (*bot*) nomeolvides *m*.
forgive *vt* perdonar.
forgiveness *n* perdón *m*.
fork *n* tenedor *m*.
form *n* forma *f*; modelo *m*; modo *m*.
formal *adj* formal.
formality *n* formalidad *f*.
format *n* formato *m*.
formation *n* formación *f*.
formative *adj* formativo/va.
former *adj* precedente; anterior.
formidable *adj* formidable.
formula *n* fórmula *f*.
formulate *vt* formular.
forsake *vt* dejar.
fort *n* castillo *m*.
forthright *adj* franco/ca.
forthwith *adj* inmediatamente.
fortieth *adj*, *n* cuadragésimo *m*.
fortification *n* fortificación *f*.
fortify *vt* fortificar.
fortitude *n* fortaleza *f*.
fortnight *n* quince días *mpl*.
fortress *n* (*mil*) fortaleza *f*.
fortuitous *adj* impensado/da.
fortunate *adj* afortunado/da.
fortune *n* fortuna, suerte *f*.
fortune-teller *n* sortílego/ga.
forty *adj*, *n* cuarenta.
forum *n* foro *m*.
forward *adj* avanzado/da; delantero/ra.
forwardness *n* precocidad *f*; audacia *f*.
fossil *adj*, *n* fósil *m*.
foster *vt* criar.
foul *adj* sucio/cia, puerco/ca; impuro/ra.
found *vt* fundar, establecer.
foundation *n* fundación *f*.
founder *n* fundador/a *m/f*.
foundling *n* niño expósito *m*, niña expósita *f*.
foundry *n* fundería *f*.
fount, fountain *n* fuente *f*.
fountainhead *n* origen de fuente *m*.
four *adj*, *n* cuatro.
fourfold *adj* cuádruple.
fourteen *adj*, *n* catorce.
fourteenth *adj*, *n* decimocuarto/ta.
fourth *adj*, *n* cuarto/ta:—*n* cuarto *m*: —**~ly** *adv* en cuarto lugar.
fowl *n* ave *f*.
fox *n* zorra *f*.
fracas *n* riña *f*.
fraction *n* fracción *f*.
fracture *n* fractura *f*.
fragile *adj* frágil; débil.
fragility *n* fragilidad *f*.
fragment *n* fragmento *m*.
fragrance *n* fragancia *f*.
fragrant *adj* fragante, oloroso/sa.
frail *adj* frágil, débil.
frailty *n* fragilidad *f*; debilidad *f*.
frame *n* armazón *m*; marco, cerco *m*.
franchise *n* sufragio *m*.
frank *adj* franco/ca, liberal.
frankly *adv* francamente.
frantic *adj* frenético/ca.
fraternize *vi* hermanarse.
fraternity *n* fraternidad *f*.
fraud *n* fraude *m*.
fraudulent *adj* fraudulento/ta.
fraught *adj* cargado/da, lleno/na.
freak *n* monstruo *m*; fenómeno *m*.
freckle *n* peca *f*.
freckled *adj* pecoso/sa.
free *adj* libre; liberal; suelto/ta.
freedom *n* libertad *f*.
freehold *n* propiedad vitalicia *f*.
free-for-all *n* riña general *f*.
freelance *adj*, *adv* por cuenta propia.
freemason *n* francmasón *m*.
freemasonry *n* francmasonería *f*.
freeway *n* autopista *f*.
freewheel *vi* ir en punto muerto.
freeze *vi* helar(se).
freezer *n* congeladora *f*.
freight *n* carga *f*; flete *m*.
freighter *n* fletador *m*.
frenzy *n* frenesí *m*; locura *f*.
frequency *n* frecuencia *f*.
fresco *n* fresco *m*.
fresh *adj* fresco/ca; nuevo/va.
freshly *adv* nuevamente.
freshman *n* novicio *m*.
freshwater *adj* de agua dulce.
fret *vi* agitarse.
friar *n* fraile *m*.
friction *n* fricción *f*.
Friday *n* viernes *m*:—**Good ~** Viernes Santo *m*.
friend *n* amigo *m*; amiga *f*.
friendship *n* amistad *f*.
frieze *n* friso *m*.
frigate *n* (*mar*) fragata *f*.
fright *n* espanto, terror *m*.
frighten *vt* espantar.
frigid *adj* frío/ría, frígido/da.
fringe *n* franja *f*.
frisk *vt* cachear.
frivolity *n* frivolidad *f*.

frock *n* vestido *m*.
frog *n* rana *f*.
frolic *vi* juguetear.
from *prep* de; después; desde.
front *n* parte delantera *f*; fachada *f*; paseo marítimo *m*; frente *m*.
frontal *adj* de frente.
frontier *n* frontera *f*.
frost *n* helada *f*; hielo *m*.
froth *n* espuma (de algún líquido) *f*.
frown *vt* mirar con ceño.
frozen *adj* helado/da.
fruit *n* fruta *f*; fruto *m*.
fruiterer *n* frutero *m*.
fruiterer's (shop) *n* frutería *f*.
fruit juice *n* jugo de fruta *m*.
fruitless *adj* estéril; inútil.
fruit salad *n* ensalada de frutas *f*.
fruit tree *n* frutal *m*.
frustrate *vt* frustrar; anular.
fry *vt* freír.
frying pan *n* sartén *f*.
fuchsia *n* (*bot*) fucsia *f*.
fuel *n* combustible *m*.
fuel tank *n* deposito *m*.
fugitive *adj*, *n* fugitivo *m*.
fulcrum *n* fulcro *m*.
fulfill *vt* cumplir; realizar.
fulfillment *n* cumplimiento *m*.
full *adj* lleno/na.
full moon *n* plenilunio *m*; luna llena *f*.
fulsome *adj* exagerado/da.
fumble *vi* manejar torpemente.
fume *vi* humear; encolerizarse.
fun *n* diversión *f*; alegría *f*.
function *n* función *f*.
functional *adj* funcional.
fund *n* fondo *m*.
fundamental *adj* fundamental.
funeral *n* funerales *mpl*.
fungus *n* hongo *m*; seta *f*.
funnel *n* embudo *m*.
funny *adj* divertido/da; curioso/sa.
fur *n* piel *f*.
furious *adj* furioso/sa.
furnace *n* horno *m*; hornaza *f*.
furnish *vt* amueblar.
furnishings *npl* muebles *mpl*.
furniture *n* muebles *mpl*.
furrow *n* surco *m*.
furry *adj* peludo/da.
furthermore *adv* además.
fury *n* furor *m*; furia *f*; ira *f*.
fuse *vt*, *vi* fundir; derretirse.
fuse box *n* caja de fusibles *f*.
fusion *n* fusión *f*.
fuss *n* lío *m*; alboroto *m*.
fussy *adj* jactancioso/sa.
futile *adj* fútil, frívolo/la.
futility *n* futilidad *f*.
future *adj* futuro/ra.
fuzzy *adj* borroso/sa; muy rizado/da.

G

gable *n* aguilón *m*.
gag *n* mordaza *f*; chiste *m*.
gage *n* calibre *m*.
gaiety *n* alegría *f*.
gain *n* ganancia *f*.
gala *n* fiesta *f*.
galaxy *n* galaxia *f*.
gale *n* vendaval *m*.
gallant *adj* galante.
gallery *n* galería *f*.
gallon *n* galón *m* (medida).
gallop *n* galope *m*.
gallows *n* horca *f*.
galore *adv* en abundancia.
gambit *n* estrategia *f*.
gamble *vi* jugar; especular *f*.
gambler *n* jugador *m*.
game *n* juego *m*; pasatiempo *m*.
gamekeeper *n* guardabosques *m*.
gaming *n* juego *m*.
gammon *n* jamón *m*.
gander *n* ganso *m*.
gang *n* pandilla, banda *f*.
gangrene *n* gangrena *f*.
gangster *n* gangster *m*.
gangway *n* pasarela *f*.
gap *n* hueco *m*; claro *m*; intervalo *m*.
garage *n* garaje *m*.
garbage *n* basura *f*.
garbage can *n* cubo de la basura *m*.
garden *n* jardín *m*.
gargoyle *n* gárgola *f*.
garish *adj* ostentoso/sa.
garland *n* guirnalda *f*.
garlic *n* ajo *m*.
garment *n* prenda *f*.
garnish *vt* guarnecer *m*.
garter *n* liga *f*.
gas *n* gas *m*.
gasoline, gas *n* gasolina *f*.
gash *n* cuchillada *f*.
gasp *vi* jadear.
gastric *adj* gástrico/ca.
gastronomic *adj* gastronómico/ca.

gate *n* puerta *f*.
gateway *n* puerta *f*.
gather *vt* recoger.
gathering *n* reunión *f*.
gaudy *adj* chillón/ona.
gauze *n* gasa *f*.
gay *adj* alegre; vivo/va; gay.
gazelle *n* gacela *f*.
gazette *n* gaceta *f*.
gazetteer *n* gacetero *m*.
gear *n* atavío *m*; vestido *m*.
gearbox *n* caja de cambios *f*.
gel *n* gel *m*.
gelatin(e) *n* jaletina, jalea *f*.
gelignite *n* gelignita *f*.
gem *n* joya *f*.
Gemini *n* Géminis *m* (signo del zodiaco).
gender *n* género *m*.
gene *n* gen *m*.
genealogy *n* genealogía *f*.
general *adj* general, común.
generalize *vt* generalizar.
generation *n* generación *f*.
generic *adj* genérico/ca.
generosity *n* generosidad.
generous *adj* generoso/sa.
genetics *npl* genética *f*.
genial *adj* genial.
genitals *npl* genitales *mpl*.
genius *n* genio *m*.
genteel *adj* refinado, elegante.
gentile *n* gentil.
gentle *adj* suave.
gentleman *n* caballero *m*.
gentry *n* alta burguesía *f*.
gents *n* aseos *mpl*.
genuine *adj* genuino/na.
genus *n* genero *m*.
geographer *n* geógrafo/fa *m/f*.
geography *n* geografía *f*.
geology *n* geología *f*.
geometry *n* geometría *f*.
geranium *n* (*bot*) geranio *m*.
germ *n* (*bot*) germen *m*.
germinate *vi* brotar.
gesticulate *vi* gesticular.
gesture *n* gesto*m*.
get *vt* ganar; conseguir, obtener.
geyser *n* géiser *m m*.
ghastly *adj* espantoso/sa.
gherkin *n* pepinillo *m*.
ghost *n* fantasma *m*.
ghostly *adj* fantasmal.
giant *n* gigante *m*.
giddy *adj* vertiginoso/sa.
gift *n* regalo*m*.
giggle *vi* reírse tontamente.
gin *n* ginebra *f*.
ginger *n* jengibre *m*.
ginger-haired *adj* pelirrojo/ja.
giraffe *n* jirafa *f*.
girl *n* muchacha, chica *f*.
girlfriend *n* amiga *f*; novia *f*.
giro *n* giro postal *m*.
girth *n* cincha *f*; circunferencia *f*.
give *vt*, *vi* dar.
glacier *n* glaciar *m*.
glad *adj* alegre, contento/ta.
gladiator *n* gladiator *m*.
glamor *n* encanto*m*.
gland *n* glándula *f*.
glare *n* deslumbramiento *m*.
glass *n* vidrio.
glean *vt* espigar; recoger.
glee *n* alegría *f*; gozo *m*.
glib *adj* con poca sinceridad, elocuente pero falso.
glide *vi* resbalar.
glimmer *n* vislumbre *f*.
glimpse *n* vislumbre *f*.
glint *vi* centellear.
glisten, glitter *vi* relucir, brillar.
gloat *vi* ojear con admiración.
global *adj* mundial.
globe *n* globo *m*; esfera *f*.
gloom, gloominess *n* oscuridad *f*; melancolía.
glorify *vt* glorificar, celebrar.
glory *n* gloria, fama, celebridad *f*.
gloss *n* glosa *f*; lustre *m*.
glossary *n* glosario *m*.
glove *n* guante *m*.
glow *vi* arder; inflamarse; relucir.
glower *vi* mirar con ceño.
glue *n* cola *f*.
glum *adj* abatido/da, triste.
glut *n* hartura, abundancia *f*.
gluttony *n* glotonería *f*.
glycerine *n* glicerina *f*.
gnarled *adj* nudoso/sa.
gnash *vt*, *vi* rechinar; crujir los dientes.
gnat *n* mosquito *m*.
gnaw *vt* roer.
gnome *n* gnomo *m*.
go *vi* ir, irse.
goal *n* meta *f*; fin *m*.
goaltender *n* portero *m*.
gobble *vt* engullir, tragar.
go-between *n* mediador/a *m/f*.
goblet *n* copa *f*.
goblin *n* espíritu ambulante, duende *m*.
God *n* Dios *m*.
godchild *n* ahijado, hijo de pila *m*.
goddaughter *n* ahijada, hija de pila *f*.
goddess *n* diosa *f*.

godfather *n* padrino *m*.
godmother *n* madrina *f*.
godsend *n* don del cielo *m*.
godson *n* ahijado *m*.
goggle-eyed *adj* bizco/ca.
goggles *npl* anteojos *mpl*.
gold *n* oro *m*.
goldfish *n* pez de colores *m*.
gold-plated *adj* chapado/da en oro.
golf *n* golf *m*.
golf course *n* campo de golf *m*.
golfer *n* golfista *m/f*.
gondolier *n* gondolero/ra *m/f*.
gone *adj* ido/da; perdido/da; pasado/da; gastado/da; muerto/ta.
gong *n* atabal chino *m*.
good *adj* bueno/na.
goodbye ! *excl* ¡adiós!
Good Friday *n* Viernes Santo *m*.
good-looking *adj* guapo/pa.
goodness *n* bondad *f*.
goodwill *n* benevolencia, bondad *f*.
goose *n* ganso *m*; oca *f*.
gooseberry *n* grosella espinosa *f*.
gorge *n* barranco *m*.
gorgeous *adj* maravilloso/sa.
gorilla *n* gorila *m*.
gorse *n* aulaga *f*.
gory *adj* sangriento/ta.
goshawk *n* azor *m*.
gospel *n* evangelio *m*.
gossamer *n* vello *m*.
gossip *n* charla *f*.
gothic *adj* gótico/ca.
gout *n* gota *f* (enfermedad).
govern *vt* gobernar, dirigir.
governess *n* gobernadora *f*.
government *n* gobierno *m*.
governor *n* gobernador *m*.
gown *n* toga *f*.
grab *vt* agarrar.
grace *n* gracia.
graceful *adj* gracioso/sa.
gracious *adj* gracioso/sa.
gradation *n* gradación *f*.
grade *n* grado *m*.
grade crossing *n* paso a nivel *m*.
gradient *n* (*rail*) pendiente.
gradual *adj* gradual.
graduate *vi* graduarse.
graduation *n* graduación *f*.
graffiti *n* pintadas *fpl*.
graft *n* injerto *m*.
grain *n* grano *m*.
gram *n* gramo *m* (peso).
grammar *n* gramática *f*.
granary *n* granero *m*.
grand *adj* grande, ilustre.
grandchild *n* nieto *m*; nieta *f*.
grandad *n* abuelo *m*.
granddaughter *n* nieta *f*.
grandeur *n* grandeza *f*.
grandfather *n* abuelo *m*.
grandiose *adj* grandioso/sa.
grandma *n* abuelita *f*.
grandmother *n* abuela *f*.
grandparents *npl* abuelos *mpl*.
grand piano *n* piano de cola *m*.
grandson *n* nieto *m*.
grandstand *n* tribuna *f*.
granite *n* granito *m*.
granny *n* abuelita *f*.
grant *vt* conceder.
granule *n* gránulo *m*.
grape *n* uva *f*:—**bunch of ~s** racimo de uvas *m*.
grapefruit *n* toronja *f*.
graph *n* gráfica *f*.
graphics *n* artes gráficas *fpl*; gráficos *mpl*.
grasp *vt* empuñar.
grass *n* hierba *f*.
grasshopper *n* saltamontes *m*.
grassland *n* pampa , pradera *f*.
grass snake *n* culebra *f*.
gratify *vt* contentar; gratificar.
gratifying *adj* grato/ta.
grating *n* rejado *m*.
gratis *adv* gratis.
gratitude *n* gratitud *f*.
grave *n* sepultura *f*.
gravel *n* cascajo *m*.
gravestone *n* piedra sepulcra *f*.
graveyard *n* cementerio *m*.
gravity *n* gravedad *f*.
gravy *n* jugo de la carne *f*; salsa *f*.
gray *adj* gris.
graze *vt* pastorear.
grease *n* grasa *f*:—*vt* untar.
greasy *adj* grasiento/ta.
great *adj* gran, grande.
greatcoat *n* sobretodo *m*.
greatness *n* grandeza *f*.
greedily *adv* vorazmente.
greediness, greed *n* gula *f*; codicia *f*.
Greek *n* griego (idioma) *m*.
green *adj* verde.
greengrocer *n* verdulero *m*.
greenhouse *n* invernadero *m*.
greet *vt* saludar, congratular.
greeting *n* saludo *m*.
greeting(s) card *n* tarjeta de felicitaciones *f*.
grenade *n* (*mil*) granada *f*.
grenadier *n* granadero *m*.
greyhound *n* galgo *m*.

greyish *adj* pardusco/ca.
grid *n* reja *f*; red *f*.
grief *n* dolor *m*.
grieve *vt* agraviar.
grievous *adj* doloroso/sa.
griffin *n* grifo *m*.
grill *n* parrilla *f*.
grim *adj* feo, fea.
grimace *n* visaje *m*.
grime *n* porquería *f*.
grin *n* mueca *f*.
grind *vt* moler.
grinder *n* molinero *m*.
grip *n* asimiento *m*.
grisly *adj* horroroso/sa.
gristle *n* tendón, nervio *m*.
grit *n* gravilla *f*; valor *m*.
groan *vi* gemir, suspirar.
grocer *n* tendero/ra, abarrotero/ra *m/f*.
groceries *npl* comestibles *mpl*.
groin *n* ingle *f*.
groom *n* establero *m*.
groove *n* ranura *f*.
gross *adj* grueso/sa.
grotesque *adj* grotesco/ca.
grotto *n* gruta *f*.
ground *n* tierra *f*.
ground floor *n* planta baja *f*.
group *n* grupo *m*..
grouse *n* urogallo *m*:—*vi* quejarse.
grove *n* arboleda *f*.
grovel *vi* arrastrarse.
grow *vt* cultivar:—*vi* crecer, aumentarse.
growl *vi* regañar, gruñir.
grown-up *n* adulto *m*.
grub *n* gusano *m*.
grubby *adj* sucio/cia.
grudge *n* rencor, odio *m*; envidia *f*:—*vt*, *vi* envidiar.
gruesome *adj* horrible.
gruff *adj* brusco/ca.
grumble *vi* gruñir; murmurar.
grunt *vi* gruñir.
G-string *n* taparrabo *m*.
guarantee *n* garantía *f*.
guard *n* guardia *f*.
guardianship *n* tutela *f*.
guerrilla *n* guerrillero *m*.
guess *vt*, *vi* conjeturar; adivinar; suponer.
guest *n* huésped/a.
guffaw *n* carcajada *f*.
guide *vt* guiar, dirigir:—*n* guía *m*.
guidebook *n* guía *f*.
guild *n* gremio *m*.
guile *n* astucia *f*.
guilt *n* culpabilidad *f*.
guilty *adj* reo, rea, culpable.
guinea pig *n* cobayo *m*.
guise *n* manera *f*.
guitar *n* guitarra *f*.
gulf *n* golfo *m*.
gull *n* gaviota *f*.
gullet *n* esófago *m*.
gullible *adj* crédulo/la.
gully *n* barranco *m*.
gulp *n* trago *m*.
gum *n* goma *f*.
gum tree *n* árbol gomero *m*.
gun *n* pistola *f*; escopeta *f*.
gunboat *n* cañonera *f*.
gunpowder *n* pólvora *f*.
gunshot *n* escopetazo *m*.
gurgle *vi* gorgotear.
guru *n* gurú *m*.
gush *vi* brotar.
gusset *n* escudete *m*.
gut *n* intestino *m*.
gutter *n* canalón *m*; arroyo *m*.
guy *n* tío *m*; tipo *m*.
gym(nasium) *n* gimnasio *m*.
gymnast *n* gimnasta *m/f*.
gynecologist *n* ginecólogo/ga *m/f*.
Gypsy *n* gitano/na *m/f*.
gyrate *vi* girar.

H

haberdasher *n* camisero/ra, mercero/ra *m/f*.
habit *n* costumbre *f*.
habitable *adj* habitable.
habitat *n* hábitat *m*.
habitual *adj* habitual.
haddock *n* merlango *m*.
hag *n* bruja *f*.
hail *n* granizo *m*.
hair *n* pelo; cabello *m*.
hairbrush *n* cepillo *m*.
haircut *n* corte de pelo *m*.
hairdresser *n* peluquero *m*.
hairdryer *n* secador de pelo *m*.
hairspray *n* laca *f*.
hairstyle *n* peinado *m*.
half *n* mitad *f*.
half-caste *adj* mestizo/za.

hall *n* vestíbulo *m*.
hallow *vt* consagrar, santificar.
hallucination *n* alucinación *f*.
halo *n* halo *m*.
halt *vi* parar.
halve *vt* partir por mitad.
ham *n* jamón *m*.
hamburger *n* hamburguesa *f*.
hamlet *n* aldea *f*.
hammer *n* martillo *m*.
hammock *n* hamaca *f*.
hamper *n* cesto *f*.
hamstring *vt* desjarretar.
hand *n* mano *f*.
handbag *n* cartera *f*
handful *n* puñado *m*.
handicap *n* desventaja *f*.
handicraft *n* artesanía *f*.
handkerchief *n* pañuelo *m*.
handle *n* mango, puño *m*; asa; manija *f*.
handshake *n* apretón de manos *m*.
handsome *adj* guapo/pa.
handwriting *n* letra *f*.
handy *adj* practico/ca.
hang *vt* colgar.
hanger *n* percha *f*.
hangover *n* resaca *f*.
happen *vi* pasar; acontecer.
happiness *n* felicidad *f*.
happy *adj* feliz.
harass *vt* cansar, fatigar.
harbinger *n* precursor *m*.
harbor *n* puerto *m*.
hard *adj* duro/ra, firme.
harden *vt*, *vi* endurecer(se).
hardiness *n* robustez *f*.
hardly *adv* apenas.
hardship *n* penas *fpl*.
hard-up *adj* sin plata.
hardware store *n* ferretería *f*.
hardy *adj* fuerte.
hare *n* liebre *f*.
hare-lipped *adj* labihendido/da.
haricot *n* alubia *f*.
harlequin *n* arlequín *m*.
harm *n* mal, daño *m*.
harmful *adj* perjudicial.
harmless *adj* inocuo/cua.
harmonic *adj* armónico/ca.
harmonious *adj* armonioso/sa.
harmonize *vt* armonizar.
harmony *n* armonía *f*.
harp *n* arpa *f*.
harpoon *n* arpón *m*.
harsh *adj* duro/ra; austero/ra.
harvest *n* cosecha *f*.
harvester *n* cosechadora *f*.
hash *n* hachís *m*.
hassock *n* cojín de paja *m*.
haste *n* apuro *m*.
hasten *vt* acelerar.
hasty *adj* apresurado/da.
hat *n* sombrero *m*.
hatch *vt* incubar; tramar*f*.
hatchet *n* hacha *f*.
hatchway *n* (*mar*) escotilla *f*.
hate *n* odio.
hateful *adj* odioso/sa.
hatred *n* odio, aborrecimiento *m*.
haughty *adj* altanero/ra, orgulloso/sa.
haul *vt* tirar;—*n* botín *m*.
hauler *n* transportista *m/f*.
haunch *n* anca *f*.
haunt *vt* frecuentar, rondar.
have *vt* haber; tener, poseer.
haven *n* asilo *m*.
havoc *n* estrago *m*.
hawk *n* halcón *m*.
hawthorn *n* espino blanco *m*.
hay *n* heno *m*.
hazard *n* riesgo *m*.
haze *n* niebla *f*.
hazel *n* avellano *m*.
hazelnut *n* avellana *f*.
hazy *adj* oscuro/ra.
he *pn* el. **head** *n* cabeza *f*.
head *n* cakeza *f*.
headache *n* dolor de cabeza *m*.
headlamp *n* faro *m*.
headline *n* titular *m*.
headmaster *n* director *m*.
headphones *npl* auriculares *mpl*.
heal *vt*, *vi* curar.
health *n* salud *f*
healthy *adj* sano/na.
heap *n* montón *m*.
hear *vt* oír; escuchar.
hearing *n* oído *m*.
hearing aid *n* audífono *m*.
hearse *n* coche fúnebre *m*.
heart *n* corazón *m*.
heart attack *n* infarto *m*.
heartburn *n* acedia *f*.
hearth *n* hogar *m*.
heartily *adv* sinceramente.
heartless *adj* cruel.
hearty *adj* cordial.
heat *n* calor *m*.
heater *n* calentador *m*.
heathen *n* pagano *m*.
heating *n* calefacción *f*.
heatwave *n* ola de calor *f*.
heaven *n* cielo *m*.
heavily *adv* pesadamente.

heavy *adj* pesado/da.
Hebrew *n* hebreo *m*.
heckle *vt* interrumpir.
hectic *adj* agitado/da.
hedge *n* seto *m*.
hedgehog *n* erizo *m*.
heed *vt* hacer caso de.
heedless *adj* descuidado/da.
heel *n* talón *m*.
hefty *adj* grande.
heifer *n* ternera *f*.
height *n* altura *f*; altitud *f*.
heinous *adj* atroz.
heir *n* heredero/ra *m/f*.
heirloom *n* reliquia de familia *f*.
helicopter *n* helicóptero *m*.
hell *n* infierno *m*.
helm *n* (*mar*) timón *m*.
helmet *n* casco *m*.
help *vt*, *vi* ayudar, socorrer.
helper *n* ayudante *m*.
helpful *adj* útil.
helping *n* ración *f*.
helpless *adj* indefenso/sa.
hem *n* ribete *m*.
he-man *n* macho *m*.
hemisphere *n* hemisferio *m*.
hemorrhage *n* hemorragia *f*.
hemorrhoids *npl* hemorroides *mpl*.
hemp *n* cáñamo *m*.
hen *n* gallina *f*.
henchman *n* secuaz *m*.
henceforth, henceforward *adv* de aquí en adelante. **hepatitis** *n* hepatitis *f*.
her *pn* su; ella; de ella; a ella.
herald *n* heraldo *m*.
heraldry *n* heráldica *f*.
herb *n* hierba *fl*.
herbaceous *adj* herbáceo/cea.
herbalist *n* herbolario *m*.
herbivorous *adj* herbívoro/ra.
herd *n* rebaño *m*.
here *adv* aquí, acá.
hereabout(s) *adv* aquí alrededor.
hereafter *adv* en el futuro.
hereby *adv* por esto.
hereditary *adj* hereditario/ria.
heresy *n* herejía *f*.
heretic *n* hereje *m/f*.
heritage *n* patrimonio *m*.
hermetic *adj* hermético/ca.
hermit *n* ermitaño/ña *m/f*.
hermitage *n* ermita *f*.
hernia *n* hernia *f*.
hero *n* héroe *m*.
heroic *adj* heroico/ca.
heroine *n* heroína *f*.
heroism *n* heroísmo *m*.
heron *n* garza *f*.
herring *n* arenque *m*.
herself *pn* ella misma.
hesitant *adj* vacilante.
hesitate *vt* dudar; tardar.
heterosexual *adj*, *n* heterosexual *m*.
hew *vt* tajar; cortar.
heyday *n* apogeo *m*.
hi *excl* ¿hola!
hiatus *n* (*gr*) hiato *m*.
hibernate *vi* invernar.
hiccup *n* hipo *m*.
hickory *n* noguera americana *f*.
hide *vt* esconder*f*.
hideaway *n* escondite *m*.
hideous *adj* horrible.
hierarchy *n* jerarquía *f*.
hieroglyphic *adj* jeroglífico/ca.
hi-fi *n* estéreo, hi-fi *m*.
high *adj* alto/ta; elevado/da.
highlight *n* punto culminante *m*.
highway *n* carretera *f*.
hike *vi* ir de excursión.
hijack *vt* secuestrar.
hilarious *adj* alegre.
hill, hillock *n* colina *f*.
him *pn* le, lo, el.
himself *pn* el mismo, se, si mismo.
hinder *vt* impedir.
hindrance *n* impedimento, obstáculo *m*.
hinge *n* bisagra *f*.
hip *n* cadera *f*.
hippopotamus *n* hipopótamo *m*.
hire *vt* alquilar.
his *pn* su, suyo, de el.
Hispanic *adj* hispano/na; hispánico/ca.
hiss *vt*, *vi* silbar.
historian *n* historiador *m*.
history *n* historia *f*.
hit *vt* golpear.
hitch *vt* atar.
hitch-hike *vi* hacer autostop.
hive *n* colmena *f*.
hoax *n* trampa *f*.
hobble *vi* cojear.
hobby *n* pasatiempo *m*.
hockey *n* hockey *m*.
hodge-podge *n* mezcolanza *f*.
hoe *n* azadón *m*.
hog *n* cerdo, puerco *m*.
hoist *vt* alzar.
hold *vt* tener; detener; contener.
hole *n* agujero *m*.
holiday *n* día de fiesta *m*:—**~s** *pl* vacaciones *fpl*.
hollow *adj* hueco/ca.

holly *n* (*bot*) acebo *m*.
hollyhock *n* malva hortense *f*.
holocaust *n* holocausto *m*.
holster *n* pistolera *f*.
holy *adj* santo/ta.
holy week *n* semana santa *f*.
homage *n* homenaje *m*.
home *n* casa *f*.
home address *n* domicilio *m*.
homely *adj* casero/ra.
homeopathist *n* homeopatista *m/f*.
homeopathy *n* homeopatía *f*.
homesick *adj* nostálgico/ca.
homework *n* deberes *mpl*.
homicide *n* homicidio *m*; homicida *m*.
homosexual *adj*, *n* homosexual *m*.
honest *adj* honrado/da.
honesty *n* honradez *f*.
honey *n* miel *f*.
honeycomb *n* panal *m*.
honeymoon *n* luna de miel *f*.
honeysuckle *n* (*bot*) madreselva *f*.
honor *n* honra *f*; honor *m*:—*vt* honrar.
honorary *adj* honorario/ria.
hood *n* capo *m*; capucha *f*.
hoof *n* pezuña *f*.
hook *n* gancho *m*.
hooligan *n* gamberro *m*.
hoop *n* aro *m*.
hooter *n* sirena *f*.
hop *n* (*bot*) lúpulo.
hope *n* esperanza *f*.
horde *n* horda *f*.
horizon *n* horizonte *m*.
horizontal *adj* horizontal.
hormone *n* hormona *f*.
horn *n* cuerno *m*.
hornet *n* avispón *m*.
horny *adj* calloso/sa.
horoscope *n* horóscopo *m*.
horrendous *adj* horrendo/da.
horrible *adj* horrible.
horrid *adj* horrible.
horrific *adj* horroroso/sa.
horrify *vt* horrorizar.
horror *n* horror, terror *m*.
hors d'oeuvre *n* entremeses *mpl*.
horse *n* caballo *m*
horse chestnut *n* castaño de Indias *m*.
horsefly *n* moscarda *f*.
horseradish *n* rábano silvestre *m*.
horticulture *n* horticultura, jardinería *f*.
horticulturist *n* jardinero/ra *m/f*.
hosepipe *n* manga *f*.
hosiery *n* calcetería *f*.
hospital *n* hospital *m*.
hospitality *n* hospitalidad *f*.
host *n* anfitrión *m*; hostia *f*.
hostage *n* rehén *m*.
hostess *n* anfitriona *f*.
hostile *adj* hostil.
hot *adj* caliente; cálido/da.
hotbed *n* semillero *m*.
hotel *n* hotel *m*.
hotelier *n* hotelero/ra *m/f*.
hour *n* hora *f*.
hour-glass *n* reloj de arena *m*.
house *n* casa *f*.
household *n* familia *f*.
houseless *adv* sin casa.
housewife *n* ama de casa *f*.
hovel *n* choza, cabaña *f*.
hover *vi* flotar.
how *adv* cómo.
howl *vi* aullar.
hub *n* centro *m*.
hue *n* color *m*.
hug *vt* abrazar:—*n* abrazo *m*.
huge *adj* vasto/ta, enorme.
hum *vi* canturrear.
human *adv* humano/na.
humane *adv* humano/na.
humanist *n* humanista *m/f*.
humanitarian *adj* humanitario/ria.
humanity *n* humanidad *f*.
humble *adj* humilde.
humid *adj* húmedo/da.
humidity *n* humedad *f*.
humiliate *vt* humillar.
humming-bird *n* colibrí *m*.
humor *n* sentido del humor *m*.
humorist *n* humorista *m./f*
humorous *adj* gracioso/sa.
hundred *adj* ciento.
hundredth *adj* centésimo.
hundredweight *n* quintal *m*.
hunger *n* hambre *f*.
hunt *vt* cazar; perseguir.
hunter *n* cazador/a *m/f*.
hurdle *n* valla *f*.
hurricane *n* huracán *m*.
hurt *vt* hacer daño; ofender.
hurtful *adj* dañoso/sa:—**~ly** *adv* dañosamente.
husband *n* marido *m*.
hush! *excl* ¡chitón!, ¡silencio!.
husk *n* cáscara *f*.
hut *n* cabaña *f*.
hutch *n* conejera *f*.
hyacinth *n* jacinto *m*.
hydraulic *adj* hidráulico/ca.
hydrofoil *n* aerodeslizador *m*.
hydrogen *n* hidroala *f*.
hyena *n* hiena *f*.

hygiene *n* higiene *f*.
hymn *n* himno *m*.
hypermarket *n* hipermercado *m*.
hyphen *n* (*gr*) guión *m*.
hypocrisy *n* hipocresía *f*.
hypocrite *n* hipócrita *m/f*.
hysterical *adj* histérico/ca.
hysterics *npl* histeria *f*.

I

I *pn* yo.
ice *n* hielo *m*:—*vt* helar.
ice cream *n* helado *m*.
ice rink *n* pista de hielo *f*.
icicle *n* carámbano *m*.
idea *n* idea *f*.
ideal *adj* ideal.
identical *adj* idéntico/ca.
identification *n* identificación *f*.
identify *vt* identificar.
identity *n* identidad *f*.
ideology *n* ideología *f*.
idiom *n* idioma *m*.
idiosyncrasy *n* idiosincrasia *f*.
idiot *n* idiota, necio *m*.
idiotic *adj* tonto/ta, bobo/ba.
idle *adj* desocupado/da.
idol *n* ídolo *m*.
idolatry *n* idolatría *f*.
idyllic *adj* idílico/ca.
i.e. *adv* esto es.
if *conj* si, aunque.
ignite *vt* encender.
ignoble *adj* innoble.
ignorance *n* ignorancia *f*.
ignorant *adj* ignorante.
ignore *vt* no hacer caso de.
ill *adj* malo/la, enfermo/ma.
ill-advised *adj* imprudente.
illegal *adj* **~ly** *adv* ilegal(mente).
illegible *adj* ilegible.
illegitimate *adj* ilegítimo/ma.
ill feeling *n* rencor *m*.
illiterate *adj* analfabeto/ta.
illness *n* enfermedad *f*.
illogical *adj* ilógico/ca.
illuminate *vt* iluminar.
illusion *n* ilusión *f*.
illustrate *vt* ilustrar.
illustration *n* ilustración *f*.
image *n* imagen *f*.
imagination *n* imaginación *f*.
imagine *vt* imaginarse.
imbalance *n* desequilibrio *m*.
imbecile *adj* imbécil.
imitate *vt* imitar, copiar.
imitation *n* imitación, copia *f*.
immaculate *adj* inmaculado/da.
immature *adj* inmaduro/ra.
immediate *adj* inmediato/ta.
immense *adj* inmenso/sa.
immigrant *n* inmigrante *m*.
immigration *n* inmigración *f*.
imminent *adj* inminente.
immodest *adj* inmodesto/ta.
immoral *adj* inmoral.
immortal *adj* inmortal.
immune *adj* inmune.
imp *n* diablillo, duende *m*.
impact *n* impacto *m*.
impair *vt* disminuir.
impartial *adj* **~ly** *adv* imparcial(mente).
impatience *n* impaciencia *f*.
impede *vt* estorbar.
impel *vt* impeler.
impending *adj* inminente.
imperative *adj* imperativo/va.
imperfect *adj* imperfecto/ta
imperial *adj* imperial.
impersonal *adj*, **~ly** *adv* impersonal-(mente).
impetus *n* ímpetu *m*.
impiety *n* irmpiedad *f*.
implant *vt* implantar.
implement *n* herramienta.
implore *vt* suplicar.
imply *vt* suponer.
impolite *adj* maleducado/da.
import *vt* importar.
importance *n* importancia *f*.
important *adj* importante.
impose *vt* imponer.
impostor *n* impostor *m*.
impotence *n* impotencia *f*.
impotent *adj* impotente.
impound *vt* embargar.
impoverish *vt* empobrecer.
impractical *adj* poco práctico/ca.
imprecise *adj* impreciso/sa.
impress *vt* impresionar.
impression *n* impresión *f*; edición *f*.
impressive *adj* impresionante.
imprint *n* sello *m*:—*vt* imprimir; estampar.
improbable *adj* improbable.

improper *adj* impropio/pia.
improve *vt*, *vi* mejorar.
improvise *vt* improvisar.
impulse *n* impulso *m*.
impure *adj* impuro/ra.
impurity *n* impureza *f*.
in *prep* en.
inability *n* incapacidad *f*.
inaccessible *adj* inaccesible.
inaccurate *adj* inexacto/ta.
inadequate *adj* inadecuado/da, defectuoso/sa.
inadmissible *adj* inadmisible.
inadvertently *adv* sin querer.
inappropriate *adj* impropio/pia.
inaudible *adj* inaudible.
inaugurate *vt* inaugurar.
in-between *adj* intermedio/dia.
inborn, inbred *adj* innato/ta.
incapable *adj* incapaz.
incarcerate *vt* encarcelar.
incarnation *n* encarnación *f*.
incendiary *n* bomba incendiaria *f*.
incense *n* incienso *m*.
incentive *n* incentivo *m*.
incessant *adj* incesante.
incest *n* incesto *m*.
inch *n* pulgada *f*.
incident *n* incidente *m*.
incinerator *n* incinerador *m*.
inclination *n* inclinación.
incline *vt*, *vi* inclinar(se).
include *vt* incluir.
inclusive *adj* inclusivo/va.
incognito *adv* de incógnito.
incoherent *adj* incoherente.
income *n* renta *f*
incompatible *adj* incompatible.
incompetence *n* incompetencia *f*.
incomplete *adj* incompleto/ta.
incomprehensible *adj* incomprensible.
inconceivable *adj* inconcebible.
incontinence *n* incontinencia *f*.
inconvenience *n* incomodidad *f*.
incorrect *adj* incorrecto/ta.
increase *vt* acrecentar, aumentar
incredible *adj* increíble.
incubate *vi* incubar.
incubator *n* incubadora *f*.
incurable *adj* incurable.
indecency *n* indecencia *f*.
indecent *adj* indecente:—**~ly** *adv* indecentemente.
indecisive *adj* indeciso/sa.
indeed *adv* verdaderamente, de veras.
independence *n* independencia *f*.
independent *adj* independiente.
indescribable *adj* indescriptible.
index *n* índice *m*.
indicate *vt* indicar.
indifference *n* indiferencia *f*.
indigenous *adj* indígena.
indigestion *n* indigestión *f*.
indignation *n* indignación *f*.
indigo *n* añil *m*.
indirect *adj* indirecto/ta.
indiscreet *adj* indiscreto/ta.
indispensable *adj* indispensable.
indistinguishable *adj* indistinguible.
individual *adj* individual *m*.
indoors *adv* dentro.
indulge *vt*, *vi* conceder; ser indulgente.
industrialist *n* industrial *m*.
industry *n* industria *f*.
inedible *adj* no comestible.
ineffective, ineffectual *adj* ineficaz.
inefficiency *n* ineficacia *f*.
ineligible *adj* ineligible.
inept *adj* incompetente.
inequality *n* desigualdad *f*.
inevitable *adj* inevitable.
inexpensive *adj* económico/ca.
inexperience *n* inexperiencia *f*.
inexpert *adj* inexperto/ta.
inexplicable *adj* inexplicable.
infallible *adj* infalible.
infamy *n* infamia *f*.
infancy *n* infancia *f*.
infant *n* niño/ña *m/f*.
infantile *adj* infantil.
infantry *n* infantería *f*.
infatuation *n* infatuación *f*.
infect *vt* infectar.
infection *n* infección *f*.
inferior *adj* inferior.
infernal *adj* infernal.
inferno *n* infierno *m*.
infest *vt* infestar.
infidelity *n* infidelidad *f*.
infinite *adj* infinito/ta.
infinitive *n* infinitivo *m*.
infinity *n* infinito *m*; infinidad *f*.
infirm *adj* enfermo/ma.
infirmary *n* enfermería *f*.
infirmity *n* fragilidad, enfermedad *f*.
inflammation *n* inflamación *f*.
inflatable *adj* inflable.
inflate *vt* inflar, hinchar.
inflation *n* inflación *f*.
inflict *vt* imponer.
influence *n* influencia *f*.
influenza *n* gripe *f*.
inform *vt* informar.
informal *adj* informal.
information *n* información *f*.

infrastructure *n* infraestructura *f*.
infuriate *vt* enfurecer.
infusion *n* infusión *f*.
ingenious *adj* ingenioso/sa.
ingenuity *n* ingeniosidad *f*.
ingot *n* barra de metal *f*.
ingrained *adj* inveterado/da.
ingratitude *n* ingratitud *f*.
ingredient *n* ingrediente *m*.
inhabit *vt*, *vi* habitar.
inhabitant *n* habitante *m*.
inhale *vt* inhalar.
inherent *adj* inherente.
inherit *vt* heredar.
inheritance *n* herencia *f*.
inhibit *vt* inhibir.
inhospitable *adj* inhospitalario/ria.
inhuman *adj* inhumano/na.
inhumanity *n* inhumanidad, crueldad *f*.
initial *adj* inicial.
initiate *vt* iniciar.
initiative *n* iniciativa *f*.
inject *vt* inyectar.
injection *n* inyección *f*.
injure *vt* herir.
injury *n* daño *m*.
injustice *n* injusticia *f*.
ink *n* tinta *f*.
inkling *n* sospecha *f*.
inlaid *adj* taraceado/da.
in-laws *npl* suegros *mpl*.
inlay *vt* taracear.
inlet *n* entsenada *f*.
inmate *n* preso *m*.
inn *n* posada *f*; mesón *m*.
innkeeper *n* posadero/ra, mesonero/ra *m/f*.
innocence *n* inocencia *f*.
innocent *adj* inocente.
innovate *vt* innovar.
innovation *n* innovación *f*.
innuendo *n* indirecta, insinuación *f*.
inoffensive *adj* inofensivo/va.
inorganic *adj* inorgánico/ca.
inpatient *n* paciente interno *m*.
input *n* entrada *f*.
inquest *n* encuesta judicial *f*.
inquire *vt*, *vi* preguntar.
inquiry *n* pesquisa *f*.
inquisition *n* inquisición *f*.
inquisitive *adj* curioso/sa.
insane *adj* loco/ca, demente.
insanity *n* locura *f*.
inscription *n* inscripción *f*.
inscrutable *adj* inescrutable.
insect *n* insecto *m*.
insecticide *n* insecticida *m*.
insecure *adj* inseguro/ra.
insensitive *adj* insensible.
inseparable *adj* inseparable.
insert *vt* introducir.
insertion *n* inserción *f*.
inside *n* interior *m*:—*adv* dentro.
inside out *adv* al revés; a fondo.
insignia *npl* insignias *fpl*.
insignificant *adj* insignificante.
insincere *adj* poco sincero/ra.
insipid *adj* insípido/da.
insist *vi* insistir.
insole *n* plantilla *f*.
insolence *n* insolencia *f*.
insoluble *adj* insoluble.
insomnia *n* insomnio *m*.
insomuch *conj* puesto que.
inspect *vt* examinar, inspeccionar.
inspection *n* inspección *f*.
inspire *vt* inspirar.
instability *n* inestabilidad *f*.
instance *n* ejemplo *m*.
instant *adj* inmediato/ta.
instead (of) *pr* por, en lugar de, en vez de.
instill *vt* inculcar.
instinct *n* instinto *m*.
instinctive *adj* instintivo/va.
institute *vt* establecer:—*n* instituto *m*.
institution *n* institución *f*.
instruct *vt* instruir, enseñar.
instruction *n* instrucción *f*.
instrument *n* instrumento *m*.
instrumental *adj* instrumental.
insufferable *adj* insoportable.
insufficient *adj* insuficiente.
insulate *vt* aislar.
insulin *n* insulina *f*.
insult *vt* insultar:—*n* insulto *m*.
insurance *n* (*com*) seguro *m*.
insure *vt* asegurar.
intact *adj* intacto/ta.
integral *adj* íntegro/gra.
integrate *vt* integrar.
integrity *n* integridad *f*.
intellect *n* intelecto *m*.
intelligence *n* inteligencia *f*.
intend *vi* tener intención.
intense *adj* intenso/sa.
intensity *n* intensidad *f*.
intention *n* intención *f*.
inter *vt* enterrar.
interaction *n* interacción *f*.
intercourse *n* relaciones sexuales *fpl*.
interest *vt* interesar.
interesting *adj* interesante.
interest rate *n* tipo de interés *m*.
interfere *vi* entrometerse.

interference *n* interferencia *f*.
interior *adj* interior.
interlude *n* intermedio *m*.
intermediate *adj* intermedio/dia.
interment *n* entierro *m*; sepultura *f*.
intermission *n* descanso *m*.
intermittent *adj* intermitente.
internal *adj* interno/na.
international *adj* internacional.
interpret *vt* interpretar.
interpretation *n* interpretación *f*.
interpreter *n* intérprete *m/f*.
interregnum *n* interregno *m*.
interrelated *adj* interrelacionado/da.
interrogate *vt* interrogar.
interrogation *n* interrogatorio *m*.
interrogative *adj* interrogativo/va.
interrupt *vt* interrumpir.
interruption *n* interrupción *f*.
intersect *vi* cruzarse.
intersection *n* cruce *m*.
intersperse *vt* esparcir.
intertwine *vt* entretejer.
interval *n* intervalo *m*.
intervene *vi* intervenir.
intervention *n* intervención *f*.
interview *n* entrevista *f*.
interviewer *n* entrevistador/a *m/f*.
intestine *n* intestino *m*.
intimacy *n* intimidad *f*.
intimate *n* amigo/ga íntimo/ma.
intimidate *vt* intimidar.
into *prep* en, dentro, adentro.
intolerable *adj* intolerable.
intolerance *n* intolerancia *f*.
intoxicate *vt* embriagar.
intravenous *adj* intravenoso/sa.
intrepid *adj* intrépido/da.
intricate *adj* intricado/da.
intrigue *n* intriga *f*:—*vi* intrigar.
intriguing *adj* fascinante.
intrinsic *adj* intrínseco/ca.
introduce *vt* introducir.
introduction *n* introducción *f*.
introvert *n* introvertido *m*.
intrude *vi* entrometerse.
intruder *n* intruso/sa *m/f*.
intuition *n* intuición *f*.
intuitive *adj* intuitivo/va.
inundate *vt* inundar.
inundation *n* inundación *f*.
invade *vt* invadir.
invalid *adj* inválido/da.
invalidate *vt* invalidar, anular.
invaluable *adj* inapreciable.
invariable *adj* invariable.
invariably *adv* invariablemente.
invasion *n* invasión *f*.
invent *vt* inventar.
invention *n* invento *m*.
inventor *n* inventor *m*.
inventory *n* inventario *m*.
inversion *n* inversión *f*.
invert *vt* invertir.
invest *vt* invertir.
investigate *vt* investigar.
investment *n* inversión *f*.
invigilate *vt* vigilar.
invigorating *adj* vigorizante.
invincible *adj* invencible.
invisible *adj* invisible.
invitation *n* invitación *f*.
invite *vt* invitar.
invoice *n* (*com*) factura *f*.
involuntarily *adv* involuntariamente.
involve *vt* implicar.
involvement *n* compromiso *m*.
iodine *n* (*chem*) yodo *m*.
IOU (I owe you) *n* vale *m*.
irate, ireful *adj* enojado/da.
iris *n* iris *m*.
irksome *adj* fastidioso/sa.
iron *n* hierro *m*:—*adj* férreo/rea:—*vt* planchar.
ironic *adj* irónico/ca:—**~ly** *adv* con ironía.
ironwork *n* herraje *m*:—**~s** *pl* herrería *f*.
irony *n* ironía *f*.
irradiate *vt* irradiar.
irrational *adj* irracional.
irreconcilable *adj* irreconciliable.
irregular *adj* **~ly** *adv* irregular(mente).
irrelevant *adj* impertinente.
irreparable *adj* irreparable.
irresistible *adj* irresistible.
irresponsible *adj* irresponsable.
irrigate *vt* regar.
irrigation *n* riego *m*.
irritable *adj* irritable.
irritant *n* (*med*) irritante *m*.
irritate *vt* irritar.
island *n* isla *f*.
isle *n* isla *f*.
isolate *vt* aislar.
issue *n* asunto *m*.
it *pn* el, ella, ello, lo, la, le.
italic *n* cursiva *f*.
itch *n* picazón *f*:—*vi* picar.
item *n* artículo *m*.
itemize *vt* detallar.
itinerary *n* itinerario *m*.
its *pn* su, suyo.
itself *pn* el mismo, la misma, lo mismo.
ivory *n* marfil *m*.
ivy *n* hiedra *f*.

J

jab *vt* clavar.
jabber *vi* farfullar.
jack *n* gato *m*; sota *f*.
jackal *n* chacal *m*.
jackboots *npl* botas militares *fpl*.
jackdaw *n* grajo *m*.
jacket *n* chaqueta *f*.
jack-knife *vi* colear.
jackpot *n* premio gordo *m*.
jade *n* jade *m*.
jagged *adj* dentado/da.
jaguar *n* jaguar *m*.
jail *n* cárcel *f*.
jailer *n* carcelero/ra *m/f*.
jam *n* conserva *f*; mermelada de frutas *f*.
jangle *vi* sonar.
January *n* enero *m*.
jargon *n* jerigonza *f*.
jasmine *n* jazmín *m*.
jaundice *n* ictericia *f*.
jaunt *n* excursión *f*.
jaunty *adj* alegre.
javelin *n* jabalina *f*.
jaw *n* mandíbula *f*.
jay *n* arrendajo *m*.
jazz *n* jazz *m*.
jealous *adj* celoso/sa.
jealousy *n* celos *mpl*; envidia *f*.
jeans *npl* vaqueros *mpl*.
jeep *n* jeep *m*.
jeer *vi* befar.
jelly *n* jalea, gelatina *f*.
jellyfish *n* aguamar *m*; medusa *f*.
jeopardize *vt* arriesgar.
jersey *n* jersey *m*.
jest *n* broma *f*.
jester *n* bufón/ona *m/f*.
Jesuit *n* jesuita *m*.
Jesus *n* Jesús *m*.
jet *n* avión a reacción *m*
jettison *vt* desechar.
jetty *n* muelle *m*.
Jew *n* judío/día *m/f*.
jewel *n* joya *f*.
jewelry *n* joyería *f*.
Jewish *adj* judío/día.
jib *n* (*mar*) foque *m*.
jibe *n* mofa *f*.
jig *n* giga *f*.
jigsaw *n* rompecabezas *m*.
jilt *vt* dejar.
job *n* trabajo *m*.
jockey *n* jinete *m/f*.
jocular *adj* jocoso/sa, alegre.
jog *vi* hacer footing.
jogging *n* footing *m*.
join *vt* juntar, unir.
joiner *n* carpintero/ra *m/f*.
joinery *n* carpintería *f*.
joint *n* articulación *f*.
jointly *adv* conjuntamente.
joke *n* broma *f*:—*vi* bromear.
joker *n* comodín *m*.
jollity *n* alegría *f*.
jolly *adj* alegre.
jolt *vt* sacudir:—*n* sacudida *f*.
jostle *vt* codear.
journal *n* revista *f*.
journalism *n* periodismo *m*.
journalist *n* periodista *m/f*.
journey *n* viaje *m*:—*vt* viajar.
jovial *adj* jovial.
joy *n* alegría *f*; jubilo *m*.
jubilant *adj* jubiloso/sa.
jubilation *n* jubilo/la, regocijo *m*.
jubilee *n* jubileo *m*.
Judaism *n* judaísmo *m*.
judge *n* juez/a *m/f*:—*vt* juzgar.
judgment *n* juicio *m*.
judicial *adj* **~ly** *adv* judicial(mente).
judiciary *n* judicatura *m*.
judicious *adj* prudente.
judo *n* judo *m*.
juggle *vi* hacer juegos malabares.
juggler *n* malabarista *m/f*.
juice *n* jugo *m*; suco *m*.
juicy *adj* jugoso/sa.
jukebox *n* gramola *f*.
July *n* julio *m*.
jumble *vt* mezclar
jump *vi* saltar
jumper *n* suéter *m*.
jumpy *adj* nervioso/sa.
juncture *n* coyuntura *f*.
June *n* junio *m*.
jungle *n* selva *f*.
junior *adj* más joven.
juniper *n* (*bot*) enebro *m*.
junk *n* basura *f*; baratijas *fpl*.
junta *n* junta *f*.
jurisdiction *n* jurisdicción *f*.
jurisprudence *n* jurisprudencia *f*.
jurist *n* jurista *m/f*.
jury *n* jurado *m*.
just *adj* justo/ta.
justice *n* justicia *f*.
justification *n* justificación *f*.
justify *vt* justificar.

justly *adv* justamente.
justness *n* justicia *f*.
jut *vi*:—**to ~ out** sobresalir.
jute *n* yute *m*.
juvenile *adj* juvenil.
juxtaposition *n* yuxtaposición *f*.

K

kaleidoscope *n* calidoscopio *m*.
kangaroo *n* canguro *m*.
karate *n* karate *m*.
kebab *n* pincho *m*.
keel *n* (*mar*) quilla *f*.
keen *adj* agudo/da; vivo/va.
keep *vt* mantener; guardar; conservar.
keeper *n* guardián/ana *m/f*.
keepsake *n* recuerdo *m*.
keg *n* barril *m*.
kennel *n* perrera *f*.
kernel *n* fruta *f*; meollo *m*.
kerosene *n* kerosene *m*.
ketchup *n* catsup *m*.
kettle *n* hervidor *m*.
key *n* llave *f*; (*mus*) clave *f*; tecla *f*.
keyboard *n* teclado *m*.
keyhole *n* ojo de la cerradura *m*.
key ring *n* llavero *m*.
khaki *n* caqui *m*.
kick *vt*, *vi* patear.
kid *n* chico *m*.
kidnap *vt* secuestrar.
kidnapper *n* secuestrador/a *m/f*.
kidney *n* riñón *m*.
killer *n* asesino/na *m/f*.
killing *n* asesinato *m*.
kiln *n* horno *m*.
kilo *n* kilo *m*.
kilobyte *n* kiloocteto *m*.
kilogram *n* kilo *m*.
kilometer *n* kilómetro *m*.
kilt *n* falda escocesa *f*.
kin *n* parientes *mpl*.
kind *adj* cariñoso/sa:—*n* genero *m*.
kind-hearted *adj* bondadoso/sa.
kindle *vt*, *vi* encender.
kindly *adj* bondadoso/sa.
kindness *n* bondad *f*.
kindred *adj* emparentado/da.
kinetic *adj* cinético/ca.
king *n* rey *m*.
kingdom *n* reino *m*.
kingfisher *n* martín pescador *m*.
kiosk *n* quiosco *m*.
kiss *n* beso *m*:—*vt* besar.
kit *n* equipo *m*.
kitchen *n* cocina *f*.
kite *n* cometa *f*.
kitten *n* gatillo *m*.
knack *n* don *m*.
knapsack *n* mochila *f*.
knave *n* bribón
knead *vt* amasar.
knee *n* rodilla *f*.
kneel *vi* arrodillarse.
knell *n* toque de difuntos *m*.
knife *n* cuchillo *m*.
knight *n* caballero *m*.
knit *vt*, *vi* tejer.
knitting needle *n* aguja de tejer *f*.
knitwear *n* prendas de punto *fpl*.
knob *n* bulto *m*.
knock *vt*, *vi* golpear.
knocker *n* aldaba *f*.
knock-kneed *adj* patizambo/ba.
knock-out *n* K.O. *m*.
knoll *n* cima de una colina *f*.
knot *n* nudo *m*; lazo *m*:—*vt* anudar.
knotty *adj* escabroso/sa.
know *vt*, *vi* conocer; saber.
know-all *n* sabelotodo *m/f*.
know-how *n* conocimientos *mpl*.
knowing *adj* entendido/da:—**~ly** *adv* a sabiendas.
knowledge *n* conocimiento *m*.
knowledgeable *adj* bien informado/da.
knuckle *n* nudillo *m*.

L

label *n* etiqueta *f*.
laboratory *n* laboratorio *m*.
laborious *adj* laborioso/sa.
labor *n* trabajo *m*.
laborer *n* peón *m*.
labyrinth *n* laberinto *m*.
lace *n* cordón.
lacerate *vt* lacerar.
lack *vt*, *vi* faltar.
lacquer *n* laca *f*.
lad *n* muchacho *m*.
ladder *n* escalera *f*.
ladle *n* cucharón *m*.
lady *n* señora *f*.

lag *vi* quedarse atrás.
lager *n* cerveza (rubia) *f*.
lagoon *n* laguna *f*.
lake *n* lago *m*.
lamb *n* cordero *m*:—*vi* parir.
lame *adj* cojo/ja.
lament *vt*, *vi* lamentar(se).
lamp *n* lámpara *f*.
lampoon *n* sátira *f*.
lampshade *n* pantalla *f*.
lance *n* lanza *f*.
lancet *n* lanceta *f*.
land *n* país *m*; tierra *f*.
landing *n* desembarco *m*.
landmark *n* lugar conocido *m*.
landscape *n* paisaje *m*.
lane *n* callejuela *f*.
language *n* lengua *f*; lenguaje *m*.
lank *adj* lacio/cia.
lanky *adj* larguirucho.
lantern *n* linterna *f*; farol *m*.
lap *n* regazo *m*.
lapel *n* solapa *f*.
lapse *n* lapso *m*.
larceny *n* latrocinio *m*.
larch *n* alerce *m*.
lard *n* manteca de cerdo *f*.
larder *n* despensa *f*.
large *adj* grande.
lark *n* alondra *f*.
larva *n* larva, oruga *f*.
laryngitis *n* laringitis *f*.
larynx *n* laringe *f*.
lascivious *adj* lascivo/va.
laser *n* láser *m*.
lash *n* latigazo *m*.
lasso *n* lazo *m*.
last *adj* último/ma.
lasting *adj* duradero/ra, permanente.
latch *n* picaporte *m*.
late *adj* tarde; difunto/ta.
latent *adj* latente.
lathe *n* torno *m*.
lather *n* espuma *f*.
latitude *n* latitud *f*.
latter *adj* último/ma.
lattice *n* celosía *f*.
laugh *vi* reir.
laughter *n* risa *f*.
launch *vt*, *vi* lanzar(se):—*n* (*mar*) lancha *f*.
launching *n* lanzamiento *m*.
launder *vt* lavar.
laundry *n* lavandería *f*.
laurel *n* laurel *m*.
lava *n* lava *f*.
lavatory *n* water *m*.
lavender *n* (*bot*) espliego *m*, lavándula *f*.
lavish *adj* pródigo/ga:—**~ly** *adv* pródigamente:—*vt* disipar.
law *n* ley *f*; derecho *m*.
law court *n* tribunal *m*.
lawn *n* pasto *m*.
lawnmower *n* cortacésped *m*.
law suit *n* proceso *m*.
lawyer *n* abogado/da *m/f*.
laxative *n* laxante *m*.
lay *vt* poner.
layabout *n* vago/ga *m/f*.
layer *n* capa *f*.
layout *n* composición *f*.
laze *vi* holgazanear.
laziness *n* pereza *f*.
lazy *adj* perezoso/sa.
lead *n* plomo *m*.
leader *n* jefe/fa *m/f*.
leaf *n* hoja *f*.
leaflet *n* folleto *m*.
league *n* liga, alianza *f*.
leak *n* escape *m*.
lean *vt*, *vi* apoyar(se).
leap *vi* saltar
leap year *n* año bisiesto *m*.
learn *vt*, *vi* aprender.
lease *n* arriendo *m*:—*vt* arrendar.
leash *n* correa *f*.
least *adj* mínimo/ma.
leather *n* cuero *m*.
leave *n* licencia *f*; permiso *m*.
lecherous *adj* lascivo/va.
lecture *n* conferencia *f*.
ledge *n* reborde *m*.
ledger *n* (*com*) libro mayor *m*.
leech *n* sanguijuela *f*.
leek *n* (*bot*) puerro *m*.
left *adj* izquierdo/da.
left-handed *adj* zurdo/da.
leftovers *npl* sobras *fpl*.
leg *n* pierna *f*
legacy *n* herencia *f*.
legal *adj* legal.
legalize *vt* legalizar.
legend *n* leyenda *f*.
legendary *adj* legendario/ria.
legible *adj* legible.
legion *n* legión *f*.
legislate *vt* legislar.
legislation *n* legislación *f*.
leisure *n* ocio *m*:—**~ly** *adj* sin prisa: —**at ~** desocupado/da.
lemon *n* limón *m*.
lemonade *n* limonada *f*.
lend *vt* prestar.
length *n* largo *m*; duración *f*.
lenient *adj* indulgente.

lens *n* lente *f*.
Lent *n* Cuaresma *f*.
lentil *n* lenteja *f*.
leopard *n* leopardo *m*.
leotard *n* leotardo *m*.
leper *n* leproso/sa *m/f*.
leprosy *n* lepra *f*.
lesbian *n* lesbiana *f*.
less *adj* menor.
lesson *n* lección *f*.
let *vt* dejar, permitir.
lethal *adj* mortal.
lethargy *n* letargo *m*.
letter *n* letra *f*; carta *f*.
lettuce *n* lechuga *f*.
leukemia *n* leucemia *f*.
level *adj* llano/na, igual.
lever *n* palanca *f*.
leverage *n* influencia *f*.
levy *n* leva (de tropas) *f*.
lexicon *n* léxico *m*.
liability *n* responsabilidad *f*.
liable *adj* sujeto/ta; responsable.
liaise *vi* enlazar.
liaison *n* enlace *m*.
liar *n* embustero *m*.
libel *n* difamación *f*:—*vt* difamar.
liberal *adj* liberal.
liberate *vt* libertar.
liberation *n* liberación *f*.
liberty *n* libertad *f*.
Libra *n* Libra *f*.
librarian *n* bibliotecario *m*.
library *n* biblioteca *f*.
license *n* licencia *f*.
lick *vt* lamer.
lid *n* tapa *f*.
lie *n* mentira *f*.
life *n* vida *f*.
lifelike *adj* natural.
life preserver *n* chaleco salvavidas *m*.
lift *vt* levantar.
ligament *n* ligamento *m*.
light *n* luz *f*.
light bulb *n* foco *m*; bombilla *f*.
lighter *n* encendedor *m*.
lighthouse *n* (*mar*) faro *m*.
lightning *n* relámpago *m*.
like *adj* semejante; igual.
likeness *n* semejanza *f*.
lilac *n* lila *f*.
lily *n* lirio *m*.
lima beans *npl* haba gruesa *f*.
limb *n* miembro *m*.
lime *n* cal *f*; lima *f*.
limestone *n* piedra caliza *f*.
limit *n* limite*m*.
line *n* línea *f*.
linen *n* lino *m*.
liner *n* transatlántico *m*.
linger *vi* persistir.
lingerie *n* ropa interior *f*.
linguist *n* lingüista *m*.
lining *n* forro *m*.
link *n* eslabón *m*.
linoleum *n* linóleo *m*.
lintel *n* dintel *m*.
lion *n* león *m*.
lip *n* labio *m*.
liqueur *n* licor *m*.
liquid *adj* líquido/da
liquor *n* licor *m*.
liquorice *n* orozuz *m*; regalicia *f*.
lisp *vi* cecear.
list *n* lista *f*.
listen *vi* escuchar.
literature *n* literatura *f*.
lithe *adj* ágil.
lithograph *n* litografía *f*.
litigation *n* litigio *m*.
liter *n* litro *m*.
litter *n* litera *f*.
little *adj* pequeño/ña, poco/ca
live *vi* vivir; habitar.
liver *n* hígado *m*.
livestock *n* ganado *m*.
living *n* vida *f*:—*adj* vivo/va.
living room *n* sala de estar *f*.
lizard *n* lagarto *m*.
load *vt* cargar
loaf *n* pan *m*.
loam *n* marga *f*.
loan *n* préstamo *m*.
loathe *vt* aborrecer.
loathing *n* aversión *f*.
lobby *n* vestíbulo *m*.
lobe *n* lóbulo *m*.
lobster *n* langosta *f*.
local *adj* local.
locality *n* localidad *f*.
locate *vt* localizar.
location *n* situación *f*.
loch *n* lago *m*.
lock *n* cerradura *f*.
locker *n* vestuario *m*.
locket *n* medallón *m*.
locomotive *n* locomotora *f*.
locust *n* langosta *f*.
loft *n* desván *m*.
lofty *adj* alto/ta.
log *n* leño *m*.
logic *n* lógica *f*.
logo *n* logotipo *m*.
loiter *vi* merodear.

lollipop *n* pirulí *m*.
loneliness *n* soledad *f*.
long *adj* largo/ga.
longitude *n* longitud *f*.
look *vi* mirar *f*.
looking glass *n* espejo *m*.
loop *n* lazo *m*.
loose *adj* suelto/ta.
loot *vt* saquear:—*n* botín *m*.
lop *vt* desmochar.
lord *n* señor *m*.
lose *vt* perder.
loss *n* perdida *f*.
lotion *n* loción *f*.
lottery *n* lotería *f*.
loud *adj* fuerte:—**~ly** *adv* fuerte.
loudspeaker *n* altavoz *m*.
lounge *n* salón *m*.
louse *n* piojo (*pl* **lice**) *m*.
lout *n* gamberro *m*.
love *n* amor, cariño *m*.
lovely *adj* hermoso/sa.
lover *n* amante *m*.
low *adj* bajo/ja.
loyal *adj* leal; fiel.
lozenge *n* pastilla *f*.
lubricant *n* lubricante *m*.
lubricate *vt* lubricar.
luck *n* suerte *f*; fortuna *f*.
lucrative *adj* lucrativo/va.
ludricrous *adj* absurdo/da.
lug *vt* arrastrar.
luggage *n* equipaje *m*.
lull *vt* acunar:—*n* tregua *f*.
lullaby *n* nana *f*.
lumbago *n* lumbago *m*.
lumber *n* madera de construccion *f*
luminous *adj* luminoso/sa.
lump *n* terrón *m*.
lunacy *n* locura *f*.
lunar *adj* lunar.
lunatic *adj* loco/ca.
lunch, luncheon *n* merienda *f*.
lungs *npl* pulmones *mpl*.
luscious *adj* delicioso/sa.
lush *adj* exuberante.
lust *n* lujuria, sensualidad *f*.
luster *n* lustre *m*.
luxurious *adj* lujoso/sa.
luxury *n* lujo *m*.
lymph *n* linfa *f*.
lynx *n* lince *m*.
lyrical *adj* lírico/ca.
lyrics *npl* letra *f*.

M

macaroni *n* macarrones *mpl*.
macaroon *n* almendrado *m*.
mace *n* maza *f*; macis *f*.
machine *n* maquina *f*.
machinery *n* maquinaria, mecanica *f*.
mackerel *n* escombro *m*.
mad *adj* loco, furioso, rabioso.
madam *n* madama, senora *f*.
madhouse *n* casa de locos *f*.
madness *n* locura *f*.
magazine *n* revista *f*.
maggot *n* gusano *m*.
magic *n* magia *f*.
magician *n* mago *m*
magistrate *n* magistrado *m*.
magnet *n* iman *m*.
magnetic *adj* magnetico.
magnificent *adj* magnifico.
magnify *vt* aumentar.
magnifying glass *n* lupa *f*.
magnitude *n* magnitud *f*.
magpie *n* urraca *f*.
mahogany *n* caoba *f*.
mail *n* correo *m*.
mailman *n* cartero *m*.
maim *vt* mutilar.
main *adj* principal.
maintain *vt* mantener.
maintenance *n* mantenimiento *m*.
maize *n* maiz *m*.
majesty *n* majestad *f*.
major *adj* principal
make *vt* hacer, crear.
make-up *n* maquillaje *m*.
malaria *n* malaria *f*.
male *adj* masculino:—*n* macho *m*.
malice *n* malicia *f*.
malicious *adj* malicioso.
mall *n* centro comercial *m*.
malleable *adj* maleable.
mallet *n* mazo *m*.
mallows *n* (*bot*) malva *f*.
malnutrition *n* desnutricion *f*.
malpractice *n* negligencia *f*.
malt *n* malta *f*.
maltreat *vt* maltratar.
mammal *n* mamifero *m*.
mammoth *adj* gigantesco.

man *n* hombre *m*.
manage *vt*, *vi* manejar, dirigir.
management *n* direccion *f*.
manager *n* director *m*.
mandate *n* mandato *m*.
mane *n* crines del caballo *fpl*.
maneuvre *n* maniobra *f*.
mangle *n* rodillo *m*.
mangy *adj* sarnoso.
manhood *n* edad viril *f*.
mania *n* mania *f*.
maniac *n* maniaco *m*.
manipulate *vt* manejar.
mankind *n* genero humano *m*.
man-made *n* artificial.
manner *n* manera *f*; modo *m*
mansion *n* palacio *m*.
mantelpiece *n* repisa de chimenea *f*.
manual *adj*, *n* manual *m*.
manufacture *n* fabricacion *f*.
manufacturer *n* fabricante *m*.
manuscript *n* manuscrito *m*.
many *adj* muchos, muchas.
map *n* mapa *m*.
maple *n* arce *m*.
mar *vt* estropear.
marathon *n* maraton *m*.
marble *n* marmol *m*.
March *n* marzo *m*.
mare *n* yegua *f*.
margarine *n* margarina *f*.
margin *n* margen *m*; borde *m*.
marigold *n* (*bot*) calendula *f*.
marijuana *n* marijuana *f*.
marine *adj* marino*m*.
marital *adj* marital.
mark *n* marca *f*.
market *n* mercado *m*.
marmalade *n* mermelada de naranja *f*.
maroon *adj* marron.
marquee *n* entoldado *m*.
marriage *n* matrimonio *m*
marrow *n* medula *f*.
marry *vi* casar(se).
marsh *n* pantano *m*.
marshy *adj* pantanoso.
martyr *n* martir *m*.
marvel *n* maravilla *f*.
marvelous *adj* maravilloso.
marzipan *n* mazapan *m*.
mascara *n* rimel *m*.
masculine *adj* masculino.
mask *n* mascara *f*.
masochist *n* masoquista *m*.
mason *n* albanil *m*.
mass *n* masa *f*; misa *f*;
massacre *n* carniceria, matanza *f*.
massage *n* masaje *m*.
massive *adj* enorme.
mast *n* mastil *m*.
masterpiece *n* obra maestra *f*.
masticate *vt* masticar.
mat *n* estera *f*.
match *n* fosforo *m*, cerilla *f*.
mate *n* companero *m*:—*vt* acoplar.
mathematics *npl* matematicas *fpl*.
matinee *n* funcion de la tarde *f*.
mating *n* aparejamiento *m*.
matriculate *vt* matricular.
matriculation *n* matriculacion *f*.
matt *adj* mate.
matter *n* materia, substancia *f*.
mattress *n* colchon *m*.
mature *adj* maduro.
mauve *adj* de color malva.
maximum *n* maximo *m*.
May *n* mayo *m*.
mayonnaise *n* mayonesa *f*.
mayor *n* alcalde *m*.
maze *n* laberinto *m*.
me *pn* me; mi.
meal *n* comida *f*; harina *f*.
mean *adj* tacano.
meander *vi* serpentear.
meaning *n* sentido, significado *m*.
meantime, meanwhile *adv* mientras tanto.
measles *npl* sarampion *m*.
measurement *n* medida *f*.
meat *n* carne *f*.
mechanic *n* mecanico *m*.
mechanism *n* mecanismo *m*.
medal *n* medalla *f*.
media *npl* medios de comunicacion *mpl*.
medical *adj* medico.
medicate *vt* medicinar.
medicine *n* medicina *f*.
medieval *adj* medieval.
mediocre *adj* mediocre.
meditate *vi* meditar.
meditation *n* meditacion *f*.
Mediterranean *adj* mediterraneo.
medium *n* medio *m*.
meet *vt* encontrar.
meeting *n* reunion *f*.
megaphone *n* megafono *m*.
melancholy *n* melancolia *f*.
mellow *adj* maduro.
mellowness *n* madurez *f*.
melody *n* melodia *f*.
melon *n* melon *m*.
melt *vt* derretir.
member *n* miembro *m*.
membrane *n* membrana *f*.
memento *n* memento *m*.

memoir *n* memoria *f.*
memorandum *n* memorandum *m.*
memorial *n* monumento conmemorativo *m.*
memory *n* memoria *f*; recuerdo *m.*
menace *n* amenaza *f.*
menagerie *n* casa de fieras *f.*
mend *vt* reparar.
menial *adj* domestico.
meningitis *n* meningitis *f.*
menopause *n* menopausia *f.*
menstruation *n* menstruacion *f.*
mental *adj* mental.
mention *n* mencion *f.*
mentor *n* mentor *m.*
menu *n* menu *m*; carta *f.*
merchandise *n* mercancia *f.*
merchant *n* comerciante *m.*
mercury *n* mercurio *m.*
mercy *n* compasion *f.*
mere *adj* mero.
meridian *n* meridiano *m.*
merit *n* merito *m.*
mermaid *n* sirena *f.*
merry *adj* alegre.
merry-go-round *n* tiovivo *m.*
mesh *n* malla *f.*
mesmerize *vt* hipnotizar.
mess *n* lio *m.*
message *n* mensaje *m.*
metabolism *n* metabolismo *n.*
metal *n* metal *m.*
metallic *adj* metalico.
metamorphosis *n* metamorfosis *f.*
metaphor *n* metafora *f.*
meteor *n* meteoro *m.*
meteorological *adj* meteorológico.
meteorology *n* meteorologia *f.*
meter[1] *n* medidor *m.*
meter[2] *n* metro *m.*
method *n* metodo *m.*
methodical *adj* metodico.
Methodist *n* metodista *m.*
metric *adj* metrico.
metropolis *n* metropoli *f.*
metropolitan *adj* metropolitano.
mettle *n* valor *m.*
mew *vi* maullar.
mezzanine *n* entresuelo *m.*
microbe *n* microbio *m.*
microphone *n* microfono *m.*
microchip *n* microplaqueta *f.*
microscope *n* microscopio *m.*
microwave *n* horno microondas *m.*
mid *adj* medio.
midday *n* mediodia *m.*
middle *adj* medio*m.*
midge *n* mosca *f.*
midget *n* enano *m.*
midnight *n* medianoche *f.*
midst *n* medio, centro *m.*
midsummer *n* pleno verano *m.*
midwife *n* partera *f.*
might *n* poder *m*; fuerza *f.*
mighty *adj* fuerte.
migraine *n* jaqueca *f.*
migrate *vi* emigrar.
migration *n* emigracion *f.*
mike *n* microfono *m.*
mild *adj* apacible; suave.
mildew *n* moho *m.*
mileage *n* kilometraje *m.*
milieu *n* ambiente *m.*
militant *adj* militante.
military *adj* militar.
milk *n* leche *f.*
milkshake *n* batido *m*
milky *adj* lechoso:—**M~ Way** *n* Via Lactea *f.*
mill *n* molino *m.*
millennium *n* milenio *m.*
miller *n* molinero *m.*
milligram *n* miligramo *m.*
milliliter *n* mililitro *m.*
millimeter *n* milimetro *m.*
milliner *n* sombrerero.
million *n* millon *m.*
millionaire *n* millonario *m.*
millionth *adj n* millonésimo.
mime *n* mimo *m.*
mimic *vt* imitar.
mince *vt* picar.
mind *n* mente *f.*
mine *pn* mio, mia, mi:—*n* mina:—*vi* minar.
miner *n* minero *m.*
mineral *adj*, *n* mineral *m.*
mineral water *n* agua mineral *f.*
mingle *vt* mezclar.
miniature *n* miniatura *f.*
minimal *adj* minimo.
minimum *n* minimum *m.*
mining *n* explotacion minera *f.*
minister *n* ministro *m.*
mink *n* vison *m.*
minnow *n* pecicillo *m* (pez).
minor *adj* menor
mint *n* (*bot*) menta *f.*
minus *adv* menos.
minute *adj* diminuto.
minute *n* minuto *m.*
miracle *n* milagro *m.*
mirage *n* espejismo *m.*
mire *n* fango *m.*
mirror *n* espejo *m.*
mirth *n* alegria *f.*

misbehave *vi* portarse mal.
miscarry *vi* abortar.
miscellaneous *adj* varios, varias.
miser *n* avaro *m*.
miserable *adj* miserable.
miserly *adj* mezquino, tacano.
misery *n* miseria *f*.
mislay *vt* extraviar.
mislead *vt* enganar.
misogynist *n* misogino *m*.
Miss *n* senorita *f*.
miss *vt* perder; echar de menos.
missile *n* misil *m*.
mission *n* mision *f*.
missionary *n* misionero *m*.
mist *n* niebla *f*.
mistake *vt* entender mal
Mister *n* Senor *m*.
mistletoe *n* (*bot*) muerdago *m*.
mistress *n* amante *f*.
mistrust *vt* desconfiar.
mitigate *vt* mitigar.
mitigation *n* mitigacion *f*.
miter *n* mitra *f*.
mittens *npl* manoplas *fpl*.
mix *vt* mezclar.
mixer *n* licuadora *f*.
mixture *n* mezcla *f*.
moan *n* gemido *m*.
moat *n* foso *m*.
mob *n* multitud *f*.
mobile *adj* movil.
mode *n* modo *m*.
model *n* modelo *m*.
moderate *adj* moderado.
moderation *n* moderacion *f*.
modern *adj* moderno.
modernize *vt* modernizar.
modest *adj* modesto.
modesty *n* modestia *f*.
modify *vt* modificar.
module *n* modulo *m*.
mogul *n* magnate *m*.
mohair *n* mohair *m*.
moist *adj* humedo.
moisture *n* humedad *f*.
mold *n* molde *m*.
mole *n* topo *m*.
molecule *n* molecula *f*.
molest *vt* importunar.
mom *n* mama *f*.
moment *n* momento *m*.
momentum *n* impetu *m*.
mommy *n* mama *f*.
monarch *n* monarca *m*.
monarchy *n* monarquia *f*.
monastery *n* monasterio *m*.
Monday *n* lunes *m*.
monetary *adj* monetario.
money *n* moneda *f*; dinero *m*.
mongol *n* mongolico *m*.
mongrel *adj*, *n* mestizo *m*.
monk *n* monje *m*.
monkey *n* mono *m*.
monopoly *n* monopolio *m*.
monotonous *adj* monotono.
monsoon *n* (*mar*) monzon *m*.
monster *n* monstruo *m*.
month *n* mes *m*.
monthly *adj*, *adv* mensual (mente).
monument *n* monumento *m*.
mood *n* humor *m*.
moody *adj* malhumorado.
moon *n* luna *f*.
moor *n* paramo.
moorland *n* paramo *m*.
moose *n* alce *m*.
mop *n* fregona *f*.
mope *vi* estar triste.
moped *n* ciclomotor *m*.
morality *n* etica, moralidad *f*.
morbid *adj* morboso.
more *adj*, *adv* mas.
moreover *adv* ademas.
morgue *n* deposito de cadaveres *m*.
morning *n* manana *f*:—**good** ~ buenos dias *mpl*.
moron *n* imbecil *m*.
morphine *n* morfina *f*.
morse *n* morse *m*.
morsel *n* bocado *m*.
mortal *adj* mortal
mortality *n* mortalidad *f*.
mortar *n* mortero *m*.
mortgage *n* hipoteca *f*.
mortify *vt* mortificar.
mortuary *n* deposito de cadaveres *m*.
mosaic *n* mosaico *m*.
mosque *n* mezquita *f*.
mosquito *n* mosquito *m*.
moss *n* (*bot*) musgo *m*.
most *adj* la mayoria de.
motel *n* motel *m*.
moth *n* polilla *f*.
mother *n* madre *f*.
mother-in-law *n* suegra *f*.
mother-of-pearl *n* nacar *m*.
motif *n* tema *m*.
motion *n* movimiento *m*.
motive *n* motivo *m*.
motor *n* motor *m*.
motorbike *n* moto *f*.
motorcycle *n* motocicleta *f*.
motor vehicle *n* automovil *m*.

motto *n* lema *m*.
mount *n* monte *m*.
mountain *n* montana *f*.
mountaineering *n* montañismo *m*.
mourn *vt* lamentar.
mourner *n* doliente *m*.
mourning *n* luto *m*.
mouse *n* (*pl* mice) raton *m*.
mousse *n* mousse *f*.
mouth *n* boca *f*;
mouthful *n* bocado *m*.
mouthwash *n* enjuague *m*.
mouthwatering *adj* apetitoso.
move *vt* mover.
movement *n* movimiento *m*.
movies *n* pelicula *f*; el cine
moving *adj* conmovedor.
mow *vt* segar.
mower *n* cortacesped *m*; mocion *f*.
Mrs *n* senora *f*.
much *adj*, *adv* mucho.
muck *n* suciedad *f*.
mucous *adj* mocoso.
mud *n* barro *m*.
muddle *vt* confundir *m*; confusion *f*.
muffle *vt* embozar.
mug *n* jarra *f*.
mulberry *n* mora *f*.
mule *n* mulo *m*, mula *f*.
multiple *adj* multiplo *m*.
multiplication *n* multiplicacion *f*.
multiply *vt* multiplicar.
multitude *n* multitud *f*.
mumble *vt*, *vi* refunfunar.
mummy *n* momia *f*.
mumps *npl* paperas *fpl*.
munch *vt* mascar.
mundane *adj* trivial.
municipal *adj* municipal.
municipality *n* municipalidad *f*.
mural *n* mural *m*.
murder *n* asesinato *m*; homicidio *m*.
murky *adj* sombrio.
murmur *n* murmullo.
muscle *n* musculo *m*.
muse *vi* meditar.
museum *n* museo *m*.
mushroom *n* (*bot*) seta *f*; champinon *m*.
music *n* musica *f*.
musician *n* musico *m*.
musk *n* musco *m*.
muslin *n* muselina *f*.
mussel *n* marisco *m*.
must *v aux* estar obligado.
mustache *n* bigote *m*.
mustard *n* mostaza *f*.
mute *adj* mudo, silencioso.
mutilate *vt* mutilar.
mutter *vt*, *vi* murmurar.
mutton *n* carnero *m*.
mutual *adj* mutuo, mutual.
muzzle *n* bozal *m*.
my *pn* mi, mis; mio, mia; mios, mias.
myriad *n* miriada *f*.
myrrh *n* mirra *f*.
myrtle *n* mirto, arrayan *m*.
myself *pn* yo mismo.
mysterious *adj* misterioso.
mystery *n* misterio *m*.
mystic(al) *adj* mistico.
mystify *vt* dejar perplejo.
mystique *n* misterio *m*.
myth *n* mito *m*.
mythology *n* mitologia *f*.

N

nag *n* jaca *f*:—*vt* reganar.
nagging *adj* persistente.
nail *n* una *f*; garra *f*; clavo *m*.
naive *adj* ingenuo.
naked *adj* desnudo.
name *n* nombre *m*.
nameless *adj* anonimo.
namely *adv* a saber.
namesake *n* tocayo *m*.
nanny *n* ninera *f*.
nap *n* sueno ligero *m*.
nape *n* nuca *f*.
napkin *n* servilleta *f*.
narcissus *n* (*bot*) narciso *m*.
narcotic *adj*, *n* narcotico *m*.
narrate *vt* narrar.
narrative *adj* narrativo.
narrow *adj* angosto, estrecho.
nasal *adj* nasal.
nasty *adj* sucio, puerco.
natal *adj* nativo; natal.
nation *n* nacion *f*.
nationalize *vt* nacionalizar.
nationalism *n* nacionalismo *m*.
nationalist *adj*, *n* nacionalista *m*.
nationality *n* nacionalidad *f*.
native *adj* nativo *m*.
native language *n* lengua materna *f*.

Nativity *n* Navidad *f*.
natural *adj* natural.
naturalize *vt* naturalizar.
naturalist *n* naturalista *m*.
nature *n* naturaleza *f*.
naught *n* cero *m*.
naughty *adj* malo.
nausea *n* nausea.
nauseous *adj* fastidioso.
nautic(al), naval *adj* nautico, naval.
nave *n* nave (de la iglesia) *f*.
navel *n* ombligo *m*.
navigate *vi* navegar.
navigation *n* navegacion *f*.
navy *n* marina *f*
Nazi *n* nazi *m*.
near *prep* cerca de.
nearby *adj* cercano.
nearly *adv* casi.
near-sighted *adj* miope.
nebulous *adj* nebuloso.
necessarily *adv* necesariamente.
necessary *adj* necesario.
necessity *n* necesidad *f*.
neck *n* cuello *m*.
necklace *n* collar *m*.
necktie *n* corbata *f*.
nectar *n* nectar *m*.
need *n* necesidad *f*.
needle *n* aguja *f*.
needless *adj* superfluo.
needlework *n* costura *f*
needy *adj* necesitado, pobre.
negation *n* negacion *f*.
negative *adj* negativo.
neglect *vt* descuidar.
negligee *n* salto de cama *m*.
negligence *n* negligencia *f*
negligible *adj* insignificante.
negotiate *vt*, *vi* negociar (con).
negotiation *n* negociacion *f*; negocio *m*.
Negress *n* negra *f*.
Negro *adj*, *n* negro *m*.
neighbor *n* vecino *m*.
neighborhood *n* vecindad *f*; vecin- dario *m*.
neither *conj* ni:—*pn* ninguno.
neon *n* neon *m*.
neon light *n* luz de neon *f*.
nephew *n* sobrino *m*.
nepotism *n* nepotismo *m*.
nerve *n* nervio *m*; valor *m*.
nerve-racking *adj* espantoso.
nervous *adj* nervioso; nervudo.
nervous breakdown *n* crisis nerviosa *f*.
nest *n* nido *m*.
nest egg *n* (*fig*) ahorros *mpl*.
nestle *vt* anidarse.
net *n* red *f*.
netball *n* basquet *m*.
nettle *n* ortiga *f*.
network *n* red *f*.
neurosis *n* neurosis *f* invar.
neurotic *adj*, *n* neurotico *m*.
neuter *adj* (*gr*) neutro.
neutral *adj* neutral.
neutrality *n* neutralidad *f*.
neutron *n* neutron *m*.
never *adv* nunca, jamas.
nevertheless *adv* no obstante.
new *adj* nuevo.
news *npl* novedad, noticias *fpl*.
newscaster *n* presentador *m*.
newspaper *n* periodico *m*.
next *adj* proximo.
nib *n* pico *m*.
nibble *vt* picar.
nice *adj* simpatico.
niche *n* nicho *m*.
nickel *n* niquel *m*
nickname *n* mote.
nicotine *n* nicotina *f*.
niece *n* sobrina *f*.
niggling *adj* insignificante.
night *n* noche *f*.
nightclub *n* cabaret *m*.
nightfall *n* anochecer *m*.
nightingale *n* ruisenor *m*.
nightmare *n* pesadilla *f*.
nihilist *n* nihilista *m*.
nimble *adj* ligero, activo, listo, agil.
nine *adj*, *n* nueve.
nineteen *adj*, *n* diecinueve.
nineteenth *adj*, *n* decimonono.
ninetieth *adj*, *n* nonagesimo.
ninety *adj*, *n* noventa.
ninth *adj*, *n* nono, noveno.
nip *vt* pellizcar; morder.
nipple *n* pezon *m*; tetilla *f*.
nit *n* liendre *f*.
nitrogen *n* nitrogeno *m*.
no *adv* no.
nobility *n* nobleza *f*.
noble *adj* noble.
nobleman *n* noble *m*.
nobody *n* nadie, ninguna persona *f*.
nocturnal *adj* nocturnal.
noise *n* ruido *m*.
noisy *adj* ruidoso, turbulento.
nominate *vt* nombrar.
nomination *n* nominacion *f*.
nominee *n* candidato *m*.
non-alcoholic *adj* no alcoholico.
nonchalant *adj* indiferente.
nondescript *adj* no descrito.

none *adj* nadie, ninguno.
nonentity *n* nulidad *f*.
nonetheless *adv* sin embargo.
nonsense *n* disparate *m*.
noodles *npl* fideos *mpl*.
noon *n* mediodia *m*.
noose *n* lazo corredizo *m*.
nor *conj* ni.
normal *adj* normal.
north *n* norte *m*.
North America *n* America del Norte *f*.
northeast *n* nor(d)este *m*.
northerly, northern *adj* norteno.
North Pole *n* polo artico *m*.
northwest *n* nor(d)oeste *m*.
nose *n* nariz *f*
nosebleed *n* hemorragia nasal *f*.
nostalgia *n* nostalgia *f*.
nostril *n* ventana de la nariz *f*.
not *adv* no.
notable *adj* notable.
notably *adv* especialmente.
notary *n* notario *m*.
notch *n* muesca *f*.
note *n* nota, marca *f*.
notebook *n* librito de apuntes *m*.
noted *adj* afamado, celebre.
nothing *n* nada *f*.
notice *n* noticia *f*; aviso *m*.
notification *n* notificacion *f*.
notify *vt* notificar.
notion *n* nocion *f*.
notoriety *n* notoriedad *f*.
notwithstanding *conj* no obstante, aunque.
nougat *n* turron *m*.
nought *n* cero *m*.
noun *n* (*gr*) sustantivo *m*.
nourish *vt* nutrir, alimentar.
novel *n* novela *f*.
novelist *n* novelista *m*.
novelty *n* novedad *f*.
November *n* noviembre *m*.
novice *n* novicio *m*.
now *adv* ahora.
nowadays *adv* hoy (en) dia.
nowhere *adv* en ninguna parte.
noxious *adj* nocivo, danoso.
nozzle *n* boquilla *f*.
nuance *n* matiz *m*.
nuclear *adj* nuclear.
nucleus *n* nucleo *m*.
nude *adj* desnudo.
nudge *vt* dar un codazo a.
nudist *n* nudista *m*.
nudity *n* desnudez *f*.
null *adj* nulo.
nullify *vt* anular.
numb *adj* entorpecido.
number *n* numero *m*.
numerous *adj* numeroso.
nun *n* monja *f*.
nunnery *n* convento de monjas *m*.
nuptial *adj* nupcial *fpl*.
nurse *n* enfermera *f*.
nursery *n* guarderia infantil *f*
nursery rhyme *n* cancion infantil *f*.
nursery school *n* parvulario *m*.
nursing home *n* clinica de reposo *f*.
nurture *vt* criar.
nut *n* nuez *f*.
nutcrackers *npl* cascanueces *m*.
nutmeg *n* nuez moscada *f*.
nutritious *adj* nutritivo.
nut shell *n* cascara de nuez *f*.
nylon *n* nilon *m*.

O

oak *n* roble *m*.
oar *n* remo *m*.
oasis *n* oasis *f*.
oat *n* avena *f*.
oath *n* juramento *m*.
obedience *n* obediencia *f*.
obese *adj* obeso, gordo.
obey *vt* obedecer.
obituary *n* necrologia *f*.
object *n* objeto *m*:—*vt* objetar.
objective *adj*, *n* objetivo *m*.
oblige *vt* obligar.
obliterate *vt* borrar.
oblivion *n* olvido *m*.
oblong *adj* oblongo.
obnoxious *adj* odioso.
oboe *n* oboe *m*.
obscene *adj* obsceno.
obscenity *n* obscenidad *f*.
obscure *adj* oscuro.
observatory *n* observatorio *m*.
observe *vt* observar, mirar.
obsess *vt* obsesionar.
obsolete *adj* en desuso.
obstacle *n* obstaculo *m*.
obstinate *adj* obstinado.

obstruct *vt* obstruir; impedir.
obtain *vt* obtener, adquirir.
obvious *adj* obvio, evidente.
occasion *n* ocasion *f*.
occupant, occupier *n* ocupador *m*
occupation *n* ocupacion *f*; empleo *m*.
occupy *vt* ocupar.
occur *vi* pasar.
ocean *n* oceano *m*; alta mar *f*.
ocher *n* ocre *m*.
octave *n* octava *f*.
October *n* octubre *m*.
octopus *n* pulpo *m*.
odd *adj* impar.
oddity *n* singularidad.
odious *adj* odioso.
odor *n* olor *m*.
of *prep* de.
off *adv* desconectado; apagado.
offence *n* ofensa *f*.
offend *vt* ofender.
offensive *adj* ofensivo.
offer *vt* ofrecer.
offering *n* sacrificio *m*.
office *n* oficina *f*.
officer *n* oficial, empleado *m*.
official *adj* oficial.
offspring *n* prole *f*.
ogle *vt* comerse con los ojos.
oil *n* aceite *m*.
oil painting *n* pintura al oleo *f*.
oil rig *n* torre de perforacion *f*.
oil tanker *n* petrolero *m*.
ointment *n* unguento *m*.
OK, okay *excl* vale.
old *adj* viejo; antiguo.
old age *n* vejez *f*.
olive *n* olivo *m*.
omelet *n* tortilla de huevos *f*.
omen *n* agüero.
ominous *adj* ominoso.
omission *n* omisión *f*.
omit *vt* omitir.
omnipotence *n* omnipotencia *f*.
on *prep* sobre, encima, en; de; a.
one *adj* un, uno.
oneself *pn* si mismo; si misma.
ongoing *adj* continuo.
onion *n* cebolla *f*.
onlooker *n* espectador *m*.
only *adj* unico, solo.
onus *n* responsabilidad *f*.
onwards *adv* adelante.
opaque *adj* opaco.
open *adj* abierto; *vi* abrirse.
open-minded *adj* imparcial.
opera *n* opera *f*.
operate *vi* obrar.
operation *n* operacion *f*.
operational *adj* operacional.
operative *adj* operativo.
operator *n* operario *m*; operador *m*.
ophthalmic *adj* oftálmico.
opinion *n* opinion *f*.
opinion poll *n* sondeo *m*.
opponent *n* antagonista *m*.
opportune *adj* oportuno.
opportunity *n* oportunidad *f*.
oppose *vt* oponerse.
opposite *adj* opuesto; contrario.
opposition *n* oposicion *f*
oppress *vt* oprimir.
oppression *n* opresion *f*.
optic(al) *adj* optico *f*.
optician *n* optico *m*.
optimist *n* optimista *m*.
optimum *adj* optimum.
option *n* opcion *f*; deseo *m*.
opulent *adj* opulento.
or *conj* o; u.
oracle *n* oraculo *m*.
oral *adj* oral.
orange *n* naranja *f*.
orbit *n* orbita *f*.
orchard *n* huerto *m*.
orchestra *n* orquesta *f*.
orchid *n* orquidea *f*.
order *n* orden mf; regla *f*; mandar.
ordinary *adj* ordinario.
ore *n* mineral *m*.
organ *n* organo *m*.
organic *adj* organico.
organization *n* organizacion *f*.
organize *vt* organizar.
organism *n* organismo *m*.
organist *n* organista *m*.
orgasm *n* orgasmo *m*.
orgy *n* orgia *f*.
oriental *adj* oriental.
orifice *n* orificio *m*.
origin *n* origen *m*.
original *adj* original.
originate *vi* originar.
ornament *n* ornamento *m*.
ornate *adj* adornado.
orphan *adj*, *n* huerfano *m*.
orphanage *n* orfanato *m*.
orthodox *adj* ortodoxo.
orthopedic *adj* ortopedico.
oscillate *vi* oscilar.
osprey *n* aguila marina *f*.
ostensibly *adv* aparentemente.
ostentatious *adj* ostentoso.
osteopath *n* osteopata *m*.

ostrich *n* avestruz *m*.
other *pn* otro.
otter *n* nutria *f*.
ouch *excl* ¡ay!
ought *v aux* deber, ser menester.
ounce *n* onza *f*.
our, ours *pn* nuestro, nuestra, nuestros, nuestras.
ourselves *pn pl* nosotros mismos.
out *adv* fuera.
outbreak *n* erupcion *f*.
outcast *n* paria *m*.
outcome *n* resultado *m*.
outcry *n* clamor *m*.
outdo *vt* exceder a otro, sobrepujar.
outer *adj* exterior.
outermost *adj* extremo; lo mas exterior.
outfit *n* vestidos *mpl*; ropa *f*.
outlet *n* enchufe *m*.
outline *n* contorno *m*
outlook *n* perspectiva *f*.
out-of-date *adj* caducado; pasado de moda.
outpatient *n* paciente externo *m*.
output *n* rendimiento *m*.
outrage *n* ultraje *m*.
outrageous *adj* ultrajoso.
outside *n* superficie *f*; exterior *m*.
outsider *n* forastero *m*.
outskirts *npl* alrededores *mpl*.
outstanding *adj* excepcional.
outwit *vt* enganar a uno a fuerza de tretas.
oval *n* ovalo *m*:—*adj* oval.
ovary *n* ovario *m*.
oven *n* horno *m*.
ovenproof *adj* resistente al horno.
over *prep* sobre, encima.
overbearing *adj* despotico.
overcharge *vt* sobrecargar.
overcoat *n* abrigo *m*.
overdose *n* sobredosis *f*.
overdue *adj* retrasado.
overeat *vi* atracarse.
overflow *vt*, *vi* inundar.
overhaul *vt* revisar.
overkill *n* exceso de medios *m*.
overlap *vi* traslaparse.
overleaf *adv* al dorso.
overload *vt* sobrecargar.
overpower *vt* predominar, oprimir.
overseas *adv* en ultramar:—*adj* extranjero.
oversee *vt* inspeccionar.
overshadow *vt* eclipsar.
overstate *vi* exagerar.
overstep *vt* exceder, pasar de.
overtake *vt* sobrepasar.
overtime *n* horas extra *fpl*.
overtone *n* tono *m*.
owe *vt* deber.
owl *n* buho *m*.
own *adj* propio.
owner *n* dueno, propietario *m*.
ownership *n* posesion *f*.
ox *n* buey *m*.
oxidize *vt* oxidar.
oxygen *n* oxigeno *m*.
oyster *n* ostra *f*.
ozone *n* ozono *m*.

P

pa *n* papa *m*.
pace *n* paso *m*.
pacemaker *n* marcapasos *m*.
pacific(al) *adj* pacifico.
pacify *vt* pacificar.
package *n* paquete *m*.
packet *n* paquete *m*.
packing *n* embalaje *m*.
pact *n* pacto *m*.
pad *n* bloc *m*.
paddle *vi* remar
paddock *n* corral *m*.
paddy *n* arrozal *m*.
pagan *adj*, *n* pagano *m*.
page *n* pagina *f*.
pain *n* pena *f*; castigo *m*; dolor *m*.
painkiller *n* analgesico *m*.
paint *vt* pintar.
paintbrush *n* pincel *m*.
painter *n* pintor *m*.
painting *n* pintura *f*.
pair *n* par *m*.
pajamas *npl* pijama *m*.
palatial *adj* palatino.
pale *adj* palido; claro.
pallet *n* pallet *m*.
palliative *adj*, *n* paliativo *m*.
pallid *adj* palido.
pallor *n* palidez *f*.
palm *n* (*bot*) palma *f*.
Palm Sunday *n* Domingo de Ramos *m*.
palpable *adj* palpable.
paltry *adj* irrisorio; mezquino.
pamphlet *n* folleto *m*.

pan *n* cazuela *f*.
pancake *n* bunuelo *m*.
pandemonium *n* jaleo *m*.
pane *n* cristal *m*.
panel *n* panel *m*
pang *n* angustia *f*.
panic *adj*, *n* panico *m*.
pansy *n* (*bot*) pensamiento *m*.
pant *vi* jadear.
panther *n* pantera *f*.
pantry *n* despensa *f*.
pants *npl* pantalones *mpl*.
papacy *n* papado *m*.
papal *adj* papal.
paper *n* papel *m*.
paperback *n* libro de bolsillo *m*.
paper clip *n* clip *m*.
paperweight *n* sujetapapeles *m*.
paprika *n* pimienta hungara *f*.
parachute *n* paracaidas *m*.
paradise *n* paraiso *m*.
paradox *n* paradoja *f*.
paragon *n* modelo perfecto *m*.
paragraph *n* parrafo *m*.
parallel *adj* paralelo.
paralysis *n* paralisis *f*.
paralytic(al) *adj* paralitico.
paralyze *vt* paralizar.
paramedic *n* ambulanciero *m*.
paramount *adj* supremo.
paranoid *adj* paranoico.
parasite *n* parásito *m*.
parasol *n* parasol *m*.
parcel *n* paquete *m*.
parch *vt* resecar.
pardon *n* perdon *m*.
parent *n* padre *m*; madre *f*.
parentage *n* parentela *f*.
parental *adj* paternal.
parenthesis *n* parentesis *m*.
parish *n* parroquia *f*.
parity *n* paridad *f*.
park *n* parque *m*.
parliament *n* parlamento *m*.
parlor *n* sala de recibimiento *f*.
parody *n* parodia *f*.
parrot *n* papagayo *m*.
parsley *n* (*bot*) perejil *m*.
parsnip *n* (*bot*) chirivia *f*.
part *n* parte *f*.
participate *vi* participar (en).
particle *n* particula *f*.
particular *adj* particular.
parting *n* separacion *f*.
partition *n* particion.
partner *n* socio, companero *m*.
partridge *n* perdiz *f*.
party *n* partido *m*; fiesta *f*.
pass *vt* pasar.
passage *n* pasaje *m*
passbook *n* libreta de depositos *f*.
passenger *n* pasajero *m*.
passion *n* pasion *f*
passionate *adj* apasionado.
passive *adj* pasivo.
Passover *n* Pascua *f*.
passport *n* pasaporte *m*.
password *n* contrasena *f*.
past *adj* pasado.
pasta *n* pasta *f*.
paste *n* pasta *f*.
pastime *n* pasatiempo *m f*.
pastor *n* pastor *m*.
pastry *n* pasteleria *f*.
pasture *n* pasto *m*.
patch *n* remiendo *m*; parche *m*.
patent *adj* patente.
pathetic *adj* patetico.
patience *n* paciencia *f*.
patient *adj* paciente.
patio *n* patio *m*.
patriot *n* patriota *m*.
patriotism *n* patriotismo *m*.
patrol *n* patrulla *f*.
patron *n* patron *m*.
patronize *vt* patrocinar.
pattern *n* patron *m*; dibujo *m*.
pauper *n* pobre *m*.
pause *n* pausa *f*.
pave *vt* empedrar.
pavilion *n* pabellon *m*.
paw *n* pata *f*.
pay *vt* pagar.
pea *n* guisante *m*.
peace *n* paz *f*.
peach *n* melocoton *m*.
peacock *n* pavon, pavo real *m*.
peak *n* cima *f*.
peanut *n* cacahuete *m*.
pear *n* pera *f*.
pearl *n* perla *f*.
peasant *n* campesino *m*.
pebble *n* guija *f*.
peculiar *adj* peculiar.
pedal *n* pedal *m*.
pedestal *n* pedestal *m*.
pedestrian *n* peaton *m*.
pedigree *n* genealogia *f*.
peel *vt* pelar.
peg *n* clavija *f*.
pelican *n* pelicano *m*.
pen *n* boligrafo *m*; pluma *f*
penal *adj* penal.
pence *n* d *pl* of penny.

pencil *n* lapiz *m*.
pendulum *n* pendulo *m*.
penetrate *vt* penetrar.
penguin *n* pinguino *m*.
penicillin *n* penicilina *f*.
peninsula *n* peninsula *f*.
penis *n* pene *m*.
penitence *n* penitencia *f*.
penitentiary *n* encierro *m*.
penknife *n* navaja *f*.
penny *n* penique *m*.
pension *n* pension *f*.
pensive *adj* pensativo.
Pentecost *n* Pentecostes *m*.
penthouse *n* atico *m*.
people *n* pueblo *m*; nacion *f*; gente *f*.
pepper *n* pimienta *f*.
peppermint *n* menta *f*.
perceive *vt* percibir.
percentage *n* porcentaje *m*.
perception *n* percepcion*f*.
percolator *n* cafetera de filtro *f*.
percussion *n* percusion *f*; golpe *m*.
perennial *adj* perenne; perpetuo.
perfect *adj* perfecto.
perform *vt* ejecutar.
performance *n* ejecucion *f*.
perfume *n* perfume *m*; fragancia *f*:—*vt* perfumar.
perhaps *adv* quiza, quizas.
peril *n* peligro *m*.
period *n* periodo *m*.
periodical *n* jornal, periodico *m*.
perk *n* extra *m*.
perm *n* permanente *f*.
permanent *adj*, **~ly** *adv* perma-nente (mente).
permissible *adj* licito.
permission *n* permiso *m*.
permit *vt* permitir.
perplex *vt* confundir.
persecute *vt* perseguir.
persevere *vi* perseverar.
persist *vi* persistir.
person *n* persona *f*.
personality *n* personalidad *f*.
personnel *n* personal *m*.
perspective *n* perspectiva *f*.
perspiration *n* transpiracion *f*.
perspire *vi* transpirar.
persuade *vt* persuadir.
perturb *vt* perturbar.
peruse *vt* leer.
perverse *adj* perverso.
pessimist *n* pesimista *m*.
pester *vt* molestar.
pet *n* animal domestico *m*.
petal *n* (*bot*) petalo *m*.
petition *n* presentacion, peticion *f*.
petroleum *n* petroleo *m*.
petticoat *n* enaguas *fpl*.
petty *adj* mezquino.
pewter *n* peltre *m*.
phantom *n* fantasma *m*.
pharmacist *n* farmacéutico *m*.
pharmacy *n* farmacia *f*.
phase *n* fase *f*.
pheasant *n* faisan *m*.
phenomenon *n* fenomeno *m*.
phial *n* redomilla *f*.
philosopher *n* filosofo *m*.
philosophy *n* filosofia *f*.
phlegm *n* flema *f*.
phobia *n* fobia *f*.
phone *n* telefono *m*.
photocopier *n* fotocopiadora *f*.
photocopy *n* fotocopia *f*.
photograph *n* fotografia *f*:—*vt* fotografiar.
photographic *adj* fotografico.
photography *n* fotografia *f*.
phrase *n* frase *f*.
physical *adj* fisico.
physician *n* medico *m*.
physicist *n* fisico *m*.
physiotherapy *n* fisioterapia *f*.
physique *n* fisico *m*.
pianist *n* pianista *m,f*.
piano *n* piano *m*.
piccolo *n* flautin *m*.
pick *vt* escoger, elegir.
pickle *n* escabeche *m*.
picnic *n* comida, merienda *f*.
picture *n* pintura *f*.
picturesque *adj* pintoresco.
pie *n* pastel *m*; tarta *f*.
piece *n* pedazo *m*; pieza *f*.
pierce *vt* penetrar, agujerear.
pig *n* cerdo *m*.
pigeon *n* paloma *f*.
pigtail *n* trenza *f*.
pike *n* lucio *m*; pica *f*.
pile *n* estaca *f*; pila *f*; monton *m*.
pilgrim *n* peregrino *m*.
pill *n* pildora *f*.
pillar *n* pilar *m*.
pillow *n* almohada *f*.
pilot *n* piloto *m*.
pimple *n* grano *m*.
pin *n* alfiler *m*.
pinball *n* fliper *m*.
pincers *n* pinzas *fpl*.
pinch *vt* pellizcar.
pine *n* (*bot*) pino *m*.
pineapple *n* pina *f*, ananas *m*.

pink *n* rosa *f*.
pinnacle *n* cumbre *f*.
pint *n* pinta *f*.
pioneer *n* pionero *m*.
pious *adj* pio.
pip *n* pepita *f*.
pipe *n* tubo.
pirate *n* pirata *m*.
pirouette *n* pirueta.
Pisces *n* Piscis *m* (signo del zodiaco).
piss *n* (*sl*) meados *mpl*.
pistol *n* pistola *f*.
piston *n* embolo *m*.
pit *n* hoyo *m*; mina *f*.
pitcher *n* cantaro, jarro *m*.
pitchfork *n* horca *f*.
pity *n* piedad, compasion *f*.
pivot *n* eje *m*.
pizza *n* pizza *f*.
placard *n* pancarta *f*.
placate *vt* apaciguar.
place *n* lugar, sitio *m*.
placid *adj* placido.
plagiarism *n* plagio *m*.
plague *n* peste, plaga *f*.
plaice *n* platija *f* (pez).
plaid *n* tartan *m*.
plain *adj* liso, llano
plaintiff *n* (*law*) demandador *m*.
plan *n* plano *m*.
plane *n* avion *m*; plano *m*.
planet *n* planeta *m*.
plank *n* tabla *f*.
plant *n* planta *f*.
plantation *n* plantacion *f*.
plaque *n* placa *f*.
plaster *n* yeso *m*.
plastic *adj* plastico.
plate *n* plato *m*.
plateau *n* meseta *f*.
platform *n* plataforma *f*.
platinum *n* platino *m*.
platoon *n* (*mil*) peloton *m*.
play *n* juego *m*.
playboy *n* playboy *m*.
player *n* jugador *m*
plea *n* defensa *f*.
pleasant *adj* agradable.
please *vt* agradar.
pleasure *n* gusto, placer *m*.
pleat *n* pliegue *m*.
plentiful *adj* copioso.
plethora *n* pletora, replecion *f*.
pleurisy *n* pleuresia *f*.
pliers *npl* alicates *mpl*.
plinth *n* plinto *m*.
plough *n* arado *m*.
ploy *n* truco *m*.
plug *n* tapon *m*.
plum *n* ciruela *f*.
plumage *n* plumaje *m*.
plumb *n* plomada *f*.
plumber *n* plomero *m*.
plume *n* pluma *f*.
plump *adj* gordo.
plunder *vt* saquear.
plunge *vi* sumergir(se), precipitarse.
pluperfect *n* (*gr*) pluscuamperfecto *m*.
plural *adj*, *n* plural *m*.
plus *n* signo de mas *m*.
plush *adj* de felpa.
plutonium *n* plutonio *m*.
plywood *n* madera contrachapada *f*.
pneumatic *adj* neumatico.
pneumonia *n* pulmonia *f*.
poach *vt* escalfar.
pocket *n* bolsillo *m*.
pod *n* vaina *f*.
poem *n* poema *m*.
poet *n* poeta *m*.
poetry *n* poesia *f*.
poignant *adj* punzante.
point *n* punta *f*; punto *m*.
point-blank *adv* directamente.
poise *n* peso *m*; equilibrio *m*.
poison *n* veneno *m*.
poker *n* atizador *m*; poker *m*.
polar *adj* polar.
pole *n* polo *m*.
police *n* policia *f*.
policy *n* politica *f*.
polio *n* polio *f*.
polish *vt* pulir, alisar.
polite *adj* pulido, cortes.
politician *n* politico *m*.
politics *npl* politica *f*.
polka *n* polca *f*.
pollen *n* (*bot*) polen *m*.
pollute *vt* ensuciar.
pollution *n* polucion, contaminacion *f*.
polo *n* polo *m*.
polyester *n* poliester *m*.
polytechnic *n* politecnico *m*.
pomegranate *n* granada *f*.
pomp *n* pompa *f*; esplendor *m*.
pompom *n* borla *f*.
pompous *adj* pomposo.
pond *n* estanque *m*.
ponder *vt* ponderar, considerar.
ponderous *adj* ponderoso, pesado.
pontoon *n* ponton *m*.
pony *n* jaca *f*.
pool *n* charca *f*; piscina.
poor *adj* pobre.

pop *n* papá *m*.
popcorn *n* palomitas *fpl*.
Pope *n* papa *m*.
poplar *n* alamo *m*.
poppy *n* (*bot*) amapola *f*.
popular *adj*, **~ly** *adv* popular(mente).
populate *vi* poblar.
population *n* poblacion *f*.
porcelain *n* porcelana *f*.
porch *n* portico *m*.
porcupine *n* puerco espin *m*.
pore *n* poro *m*.
pork *n* carne de puerco *f*.
pornography *n* pornografia *f*.
porous *adj* poroso.
porpoise *n* marsopa *f*.
porridge *n* gachas de avena *fpl*.
port *n* puerto *m m*.
portable *adj* portatil.
portal *n* portal *m f*.
porter *n* portero *m*.
portfolio *n* cartera *f*.
porthole *n* portilla *f*.
portico *n* portico *m*.
portion *n* porcion*f*.
portly *adj* rollizo.
portrait *n* retrato *m*.
portray *vt* retratar.
pose *n* postura *f*; pose *f*.
posh *adj* elegante.
position *n* posicion *f*.
positive *adj* positivo.
posse *n* peloton *m*.
possess *vt* poseer.
possession *n* posesion *f*.
possibility *n* posibilidad *f*.
possible *adj* posible.
post *n* correo *m*; puesto *m*.
postage stamp *n* sello *m*.
postcard *n* tarjeta postal *f*.
poster *n* cartel *m*.
posterior *n* trasero *m*.
posterity *n* posteridad *f*.
postgraduate *n* posgraduado *m*.
posthumous *adj* postumo.
post office *n* correos *m*.
postpone *vt* diferir.
posture *n* postura *f*.
posy *n* ramillete de flores *m*.
pot *n* marmita *f*.
potato *n* patata *f*; papa *f*.
potent *adj* potente.
potential *adj* potencial.
pothole *n* bache *m*.
potion *n* pocion *f*.
potter *n* alfarero *m*.
pottery *n* cerámica *f*.
pouch *n* bolsa *f*.
poultice *n* cataplasma *f*.
poultry *n* aves caseras *fpl*.
pound *n* libra *f*; libra esterlina *f*.
pour *vt* echar; servir.
pout *vi* ponerse cenudo.
poverty *n* pobreza *f*.
powder *n* polvo *m*.
power *n* poder *m*.
practicable *adj* practicable; hacedero.
practical *adj* práctico:—**~ly** *adv* prácticamente.
practicality *n* factibilidad *f*.
practice *n* practica *f*.
pragmatic *adj* pragmático.
prairie *n* pampa *f*.
praise *n* renombre *m*.
prattle *vi* charlar:—*n* charla *f*.
prawn *n* gamba *f*.
pray *vi* rezar.
prayer *n* oracion *f*.
preach *vi* predicar.
preacher *n* pastor *m*.
precaution *n* precaucion *f*.
precede *vt* anteceder.
precious *adj* precioso.
precise *n* preciso.
precision *n* precision *f*.
preconception *n* preocupacion *f*.
predator *n* animal de rapina *m*.
predict *vt* predecir.
prediction *n* prediccion *f*.
predominant *adj* predominante.
predominate *vt* predominar.
preface *n* prefacio *m*.
prefer *vt* preferir.
preference *n* preferencia *f*.
prefix *vt* prefijar.
pregnancy *n* embarazo *m*.
pregnant *adj* embarazada.
prehistoric *adj* prehistorico.
prejudice *n* perjuicio *m*.
preliminary *adj* preliminar.
prelude *n* preludio *m*.
premature *adj* prematuro.
premier *n* primer ministro *m*.
premises *npl* establecimiento *m*.
premium *n* premio *m*.
premonition *n* presentimiento *m*.
prepare *vt* preparar(se).
preposition *n* preposicion *f*.
preposterous *adj* prepostero; absurdo.
prerequisite *n* requisito *m*.
prerogative *n* prerrogativa *f*.
prescribe *vi* prescribir; recetar.
prescription *n* prescripcion *f*.
present *n* regalo *m*.

presentation *n* presentacion *f.*
preservation *n* preservacion *f.*
preservative *n* preservativo *m.*
preserve *vt* preservar.
preside *vi* presidir.
presidency *n* presidencia *f.*
president *n* presidente *m.*
press *vt* empujar *n* prensa.
pressure *n* presion *f.*
prestige *n* prestigio *m.*
presume *vt* presumir, suponer.
pretence *n* pretexto *m*; pretension *f.*
pretend *vi* pretender.
preterite *n* preterito *m.*
pretext *n* pretexto *m.*
pretty *adj* lindo.
prevent *vt* prevenir.
preview *n* preestreno *m.*
previous *adj* previo.
prey *n* presa *f.*
price *n* precio *m*; premio *m.*
prick *vt* punzar, picar.
pride *n* orgullo *m.*
priest *n* sacerdote *m.*
priggish *adj* afectado.
prim *adj* peripuesto.
primary *adj* primario.
primate *n* primado *m.*
primeval *adj* primitivo.
primitive *adj* primitivo.
primrose *n* (*bot*) primula *f.*
prince *n* principe *m.*
princess *n* princesa *f.*
principle *n* principio *m.*
printer *n* impresor *m.*
prior *adj* anterior.
priority *n* prioridad *f.*
priory *n* priorato *m.*
prism *n* prisma *m.*
prison *n* prision, carcel *f.*
prisoner *n* prisionero *m.*
pristine *adj* pristino.
privacy *n* soledad *f.*
private *adj* secreto, privado; particular.
private eye *n* detective privado *m.*
privet *n* alhena *f.*
privilege *n* privilegio *m.*
prize *n* premio *m.*
probability *n* probabilidad *f.*
probable *adj* probable.
probation *n* prueba *f.*
problem *n* problema *m.*
procedure *n* procedimiento
proceed *vi* proceder.
process *n* proceso *m.*
procession *n* procesion *f.*
proclaim *vt* proclamar.
proclamation *n* proclamacion *f.*
procure *vt* procurar.
prod *vt* empujar.
prodigal *adj* prodigo.
prodigious *adj* prodigioso.
prodigy *n* prodigio *m.*
produce *vt* producir
product *n* producto *m*; obra *f*; efecto *m.*
production *n* produccion *f.*
profane *adj* profano.
profess *vt* profesar.
profession *n* profesion *f.*
professor *n* profesor, catedrático *m.*
proficient *adj* proficiente.
profile *n* perfil *m.*
profit *n* ganancia *f.*
profound *adj* profundo.
profuse *adj* profuso.
program *n* programa *m.*
progress *n* progreso *m.*
prohibit *vt* prohibir.
project *vt* proyectar
prominent *adj* prominente, saledizo.
promiscuous *adj* promiscuo.
promise *n* promesa *f.*
promontory *n* promontorio *m.*
promote *vt* promover.
promotion *n* promocion *f.*
prone *adj* inclinado.
prong *n* diente *m.*
pronoun *n* pronombre *m.*
pronounce *vt* pronunciar.
proof *n* prueba *f.*
propaganda *n* propaganda *f.*
propel *vt* impeler.
propeller *n* helice *f.*
propensity *n* propension *f.*
proper *adj* propio.
property *n* propiedad *f.*
prophecy *n* profecia *f.*
prophesy *vt* profetizar.
prophet *n* profeta *m.*
prophetic *adj* profetico.
proportion *n* proporcion *f.*
proportional *adj* proporcional.
proposal *n* propuesta *f.*
propose *vt* proponer.
proposition *n* proposicion *f.*
proprietor *n* propietario *m.*
propriety *n* propiedad *f.*
pro rata *adv* a prorrateo.
prosaic *adj* prosaico.
prose *n* prosa *f.*
prosecute *vt* proseguir.
prosecution *n* prosecucion *f.*
prosecutor *n* acusador *m.*
prospect *n* perspectiva *f.*

prospectus *n* prospecto *m*.
prosper *vi* prosperar.
prosperity *n* prosperidad *f*.
prostitute *n* prostituta *f*.
prostitution *n* prostitucion *f*.
prostrate *adj* postrado.
protagonist *n* protagonista *m*.
protect *vt* proteger.
protection *n* proteccion *f*.
protective *adj* protectorio.
protector *n* protector, patrono *m*.
protege *n* protegido *m*.
protein *n* proteina *f*.
protest *vi* protestar.
Protestant *n* protestante *m*.
protester *n* manifestante *m*.
protocol *n* protocolo *m*.
prototype *n* prototipo *m*.
protracted *adj* prolongado.
protrude *vi* sobresalir.
proud *adj* soberbio, orgulloso.
prove *vt* probar.
proverb *n* proverbio *m*.
provide *vt* proveer.
provided *conj*:—~ **that** con tal que.
providence *n* providencia *f*.
province *n* provincia *f*
provincial *adj*, *n* provincial *m*.
provision *n* provision *f*.
proviso *n* estipulacion *f*.
provocation *n* provocacion *f*.
provocative *adj* provocativo.
provoke *vt* provocar.
prowess *n* proeza *f*.
prowl *vi* rondar.
proximity *n* proximidad *f*.
proxy *n* poder *m*; apoderado *m*.
prudence *n* prudencia *f*.
prudent *adj* prudente.
prudish *adj* gazmono.
prussic acid *n* acido prúsico *m*.
pry *vi* espiar, acechar.
psalm *n* salmo *m*.
pseudonym *n* seudonimo *m*.
psyche *n* psique *f*.
psychiatrist *n* psiquiatra *m*.
psychiatry *n* psiquiatria *f*.
psychic *adj* psiquico.
psychoanalysis *n* psicoanalisis *m*.
psychoanalyst *n* psicoanalista *m*.
psychological *adj* psicologico.
psychologist *n* psicologo *m*.
psychology *n* psicologia *f*.
puberty *n* pubertad *f*.
public *adj* publico
publicize *vt* publicitar.
publicity *n* publicidad *f*.
publish *vt* publicar.
publisher *n* publicador *m*.
pucker *vt* arrugar, hacer pliegues.
puddle *n* charco *m*.
puff *n* soplo *m*.
pull *vt* tirar.
pulley *n* polea *f*.
pullover *n* jersey *m*.
pulp *n* pulpa *f*.
pulpit *n* pulpito *m*.
pulsate *vi* pulsar.
pulse *n* pulso *m*; legumbres *fpl*.
pumice *n* piedra pomez *f*.
pummel *vt* aporrear.
pump *n* bomba *f*.
pumpkin *n* calabaza *f*.
pun *n* equivoco, chiste *m*.
punch *n* punetazo *m*.
punctual *adj* puntual.
punctuate *vi* puntuar.
punctuation *n* puntuacion *f*.
pungent *adj* picante.
punish *vt* castigar.
punishment *n* castigo *m*.
punk *n* punki *m*.
punt *n* barco llano *m*.
pup *n* cachorro *m*.
pupil *n* alumno *m*.
puppet *n* titere *m*.
puppy *n* perrito *m*.
purchase *vt* comprar.
pure *adj* puro.
puree *n* pure *m*.
purification *n* purificacion *f*.
purify *vt* purificar.
puritan *n* puritano *m*.
purity *n* pureza *f*.
purple *adj* purpureo.
purpose *n* intencion *f*.
purr *vi* ronronear.
purse *n* bolsa *f*; cartera *f*.
pursue *vi* perseguir.
pursuit *n* perseguimiento *m*.
purveyor *n* abastecedor *m*.
push *vt* empujar
pusher *n* traficante de drogas *m*.
push-up *n* plancha *f*.
put *vt* poner, colocar.
putrid *adj* podrido.
putty *n* masilla *f*.
puzzle *n* acertijo *m*.
puzzling *adj* extrano.
pylon *n* torre de conduccion electrica *f*.
pyramid *n* piramide *f*.
python *n* piton atigrado *m*.

Q

quack *vi* graznar.
quadrangle *n* cuadrangulo *m*.
quadrant *n* cuadrante *m*.
quadrilateral *adj* cuadrilatero.
quadruped *n* cuadrupedo *m*.
quadruple *adj* cuadruplo.
quadruplet *n* cuatrillizo *m*.
quagmire *n* tremedal *m*.
quail *n* codorniz *f*.
quaint *adj* pulido; exquisito.
quake *vi* temblar; tiritar.
qualification *n* calificacion *f*.
qualify *vt* calificar.
quality *n* calidad *f*.
qualm *n* escrupulo *m*.
quandary *n* incertidumbre *f*.
quantitative *adj* cuantitativo.
quantity *n* cantidad *f*.
quarantine *n* cuarentena *f*.
quarrel *n* rina, contienda *f*.
quarrelsome *adj* pendenciero.
quarry *n* cantera *f*.
quarter *n* cuarto *mr*.
quarterly *adj* trimestral.
quartermaster *n* (*mil*) comisario *m*.
quartet *n* (*mus*) cuarteto *m*.
quartz *n* (*min*) cuarzo *m*.
quash *vt* fracasar; anular.
quay *n* muelle *m*.
queasy *adj* nauseabundo.
queen *n* reina *f*.
queer *adj* extrano.
quell *vt* calmar.
quench *vt* apagar.
query *n* cuestion.
quest *n* pesquisa *f*.
question *n* pregunta *f*; cuestion *f*.
questionable *adj* cuestionable.
question mark *n* punto de interrogación *m*.
questionnaire *n* cuestionario *m*.
quibble *vi* buscar evasivas.
quick *adj* rapido.
quicken *vt* apresurar.
quicksand *n* arena movediza *f*.
quicksilver *n* azogue, mercurio *m*.
quick-witted *adj* agudo, perspicaz.
quiet *adj* callado.
quinine *n* quinina *f*.
quintet *n* (*mus*) quinteto *m*.
quintuple *adj* quintuplo.
quintuplet *n* quintillizo *m*.
quip *n* indirecta *f*:—*vt* echar pullas.
quirk *n* peculiaridad *f*.
quit *vt* dejar.
quite *adv* bastante.
quits *adv* ien paz!.
quiver *vi* temblar.
quixotic *adj* quijotesco.
quiz *n* concurso *m*.
quizzical *adj* burlon.
quota *n* cuota *f*.
quotation *n* citacion, cita *f*.
quotation marks *npl* comillas *fpl*.
quote *vt* citar.
quotient *n* cociente *m*.

R

rabbi *n* rabi *m*.
rabbit *n* conejo *m*.
rabble *n* gentuza *f*.
rabid *adj* rabioso.
rabies *n* rabia *f*.
race *n* raza.
rack *n* rejilla *f*.
racket *n* ruido *m*; raqueta *f*.
racy *adj* picante.
radiance *n* brillantez *f*.
radiant *adj* radiante.
radiate *vt*, *vi* radiar.
radiation *n* radiacion *f*.
radiator *n* radiador *m*.
radical *adj*, **~ly** *adv* radical(mente).
radio *n* radio *f*.
radioactive *adj* radioactivo.
radish *n* rabano *m*.
radius *n* radio *f*.
raffle *n* rifa *f*.
raft *n* balsa *f*.
rafter *n* par *m*; viga *f*.
rag *n* trapo *m*.
rage *n* rabia *f*.
raid *n* incursion *f*.
rail *n* baranda, barandilla *f*.

railroad, railway *n* ferrocarril *m*.
rain *n* lluvia *f*.
rainbow *n* arco iris *m*.
raise *vt* levantar, alzar.
raisin *n* pasa *f*.
rake *n* rastro *m*.
ram *n* carnero *m*.
ramble *vi* divagar.
ramification *n* ramificacion *f*.
ramp *n* rampa *f*.
rampant *adj* exuberante.
ramshackle *adj* en ruina.
ranch *n* hacienda *f*.
rancid *adj* rancio.
rancor *n* rencor *m*.
random *adj* fortuito, sin orden.
range *vt* colocar, ordenar.
ransack *vt* saquear.
ransom *n* rescate *m*.
rape *n* violacion *f*.
rapid *adj* rapido.
rapist *n* violador *m*.
rapture *n* rapto *m*.
rare *adj* raro.
rascal *n* picaro *m*.
rash *adj* precipitado *m*; erupción (cutánea) *f*.
raspberry *n* frambuesa *f*.
rat *n* rata *f*.
rate *n* tasa *f*, precio, valor *m*.
rather *adv* mas bien; antes.
ratification *n* ratificacion *f*.
ratify *vt* ratificar.
ratio *n* razon *f*.
ration *n* racion *f*.
rational *adj* racional.
ravage *vt* saquear.
rave *vi* delirar.
raven *n* cuervo *m*.
ravine *n* barranco *m*.
ravish *vt* encantar.
ravishing *adj* encantador.
raw *adj* crudo.
ray *n* rayo de luz *m*; raya *f* (pez).
raze *vt* arrasar.
razor *n* navaja.
reach *vt* alcanzar.
react *vi* reaccionar.
reaction *n* reaccion *f*.
read *vt* leer.
readable *adj* legible.
reader *n* lector *m*.
readjust *vt* reajustar.
ready *adj* listo, pronto.
real *adj* real.
realization *n* realizacion *f*.
realize *adv* darse cuenta de; realizar.
reality *n* realidad *f*.
realm *n* reino *m*.
ream *n* resma *f*.
reap *vt* segar.
reappear *vi* reaparecer.
rear *n* parte trasera *fr*.
rearmament *n* rearme *m*.
reason *n* razon *f*; causa *f*:—*vt*, *vi* razonar.
reassure *vt* tranquilizar, alentar; (*com*) asegurar.
rebel *n* rebelde *m/f*.
rebellion *n* rebelion *f*.
rebound *vi* rebotar.
rebuke *vt* reprender.
rebut *vi* repercutir.
recede *vi* retroceder.
receipt *n* recibo *m*.
receive *vt* recibir.
recent *adj* reciente.
reception *n* recepcion *f*.
recess *n* descanso *m*.
recession *n* retirada *f*; (*com*) recesion *f*.
recipe *n* receta *f*.
recipient *n* recipiente *m*.
recital *n* recital *m*.
recite *vt* recitar.
reckless *adj* temerario.
reckon *vt* contar.
recline *vt*, *vi* reclinar(se).
recluse *n* recluso/a *m/f*.
recognize *vt* reconocer.
recommend *vt* recomendar.
recommendation *n* recomendacion *f*.
recompense *n* recompensa *f*.
reconcile *vt* reconciliar.
reconsider *vt* considerar de nuevo.
record *vt* registrar; grabar.
recourse *n* recurso *m*.
recover *vt* recobrar; recuperar.
recovery *n* convalecencia *f*; recobro *m*.
recreation *n* recreacion *f*; recreo *m*.
recruit *vt* reclutar.
rectangle *n* rectangulo *m*.
rectify *vt* rectificar.
rectilinear *adj* rectilineo.
rector *n* rector *m*.
recur *vi* repetirse.
red *adj* rojo; tinto:—*n* rojo *m*.
redeem *vt* redimir.
redemption *n* redencion *f*.
redhot *adj* candente, ardiente.
redress *vt* corregir.
reduce *vt* reducir.
reduction *n* reduccion *f*.
reed *n* cana *f*.
reek *n* mal olor.
refectory *n* refectorio *m*.
refer *vt*, *vi* referir.

referee *n* arbitro *m*.
reference *n* referencia.
refine *vt* refinar.
refit *vt* reparar.
reflect *vt, vi* reflejar.
reflection *n* reflexion *f*.
reflex *adj* reflejo.
reform *vt, vi* reformar(se).
refresh *vt* refrescar.
refreshment *n* refresco.
refrigerator *n* nevera *f*.
refuge *n* refugio, asilo *m*.
refugee *n* refugiado *m/f*.
refund *vt* devolver.
refurbish *vt* restaurar.
refusal *n* negativa *f*.
refuse *vt* rehusar.
refute *vt* refutar.
regal *adj* real.
regard *vt* estimar.
regardless *adv* a pesar de todo.
regatta *n* regata *f*.
regime *n* regimen *m*.
region *n* region *f*.
register *n* registro *m*.
registrar *n* registrador *m*.
registration *n* registro *m*.
registry *n* registro *m*.
regular *adj* regular.
regulation *n* regulacion *f*.
reign *n* reinado, reino *m*.
reinforce *vt* reforzar.
reinstate *vt* reintegrar.
reject *vt* rechazar.
rejection *n* rechazo *m*.
rejoice *vt, vi* regocijar(se).
relapse *vi* recaer.
relate *vt, vi* relatar.
relation *n* relacion *f*.
relationship *n* parentesco *m*; relacion *f*.
relative *adj* relativo.
relax *vt, vi* relajar.
release *vt* soltar, libertar.
relic *n* reliquia *f*.
relief *n* relieve *m*.
relieve *vt* aliviar.
religion *n* religion *f*.
rely *vi* confiar en; contar con.
remain *vi* quedar.
remains *npl* restos *mpl*.
remark *n* observacion, nota *f*.
remedial *adv* curativo.
remedy *n* remedio *m*.
remember *vt* acordarse de; recordar.
remind *vt* recordar.
remit *vt, vi* remitir.
remorse *n* remordimiento *m*.
remote *adj* remoto.
remove *vt* quitar.
renew *vt* renovar.
renovate *vt* renovar.
rent *n* renta *f*.
rental *n* alquiler *m*.
repair *vt* reparar.
repeat *vt* repetir.
repel *vt* repeler.
repetition *n* repeticion *f*.
replace *vt* reemplazar.
reply *n* respuesta *f*.
repose *vt, vi* reposar.
represent *vt* representar.
reproduce *vt* reproducir.
reproduction *n* reproduccion *f*.
reptile *n* reptil *m*.
republic *n* republica *f*.
repugnance *n* repugnancia *f*.
repulse *vt* repulsar.
request *n* peticion.
require *vt* requerir.
rescue *vt* librar.
research *vt* investigar.
resemble *vt* asemejarse.
resent *vt* resentirse.
reserve *vt* reservar.
residence *n* residencia *f*.
resign *vt, vi* resignar.
resin *n* resina *f*.
resist *vt* resistir, oponerse.
resolve *vt, vr* resolver(se).
resort *vi* recurrir.
resource *n* recurso *m*.
respect *n* respecto *m*.
respite *n* suspension *f*.
respond *vt* responder.
rest *n* reposo *m*.
restless *adj* insomne.
restore *vt* restaurar.
restrict *vt* restringir.
result *vi* resultar.
resume *vt* resumir.
résumé *n* currículum *m*.
resurrection *n* resurreccion *f*.
resuscitate *vt* resucitar.
retail *vt* revender *f*.
retain *vt* retener.
reticence *n* reticencia *f*.
retina *n* retina *f*.
retire *vt, vi* retirar(se).
retreat *n* retirada *f*.
return *vt* retribuir; restituir; devolver.
reveal *vt* revelar.
revenge *vt* vengar:—*n* venganza *f*.
revenue *n* renta *f*.
revere *vt* reverenciar.

reverse *vt* trastrocar.
review *vt* rever.
revise *vt* rever; repasar.
revival *n* restauracion *f*.
revolt *vi* rebelarse.
revolution *n* revolucion *f*.
revolve *vt* revolver.
revue *n* revista *f*.
reward *n* recompensa *f*.
rheumatism *n* reumatismo *m*.
rhinoceros *n* rinoceronte *m*.
rhombus *n* rombo *m*.
rhubarb *n* ruibarbo *m*.
rhyme *n* rima *f*.
rhythm *n* ritmo *m*.
rib *n* costilla *f*.
ribbon *n* liston *m*.
rice *n* arroz *m*.
rich *adj* rico.
riches *npl* riqueza *f*.
rickets *n* raquitis *f*.
rid *vt* librar.
riddle *n* enigma *m*.
ride *vi* cabalgar.
ridge *n* espinazo.
ridiculous *adj* ridiculoso.
rifle *n* rifle *m*.
right *adj* derecho, recto; justo.—*n* derecho *m*; título *m*; privilegio *m*.
rigid *adj* rigido.
rigor *n* rigor *m*.
rind *n* corteza *f*.
rinse *vt* lavar, limpiar.
rise *vi* levantarse.
risk *n* riesgo, peligro *m*.
rite *n* rito *m*.
ritual *adj*, *n* ritual *m*.
rival *adj* emulo.
river *n* rio *m*.
road *n* camino *m*.
roadsign *n* senal de trafico *f*.
roar *vi* rugir.
roast *vt* asar.
rob *vt* robar.
robber *n* robador, ladron *m*.
robbery *n* robo *m*.
robust *adj* robusto.
rock *n* roca *f*.
rocket *n* cohete *m*.
rodent *n* roedor *m*.
rogue *n* bribon *m*.
roll *vt* rodar.
Roman Catholic *adj*, *n* catolico/a *m/f* (romano/a).
romance *n* romance *m*.
roof *n* tejado *m*.
room *n* habitacion, sala *f*.
roomy *adj* espacioso.
root *n* raiz *f*.
rope *n* cuerda *f*.
rosary *n* rosario *m*.
rose *n* rosa *f*.
rosebed *n* campo de rosales *m*.
rosebud *n* capullo de rosa *m*.
rosemary *n* (*bot*) romero *m*.
rosette *n* roseta *f*.
rot *vi* pudrirse.
rotten *adj* podrido.
rouble *n* rublo *m*.
rouge *n* arrebol *m*.
rough *adj* aspero.
roulette *n* ruleta *f*.
round *adj* redondo.
rouse *vt* despertar.
route *n* ruta *f*.
routine *adj* rutinario.
row *n* camorra *f*.
row *n* (line) hilera, fila *f*:—*vt* (*mar*) remar, bogar.
royal *adj* real.
royalty *n* realeza, dignidad real *f*.
rub *vt* estregar, fregar, frotar.
rubber *n* caucho *m*, goma *f*.
rubber-band *n* goma, gomita *f*.
rubric *n* rubrica *f*.
ruby *n* rubi *m*.
rudder *n* timon *m*.
rude *adj* rudo, brutal.
rudiment *n* rudimentos *mpl*.
rue *vi* compadecerse.
rug *n* alfombra *f*.
rugby *n* rugby *m*.
ruin *n* ruina *f*.
ruinous *adj* ruinoso.
rule *n* mando *m*; regla *f*.
ruler *n* gobernador *m*; regla *f*.
rum *n* ron *m*.
rumor *n* rumor *m*.
run *vt* dirigir; organizar, *vi* correr.
runaway *n* fugitivo.
rung *n* escalon.
runway *n* pista de aterrizaje *f*.
rupture *n* rotura *f*.
rural *adj* rural.
ruse *n* astucia *f*.
rush *n* junco *m*; rafaga *f*.
rusk *n* galleta *f*.
russet *adj* bermejo.
rust *n* herrumbre *f*.
rustic *adj* rustico.
rustle *vi* crujir.
rut *n* celo *m*.
ruthless *adj* cruel.
rye *n* (*bot*) centeno *m*.

S

Sabbath *n* sabado *m*.
sabotage *n* sabotaje *m*.
saccharin *n* sacarina *f*.
sachet *n* sobrecito *m*.
sack *n* saco *m*:—*vt* despedir.
sacrament *n* sacramento *m*.
sacred *adj* sagrado.
sacredness *n* santidad *f*.
sacrifice *n* sacrificio *m*.
sacrilege *n* sacrilegio *m*.
sad *adj* triste.
saddle *n* silla *f*.
sadness *n* tristeza *f*.
safari *n* safari *m*.
safe *adj* seguro; *n* caja fuerte *f*.
safety *n* seguridad *f*
saffron *n* azafran *m*.
sage *n* (*bot*) salvia *f*.
Sagittarius *n* Sagitario *m* (signo del zodiaco).
sago *n* (*bot*) zagu *m*.
sail *n* vela *f*.
sailor *n* marinero *m*.
saint *n* santo *m*; santa *f*.
sake *n* causa, razon *f*.
salad *n* ensalada *f*.
salamander *n* salamandra *f*.
salary *n* sueldo *m*.
sale *n* venta *f*.
sales clerk *n* dependiente *m*.
salient *adj* saliente.
saline *adj* salino.
saliva *n* saliva *f*.
salmon *n* salmon *m*.
salmon trout *n* trucha salmonada *f*.
saloon *n* bar *m*.
salt *n* sal *f*.
salubrious *adj* salubre.
salutation *n* salutacion *f*.
salute *vt* saludar.
same *adj* mismo, idéntico/a
sample *n* muestra *f*; ejemplo *m*.
sanctify *vt* santificar.
sanctuary *n* santuario *m*.
sand *n* arena *f*.
sandal *n* sandalia *f*.
sandstone *n* piedra arenisca *f*.
sandwich *n* bocadillo *m*.
sane *adj* sapo.
sanitarium *n* sanatorio *m*.
sanity *n* juicio sano *m*.
sap *n* savia *f*.
sapling *n* arbolito *m*.
sapphire *n* zafir *m*.
sarcasm *n* sarcasmo *m*.
sarcophagus *n* sarcofago.
sardine *n* sardina *f*.
Satan *n* Satanas *m*.
satchel *n* mochila *f*.
satellite *n* satelite *m*.
satin *n* raso *m*.
satire *n* satira *f*.
satisfaction *n* satisfaccion *f*.
satisfy *vt* satisfacer.
Saturday *n* sabado *m*.
satyr *n* satiro *m*.
sauce *n* salsa *f*.
saucepan *n* cazo *m*.
saucer *n* platillo *m*.
sausage *n* salchicha *f*.
savage *adj* salvaje
savagery *n* crueldad *f*.
savannah *n* sabana *f*.
save *vt* salvar.
saveloy *n* chorizo *m*.
Savior *n* Salvador *m*.
savory *adj* sabroso.
saw *n* sierra *f*.
saxophone *n* saxofono *m*.
say *vt* decir.
saying *n* dicho *m*.
scab *n* rona *f*.
scald *vt* escaldar.
scale *n* balanza *f*.
scalp *n* cabellera *f*.
scamp *n* bribon.
scampi *npl* gambas *fpl*.
scan *vt* escudrinar.
scandal *n* escandalo *m*.
scandalize *vt* escandalizar.
scar *n* cicatriz *f*.
scarce *adj* raro.
scare *vt* espantar.
scarf *n* bufanda *f*.
scarlet *n* escarlata *f*.
scarp *n* escarpa *f*.
scene *n* escena *f*.
scenery *n* vista *f*.
schedule *n* horario *m*.
scheme *n* proyecto, plan *m*.
schism *n* cisma *m*.
scholar *n* estudiante *m*
school *n* escuela *f*.
schoolteacher *n* maestro, tra *m/f*; profesor, ra *m/f*.
science *n* ciencia *f*.
scientist *n* cientifico, ca *m/f*.
scissors *npl* tijeras *fpl*.

scooter *n* moto *f.*
scorch *vt* quemar.
scorn *vt*, *vi* despreciar.
Scorpio *n* Escorpion *m* (signo del zodiaco).
scorpion *n* escorpion *m*.
Scotch *n* whisky escoces *m*.
scoundrel *n* picaro *m*.
scramble *vi* arrapar.
scrap *n* migaja *f*; sobras *fpl.*
scrape *vt*, *vi* raer, raspar.
scraper *n* rascador *m*.
scratch *vt* rascar.
scrawl *vt*, *vi* garrapatear.
scream, screech *vi* chillar.
screen *n* pantalla *f.*
screenplay *n* guion *m*.
screw *n* tornillo *m*.
screwdriver *n* destornillador *m*.
scribble *vt* escarabajear.
scribe *n* escritor *m*.
script *n* guion *m*; letra *f.*
Scripture *n* Escritura sagrada *f.*
scruffy *adj* desalinado.
scruple *n* escrupulo *m*.
scullery *n* fregadero *m*.
sculptor *n* escultor, ra *m/f.*
sculpture *n* escultura *f.*
scum *n* espuma *f*; escoria *f.*
scurvy *n* escorbuto *m*.
scythe *n* guadana *f.*
sea *n mar m/f:—adj* de *mar*.
sea breeze *n* viento de *mar m*.
seafood *n* mariscos *mpl*.
sea front *n* paseo maritimo *m*.
seagull *n* gaviota *f.*
sea horse *n* hipocampo *m*.
seal *n* sello *m*; foca *f.*
seam *n* costura *f.*
seaman *n* marinero *m*.
sea plane *n* hidroavion *m*.
sear *vt* cauterizar.
search *vt* examinar, buscar.
seashore *n* ribera *f*, litoral *m*.
seasick *adj* mareado.
season *n* estacion *f.*
seasoning *n* condimento *m*.
seat *n* asiento *m*; silla *f.*
seat belt *n* cinturon de seguridad *m*.
seaweed *n* alga marina *f.*
seclude *vt* apartar.
seclusion *n* separacion *f.*
second *adj* segundo.
secondary *adj* secundario.
secondhand *n* segunda mano *f.*
secret *adj*, *n* secreto *m*.
secretary *n* secretario, ria *m/f.*
sect *n* secta *f.*
section *n* seccion *f.*
sector *n* sector *m*.
secular *adj* secular.
secure *adj* seguro.
security *n* seguridad *f.*
sedate *adj* sosegado.
sedative *n* sedativo *m*.
sedge *n* (*bot*) junco *m*.
sediment *n* sedimento *m*
sedition *n* sedicion *f.*
seduce *vt* seducir.
seducer *n* seductor *m*.
seduction *n* seduccion *f.*
seductive *adj* seductivo.
see *vt*, *vi* ver
seed *n* semilla.
seedy *adj* desaseado.
seek *vt*, *vi* buscar.
seem *vi* parecer.
seemliness *n* decensia *f.*
seesaw *n* vaiven *m*.
seethe *vi* hervir.
segment *n* segmento *m*.
seize *vt* asir.
seizure *n* captura *f.*
seldom *adv* raramente.
select *vt* elegir.
selection *n* seleccion *f.*
self *n* uno mismo.
selfish *adj* egoista.
self-portrait *n* autorretrato *m*.
selfsame *adj* identico.
sell *vt*, *vi* vender.
semen *n* semen *m*.
semester *n* semestre *m*.
semicircle *n* semicirculo *m*.
semicircular *adj* semicircular.
semicolon *n* punto y coma *m*.
seminary *n* seminario *m*.
senate *n* senado *m*.
senator *n* senador, ra *m/f.*
send *vt* enviar.
sender *n* remitente *m*.
senile *adj* senil.
senior *n* mayor *m*.
senna *n* (*bot*) sena *f.*
sensation *n* sensacion *f.*
sense *n* sentido *m*.
sensibility *n* sensibilidad *f.*
sensible *adj* sensato/a, juicioso/a..
sensitive *adj* sensitivo.
sensual, sensuous *adj* sensual.
sensuality *n* sensualidad *f.*
sentence *n* oracion *f*; sentencia *f.*
sentiment *n* sentimiento *m*.
sentinel, sentry *n* centinela *m*.
separate *vt* (*vi*) separar(se).

separation *n* separacion *f.*
September *n* se(p)tiembre *m.*
sepulcher *n* sepulcro *m.*
sequel *n* continuacion *f.*
sequence *n* serie *f.*
seraph *n* serafin *m.*
serenade *n* serenata *f.*
serene *adj* seneno.
serenity *n* serenidad *f.*
serf *n* siervo *m.*
sergeant *n* sargento *m.*
serial *adj* consecutivo.
series *n* serie *f.*
serious *adj* serio, grave.
sermon *n* sermon *f.*
serious *adj* seroso.
serpent *n* serpiente *f.*
serpentine *adj* serpentino.
serrated *adj* serrado.
serum *n* suero *m.*
servant *n* criado *m*; criada *f.*
serve *vt*, *vi* servir.
service *n* servicio *m.*
servile *adj* servil.
session *n* junta *f*; sesion *f.*
set *vt* poner, colocar, fijar.
setter *n* perro de muestra *m.*
seven *adj*, *n* siete.
seventeen *adj*, *n* diez y siete, diecisiete.
seventeenth *adj*, *n* decimoseptimo.
seventh *adj*, *n* septimo.
seventieth *adj*, *n* septuagesimo.
seventy *adj*, *n* setenta.
sever *vt*, *vi* separar.
several *adj*, pn varios.
severance *n* separacion *f.*
severe *adj* severo.
severity *n* severidad *f.*
sew *vt*, *vi* coser.
sewer *n* albanal *m.*
sex *n* sexo *m.*
sexist *adj n* sexista *m/f.*
sexual *adj* sexual.
sexy *adj* sexy.
shade *n* sombra.
shadow *n* sombra *f.*
shaft *n* flecha, saeta *f.*
shake *vt* sacudir; agitar.
shallow *adj* somero.
sham *vt* enganar.
shame *n* verguenza *f.*
shamefaced *adj* vergonzoso.
shampoo champu *m.*
shamrock *n* trebol *m.*
shank *n* pierna *f.*
shanty *n* chabola *f.*
shantytown *n* barrio de chabolas *m.*
shape *vt*, *vi* formar; *n* forma *m.*
shapeless *adj* informe.
shapely *adj* bien hecho.
share *n* parte, porcion *f*; compartir.
shark *n* tiburon *m.*
sharp *adj* agudo.
shatter *vt* destrozar.
shave *vt* afeitar.
shaver *n* maquina de afeitar *f.*
shawl *n* chal *m.*
she *pn* ella.
sheaf *n* gavilla *f*
shear *vt* atusar.
sheath *n* vaina *f.*
shed *vt* verter; cabana *f.*
sheen *n* resplandor *m.*
sheep *n* oveja *f.*
sheer *adj* puro, claro.
sheet *n* sabana *f.*
sheet lightning *n* relampagueamiento *m.*
shelf *n* anaquel *m.*
shell *n* cascara *f*; concha *f.*
shelter *n* guardia *f*; amparo *m.*
shepherd *n* pastor *m.*
sherbet *n* sorbete *m.*
sheriff *n* sherif *m.*
sherry *n* jerez *m.*
shield *n* escudo *m.*
shift *vi* cambiarse.
shinbone *n* espinilla *f.*
shine *vi* lucir, brillar.
shiny *adj* brillante.
ship *n* nave *f*; barco *m.*
shipwreck *n* naufragio *m.*
shirt *n* camisa *f.*
shit *excl* (*sl*) imierda!
shiver *vi* tiritar de frio.
shoal *n* banco *m.*
shock *n* choque *m.*
shock absorber *n* amortiguador *m.*
shoddy *adj* de pacotilla.
shoe *n* zapato *m.*
shoelace *n* correa de zapato *f.*
shoemaker *n* zapatero *m.*
shoot *vt* tirar.
shopper *n* comprador, ra *m/f.*
shopping *n* compras *fpl.*
shopping mall *n* centro comercial *m.*
shore *n* costa, ribera *f.*
short *adj* corto breve.
short-sighted *adj* corto de vista.
shot *n* tiro *m.*
shotgun *n* escopeta *f.*
shoulder *n* hombro *m.*
shout *vi* gritar, aclamar.
shove *vt*, *vi* empujar.
shovel *n* pala *f.*

show *vt* mostrar.
shower *n* nubada *f*; llovizna *f*; ducha *f*.
showy *adj* ostentoso.
shred *n* cacho, pedazo.
shrewd *adj* astuto.
shriek *vt*, *vi* chillar
shrimp *n* camaron *m*.
shrine *n* relicario *m*.
shrink *vi* encogerse.
shroud *n* cubierta *f*.
Shrove Tuesday *n* martes de carnaval *m*.
shrub *n* arbusto *m*.
shrug *vt* encogerse de hombros.
shun *vt* huir, evitar.
shut *vt* cerrar.
shutter *n* contraventana *f*.
shuttle *n* lanzadera *f*.
shuttlecock *n* volante *m*.
shy *adj* timido.
shyness *n* timidez *f*.
sick *adj* malo, enfermo.
sickle *n* hoz *f*.
sickness *n* enfermedad *f*.
side *n* lado *m*.
sideboard *n* aparador *m*; alacena *f*.
sidewalk *n* calzada *f*.
siege *n* (*mil*) sitio *m*.
sieve *n* tamiz *m*.
sift *vt* cerner.
sigh *vi* suspirar.
sight *n* vista *f*.
sightseeing *n* excursionismo, turismo *m*.
sign *n* senal *f*.
signal *n* senal *f*.
signature *n* firma *f*.
significance *n* importancia *f*.
signify *vt* significar.
signpost *n* indicador *m*.
silence *n* silencio *m*.
silk *n* seda *f*.
silky *adj* hecho de seda; sedeno.
sill *n* repisa *f*.
silly *adj* tonto.
silver *n* plata *f*.
similar *adj* similar; semejante.
similarity *n* semejanza *f*.
simile *n* simil *m*.
simmer *vi* hervir a fuego lento.
simple *adj* simple.
simplicity *n* sencillez *ff*.
simulate *vt* simular.
simulation *n* simulacion *f*.
sin *n* pecado *m*.
since *adv* desde.
sincerity *n* sinceridad *f*.
sinew *n* tendon *m*; nervio *m*.
sing *vi*, *vt* cantar.
singe *vt* chamuscar.
singer *n* cantor *m*; cantora *f*.
single *adj* solo; soltero, soltera.
singly *adv* separadamente.
singular *adj* singular.
sinister *adj* siniestro.
sink *vi* hundirse.
sinner *n* pecador *m*; pecadora *f*.
sinus *n* seno *m*.
sip *vt* sorber:—*n* sorbo *m*.
siphon *n* sifon *m*.
sir *n* senor *m*.
siren *n* sirena *f*.
sister *n* hermana *f*.
sister-in-law *n* cunada *f*.
sisterly *adj* con hermandad.
sit *vi* sentarse.
site *n* sitio *m*; situacion *f*.
sit-in *n* ocupacion *f*.
sitting room *n* sala de estar *f*.
situation *n* situacion *f*.
six *adj*, *n* seis.
sixteen *adj*, *n* diez y seis, dieciseis.
sixteenth *adj*, *n* decimosexto.
sixth *adj*, *n* sexto.
sixtieth *adj*, *n* sexagesimo.
sixty *adj*, *n* sesenta.
size *n* tamano *m*.
skate *n* patin *m*:—*vi* patinar.
skeleton *n* esqueleto *m*.
skeptic *n* esceptico.
skepticism *n* escepticismo *m*.
sketch *n* esbozo *m*.
ski *n* esqui *m*:—*vi* esquiar.
skid *n* patinazo *m*.
skill *n* destreza *f*.
skim *vt* espumar.
skin *n* piel *f*; cutis *m/f*.
skip *vi* saltar, brincar.
skirt *n* falda.
skittle *n* bolo *m*.
skulk *vi* escuchar, acechar.
skull *n* craneo *m*.
sky *n* cielo *m*.
skyscraper *n* rascacielos *m invar*.
slab *n* losa *f*.
slack *adj* flojo.
slag *n* escoria *f*.
slander *vt* calumniar *f*.
slang *n* argot *m f*.
slap *n* manotada *f*.
slate *n* pizarra *f*.
slave *n* esclavo *m*.
slaver *n* baba *f*:—*vi* babosear.
slay *vt* matar.
sled, sleigh *n* trineo *m*.
sleek *adj* liso.

sleep *vi* dormir.
sleeping bag *n* saco de dormir *m*.
sleeping pill *n* somnifero *m*.
sleepwalking *n* sonambulismo *m*.
sleet *n* aguanieve *f*.
sleeve *n* manga *f*.
slender *adj* delgado.
slice *n* rebanada *f*.
slide *vi* resbalar, deslizarse.
slight *adj* ligero.
slim *adj* delgado.
slime *n* lodo *m/f*.
slimy *adj* viscoso, pegajoso.
sling *n* honda *f*; cabestrillo *m*.
slingshot *n* catapulta *f*.
slip *vi* resbalar; escapar.
slipper *n* zapatilla *f*.
slogan *n* eslogan, lema *m*.
slope *n* cuesta *f*.
slow *adj* tardio, lento, torpe.
slum *n* tugurio *m*.
slump *n* depresion *f*.
slur *vt* ensuciar; calumniar.
slut *n* marrana *f*.
sly *adj* astuto.
smack *n* sabor, gusto *m*; chasquido de latigo *m*.
small *adj* pequeno.
smallpox *n* viruelas *fpl*.
smalltalk *n* charla, prosa *f*.
smart *adj* elegante; listo.
smash *vt* romper, quebrantar
smell *vt*, *vi* oler.
smile *vi* sonreirse:—*n* sonrisa *f*.
smoke *n* humo *m*; fumar.
smoker *n* fumador, ra *m/f*.
smooth *adj* liso.
smug *adj* presumido.
smut *n* tiznon *m*.
snack *n* bocado*m*.
snag *n* problema *m*.
snail *n* caracol *m*.
snake *n* culebra *f*.
snap *vt*, *vi* romper.
snapdragon *n* (*bot*) antirrino *m*.
snatch *vt* arrebatar.
sneeze *vi* estornudar.
sniff *vt* oler:—*vi* resollar con fuerza.
snob *n* (e)snob *m/f*.
snore *vi* roncar.
snow *n* nieve *f*.
snowdrop *n* (*bot*) campanilla blanca *f*.
snowman *n* figura de nieve *f*.
snub *vt* reprender.
snuff *n* rape *m*.
so *adv* asi; de este modo; tan.
soap *n* jabon *m*.
soap opera *n* telenovela *f*.
soar *vi* remontarse.
sob *n* sollozo *m*:—*vi* sollozar.
soccer *n* balón *m*; fútbol *m*.
soccer player *n* futbolista *m/f*.
sociable *adj* sociable.
social *adj* social.
socialism *n* socialismo *m*.
society *n* sociedad *f*.
sociologist *n* sociologo, ga *m/f*.
sociology *n* sociologia *f*.
sock *n* calcetin *m*.
sod *n* cesped *m*.
soda *n* sosa *f*.
sofa *n* sofa *m*.
soft *adj* blando.
soil *vt* ensuciar, tierra *f*.
solar *adj* solar.
soldier *n* soldado *m*.
sole *n* planta del pie *f*.
solemn *adj*, **~ly** *adv* solemne(mente).
solicitor *n* representante, agente *m/f*.
solid *adj* solido.
solitaire *n* solitario *m*; grueso diamante *m*.
solitude *n* soledad *f*.
solo *n* (*mus*) solo *m*.
solstice *n* solsticio *m*.
soluble *adj* soluble.
solution *n* solucion *f*.
solve *vt* resolver.
some *adj* algo de, un poco, algun, alguno, alguna, unos, pocos, ciertos.
somebody *n* alguien *m*.
something *n* alguna cosa, algo.
sometimes *adv* a veces.
somnambulism *n* somnambulismo *m*.
somnambulist *n* somnambulo *m*.
somnolence *n* somnolencia *f*.
son *n* hijo *m*.
sonata *n* (*mus*) sonata *f*.
song *n* cancion.
son-in-law *n* yerno *m*.
sonnet *n* soneto *m*.
soon *adv* pronto.
soot *n* hollin *m*.
soothe *vt* adular; calmar.
sop *n* sopa *f*.
sophisticate *vt* sofisticar.
sophisticated *adj* sofisticado.
sorcerer *n* hechicero *m*.
sorcery *n* hechizo*m*.
sordid *adj* sordido.
sore *n* llaga, ulcera *f*.
sorrow *n* pesar *m*; tristeza *f*.
sorry *adj* triste.
soul *n* alma *f*.
sound *adj* sano; sonido,*vi* sonar.

soup *n* sopa *f*.
sour *adj* agrio.
souvenir *n* recuerdo *m*.
south *n* sur *m*.
sovereign *adj*, *n* soberano, na (*m/f*).
sovereignty *n* soberania *f*.
sow *n* puerca *f*.
sow *vt* sembrar.
space *n* espacio *m*.
spacious *adj* espacioso.
spade *n* laya.
spaghetti *n* espaguetis *mpl*.
span *n* palmo *m*.
spangle *n* lentejuela *f*.
spaniel *n* perro de aguas *m*.
Spanish *adj* espanol(a)
spar *n* palo *m*.
spark *n* chispa *f*.
sparkle *n* centella.
sparrow *n* gorrion *m*.
sparse *adj* delgado.
spasm *n* espasmo *m*.
spatula *n* espatula *f*.
spawn *n* freza *f*.
speak *vt*, *vi* hablar.
spear *n* lanza *f*.
special *adj* especial.
species *n* especie *f*.
specific *adj* especifico *m*.
specimen *n* muestra *f*.
spectacle *n* espectaculo *m*.
spectator *n* espectador, ra *m/f*.
specter *n* espectro *m*.
speculate *vi* especular.
speculation *n* especulacion *f*.
speed *n* prisa *f*; velocidad *f*.
spell *n* hechizo*m*.
spelling *n* ortografia *f*.
spend *vt* gastar.
sperm *n* esperma *f*.
spew *vi* (*sl*) vomitar.
sphere *n* esfera *f*.
spherical *adj* esferico.
spice *n* especia *f*.
spicy *adj* aromatico.
spider *n* arana *f*.
spike *n* espigon *m*.
spill *vt* derramar.
spin *vt* hilar.
spinach *n* espinaca *f*.
spinal *adj* espinal.
spine *n* espinazo *m*.
spinster *n* soltera *f*.
spiral *adj* espiral.
spire *n* espira *f*.
spirit *n* aliento *m*; espiritu *m*.
spiritual *adj*, **~ly** *adv* espiritual(men-te).
spiritualist *n* espiritualista *m*.
spit *n* asador *m*; saliva *f*.
spite *n* rencor *m*.
splash *vt* salpicar.
spleen *n* bazo *m*.
splendid *adj* esplendido.
splendor *n* esplendor *m*.
splint *n* tablilla *f*.
splinter *n* cacho *m*.
split *n* hendedura *f*.
spoil *vt* despojar.
spoke *n* rayo de la rueda *m*.
spokesman *n* portavoz *m*.
sponge *n* esponja *f*.
sponsor *n* fiador *m*.
spontaneity *n* espontaneidad *f*.
spool *n* carrete *m*.
spoon *n* cuchara *f*.
spoonful *n* cucharada *f*.
sport *n* deporte *m*
spot *n* mancha *f*.
spouse *n* esposo *m*; esposa *f*.
sprain *adj* descoyuntar.
sprat *n* meleta, nuesa *f* (pez).
sprawl *vi* revolcarse.
spray *n* rociada *f*; espray *m*.
spread *vt* extender
spree *n* fiesta *f*; juerga *f*.
sprig *n* ramito *m*.
sprinkle *vt* rociar.
spur *n* espuela *f*.
spurn *vt* despreciar.
spy *n* espia *m*.
squad *n* escuadra *f*.
squadron *n* (*mil*) escuadron *m*.
squalid *adj* sucio.
squall *n* rafaga *f*.
squalor *n* porqueria *f*.
squander *vt* malgastar.
square *adj* cuadrado *m*; plaza *f*.
squash *vt* aplastar.
squaw *n* hembra de un indiano *f*.
squeak *vi* planir.
squeamish *adj* fastidioso.
squeeze *vt* apretar.
squid *n* calamar *m*.
squint *adj* bizco.
squirrel *n* ardilla *f*.
stable *n* establo *m*.
stack *n* pila *f*.
staff *n* personal *m*.
stag *n* ciervo *m*.
stage *n* etapa *f*; escena *f*.
stagnate *vi* estancarse.
stain *vt* manchar.
stair *n* escalon *m*.
staircase *n* escalera *f*.

stale *adj* anejo.
stalk, tronco *m*.
stall *n* pesebre *m*; tienda portatil *f*.
stallion *n* semental *m*.
stamina *n* resistencia *f*.
stammer *vi* tartamudear.
stamp estampar, imprimir; sello *m*.
stampede *n* estampida *f*.
stand *vi* estar de pie o derecho; stand *m*.
standard *n* estandarte *m*.
staple *n* grapa *f*.
star *n* estrella *f*.
starch *n* almidon *m*.
stark *adj* fuerte, aspero.
starling *n* estornino *m*.
start *vi* empezar.
startle *vt* sobresaltar.
starvation *n* hambre *f*.
state *n* estado *m*; condicion *f*.
statement *n* afirmacion *f*.
static *adj* estatico.
station *n* estacion *f*.
stationary *adj* estacionario, fijo.
stationery *n* papeleria *f*.
statistics *npl* estadistica *f*.
statuary *n* estatuario *m*.
statue *n* estatua *f*.
stature *n* estatura *f*.
statute *n* estatuto *m*.
stay *n* estancia *f*.
steak *n* filete *m*; bistec *m*.
steal *vt*, *vi* robar.
stealth *n* hurto *m*.
steam *n* vapor *m*.
steel *n* acero *m*.
steep *adj* escarpado.
steeple *n* torre *f*; campanario *m*.
steer *n* novillo *m*:—*vt* manejar, conducir.
steering wheel *n* volante *m*.
stem *n* vastago.
stench *n* hedor *m*.
stencil *n* cliche *m*.
stenographer *n* taquigrafo, fa *m/f*.
stenography *n* taquigrafia *f*.
step *n* paso, escalon *m*.
stepbrother *n* hermanastro *m*.
stepdaughter *n* hijastra *f*.
stepfather *n* padrastro *m*.
stepmother *n* madrastra *f*.
stepsister *n* hermanastra *f*.
stepson *n* hijastro *m*.
stereo *n* estereo *m*.
stereotype *n* estereotipo *m*.
sterile *adj* esteril.
sterling *n* libras esterlinas *fpl*.
stethoscope *n* (*med*) estetoscopio *m*.
stew *vt* estofar *f*.
steward *n* mayordomo *m*
stick *n* palo, pegarse.
stiff *adj* tieso.
stifle *vt* sufocar.
stigma *n* estigma *m*.
stigmatize *vt* infamar.
stiletto *n* estilete *m*
still tranquilo; *adv* todavia.
stillborn *adj* nacido muerto.
stilts *npl* zancos *mpl*.
stimulant *n* estimulante *m*.
stimulate *vt* estimular.
stimulus *n* estimulo *m*.
sting *vt* picar o morder (un insecto).
stingy *adj* mezquino.
stink *vi* heder.
stint *n* tarea *f*.
stipulate *vt* estipular.
stipulation *n* estipulacion *f*.
stir *vt* agitar.
stirrup *n* estribo *m*.
stitch *vt* coser.
stoat *n* comadreja *f*.
stock *n* ganado *m*; caldo *m*.
stockbroker *n* agente de bolsa *m/f*.
stock exchange *n* bolsa *f*.
stocking *n* media *f*.
stock market *n* bolsa *f*.
stoic *n* estoico *m*.
stoical *adj* estoico.
stole *n* estola *f*.
stomach *n* estomago *m*.
stone *n* piedra *f*.
stop *vt* detener, parar.
stopwatch *n* cronometro *m*.
store *n* provision *f*; almacen *m*.
stork *n* ciguena *f*.
storm *n* tempestad.
story *n* historia *f*.
stout *adj* robusto.
stove *n* estufa *f*.
straight *adj* derecho.
strain *vt* colar, filtrar; *n* tension *f*.
strainer *n* colador *m*.
strange *adj* raro/a, extranjero.
stranger *n* desconocido *m*; extranjero, ra *m/f*.
strangle *vt* ahogar.
strap *n* correa.
strapping *adj* abultado.
stratagem *n* estratagema *f*; astucia *f*.
strategic *adj* estrategico *m*.
strategy *n* estrategia *f*.
stratum *n* estrato *m*.
straw *n* paja *m*; pajita *f*.
strawberry *n* fresa *f*.
stray *vi* extraviarse.

streak *n* raya.
street *n* calle *f.*
streetcar *n* tranvia *f.*
strength *n* fuerza.
strenuous *adj* arduo.
stress *n* presion *f*; estres *m.*
stretch *vt*, *vi* extender.
stretcher *n* camilla *f.*
strew *vt* esparcir.
strict *adj* estricto.
stride *n* tranco *m.*
string *n* cordon *m.*
stringent *adj* astringente.
strip *vt* desnudar.
stripe *n* raya.
strive *vi* esforzarse.
stroll *n* paseo.
strong *adj* fuerte.
strongbox *n* cofre fuerte *m.*
structure *n* estructura *f.*
struggle *vi* esforzarse.
strum *vt* (*mus*) rasguear.
strut *vi* pavonearse.
stubborn *adj* obstinado.
stucco *n* estuco *m.*
stud *n* corchete *m.*
student *n* estudiante *m/f.*
studio *n* estudio de un artista *m.*
studious *adj* estudioso.
study *n* estudio *m.*
stuff *n* materia *f.*
stuffing *n* relleno *m.*
stumble *vi* tropezar
stump *n* tronco *m.*
stun *vt* aturdir.
stunt *n* vuelo acrobático *m*; truco publicitario *m.*
stuntman *n* especialista *m.*
stupid *adj* estupido.
sturdy *adj* fuerte.
sturgeon *n* esturion *m.*
stutter *vi* tartamudear.
sty *n* zahurda *f.*
stye *n* orzuelo *m.*
style *n* estilo *m.*
stylish *adj* elegante.
suave *adj* afable.
subdivide *vt* subdividir.
subdue *vt* sojuzgar, sujetar.
subject *adj* sujeto.
subjunctive *n* subjuntivo *m.*
sublime *adj* sublime
submarine *adj* submarino.
submerge *vt* sumergir.
submit *vt*, (*vi*) someter(se).
subordinate *adj* subordinado, inferior:—*vt* subordinar.
subscribe *vt*, *vi* suscribir.
subsequent *adj*, ~**ly** *adv* subsiguien-te (mente).
subservient *adj* subordinado.
subside *vi* sumergirse.
subsidence *n* derrumbamiento *m.*
subsidiary *adj* subsidiario.
subsidize *vt* subvencionar.
subsidy *n* subvencion *f.*
substance *n* substancia *f.*
substitute *vt* sustituir.
substratum *n* lecho *m.*
subterranean *adj* subterraneo.
subtitle *n* subtitulo *m.*
subtle *adj* sutil.
suburb *n* suburbio *m.*
subversion *n* subversion *f.*
subway *n* metro *m.*
succeed *vt*, *vi* seguir; conseguir, lograr, tener exito.
success *n* exito *m.*
succumb *vi* sucumbir.
such *adj* tal.
suck *vt*, *vi* chupar.
sudden *adj* repentino, no previsto.
sue *vt* poner por justicia; suplicar.
suede *n* ante *m.*
suffer *vt*, *vi* sufrir, padecer.
sufficient *adj* suficiente.
suffocate *vt* sufocar.
suffrage *n* sufragio.
sugar *n* azucar *m.*
sugar cane *n* cana de azucar *f.*
suggest *vt* sugerir.
suggestion *n* sugestion *f.*
suicide *n* suicidio *m.*
suit *n* conjunto *m*; traje *m.*
suitcase *n* maleta *f.*
suitor *n* suplicante *m.*
sultan *n* sultan *m.*
sultana *n* sultana *f.*
sum *n* suma *f.*
summary *adj*, *n* sumario (*m*).
summer *n* verano *m.*
summit *n* apice *m.*
summon *vt* citar.
summons *n* citacion *f.*
sumptuous *adj* suntuoso.
sun *n* sol *m.*
sunbathe *vi* tomar el sol.
Sunday *n* domingo *m.*
sundial *n* reloj de sol *m.*
sundry *adj* varios.
sunflower *n* girasol *m.*
sunglasses *npl* gafas o antojos de sol *mpl.*
sunlight *n* luz del sol *f.*

sunrise *n* salida del sol *f*.
sunset *n* puesta del sol *f*.
sunshade *n* quitasol *m*.
sunstroke *n* insolacion *f*.
suntan *n* bronceado *m*.
suntan oil *n* aceite bronceador *m*.
superb *adj* magnifico.
superficial *adj* superficial.
superfluity *n* superfluidad *f*.
superior *adj*, *n* superior (*m*).
supermarket *n* supermercado *m*.
supernatural *n* sobrenatural.
superpower *n* superpotencia *f*.
superstition *n* supersticion *f*.
supertanker *n* superpetrolero *m*.
supervise *vt* inspeccionar.
supper *n* cena *f*.
supple *adj* flexible.
supplement *n* suplemento *m*.
supplementary *adj* adicional.
suppleness *n* flexibilidad *f*.
suppli(c)ant *n* suplicante *m*.
supplicate *vt* suplicar.
supplication *n* suplica, suplicacion *f*.
supplier *n* distribuidor, ra *m/f*.
supply *vt* suministrar; suplir, completar; surtir:—*n* provision *f*; suministro *m*.
support *vt* sostener; soportar, asistir: —*n* apoyo *m*.
supportable *adj* soportable.
supporter *n* partidario, ria; aficionado, da *m/f*.
suppose *vt*, *vi* suponer.
supposition *n* suposicion *f*.
suppress *vt* suprimir.
suppression *n* supresion *f*.
supremacy *n* supremacia *f*.
supreme *adj* supremo:—**~ly** *adv* supremamente.
surcharge *vt* sobrecargar:—*n* sobretasa *f*.
sure *adj* seguro, cierto; firme; estable:—**to be ~** sin duda; ya se ve:—**~ly** *adv* ciertamente, seguramente, sin duda.
sureness *n* certeza, seguridad *f*.
surety *n* seguridad *f*; fiador *m*.
surf *n* (*mar*) resaca *f*.
surface *n* superficie *f*:—*vt* revestir:—*vi* salir a la superficie.
surfboard *n* plancha (de surf) *f*.
surfeit *n* exceso *m*.
surge *n* ola, onda *f*:—*vi* avanzar en tropel.
surgeon *n* cirujano, na *m/f*.
surgery *n* cirujia *m*.
surgical *adj* quirurgico.
surliness *n* mal humor *m*.
surly *adj* aspero de genio.
surmise *vt* sospechar:—*n* sospecha *f*.
surmount *vt* sobrepujar.
surmountable *adj* superable.
surname *n* apellido, sobrenombre *m*.
surpass *vt* sobresalir, sobrepujar, exceder, aventajar.
surpassing *adj* sobresaliente.
surplice *n* sobrepelliz *f*.
surplus *n* excedente *m*; sobrante *m*:—*adj* sobrante.
surprise *vt* sorprender:—*n* sorpresa *f*.
surprising *adj* sorprendente.
surrender *vt*, *vi* rendir; ceder; rendirse:—*n* rendicion *f*.
surreptitious *adj* subrepticio:—**~ly** *adv* subrepticiamente.
surrogate *vt* subrogar:—*n* subrogado *m*.
surrogate mother *n* madre portadora *f*.
surround *vt* circundar, cercar, rodear.
survey *vt* inspeccionar, examinar; apear: —*n* inspeccion *f*; apeo (de tierras) *m*.
survive *vi* sobrevivir:—*vt* sobrevivir a.
survivor *n* sobreviviente *m/f*.
susceptibility *n* susceptibilidad *f*.
susceptible *adj* susceptible.
suspect *vt*, *vi* sospechar:—*n* sospechoso, sa *m/f*.
suspend *vt* suspender.
suspense *n* suspense *m*; detencion *f*; incertidumbre *f*.
suspension *n* suspension *f*.
suspension bridge *n* puente colgante o colgado *m*.
suspicion *n* sospecha *f*.
suspicious *adj* suspicaz:—**~ly** *adv* sospechosamente.
suspiciousness *n* suspicacia *f*.
sustain *vt* sostener, sustentar, mantener; apoyar; sufrir.
sustenance *n* sostenimiento, sustento *m*.
suture *n* sutura, costura *f*.
swab *n* algodon *m*; frotis *m* invar.
swaddle *vt* fajar.
swaddling-clothes *npl* panales *mpl*.
swagger *vi* baladronear.
swallow *n* golondrina *f*:—*vt* tragar, engullir.
swamp *n* pantano *m*.
swampy *adj* pantanoso.
swan *n* cisne *m*.
swap *vt* canjear:—*n* intercambio *m*.
swarm *n* enjambre *m*; gentio *m*; hormiguero *m*:—*vi* enjam brar; hormiguear de gente; abundar.
swarthy *adj* atezado.
swarthiness *n* tez morena *f*.
swashbuckling *adj* fanfarron.
swath *n* tranco *m*.

swathe *vt* fajar:—*n* faja *f*.
sway *vt* mover:—*vi* ladearse, inclinarse:—*n* balanceo *m*; poder, imperio, influjo *m*.
swear *vt*, *vi* jurar; hacer jurar; juramentar.
sweat *n* sudor *m*:—*vi* sudar; trabajar con fatiga.
sweater, sweatshirt *n* sueter *m*.
sweep *vt*, *vi* barrer; arrebatar; deshollinar; pasar o tocar liger amente; oscilar:—*n* barredura *f*; vuelta *f*; giro *m*.
sweeping *adj* rapido:—**~s** *pl* barreduras *fpl*.
sweepstake *n* loteria *f*.
sweet *adj* dulce, grato, gustoso; suave; oloroso; melodioso; hermoso; amable:—*adv* dulcemente, suavemente.
sweetbread *n* mellejas de ternera *fpl*.
sweeten *vt* endulzar; suavizar; aplacar; perfumar.
sweetener *n* edulcorante *m*.
sweetheart *n* novio, via *m/f*; querida *f*.
sweetmeats *npl* dulces secos *mpl*.
sweetness *n* dulzura, suavidad *f*.
swell *vi* hincharse; ensoberbecerse; embravecerse:—*vt* hin char, inflar, agravar:—*n* marejada *f*:—*adj* (*fam*) estupendo, fenomenal.
swelling *n* hinchazon *f*; tumor *m*.
swelter *vi* ahogarse de calor.
swerve *vi* vagar; desviarse.
swift *adj* veloz, ligero, rapido:—*n* vencejo, *m*.
swiftly *adv* velozmente.
swiftness *n* velocidad, rapidez *f*.
swill *vt* beber con exceso:—*n* bazofia *f*.
swim *vi* nadar; abundar en:—*vt* pasar a nado:—*n* nadada *f*.
swimming *n* natacion *f*; vertigo *m*.
swimming pool *n* piscina *f*.
swimsuit *n* traje de bano *m*.
swindle *vt* estafar.
swindler *n* trampista *m*.
swine *n* puerco, cochino *m*.
swing *vi* balancear, columpiarse; vibrar; agitarse:—*vt* colum piar; balancear; girar:—*n* vibracion *f*; balanceo *m*.
swinging *adj* (*fam*) alegre.
swinging door *n* puerta giratoria *f*.
swirl *n* hacer remolinos (en el agua).
switch *n* varilla *f*; interruptor *m*; (*rail*) aguja *f*:—*vt* cambiar de:—**to ~ off** apagar; parar:—**to ~ on** encender, prender.
switchboard *n* centralita (de teléfonos) *f*.
swivel *vt* girar.
swoon *vi* desmayarse:—*n* desmayo, deliquio, pasmo *m*.
swoop *vi* calarse:—*n* calada; redada *f*:— **in one ~** de un golpe.
sword *n* espada *f*.
swordfish *n* pez espada *f*.
swordsman *n* guerrero *m*.
sycamore *n* sicomoro *m* (arbol).
sycophant *n* sicofante *m*.
syllabic *adj* silabico.
syllable *n* silaba *f*.
syllabus *n* programa de estudios *m*.
syllogism *n* silogismo *m*.
sylph *n* silfio *m*; silfida *f*.
symbol *n* simbolo *m*.
symbolic(al) *adj* simbolico.
symbolize *vt* simbolizar.
symmetrical *adj* simetrico:—**~ly** *adv* con simetria.
symmetry *n* simetria *f*.
sympathetic *adj* simpatico:—**~ally** *adv* simpaticamente.
sympathize *vi* compadecerse.
sympathy *n* simpatia *f*.
symphony *n* sinfonia *f*.
symposium *n* simposio *m*.
symptom *n* sintoma *m*.
synagogue *n* sinagoga *f*.
synchronism *n* sincronismo *m*.
syndicate *n* sindicato *m*.
syndrome *n* sindrome *m*.
synod *n* sinodo *m*.
synonym *n* sinonimo *m*.
synonymous *adj* sinonimo:—**~ly** *adv* con sinonimia.
synopsis *n* sinopsis *f*; sumario *m*.
synoptical *adj* sinoptico.
syntax *n* sintaxis *f*.
synthesis *n* sintesis *f*.
syringe *n* jeringa, lavativa *f*:—*vt* jeringar.
system *n* sistema *m*.
systematic *adj* sistematico:—**~ally** *adv* sistematicamente.
systems analyst *n* analista de sistemas *m/f*.

T

table *n* mesa *f m*.
tablecloth *n* mantel *m*.
tablespoon *n* cuchara para comer *f*.
tablet *n* tableta *f m*.
table tennis *n* ping-pong *m*.
taboo *adj* tabu.
tacit *adj* tacito.
taciturn *adj* taciturno.

tack *n* tachuela *f*.
tact *n* tacto *m*.
tactician *n* tactico *m*.
tactics *npl* tactica *f*.
tadpole *n* ranilla *f*.
taffeta *n* tafetan *m*.
tag *n* herrete *m*.
tail *n* cola *f*.
tailor *n* sastre *m*.
tailor-made *adj* hecho a la medida.
taint *vt* tachar.
take *vt* tomar, coger.
takeoff *n* despegue *m*.
takings *npl* ingresos *mpl*.
talc *n* talco *m*.
talent *n* talento *m*.
talisman *n* talisman *m*.
talk *vi* hablar.
talkative *adj* locuaz.
tall *adj* alto.
talon *n* garra de ave de rapina *f*.
tambourine *n* pandereta *f*.
tame *adj* amansado.
tamper *vi* tocar.
tampon *n* tampon *m*.
tan *vt* broncear.
tang *n* sabor fuerte *m*.
tangerine *n* mandarina *f*.
tangle *vt* enredar.
tank *n* cisterna *f*; aljibe *m*.
tanned *adj* bronceado.
tantrum *n* rabieta *f*.
tape *n* cinta *f*.
tape measure *n* metro *m*.
tapestry *n* tapiz *mf*.
tar *n* brea *f*.
target *n* blanco *m* (para tirar).
tariff *n* tarifa *f*.
tarmac *n* pista *f*.
tarnish *vt* deslustrar.
tarpaulin *n* alquitranado *m*.
tarragon *n* (*bot*) estragon *m*.
tartan *n* tela escocesa *f*.
tartar *n* tartaro *m*.
task *n* tarea *f*.
tassel *n* borlita *f*.
taste *n* gusto *m*; sabor *m*.
tasty *adj* sabroso.
tattoo *n* tatuaje *m*.
taunt *vt* mofar.
Taurus *n* Tauro *m*.
tax *n* impuesto *m*.
taxi *n* taxi *m*.
tea *n* te *m*.
teach *vt* ensenar.
teacher *n* profesor, ra *m/f*.
teak *n* teca *f* (arbol).
team *n* equipo *m*.
teamster *n* camionero *m*.
teapot *n* tetera *f*.
tear *vt* despedazar, rasgar.
tear *n* lagrima *f*.
tease *vt* tomar el pelo.
teaspoon *n* cucharita *f*.
teat *n* ubre, teta *f*.
technical *adj* tecnico.
technician *n* tecnico *m*.
technique *n* tecnica *f*.
technology *n* tecnologia *f*.
teddy (bear) *n* osito de felpa *m*.
tedious *adj* tedioso.
tedium *n* tedio *m*.
tee-shirt *n* camiseta *f*.
teeth *npl* de tooth.
telegraph *n* telegrafo *m*.
telegraphic *adj* telegrafico.
telepathy *n* telepatia *f*.
telephone *n* telefono *m*.
telescope *n* telescopio *m*.
telescopic *adj* telescopico.
television *n* television *f*.
tell *vi* decir.
teller *n* cajero *m*.
temper *vt* templar:—*n* mal genio *m*.
temperament *n* temperamento *m*.
temperate *adj* templado.
temperature *n* temperatura *f*.
template *n* plantilla *f*.
temple *n* templo *m*.
temporary *adj* temporal.
tempt *vt* tentar.
temptation *n* tentacion *f*.
ten *adj*, *n* diez.
tenacity *n* tenacidad *f*.
tenancy *n* tenencia *f*.
tenant *n* arrendador *m*.
tend *vt* guardar.
tendency *n* tendencia *f*.
tender *adj* tierno, estimar.
tendon *n* tendon *m*.
tennis *n* tenis *m*.
tense *adj* tieso, tenso.
tension *n* tension *f*.
tent *n* tienda de campana *f*.
tentacle *n* tentaculo *m*.
tenth *adj*, *n* decimo.
tenure *n* tenencia *f*.
tepid *adj* tibio.
term *n* termino *m*.
terminal *adj* mortal.
termination *n* terminacion *f*.
terminus *n* terminal *f*.
terrace *n* terraza *f*.
terrain *n* terreno *m*.

terrestrial *adj* terrestre.
terrible *adj* terrible.
terrier *n* terrier *m*.
terrific *adj* fantastico.
terrify *vt* aterrar.
territorial *adj* territorial.
territory *n* territorio, distrito *m*.
terror *n* terror *m*.
terrorism *n* terrorismo *m*.
test *n* examen *m*.
testament *n* testamento *m*.
testicles *npl* testiculos *mpl*.
testify *vt* testificar.
testimony *n* testimonio *m*.
tetanus *n* tetano *m*.
tether *vt* atar.
text *n* texto *m*.
textiles *npl* textiles *mpl*.
texture *n* textura *f*.
than *adv* que, de.
thank *vt* agradecer.
thanks *npl* gracias *fpl*.
that *pn* aquel, aquello, aquella; que; este.
thaw *n* deshielo *m*.
the *art* el, la, lo; los, las.
theater *n* teatro *m*.
theft *n* robo *m*.
their *pn* su, suyo, suya; de ellos, de ellas:—~**s** el suyo, la suya, los suyos, las suyas; de ellos, de ellas.
them *pn* los, las, les; ellos, ellas.
theme *n* tema *m*.
themselves *pn pl* ellos mismos, ellas mismas; si mismos; se.
then *adv* entonces, despues.
theology *n* teologia *f*.
theory *n* teoria *f*.
therapist *n* terapeuta *m*.
therapy *n* terapia *f*.
there *adv* alli, alla.
thermal *adj* termal.
thermometer *n* termometro *m*.
thesaurus *n* tesoro *m*.
these *pn pl* estos, estas.
thesis *n* tesis *f*.
they *pn pl* ellos, ellas.
thick *adj* espeso.
thicken *vi* espesar.
thief *n* ladron *m*.
thigh *n* muslo *m*.
thimble *n* dedal *m*.
thin *adj* delgado.
thing *n* cosa *f*.
think *vi* pensar.
third *adj* tercero.
thirst *n* sed *f*.
thirteen *adj*, *n* trece.
thirteenth *adj*, *n* decimotercio.
thirtieth *adj*, *n* trigesimo.
thirty *adj*, *n* treinta.
this *adj* este, esta, esto:—*pn* este, esta, esto.
thorn *n* espino *m*; espina *f*.
those *pn pl* esos, esas; aquellos, aquellas:—*adj* esos, esas; aquellos, aquellas.
thought *n* pensamiento *m*.
thousand *adj*, *n* mil.
thousandth *adj*, *n* milesimo.
thrash *vt* golpear.
thread *n* hilo *m*.
threat *n* amenaza *f*.
threaten *vt* amenazar.
three *adj*, *n* tres.
threshold *n* umbral *m*.
thrifty *adj* economico.
thrill *vt* emocionar.
thrive *vi* prosperar.
throat *n* garganta *f*.
throb *vi* palpitar.
throne *n* trono *m*.
through *prep* por; durante; mediante.
throw *vt* echar.
thrush *n* tordo *m* (ave).
thrust *vt* empujar.
thug *n* gamberro *m*.
thumb *n* pulgar *m*.
thump *n* golpe *m*.
thunder *n* trueno *m*.
Thursday *n* jueves *m*.
thus *adv* asi, de este modo.
thyme *n* (*bot*) tomillo *m*.
thyroid *n* tiroides *m*.
tiara *n* tiara *f*.
tic *n* tic *m*.
ticket *n* billete *m* .
tickle *vt* hacer cosquillas.
tidal *adj* (*mar*) de marea.
tide *n* marea *f*.
tidy *adj* ordenado.
tie *vt* anudar, atar
tiger *n* tigre *m*.
tight *adj* tirante, apretado/a.
tile *n* azulejo *m*.
till *n* caja *f*:—*vt* cultivar.
time *n* tiempo; epoca *f*.
timer *n* interruptor *m*.
timid *adj* timido.
timidity *n* timidez *f*.
tin *n* estano *m*.
tinfoil *n* papel de estano *m*.
tinsel *n* oropel *m*.
tint *n* tinte *m*.
tiny *adj* pequeno, chico.
tip *n* punta, extremidad *f*; propina *f*.
tire *vt* cansar, fatigar:—*n* neumático *m*.

tissue *n* tejido *m*.
title *n* titulo *m*.
titular *adj* titular.
to *prep* a; para; por; de; hasta; en; con; que.
toad *n* sapo *m*.
toadstool *n* (*bot*) hongovejin *m*.
toast *vt* tostar; brindar.
toaster *n* tostadora *f*.
tobacco *n* tabaco *m*.
tobacco shop *n* tabaqueria *f*.
today *adv* hoy.
toe *n* dedo del pie *m*.
together *adv* juntamente.
toilet paper *n* papel higienico *m*.
token *n* senal *f*.
tolerate *vt* tolerar.
tomato *n* tomate *m*.
tomb *n* tumba *f*.
tomboy *n* muchachota *f*.
tombstone *n* piedra sepulcral *f*.
tomcat *n* gato *m*.
tomorrow *adv*, *n* manana *f*.
ton *n* tonelada *f*.
tongs *npl* tenacillas *fpl*.
tongue *n* lengua *f*.
tonic *n* (*med*) tonico.
tonight *adv*, *n* esta tarde (*f*).
tonsil *n* amigdala *f*.
too *adv* demasiado; tambien.
tool *n* herramienta *f*.
tooth *n* diente *m*.
toothache *n* dolor de muelas *m*.
top *n* cima.
topaz *n* topacio *m*.
topic *n* tema *m*.
topless *adj* topless.
topographic(al) *adj* topografico.
topography *n* topografia *f*.
torment *vt* atormentar.
tornado *n* tornado *m*.
torrent *n* torrente *m*.
torrid *adj* apasionado.
tortoise *n* tortuga *f*.
tortoiseshell *adj* de carey.
tortuous *adj* tortuoso.
torture *n* tortura *f*.
toss *vt* tirar, lanzar.
total *adj* total.
totalitarian *adj* totalitario.
totality *n* totalidad *f*.
totter *vi* vacilar.
touch *vt* tocar.
touchdown *n* aterrizaje *m*.
touching *adj* patetico, conmovedor.
tough *adj* duro.
toupee *n* tupe *m*.
tour *n* viaje *m*.
touring *n* viajes turisticos *mpl*.
tourism *n* turismo *m*.
tourist *n* turista *m/f*.
tourist office *n* oficina de turismo *f*.
tournament *n* torneo *m*.
tow *n* remolque *m*.
toward(s) *prep*, *adv* hacia.
towel *n* toalla *f*.
tower *n* torre *m*.
town *n* ciudad *f*.
town hall *n* ayuntamiento *m*.
toy *n* juguete *m*.
toy store *n* jugueteria *f*.
trace *n* huella *f*:—*vt* trazar.
trade *n* comercio *m*; ocupacion *f*.
trade(s) union *n* sindicato *m*.
tradition *n* tradicion *f*.
traditional *adj* tradicional.
traffic *n* trafico *m*.
traffic lights *npl* semaforo *m*.
tragedy *n* tragedia *f*.
tragic *adj* tragico.
trail *vt*, *vi* rastrear:— *n* senda *f*.
trailer *n* caravana *f*.
train *vt* entrenar * *n* tren *m*.
trainee *n* aprendiz *m*.
trainer *n* entrenador *m*.
trait *n* rasgo *m*.
traitor *n* traidor *m*.
tramp *n* vagabundo *m*.
trample *vt* pisotear.
trampoline *n* trampolin *m*.
trance *n* rapto *m*.
tranquil *adj* tranquilo.
tranquillizer *n* tranquilizante *m*.
transact *vt* negociar.
transaction *n* transaccion *f*.
transatlantic *adj* transatlántico.
transcription *n* traslado *m*.
transfer *vt* transferir.
transform *vt* transformar.
transformation *n* transformacion *f*.
transfusion *n* transfusion *f*.
transit *n* transito *m*.
transition *n* transito *m*; transicion *f*.
translate *vt* traducir.
translation *n* traduccion *f*.
translator *n* traductor, ra *m/f*.
transmit *vt* transmitir.
transparent *adj* transparente.
transpire *vi* resultar.
transplant *vt* trasplantar.
transport *vt* transportar.
trap *n* trampa *f*.
trapeze *n* trapecio *m*.
trappings *npl* adornos *mpl*.
trash *n* pacotilla *f*; basura *f*.

travel *vi* viajar.
trawler *n* pesquero de arrastre *m*.
tray *n* bandeja *f*
treachery *n* traicion *f*.
tread *vi* pisar.
treason *n* traicion *n*.
treasure *n* tesoro *m*.
treasurer *n* tesorero *m*.
treat *vt* tratar.
treatise *n* tratado *m*.
treatment *n* trato *m*.
treaty *n* tratado *m*.
treble *adj* triple.
treble clef *n* clave de sol *f*.
tree *n* arbol *m*.
trellis *n* enrejado *m*.
tremble *vi* temblar.
tremendous *adj* tremendo.
tremor *n* temblor *m*.
trench *n* foso *m*.
trend *n* tendencia *f*.
trendy *adj* de moda.
trespass *vt* transpasar.
tress *n* trenza *f*.
trestle *n* caballete de serrador *m*.
trial *n* proceso *m*.
triangle *n* triangulo *m*.
triangular *adj* triangular.
tribal *adj* tribal.
tribe *n* tribu *f*.
tribunal *n* tribunal *m*.
tributary *adj*, *n* tributario *m*.
tribute *n* tributo *m*.
trice *n* momento, tris *m*.
trick *n* engano.
trickle *vi* gotear.
tricky *adj* dificil.
tricycle *n* triciclo *m*.
trifle *n* bagatela.
trigger *n* gatillo *m*.
trigonometry *n* trigonometria *f*.
trim *adj* aseado.
Trinity *n* Trinidad *f*.
trinket *n* joya.
trio *n* (*mus*) trio *m*.
trip *vt* hacer caer; viaje corto *m*.
tripe *n* callos *mpl*.
triple *adj* triple.
triplets *npl* trillizos *mpl*.
triplicate *n* triplicado *m*.
tripod *n* tripode *m*.
triumph *n* triunfo *m*.
triumphal *adj* triunfal.
triumphant *adj* triunfante.
trivia *npl* trivialidades *fpl*.
trivial *adj* trivial.
trolley *n* carrito *m*.
trombone *n* trombon *m*.
trophy *n* trofeo *m*.
tropical *adj* tropico.
trot *n* trote *m*.
trouble *vt* afligir.
trough *n* abrevadero *m*.
trout *n* trucha *f*.
trowel *n* paleta *f*.
truce *n* tregua *f*.
truck *n* camion *m*
true *adj* verdadero.
truffle *n* trufa *f*.
truly *adv* en verdad.
trumpet *n* trompeta *f*.
trunk *n* baul, cofre *m*; trompa *f*.
trust *n* confianza *f*.
truth *n* verdad *f*.
try *vt* examinar, tentar.
tub *n* balde, cubo *m*.
tuba *n* tuba *f*.
tube *n* tubo *m*.
tuberculosis *n* tuberculosis *f*.
Tuesday *n* martes *m*.
tuition *n* enseñanza. *f*.
tulip *n* tulipan *m*.
tumble *vi* caer.
tumbler *n* vaso *m*.
tummy *n* barriga *f*.
tumor *n* tumor *m*.
tumultuous *adj* tumultuoso.
tuna *n* atun *m*.
tune *n* tono *m*.
tunic *n* tunica *f*.
tunnel *n* tunel *m*.
turban *n* turbante *m*.
turbine *n* turbina *f*.
turbulence *n* turbulencia *f*.
tureen *n* sopera *f*.
turf *n* cesped *m*.
turgid *adj* pesado.
turkey *n* pavo *m*.
turmoil *n* disturbio *m*.
turn *vi* volver.
turncoat *n* desertor *m*.
turnip *n* nabo *m*.
turnover *n* facturacion *f*.
turnstile *n* torniquete *m*.
turpentine *n* trementina *f*.
turquoise *n* turquesa *f*.
turret *n* torrecilla *f*.
turtle *n* galapago *m*.
turtledove *n* tortola *f*.
tusk *n* colmillo *m*.
tussle *n* pelea *f*.
tutor *n* tutor *m*.
tuxedo *n* smoking *m*.
twang *n* gangueo *m*.

tweezers *npl* tenacillas *fpl*.
twelfth *adj*, *n* duodecimo.
twelve *adj*, *n* doce.
twentieth *adj*, *n* vigesimo.
twenty *adj*, *n* veinte.
twice *adv* dos veces.
twig *n* ramita *f*:—*vi* caer en la cuenta.
twilight *n* crepusculo *m*.
twin *n* gemelo *m*.
twist *vt* torcer.
twit *n* (*col*) tonto *m*.
twitch *vi* moverse nerviosamente.
two *adj*, *n* dos.
two-faced *adj* falso.
tycoon *n* magnate *m*.
type *n* tipo *m*; letra *f*; modelo *m*:—*vt* escribir a maquina.
typewriter *n* maquina de escribir *f*.
typical *adj* tipico.
tyrannical *adj* tiranico.
tyranny *n* tirania *f*.
tyrant *n* tirano *m*.

U

ubiquitous *adj* ubicuo.
udder *n* ubre *f*.
ugh *excl* ¡uf!
ugliness *n* fealdad *f*.
ugly *adj* feo; peligroso.
ulcer *n* ulcera *f*.
ulterior *adj* ulterior.
ultimate *adj* ultimo.
ultimatum *n* ultimatum *m*.
umbrella *n* paraguas *m invar*.
umpire *n* arbitro *m*.
unable *adj* incapaz.
unaccompanied *adj* solo.
unaccustomed *adj* desacostumbrado.
unanimity *n* unanimidad *f*.
unanimous *adj* unanime.
unanswerable *adj* incontrovertible.
unapproachable *adj* inaccesible.
unbearable *adj* intolerable.
unbecoming *adj* indecente.
unbutton *vt* desabotonar.
uncanny *adj* extraordinario.
unchanged *adj* no alterado.
uncharitable *adj* nada caritativo.
uncle *n* tio.
uncomfortable *adj* incomodo.
uncommon *adj* raro.
uncompromising *adj* irreconciliable.
unconscious *adj* inconsciente.
unconventional *adj* poco convencional.
uncork *vt* destapar.
uncouth *adj* grosero.
uncover *vt* descubrir.
undaunted *adj* intrepido.
under *prep* debajo de.
under-age *adj* menor de edad.
underclothing *n* ropa intima *f*.
underdeveloped *adj* subdesarrollado.
underdog *n* desvalido *m*.
underestimate *vt* subestimar.
undergo *vt* sufrir.
undergraduate *n* estudiante *m*.
underground *n* movimiento clandestino *m*.
underline *vt* subrayar.
underpaid *adj* mal pagado.
undershirt *n* camiseta *f*.
understand *vt* entender, comprender.
understatement *n* subestimacion *f*.
underwear *n* ropa intima *f*.
underworld *n* hampa *f*.
undetermined *adj* indeterminado, indeciso.
undigested *adj* indigesto.
undisciplined *adj* indisciplinado.
undismayed *adj* intrepido.
undisputed *adj* incontestable.
undisturbed *adj* quieto, tranquilo.
undivided *adj* indiviso, entero.
undo *vt* deshacer, destar.
undoubted *adj* indudable.
undress *vi* desnudarse.
undue *adj* indebido.
undulating *adj* ondulante.
unduly *adv* indebidamente.
undying *adj* inmortal.
unearth *vt* desenterrar.
uneasy *adj* inquieto.
uneducated *adj* ignorante.
unemployed *adj* parado.
unemployment *n* paro *m*.
unenlightened *adj* no iluminado.
unenviable *adj* poco envidiable.
unequal *adj* desigual.
unequaled *adj* incomparable.
uneven *adj* desigual.
unexpected *adj* inesperado.
unexplored *adj* inexplorado.
unfair *adj* injusto.
unfaithful *adj* infiel.
unfamiliar *adj* desacostumbrado.
unfashionable *adj* pasado de moda.
unfasten *vt* desatar.
unfavorable *adj* desfavorable.
unfeeling *adj* insensible.

unfit *adj* indispuesto.
unfold *vt* desplegar.
unforeseen *adj* imprevisto.
unforgettable *adj* inolvidable.
unforgivable *adj* imperdonable.
unforgiving *adj* implacable.
unfortunate *adj* desafortunado.
unfounded *adj* sin fundamento.
unfriendly *adj* antipatico.
unfruitful *adj* esteril; infructuoso.
unfurnished *adj* sin muebles.
ungrateful *adj* ingrato.
unhappily *adv* infelizmente.
unhappy *adj* infeliz.
unhealthy *adj* malsano.
unhook *vt* desenganchar; descolgar; desabrochar.
unhoped(-for) *adj* inesperado.
unhurt *adj* ileso.
unicorn *n* unicornio *m*.
uniform *adj* uniforme:—*n* uniforme *m*.
uniformity *adj* uniformidad *f*.
unify *vt* unificar.
unimaginable *adj* inimaginable.
unimportant *adj* nada importante.
uninformed *adj* ignorante.
uninhabitable *adj* inhabitable.
uninhabited *adj* inhabitado, desierto.
uninjured *adj* ileso, no danado.
unintelligible *adj* ininteligible.
unintentional *adj* involuntario.
uninterested *adj* desinteresado.
uninteresting *adj* poco interesante.
uninvited *adj* no convivado.
union *n* union *f*; sindicato *m*.
unionist *n* unitario *m*.
unique *adj* unico, uno, singular.
unit *n* unidad *f*.
unite *vt vi* unir(se), juntarse.
United States (of America) *npl* Estados Unidos (de América) *mpl*.
unity *n* unidad *f*.
universal *adj* universal.
universe *n* universo *m*.
university *n* universidad *f*.
unjust *adj* injusto.
unkind *adj* poco amable.
unknown *adj* incognito.
unlawful *adj* ilícito/a.
unless *conj* a menos que, si no.
unload *vt* descargar.
unluckily *adv* desafortunadamente.
unlucky *adj* desafortunado.
unmarried *adj* soltero; soltera.
unmerited *adj* desmerecido.
unmistakable *adj* evidente.
unmoved *adj* inmoto, firme.
unnatural *adj* antinatural.
unnecessary *adj* inutil, innecesario.
unnoticed *adj* no observado.
unobserved *adj* invertido/a.
unobtainable *adj* inconseguible.
unobtrusive *adj* modesto.
unoccupied *adj* desocupado.
unofficial *adj* no oficial.
unpack *vt* desempacar; desenvolver.
unpaid *adj* no pagado.
unpleasant *adj* desagradable.
unpopular *adj* no popular.
unpracticed *adj* inexperto.
unprecedented *adj* sin ejemplo.
unpredictable *adj* imprevisible.
unprepared *adj* no preparado.
unprofitable *adj* inútil, vano; poco lucrativo.
unpunished *adj* impune.
unqualified *adj* sin titulos; total.
unquestionable *adj* indubitable.
unravel *vt* desenredar.
unrealistic *adj* poco realista.
unreasonable *adv* irracionalmente.
unrelated *adj* sin relacion; inconexo.
unrelenting *adj* incompasivo, inflexible.
unreliable *adj* poco fiable.
unrestrained *adj* desenfrenado; ilimitado.
unripe *adj* inmaduro.
unrivaled *adj* sin rival.
unroll *vt* desenrollar.
unsafe *adj* inseguro.
unsatisfactory *adj* insatisfactorio.
unscrew *vt* destornillar.
unscrupulous *adj* sin escrupulos.
unseemly *adj* indecente.
unseen *adj* invisible.
unselfish *adj* desinteresado.
unsettle *vt* perturbar.
unshaken *adj* firme, estable.
unskilled *adj* inhabil.
unsociable *adj* insociable.
unspeakable *adj* inefable.
unstable *adj* instable, inconstante.
unsteady *adj* inestable.
unsuccessful *adj* infeliz, desafortunado.
unsuitable *adj* inapropiado; inoportuno.
unsure *adj* inseguro.
unsympathetic *adj* inompasivo.
untapped *adj* sin explotar.
untenable *adj* insostenible.
unthinkable *adj* inconcebible.
unthinking *adj* desatento, irreflexivo.
untidiness *n* desalino *m*.
untidy *adj* desordenado; sucio.
untie *vt* desatar, deshacer, soltar.
until *prep* hasta:—*conj* hasta que.

untimely *adj* intempestivo.
untiring *adj* incansable.
untold *adj* nunca dicho; indecible; incalculable.
untouched *adj* intacto.
untoward *adj* impropio; adverso.
untried *adj* no ensayado o probado.
untroubled *adj* no perturbado, tranquilo.
untrue *adj* falso.
untrustworthy *adj* indigno de confianza.
untruth *n* falsedad, mentira *f*.
unused *adj* isin usar, no usado.
unusual *adj* inusitado, raro:—**~ly** *adv* inusitadamente, raramente.
unveil *vt* quitar el velo, descubrir.
unwavering *adj* inquebrantable.
unwelcome *adj* desagradable, inoportuno.
unwell *adj* enfermizo, malo.
unwieldy *adj* pesado.
unwilling *adj* desinclinado:—**~ly** *adv* de mala gana.
unwillingness *n* mala gana, repugnancia *f*.
unwind *vt* desenredar, desenmaranar: —*vi* relajarse.
unwise *adj* imprudente.
unwitting *adj* inconsciente.
unworkable *adj* poco practico.
unworthy *adj* indigno.
unwrap *vt* desenvolver.
unwritten *adj* no escrito.
up *adv* arriba, en lo alto; levantado:—*prep* hacia; hasta.
upbringing *n* educacion *f*.
update *vt* poner al dia.
upheaval *n* agitacion *f*.
uphill *adj* dificil, penoso:—*adv* cuesta arriba.
uphold *vt* sos tener, apoyar.
upholstery *n* tapiceria *f*.
upkeep *n* manteniniento *m*.
uplift *vt* levantar.
upon *prep* sobre, encima.
upper *adj* superior; mas elevado.
upper-class *adj* de la clase alta.
upper-hand *n* (*fig*) superioridad *f*.
uppermost *adj* mas alto, supremo:—**to be ~** predominar.
upright *adj* derecho, perpendicular, recto; puesto en pie; hon rado.
uprising *n* sublevacion *f*.
uproar *n* tumulto, alboroto *m*.
uproot *vt* desarraigar.
upset *vt* trastornar; derramar, volcar:—*n* reves *m*; trastorno *m*:—*adj* molesto; revuelto.
upshot *n* remate *m*; fin *m*; conclusion *f*.
upside-down *adv* de arriba abajo.
upstairs *adv* de arriba.
upstart *n* advenedizo *m*.
uptight *adj* nervioso.
up-to-date *adj* al dia.
upturn *n* mejora *f*.
upward *adj* ascendente:—**~s** *adv* hacia arriba.
urban *adj* urbano.
urbane *adj* cortes.
urchin *n* golfillo *m*.
urge *vt* animar:—*n* impulso *m*; deseo *m*.
urgency *n* urgencia *f*.
urgent *adj* urgente.
urinal *n* orinal *m*.
urinate *vi* orinar.
urine *n* orina *f*.
urn *n* urna *f*.
us *pn* nos; nosotros.
usage *n* tratamiento *m*; uso *m*.
use *n* uso *m*; utilidad, practica *f*:—*vt* usar, emplear.
used *adj* usado.
useful *adj* , **~ly** *adv* util(mente).
usefulness *n* utilidad *f*.
useless *adj* inútil:—**~ly** *adv* inútilmente.
uselessness *n* inutilidad *f*.
user-friendly *adj* amistoso.
usher *n* ujier *m*; acomodador *m*.
usherette *n* acomodadora *f*.
usual *adj* usual, comun, normal:—**~ly** *adv* normalmente.
usurer *n* usurero *m*.
usurp *vt* usurpar.
usury *n* usura *f*.
utensil *n* utensilio *m*.
uterus *n* utero *m*.
utilize *vt* utilizar.
utility *n* utilidad *f*.
utmost *adj* extremo, sumo; ultimo.
utter *adj* total; todo; entero:—*vt* proferir; expresar; publicar.
utterance *n* expresion *f*.
utterly *adv* enteramente, del todo.

V

vacancy *n* cuarto libre *m*.
vacant *adj* vacio; desocupado.
vacate *vt* desocupar.
vacation *n* vacaciones *fpl*.
vaccinate *vt* vacunar.
vaccination *n* vacunacion *f*.

vaccine *n* vacuna *f.*
vacuous *adj* necio/a, bobo/a.
vacuum *n* vacio *m.*
vagina *n* vagina *f.*
vagrant *n* vagabundo.
vague *adj* vago.
vain *adj* vano.
valet *n* criado *m.*
valiant *adj* valiente.
valid *adj* valido.
valley *n* valle *m.*
valor *n* valor *m.*
valuable *adj* precioso.
valuation *n* tasa, valuacion *f.*
value *n* valor.
valued *adj* apreciado.
valve *n* valvula *f.*
vampire *n* vampiro *m.*
vandal *n* gamberro *m.*
vandalize *vt* danar.
vandalism *n* vandalismo *m.*
vanguard *n* vanguardia *f.*
vanilla *n* vainilla *f.*
vanish *vi* desvanecerse.
vanity *n* vanidad *f.*
vanquish *vt* vencer.
vantage point *n* punto panoramico *m.*
vapor *n* vapor *m.*
variable *adj* variable.
variance *n* discordia *f.*
variation *n* variacion *f.*
varicose vein *n* variz *f.*
varied *adj* variado.
variety *n* variedad *f.*
various *adj* vario.
varnish *n* barniz *m.*
vary *vt, vi* variar.
vase *n* florero *m.*
vast *adj* vasto.
vat *n* tina *f.*
vault *n* boveda *f.*
veal *n* ternera *f.*
veer *vi* (*mar*) virar.
vegetable *adj* vegetal, *n* **~s** *pl* legumbres *fpl.*
vegetable garden *n* huerta *f.*
vegetarian *n* vegetariano, na *m/f.*
vegetate *vi* vegetar.
vegetation *n* vegetacion *f.*
vehemence *n* vehemencia *f.*
vehement *adj* vehemente.
vehicle *n* vehiculo *m.*
veil *n* velo *m.*
vein *n* vena *f.*
velocity *n* velocidad *f.*
velvet *n* terciopelo *m.*
vendor *n* vendedor *m.*
veneer *n* chapa *f.*
venerable *adj* venerable.
venerate *vt* venerar.
veneration *n* veneracion *f.*
venereal *adj* venereo.
vengeance *n* venganza *f.*
venial *adj* venial.
venison *n* (carne de) venado *f.*
venom *n* veneno *m.*
venomous *adj* venenoso.
vent *n* respiradero *m*; salida *f.*
ventilate *vt* ventilar.
ventilation *n* ventilacion *f.*
ventilator *n* ventilador *m.*
ventriloquist *n* ventrilocuo *m.*
venture *n* empresa *f*:—*vi* aventurarse.
venue *n* lugar de reunion *m.*
veranda(h) *n* terraza *f.*
verb *n* (*gr*) verbo *m.*
verbal *adj* verbal.
verdict *n* (law) veredicto *m.*
verification *n* verificacion *f.*
verify *vt* verificar.
veritable *adj* verdadero.
vermin *n* bichos *mpl.*
vermouth *n* vermut *m.*
versatile *adj* versatil.
verse *n* verso *m.*
versed *adj* versado.
version *n* version *f.*
versus *prep* contra.
vertebra *n* vertebra *f.*
vertebral, vertebrate *adj* vertebral.
vertical *adj* , **~ly** *adv* vertical(mente).
vertigo *n* vertigo *m.*
very *adj adv* muy, mucho.
vessel *n* vasija *f.*
vest *n* chaleco *m.*
vestibule *n* vestibulo *m.*
vestige *n* vestigio *m.*
vestry *n* sacristia *f.*
veteran *adj, n* veterano (*m*).
veterinary *adj* veterinario.
veto *n* veto *m.*
vex *vt* molestar.
via *prep* por.
viaduct *n* viaducto *m.*
vial *n* redoma *f.*
vibrate *vi* vibrar.
vibration *n* vibracion *f.*
vicarious *adj* sustituto.
vice *n* vicio *m.*
vice versa *adv* viceversa.
vicinity *n* vecindad *f.*
vicious *adj* vicioso.
victim *n* victima *f.*
victimize *vt* victimizar.

victor *n* vencedor *m*.
victorious *adj* victorioso.
victory *n* victoria *f*.
video *n* videofilm *m*; video cassette *f*; videograbadora *f*.
video tape *n* cinta de video *f*.
vie *vi* competir.
view *n* vista *f*.
viewpoint *n* punto de vista *m*.
vigilance *n* vigilancia *f*.
vigilant *adj* vigilante.
vigorous *adj* vigoroso.
vigor *n* vigor *m*.
vile *adj* vil.
vilify *vt* envilecer.
villa *n* chalet *m*.
village *n* aldea *f*.
villain *n* malvado *m*.
vindicate *vt* vindicar.
vindication *n* vindicacion *f*.
vindictive *adj* vengativo.
vine *n* vid *f*.
vinegar *n* vinagre *m*.
vineyard *n* vina *f*.
vintage *n* vendimia *f*.
vinyl *n* vinilo *m*.
viola *n* (*mus*) viola *f*.
violate *vt* violar.
violation *n* violacion *f*.
violence *n* violencia *f*.
violent *adj* violento.
violet *n* (*bot*) violeta *f*.
violin *n* (*mus*) violin *m*.
viper *n* vibora *f*.
virgin *n* virgen *f*.
virginity *n* virginidad *f*.
Virgo *n* Virgo *f* (signo del zodiaco).
virile *adj* viril.
virility *n* virilidad *f*.
virtual *adj* , **~ly** *adv* virtual(mente).
virtue *n* virtud *f*.
virtuous *adj* virtuoso.
virulent *adj* virulento.
virus *n* virus *m*.
visa *n* visado *m*, visa *f*.
vis-a-vis *prep* con respecto a.
visibility *n* visibilidad *f*.
visible *adj* visible.
vision *n* vista *f*.
visit *vt* visitar:—*n* visita *f*.
visitor *n* visitante *m/f*.
visor *n* visera *f*.
vista *n* vista, perspectiva *f*.
visual *adj* visual.
visualize *vt* imaginarse.
vital *adj* vital.
vitality *n* vitalidad *f*.
vitamin *n* vitamina *f*.
vitiate *vt* viciar.
vivacious *adj* vivaz.
vivid *adj* vivo.
vivisection *n* viviseccion *f*.
vocabulary *n* vocabulario *m*.
vocal *adj* vocal.
vocation *n* vocacion *f*.
vociferous *adj* vocinglero.
vodka *n* vodka *m*.
vogue *n* moda *f*; boga *f*.
voice *n* voz *f*:—*vt* expresar.
void *adj* nulo:—*n* vacio *m*.
volatile *adj* volatil; voluble.
volcanic *adj* volcanico.
volcano *n* volcan *m*.
volition *n* voluntad *f*.
volley *n* descarga *f*; salva *f*; rociada *f*; volea *f*.
volleyball *n* voleibol *m*.
volt *n* voltio *m*.
voltage *n* voltaje *m*.
voluble *adj* locuaz.
volume *n* volumen *m*.
voluntarily *adv* voluntariamente.
voluntary *adj* voluntario.
volunteer *n* voluntario *m*.
voluptuous *adj* voluptuoso.
vomit *vt*, *vi* vomitar.
vortex *n* remolino *m*.
vote *n* voto.
voter *n* votante *m/f*.
voting *n* votacion *f*.
voucher *n* vale *m*.
vow *n* voto *m*.
vowel *n* vocal *f*.
voyage *n* viaje *m*.
vulgar *adj* ordinario.
vulgarity *n* groseria.
vulnerable *adj* vulnerable.
vulture *n* buitre *m*.

W

wad *n* fajo *m*.
waddle *vi* anadear.
wade *vi* vadear.
wafer *n* galleta *f*.
waffle *n* gofre *m*.
wag *vt* menear.
wage *n* salario *m*.
waggon *n* carro *m*.

wail *n* lamento *m*.
waist *n* cintura *f*.
wait *vi* esperar.
waiter *n* camarero *m*.
waiting list *n* lista de espera *f*.
waiting room *n* sala de espera *f*.
waive *vt* suspender.
wake *vi* despertarse.
waken *vt*, (*vi*) despertar(se).
walk *vt*, *vi* pasear; andar.
walking stick *n* baston *m*.
wall *n* pared *f*; muralla *f*; muro *m*.
wallflower *n* (*bot*) aleli *m*.
wallpaper *n* papel pintado *m*.
walnut *n* nogal *m*; nuez *f*.
walrus *n* morsa *f*.
waltz *n* vals *m* (baile).
wan *adj* palido.
wand *n* varita magica *f*.
wane *vi* menguar.
want *vt* querer.
wanton *adj* lascivo.
war *n* guerra *f*.
ward *n* sala *f*
wardrobe *n* guardarropa *f*.
warehouse *n* almacen *m*.
warm *adj* calido; caliente.
warm-hearted *adj* afectuoso.
warmth *n* calor *m*.
warn *vt* avisar.
warning *n* aviso *m*.
warp *vi* torcerse.
warrant *n* orden judicial *f*.
warranty *n* garantia *f*.
warren *n* conejero *m*.
warrior *n* guerrero *m*.
wart *n* verruga *f*.
wary *adj* cauto.
wash *vt* lavar.
washbowl *n* lavabo *m*.
washing machine *n* lavadora *f*.
washing-up *n* fregado *m*.
washroom *n* servicios *mpl*.
wasp *n* avispa *f*.
waste *vt* malgastar.
watch *n* reloj *m*; vigilar.
watchdog *n* perro guardian *m*.
water *n* agua *f*.
watercolor *n* acuarela *f*.
waterfall *n* cascada *f*.
watering-can *n* regadera *f*.
waterlily *n* ninfea *f*.
water melon *n* sandia *f*.
watertight *adj* impermeable.
watt *n* vatio *m*.
wave *n* ola, onda *f*.
waver *vi* vacilar.
wax *n* cera *f*.
way *n* camino *m*; via *f*.
we *pn* nosotros, nosotras.
weak *adj* , **~ly** *adv* debil(mente).
wealth *n* riqueza *f*.
wealthy *adj* rico.
weapon *n* arma *f*.
wear *vt* gastar, consumir; usar, llevar.
weary *adj* cansado.
weasel *n* comadreja *f*.
weather *n* tiempo *m*.
weave *vt* tejer; trenzar.
weaving *n* tejido *m*.
web *n* telarana *f*.
wed *vt*, *vi* casar(se).
wedge *n* cuna *f*.
Wednesday *n* miercoles *m*.
wee *adj* pequenito.
weed *n* mala hierba *f*.
week *n* semana *f*.
weekend *n* fin de semana *m*.
weekly *adj* semanal.
weep *vt*, *vi* llorar.
weeping willow *n* sauce lloron *m*.
weigh *vt*, *vi* pesar.
weight *n* peso *m*.
welcome *adj* recibido con agrado:**—~!** ¡bienvenido!.
weld *vt* soldar.
welfare *n* prosperidad *f*
well *n* fuente *f* *adv* bien.
wench *n* mozuela *f*.
west *n* oeste, occidente *m*.
wet *adj* humedo, mojado.
whale *n* ballena *f*.
wharf *n* muelle *m*.
what *pn* que, qué?, el que, la que, lo que.
whatever *pn* cualquier o cualquiera cosa que.
wheat *n* trigo *m*.
wheel *n* rueda *f*.
wheelbarrow *n* carretilla *f*.
wheelchair *n* sillita de ruedas *f*.
wheeze *vi* jadear.
when *adv* cuando.
whenever *adv* cuando; cada vez que.
where *adv* dónde? *conj* donde.
whether *conj* si.
which *pn* que; lo que; el que, el cual; cual: *—adj* qué?; cuyo.
while *n* rato *m*; vez *f*:*—conj* durante; mientras; aunque.
whim *n* antojo *m*.
whine *vi* llorar, lamentar
whinny *vi* relinchar.
whip *n* azote *m*; latigo *m*.
whirlpool *n* vortice *m*.
whirlwind *n* torbellino *m*.

whiskey *n* whisky *m*.
whisper *vi* cuchichear.
whistle *vi* silbar.
white *adj* blanco.
who *pn* quién?, que.
whoever *pn* quienquiera, cualquiera.
whole *adj* todo.
wholemeal *adj* integral.
wholly *adv* enteramente.
whom *pn* quién? que.
whooping cough *n* tos ferina *f*.
whore *n* puta *f*.
why *n* por qué?
wick *n* mecha *f*.
wicked *adj* malvado.
wide *adj* ancho.
widen *vt* ensanchar.
widow *n* viuda *f*.
widower *n* viudo *m*.
width *n* anchura *f*.
wield *vt* manejar.
wife *n* esposa *f*.
wig *n* peluca *f*.
wild *adj* silvestre.
wilderness *n* desierto *m*.
wild life *n* fauna *f*.
will *n* voluntad *f*.
willful *adj* deliberado; testarudo.
willow *n* sauce *m* (arbol).
willpower *n* fuerza de voluntad *f*.
wilt *vi* marchitarse.
wily *adj* astuto.
win *vt* ganar.
wince *vi* encogerse, estremecerse.
winch *n* torno *m*.
wind *n* viento *m*.
wind *vt* enrollar.
windfall *n* golpe de suerte *m*.
winding *adj* tortuoso.
windmill *n* molino de viento *m*.
window *n* ventana *f*.
window box *n* jardinera de ventana *f*.
window ledge *n* repisa *f*.
window pane *n* cristal *m*.
window sill *n* repisa *f*.
windpipe *n* traquea *f*.
windshield *n* parabrisas *m* invar.
windy *adj* de mucho viento.
wine *n* vino *m*.
wine cellar *n* bodega *f*.
wine glass *n* copa *f*.
wing *n* ala *f*.
winged *adj* alado.
wink *vi* guinar.
winner *n* ganador.
winter *n* invierno *m*.
wintry *adj* invernal.
wipe *vt* limpiar.
wire *n* telegrama *m*.
wisdom *n* sabiduria *f*.
wisdom teeth *npl* muelas de juicio *fpl*.
wise *adj* sabio.
wisecrack *n* broma *f*.
wish *vt* querer.
wishful *adj* deseoso.
wit *n* entendimiento *m*.
witch *n* bruja *f*.
witchcraft *n* brujeria *f*.
with *prep* con; por, de, a.
withdraw *vt* quitar.
withdrawal *n* retirada *f*.
withdrawn *adj* reservado.
withhold *vt* detener.
within *prep* dentro de.
without *prep* sin.
withstand *vt* resistir.
witless *adj* necio.
witness *n* testigo *m*.
witticism *n* ocurrencia *f*.
wittily *adv* ingeniosamente.
witty *adj* ingenioso.
wizard *n* brujo *m*.
woe *n* dolor *m*; miseria *f*.
woeful *adj* triste.
wolf *n* lobo *m*.
woman *n* mujer *f*.
womb *n* utero *m*.
wonder *n* milagro *m*.
wonderful *adj* maravilloso.
won't *abrev* de will not.
woo *vt* cortejar.
wood *n* bosque *m*; selva *f*; madera *f*; lena *f*.
woodland *n* arbolado *m*.
woodlouse *n* cochinilla *f*.
woodpecker *n* picamaderos *m* invar.
woodworm *n* carcoma *f*.
wool *n* lana *f*.
woolen *adj* de lana.
word *n* palabra *f*.
wordy *adj* verboso.
work *vi* trabajar; obrar.
world *n* mundo *m*.
worm *n* gusano *m*.
worn-out *adj* gastado.
worried *adj* preocupado.
worry *vt* preocupar.
worse *adj*, *adv* peor.
worship *n* culto *m*; adoracion *f*.
worst *adj* el/la peor.
worth *n* valor *m*.
worthwhile *adj* que vale la pena; valioso.
worthy *adj* digno.
wound *n* herida *f*.
wrangle *vi* renir *f*.

wrap *vt* envolver.
wrath *n* ira *f*.
wreath *n* corona *f*.
wreck *n* naufragio *m*; ruina *f*.
wreckage *n* restos *mpl*.
wren *n* reyezuelo *m* (avecilla).
wrestle *vi* luchar; disputar.
wrestling *n* lucha *f*.
wretched *adj* infeliz, miserable.
wring *vt* torcer.
wrinkle *n* arruga *f*.
wrist *n* muneca *f*.
wristband *n* puno de camisa *m*.
wristwatch *n* reloj de pulsera *m*.
writ *n* escrito *m*; escritura *f*.
write *vt* escribir.
write-off *n* perdida total *f*.
writer *n* escritor, ra, *m/f*; autor, ra *m/f*.
writhe *vi* retorcerse.
writing *n* escritura *f*
writing desk *n* escritorio *m*.
writing paper *n* papel para escribir *m*.
wrong *n* injuria *f*; injusticia *f*.
wrongful *adj* injusto.
wrongly *adv* injustamente.
wry *adj* ironico.

XYZ

Xmas *n* Navidad *f*.
X-ray *n* radiografia *f*.
xylophone *n* xilofano *m*.
yacht *n* yate *m*.
yachting *n* balandrismo *m*.
Yankee *n* yanqui *m*.
yard *n* corral *m*; yarda *f*.
yardstick *n* criterio *m*.
yarn *n* estambre *m*; hilo de lino *m*.
yawn *vi* bostezar
yeah *adv* si.
year *n* ano *m*.
yearling *n* primal *m*, ala *f*.
yearly *adj* anual.
yearn *vi* anorar.
yearning *n* anoranza *f*.
yeast *n* levadura *f*.
yell *vi* aullar.
yellow *adj* amarillo.
yelp *vi* latir, ganir.
yes *adv*, *n* si (*m*).
yesterday *adv*, *n* ayer (*m*).
yet *conj* sin embargo; pero:—*adv* todavia.
yew *n* tejo *m*.
yield *vt* dar, producir.
yoga *n* yoga *m*.
yog(h)urt *n* yogur *m*.
yoke *n* yugo *m*.
yolk *n* yema de huevo *f*.
yonder *adv* alla.
you *pn* vosotros, tu, usted, ustedes.
young *adj* joven.
youngster *n* jovencito, ta *m/f*.
your(s) *pn* tuyo, vuestro, suyo:—**sincerely ~s** su seguro ser vidor.
yourself *pn* tu mismo, usted mismo, vosotros mismos, ustedes mismos.
youth *n* juventud *f*.
youthful *adj* juvenil.
youthfulness *n* juventud *f*.
yuppie *adj*, *n* yuppie *m/f*.
zany *adj* estrafalario.
zap *vt* borrar.
zeal *n* celo *m*; ardor *m*.
zealous *adj* celoso.
zebra *n* cebra *f*.
zenith *n* cenit *m*.
zero *n* zero, cero *m*.
zest *n* animo *m*.
zigzag *n* zigzag *m*.
zinc *n* zinc *m*.
zip, zipper *n* cremallera *f*.
zodiac *n* zodiaco *m*.
zone *n* banda, faja *f*; zona *f*.
zoo *n* zoo *m*.
zoological *adj* zoologico.
zoologist *n* zoologo, ga *m/f*.
zoology *n* zoologia *f*.
zoom *vi* zumbar.
zoom lens *n* zoom *m*.

Verbos Irregulares en Ingles

Present tense	Past tense	Past participle
arise	arose	arisen
awake	awoke	awaked, awoke
be [I am, you/we/they are, he/she/it is, gerund being]	was, were	been
bear	bore	borne
beat	beat	beaten
become	became	become
begin	began	begun
behold	beheld	beheld
bend	bent	bent
beseech	besought, beseeched	besought, beseeched
beset	beset	beset
bet	bet, betted	bet, betted
bid	bade, bid	bid, bidden
bite	bit	bitten
bleed	bled	bled
bless	blessed, blest	blessed, blest
blow	blew	blown
break	broke	broken
breed	bred	bred
bring	brought	brought
build	built	built
burn	burnt, burned	burnt, burned
burst	burst	burst
buy	bought	bought
can	could	(been able)
cast	cast	cast
catch	caught	caught
choose	chose	chosen
cling	clung	clung
come	came	come
cost	cost	cost
creep	crept	crept
cut	cut	cut
deal	dealt	dealt
dig	dug	dug
do [he/she/it does]	did	done
draw	drew	drawn
dream	dreamed, dreamt	dreamed, dreamt

Present tense	Past tense	Past participle
drink	drank	drunk
drive	drove	driven
dwell	dwelt, dwelled	dwelt, dwelled
eat	ate	eaten
fall	fell	fallen
feed	fed	fed
feel	felt	felt
fight	fought	fought
find	found	found
flee	fled	fled
fling	flung	flung
fly [he/she/it flies]	flew	flown
forbid	forbade	forbidden
forecast	forecast	forecast
forget	forgot	forgotten
forgive	forgave	forgiven
forsake	forsook	forsaken
forsee	foresaw	foreseen
freeze	froze	frozen
get	got	got, gotten (US)
give	gave	given
go [he/she/it goes]	went	gone
grind	ground	ground
grow	grew	grown
hang	hung, hanged	hung, hanged
have [I/you/we/they have, he/she/it has,gerund having]	had	had
hear	heard	heard
hide	hid	hidden
hit	hit	hit
hold	held	held
hurt	hurt	hurt
keep	kept	kept
kneel	knelt	knelt
know	knew	known
lay	laid	laid
lead	led	led
lean	leant, leaned	leant, leaned
leap	leapt, leaped	leapt, leaped
learn	learnt, learned	learnt, learned
leave	left	left
lend	lent	lent
let	let	let
lie [gerund lying]	lay	lain
light	lighted, lit	lighted, lit

Present tense	Past tense	Past participle
lose	lost	lost
make	made	made
may	might	—
mean	meant	meant
meet	met	met
mistake	mistook	mistaken
mow	mowed	mowed, mown
must	(had to)	(had to)
overcome	overcame	overcome
pay	paid	paid
put	put	put
quit	quit, quitted	quit, quitted
read	read	read
rid	rid	rid
ride	rode	ridden
ring	rang	rung
rise	rose	risen
run	ran	run
saw	sawed	sawn, sawed
say	said	said
see	saw	seen
seek	sought	sought
sell	sold	sold
send	sent	sent
set	set	set
sew	sewed	sewn, sewed
shake	shook	shaken
shall	should	—
shear	sheared	sheared, shorn
shed	shed	shed
shine	shone	shone
shoot	shot	shot
show	showed	shown, showed
shrink	shrank	shrunk
shut	shut	shut
sing	sang	sung
sink	sank	sunk
sit	sat	sat
slay	slew	slain
sleep	slept	slept
slide	slid	slid
sling	slung	slung
smell	smelt, smelled	smelt, smelled
sow	sowed	sown, sowed
speak	spoke	spoken

Present tense	Past tense	Past participle
speed	sped, speeded	sped, speeded
spell	spelt, spelled	spelt, spelled
spend	spent	spent
spill	spilt, spilled	spilt, spilled
spin	spun	spun
spit	spat	spat
split	split	split
spoil	spoilt	spoilt
spread	spread	spread
spring	sprang	sprung
stand	stood	stood
steal	stole	stolen
stick	stuck	stuck
sting	stung	stung
stink	stank	stunk
stride	strode	stridden
strike	struck	struck
strive	strove	striven
swear	swore	sworn
sweep	swept	swept
swell	swelled	swelled, swollen
swim	swam	swum
swing	swung	swung
take	took	taken
teach	taught	taught
tear	tore	torn
tell	told	told
think	thought	thought
throw	threw	thrown
thrust	thrust	thrust
tread	trod	trodden, trod
understand	understood	understood
upset	upset	upset
wake	woke	woken
wear	wore	worn
weave	wove,	wove, woven
wed	wedded	wed, wedded
weep	wept	wept
win	won	won
wind	wound	wound
withdraw	withdrew	withdrawn
withhold	withheld	withheld
withstand	withstood	withstood
wring	wrung	wrung
write	wrote	written

Spanish Verbs

Regular

	comprar	temer	partir
	to buy	to fear	to divide
Gerund	compr**ando**	tem**iendo**	part**iendo**
Part participle	compr**ado**	tem**ido**	part**ido**
Present indicative	compr**o**	tem**o**	part**o**
	compr**as**	tem**es**	part**es**
	compr**a**	tem**e**	part**e**
	compr**amos**	tem**emos**	part**imos**
	compr**áis**	tem**éis**	part**ís**
	compr**an**	tem**en**	part**en**
Imperfect indicative	compr**aba**	tem**ía**	part**ía**
	compr**abas**	tem**ías**	part**ías**
	compr**aba**	tem**ía**	part**ía**
	compr**ábamos**	tem**íamos**	part**íamos**
	compr**abais**	tem**íais**	part**íais**
	compr**aban**	tem**ían**	part**ían**
Past absolute (or preterit)	compr**é**	tem**í**	part**í**
	compr**aste**	tem**iste**	part**iste**
	compr**ó**	tem**ió**	part**ió**
	compr**amos**	tem**imos**	part**imos**
	compr**asteis**	tem**isteis**	part**isteis**
	compr**aron**	tem**ieron**	part**ieron**
Future	compr**aré**	tem**eré**	part**iré**
	compr**arás**	tem**erás**	part**irás**
	compr**ará**	tem**erá**	part**irá**
	compr**aremos**	tem**eremos**	part**iremos**
	compr**aréis**	tem**eréis**	part**iréis**
	compr**arán**	tem**erán**	part**irán**
Conditional	compr**aría**	tem**ería**	part**iría**
	compr**arías**	tem**erías**	part**irías**
	compr**aría**	tem**ería**	part**iría**
	compr**aríamos**	tem**eríamos**	part**iríamos**
	compr**aríais**	tem**eríais**	part**iríais**
	compr**arían**	tem**erían**	part**irían**

Imperative	compra	teme	parte
	compre	tema	parta
	compremos	temamos	partamos
	comprad	temed	partid
	compren	teman	partan
Present subjunctive	compre	tema	parta
	compres	temas	partas
	compre	tema	parta
	compreemos	temamos	partamos
	compreéis	temáis	partáis
	compren	teman	partan
Imperfect subjunctive	comprara	temiera	partiera
	ase	iese	iese
	compraras	temieras	partieras
	ases	ieses	ieses
	comprara	temiera	partiera
	ase	iese	iese
	compráramos	temiéramos	partiéramos
	ásemos	iésemos	iésemos
	comprarais	temierais	partierais
	aseis	ieseis	ieseis
	compraran	temieran	partieran
	asen	iesen	iesen

Auxiliary Verbs

Infinitive	haber	ser	tener	estar
	to have	to be	to have	to be
Gerund	habiendo	siendo	teniendo	estando
Part participle	habido	sido	tenido	estado
Present indicative	he	soy	tengo	estoy
	has	eres	tienes	estás
	ha	es	tiene	está
	hemos	somos	tenemos	estamos
	habéis	sois	tenéis	estáis
	han	son	tienen	están
Imperfect indicative	había	era	tenía	estaba
	habías	eras	tenías	estabas
	había	era	tenía	estaba
	habíamos	éramos	teníamos	estábamos
	habíais	erais	teníais	estabais
	habían	eran	tenían	estaban

Past absolute	hube	fui	tuve	estuve
(or preterit)	hubiste	fuiste	tuviste	estuviste
	hubo	fue	tuvo	estuvo
	hubimos	fuimos	tuvimos	estuvimos
	hubisteis	fuisteis	tuvisteis	estuvisteis
	hubieron	fueron	tuvieron	estuvieron
Future	habré	seré	tendré	estaré
	habrás	serás	tendrás	estarás
	habrá	será	tendrá	estará
	habremos	seremos	tendremos	estaremos
	habréis	seréis	tendréis	estaréis
	habrán	serán	tendrán	estarán
Conditional	habría	sería	tendría	estaría
	habrías	serías	tendrías	estarías
	habría	sería	tendría	estaría
	habríamos	seríamos	tendríamos	estaríamos
	habríais	seríais	tendríais	estaríais
	habrían	serían	tendrían	estarían
Imperative	–	sé(tu)	ten(tu)	está(tu)
Present subjunctive	haya	sea	tenga	esté
	hayas	seas	tengas	estés
	haya	sea	tenga	esté
	hayamos	seamos	tengamos	estémos
	hayáis	seáis	tengáis	estéis
	hayan	sean	tengan	estén
Imperfect subjunctive	hubiera	fuera	tuviera	estuviera
	iese	ese	iese	iese
	hubieras	fueras	tuvieras	estuvieras
	ieses	eses	ieses	ieses
	hubiera	fuera	tuviera	estuviera
	iese	ese	iese	iese
	hubiéramos	fuéramos	tuviéramos	estuviéramos
	iésemos	ésemos	iésemos	iésemos
	hubierais	fuerais	tuvierais	estuvierais
	ieseis	eseis	ieseis	ieseis
	hubieran	fueran	tuvieran	estuvieran
	iesen	esen	iesen	iesen